THEORY AND INTERPRETATION OF NARRATIVE
James Phelan, Peter J. Rabinowitz, and Robyn Warhol, Series Editors

The SUBMERGED PLOT and the MOTHER'S PLEASURE from JANE AUSTEN to ARUNDHATI ROY

Kelly A. Marsh

THE OHIO STATE UNIVERSITY PRESS
COLUMBUS

Copyright © 2016 by The Ohio State University.
All rights reserved.

Library of Congress Cataloging-in-Publication Data

Names: Marsh, Kelly A., 1968– author.
Title: The submerged plot and the mother's pleasure from Jane Austen to Arundhati
  Roy / Kelly A. Marsh.
Other titles: Theory and interpretation of narrative series.
Description: Columbus : The Ohio State University Press, [2015] | "2016" | Series:
  Theory and interpretation of narrative | Includes bibliographical references and
  index.
Identifiers: LCCN 2015034052 | ISBN 9780814212974 (cloth : alk. paper)
Subjects: LCSH: Narration (Rhetoric) | Sex in literature. | Feminism in literature. |
  Fiction—History and criticism. | Daughters in literature.
Classification: LCC PN3383.N35 M37 2015 | DDC 823.009/3522—dc23
LC record available at http://lccn.loc.gov/2015034052

Cover design by Regina Starace
Type set in Adobe Sabon
Printed by Thomson-Shore, Inc.

Lines from "Autobiography" quoted from *Collected Poems: 1925–1948* by Louis
MacNeice. First published by Faber and Faber Ltd. Reprinted by permission of David
Higham Associates.

∞ The paper used in this publication meets the minimum requirements of the American National Standard for Information Sciences—Permanence of Paper for Printed
Library Materials. ANSI Z39.48-1992.

9 8 7 6 5 4 3 2 1

*For my mother,
Margaret Sharrow Steele*

CONTENTS

Acknowledgments — ix

INTRODUCTION
Plot, Progression, and the Search for the
Mother's Unnarratable Pleasure — 1

CHAPTER 1
The Submerged Plot and the Interrelation of
Progression and Character: *Persuasion* and *Jane Eyre* — 26

CHAPTER 2
Dual and Serial Narration and the Disclosure of the
Submerged Plot: *Bleak House* and *The Woman in White* — 66

CHAPTER 3
The House, the Journey, and the Spaces of the
Submerged Plot: *The House of Mirth* and
The Last September — 112

CHAPTER 4
Surviving the Submerged Plot and the Work of Character
Narration: *The Color Purple*, *A Thousand Acres*, and
Bastard Out of Carolina — 153

CHAPTER 5
The End of Pleasure and the Function of Time
in the Submerged Plot: *Talking to the Dead* and
The God of Small Things — 205

CONCLUSION
The Evolution of the Search — 247

Notes — 253
Works Cited — 267
Index — 277

ACKNOWLEDGMENTS

My first thanks go to three people without whom this book could not have been written: James Phelan, Kathryn Hume, and Brian Anderson. I am also very grateful for the advice and guidance of Robyn Warhol, Margaret Homans, and Kay Young. All of the editors at The Ohio State University Press have been a great help, including Lindsay Martin and Tara Cyphers. The National Endowment for the Humanities supported my participation in the summer seminar on "Narrative Theory: Rhetoric and Ethics in Fiction and Non-Fiction," which was crucial to the development of the project. Mississippi State University has supported my work by granting me time and resources, especially the Office of the Provost, the Office of Research and Economic Development, the College of Arts and Sciences, and the Department of English. I would particularly like to thank Richard Raymond, Matthew Little, Gregory Dunaway, and Gary Myers, as well as my colleagues in the English Department, past and present. I am grateful for permission to reproduce earlier versions of the material in chapter 1, which appeared as "Jane Eyre and the Pursuit of the Mother's Pleasure" in *South Atlantic Review* 69.3/4 (2004) 81–106 and "The Mother's Unnarratable Pleasure and the Submerged Plot of *Persuasion*" in *Narrative* 17:1 (2009) 76–94.

INTRODUCTION

Plot, Progression, and the Search for the Mother's Unnarratable Pleasure

The protagonist as motherless daughter is a novelistic convention that was already well established by the time Jane Austen commented ironically on it in her own first novel. *Northanger Abbey* begins with this description of the protagonist's mother: "she had three sons before Catherine was born; and instead of dying in bringing the latter into the world, as any body might expect, she still lived on" (37). Austen conveys clearly that the absent mother is a convention of the eighteenth-century novel, that readers have developed expectations regarding such conventions, and that these will be challenged by her novel.[1] The expectations are dramatized in Catherine Morland's responses to the Tilney family, which reveal her assumption that a missing mother necessarily represents a mystery, the solution to which will be revealed as the unprotected daughter becomes victim of the same forces that took the mother's life. By defusing the "mystery" of Mrs. Tilney's absence and mitigating Eleanor Tilney's suffering, Austen consciously opens the door to the varied deployments of this literary convention that would follow and the complex interpretive strategies that would develop in response to them.

Two centuries later, the interpretive strategies we bring to novels of motherless daughters have been influenced by the groundbreaking work of Margaret Homans, Marianne Hirsch, Carolyn Dever, Susan Greenfield, and others. These very different studies share a feminist psychoanalytic approach to the study of narrative, and all extend the critique of patriarchy begun in those eighteenth-century novels of motherless daughters with which Austen and her contemporaries were so familiar. Carolyn Dever analyzes the cultural imperative for the mother's absence in *Death and the Mother from Dickens to Freud* (1998). She maintains the focus on maternal absence as mystery in her analysis of this plot in Victorian fiction: "The mother's absence creates a mystery for her child to solve, motivating time and again the redefinition—in the absence of role-models—of female decorum, gender roles, and sexuality" (xi). For Dever, the mother's absence is in service of the cultural mandate for "the containment of all that is potentially transgressive in the mother embodied" (xii). In Dever's analysis, "the representational conundrum of the eroticized adult female is accommodated in the disguise of a dead—and therefore virtuous, pure, noble, and true—mother" (xi). She traces the ways nineteenth-century writers are influenced by and attempt to subvert this assumption that only an idealized, absent mother is acceptable as a model for her daughter.

Margaret Homans's *Bearing the Word* (1986) also seeks to account for the prevalence of missing mothers in nineteenth-century fiction. She finds the source of this convention in what she calls "the dominant myth of language" (5), that "the death or absence of the mother sorrowfully but fortunately makes possible the construction of language and of culture" (2). Homans traces the engagement of nineteenth-century women writers with this destructive foundational myth that the daughter can only enter into the symbolic in her mother's absence. She concludes that "for nineteenth-century women writers, the collision between the urgent need to represent female experience and women's silencing within language and literary history remained a collision, articulated but not resolved" (xiii). Like Homans, Marianne Hirsch, in her *The Mother/Daughter Plot: Narrative, Psychoanalysis, Feminism* (1989), attributes the absence and silencing of mothers to the damaging cultural myth defining women as outside of language. Considering narratives by women from the nineteenth and twentieth centuries, Hirsch focuses on the absence of mothers' stories, which she attributes to the "myths we read and take to be basic," especially that of Oedipus (2). Locating not only a mother's story but a "maternal narrative" in Toni Morrison's

Beloved (198), Hirsch "traces the transformations, within narrative conventions, psychoanalytic theories, and feminist thinking, which enable the silent Jocasta gradually to give way to the vocal Sethe" (8). For Hirsch, the suppression of "maternal speech" (16) in the Western tradition is a product of "a sex-gender system which [...] identifies writing as masculine and insists on the incompatibility of creativity and procreativity" (8). In this system, even when daughters do begin to speak, mothers' stories remain repressed. Although she sees progress away from this model in contemporary fiction, Hirsch nevertheless concludes,

> All of these variations, however, are based on the heroines' refusal of conventional heterosexual romance and marriage plots and, furthermore, on their disidentification from conventional constructions of femininity. Mothers—the ones who are not singular, who did succumb to convention inasmuch as they are mothers—thereby become the targets of this process of disidentification and the primary negative models for the daughter. (10–11)

Hirsch finds that cultural constraints demand that the daughter "disidentify" with her mother, and much of the scholarship considered in what follows maintains this emphasis on mothers in fiction who, silenced and trapped, pass a legacy of oppression on to their daughters that must be resisted and overcome by them. This approach has been crucial to our understanding of the painful process by which women access authority even given a history of gender oppression.

The work done by all of these studies has been rightly influential: feminist theorists combining psychoanalytic and narratological approaches have exposed and explored cultural and psychological threats to maternal speech and to the connection between mother and daughter that would be impossible to access without the complexity of their vision. Like any set of interpretive strategies, however, even as they revolutionize our apprehension of certain elements of a text, they necessarily leave other elements unaccounted for. Even as we finally learn to read hitherto illegible workings of a text, we may still be underreading others. In my analysis of novels of motherless daughters from Austen's *Persuasion* to Arundhati Roy's *The God of Small Things*, I consider yet other forces, primarily social and conventional, that silence maternal speech and threaten to divide mothers and daughters. My analysis points to narrative structures that, although they do not give voice to the mother, do reveal her story and emphasize that the daughter protagonist's progress depends on that story. Although culture demands containment of the eroticized mother, as Dever asserts, the daughters in these novels nevertheless seek knowledge of their mothers' pleasure. As Austen implied in *Northanger Abbey*, in many novels in which women are central, the story of the mother's hardship and death is known, but the story of her pleasure is obscured. Even in cases in which the mother's pleasure in her marriage, her children, her intellectual pursuits, or her community is evident—through the daughter's own observation or through stories she is told by others—her pleasure in sex remains not only invisible but also unnarratable. These stories of sexual pleasure I have sought to recover by emphasizing those glimmers, glimpses, traces of pleasure that are just detectable even in narratives recounting lives lived under the most stifling conditions. Indeed, I argue that the obscuring of these stories is another form of oppression of women, those who do not tell and those who do not hear. In order to access that which tends to be underread in novels of motherless daughters, I propose a revised set of strategies involving both rethinking the assumptions we bring to these texts and reconsidering the ways we progress through them. Employing this new set of strategies has the potential to influence our vision not only of these particular novels but also of the ways the unnarratable is communicated in fiction.

To reconsider the assumptions we bring to novels of motherless daughters is an important first step in becoming alert to stories of pleasure. The preconceptions we bring to literature shape our responses as we read; this is the phase of interpretation identified by Peter Rabinowitz as "before reading." Rabinowitz analyzes the ways that readers' interpretive activities as they read and after reading "are already limited by decisions made before the book is even begun" (2). Much of the power of Rabinowitz's argument is attributable to his emphasis on the most foundational and widely shared of such decisions, but assumptions established before reading can also be very complex, highly informed, and shared by a relatively small group of readers, such as literary critics. Scholars have tended to approach novels of motherless daughters as Austen did, with the wry acknowledgement that suffering—that of the mother who dies and that of the bereft daughter—is generally thought of as the most acceptable subject of fiction about women. We approach them as Homans, Dever, and others do, with the understanding that the impact of a missing parent on a protagonist must be as strongly psychological as it is material, and that psychoanalytic theories are the most productive in analyzing them. We assume that the marriage plot, which functions in many novels of motherless daughters and nearly all such novels in the nineteenth century, has a highly recognizable structure powered by identifiable desires on the part of the protagonist and the reader. And we assume that plots themselves are linear and consistently visible, however rich the interpretations they inspire. These assumptions are the product of decades of invaluable literary scholarship, but to question them may open new paths of inquiry.

Approaching novels of motherless daughters with a different set of assumptions may also influence our interpretive activities by freeing us to reconsider the ways we move through these texts, enabling us to reconfigure as we do what James Phelan calls their "narrative progression" (*Experiencing Fiction* 3). For Phelan, attention to narrative progression is a necessary strategy for apprehension of narrative form: "to account for that experience of form we need to focus on narrative progression, that is, the synthesis of both the textual dynamics that govern the movement of narrative [. . .] and the readerly dynamics [. . .] that both follow from and influence those textual dynamics" (3). Textual dynamics, in Phelan's model, are the "introduction, complication, and resolution (in whole or in part) of unstable situations within, between, or among the characters," which "may be accompanied by a dynamics of tension in the telling—unstable relations among authors, narrators, and audiences" (7). The textual dynamics of an individual work are already complex and layered, but Phelan's rhetorical approach depends on yet another set of dynamics as well: "the dynamics of audience response" (7). He argues that as readers observe the textual dynamics, we make ethical, interpretive, and aesthetic judgments. As he explains, "Thus, from the rhetorical perspective, narrativity involves the interaction of two kinds of change: that experienced by the characters and that experienced by the audience in its developing responses to the characters' changes" (7). The emphasis in Phelan's account on the judgments of the reader encountering the textual dynamics reaffirms the weight of Rabinowitz's focus on the preconceptions we bring to reading, which can limit and determine readers' judgments. Following Phelan and Rabinowitz's rhetorical approach to narrative, I will begin by questioning the assumptions we bring to novels of motherless daughters, and, having suggested alternatives to those assumptions, I will trace the textual and readerly dynamics of each novel considered here in order to reconfigure the progression of each. In the process, I will offer new responses to interpretive problems in individual novels, posit an alternative view of the workings of plot in novels of motherless daughters, and challenge our view of plot more generally.

My rhetorical approach is combined with a feminist approach to narrative, and my work participates in what Robyn Warhol calls "the study of narrative structures and strategies in the context of cultural constructions of gender" ("The Look, The Body" 21). Feminist narrative theory relating to plot has a long and influential history of locating the ways plot structures reinscribe or push against cultural constructs of gender.[2] Feminist psychoanalytic critics have done just this with reference to novels of motherless daughters, but feminist narratology offers the opportunity to look again at these texts outside the psychoanalytic paradigm to discover additional ways these texts respond to the history and politics of gender in their various times and places.

To adopt, before reading novels of motherless daughters, a feminist narratological perspective combined with a rhetorical approach to narrative, allows us to observe, as we progress through each novel, a second plot. Under the plot of maternal absence and filial disidentification, we can locate what I call a submerged plot of the daughter's search for the mother's story that surfaces at times and exerts consistent pressure on the surface plot. Although the mother's story is not narrated—is, in fact, unnarratable—the daughter discovers it in her own experience, which is narrated for us. As we study the progression of each novel, we can identify the ways in which the daughter's experiences repeat her mother's; this is evident regardless of how much or how little we know of the mother's own story. As the protagonist makes decisions that appear on the surface to be motivated by her own circumstances, we can find in those decisions additional, submerged motivations to pursue experiences like those the mother is known to have had, to learn how they feel and what insight they might yield.

An especially useful model of a text's structure for conceptualizing how this submerged plot—which some readers will recognize and some will not but all will feel the effects of—functions in a text is one offered by Susan Stanford Friedman. In her "Spatialization: A Strategy for Reading Narrative," she adapts Julia Kristeva's theory of spatializing the word and proposes a model of reading narrative that would be "relational" (20) and "fluid" (13), and she does so by envisioning a text as a series of interactions between "surface and depth" (12). Friedman's model is designed to be broad enough to accommodate all texts without imposing a specific structure: the text is represented simply by a horizontal and a vertical axis, and reading "involves an interpretation of the continuous interplay between the horizontal and vertical narrative coordinates" (14). For Friedman, the horizontal axis is "the sequence of events, whether internal or external, that 'happens' according to the ordering principles of the plot and narrative point of view" (15). Friedman places greater emphasis on theorizing the vertical axis, which "involves the space and time the writer and reader occupy as they inscribe and interpret what Kristeva calls the 'subject-in-process' constituted through the 'signifying practices' of the text and its dialogues with literary, social, and historical intertexts" (14). She introduces her detailed analysis of the vertical axis by suggesting that "instead of the single textual surface of the horizontal narrative, the vertical narrative has many superimposed surfaces, layered and overwritten like the human psyche" (15). She identifies "three distinct strands" of the vertical axis: literary conventions and intertexts; historical intertexts and "the larger social order of the writer, text, and reader"; and the psychic aspect or the "textual unconscious" (17). Friedman's work on the vertical axis is thought-provoking, and her distinctions among the three strands bring a great deal of clarity to that aspect of a narrative "that must be traced by the reader because it has no narrator of its own" (16). Also, her spatial model provides a visual metaphor that opens the way to further thinking about the construction of a text and the reader's participation in that construction. In the context of my work, Friedman's model offers a "space" for imagining the complexities of the horizontal axis that have yet to be explored.

I argue for a reconsideration of the horizontal axis; in fact, my analysis of the novels considered in this study suggests the existence of a second horizontal axis that charts what I identify as the submerged plot. This second, submerged plot is not a function of vertical communications between the writer and reader that circumvent the characters and their actions, but rather resides, as does the surface plot, in "the linear movement of the characters through the coordinates of textual space and time," as Friedman explains it (14). My readings of novels of motherless daughters in what follows depend, as all readings do in Friedman's model, on tracking the coordinates of the three strands of the vertical axis—the literary, the historical, and the psychic—as they intersect with the sequence of events narrated, and I use Phelan's model of progression as a method for tracking those coordinates.[3] However, the focus of my analysis is to demonstrate the ways that, as readers construct these texts, they do so by tracing the intersections of the vertical axis with not one but two horizontal axes.

Such complexity on the horizontal axis is necessitated in these novels by the plot's concern with a story that is unnarratable. The submerged plot of each novel considered here follows the daughter protagonist as she seeks the story of her mother's pleasure. My concept of the mother's pleasure is indebted to the ways feminist critics have used the term *jouissance*, which, when it has been translated, has appeared in English as "pleasure" and "sexual pleasure" (Gallop 119–20). The most important commonality between the two concepts is that, like *jouissance*, the mother's pleasure exceeds a culturally proscribed limit. One difference between them is that my concept of pleasure does not share what Marianne DeKoven refers to as the "utopian" element of *jouissance* (1690). As she explains, in the work of French feminists in the 1970s and 1980s, feminine *jouissance* came to be seen as the liberating product of the pre-oedipal mother/daughter bond (a concept important to the work of Hirsch and Homans), and, as such, associated with *écriture féminine*. The mother's pleasure, in contrast, describes the experiences of women within the symbolic order and is expressed in realist texts. However, the difficulties of representing women's pleasure in literary texts are multiple, as Tamar Heller finds in her work on sensationalism and maternal sexuality in Edith Wharton's *The Mother's Recompense*. Considering Wharton's novel and Ellen Price Wood's *East Lynne*, in which the mothers are not absent, she finds the twentieth-century mother character maintains the same "sacrificial silence about her sexual history" as her Victorian predecessor (136). Heller concludes, "It is still the quest-romance of feminism to imagine narratives in which the mother can tell the story of her sexuality so that both she and her daughter can freely express their desires" (141). Heller finds that the mother's sexual pleasure is difficult or impossible for the mother to communicate, even when she is present.

The signs of women's pleasure tend to be obscured in literary texts for a number of reasons, and, before reading, we can endeavor to be cognizant of the historical, cultural, and literary constraints that render the story of the mother's pleasure not just unnarrated but actually unnarratable. In Robyn Warhol's terms, unnarratability occurs in at least four forms,[4] all of which are at work to some extent in the story of the mother's pleasure. First, sexual pleasure itself is difficult to represent, placing such a story within the realm of the "supranarratable," or "what can't be told because it's 'ineffable'" (223). Whereas sex can be narrated in a wide range of registers, and physical sensation can be described minutely, pleasure is more encompassing than either of these. Pleasure tends to be expressed indirectly, made explicit primarily by being "unnarrated," as Warhol explains of "highly charged emotional scenes" in other contexts (223) that are indicated by the narrator's admission that words cannot express the feelings attending an event. Sexual pleasure is not necessarily universally supranarratable; as Warhol asserts, "shifts in the category of the unnarratable [. . .] both reflect and constitute their audiences' developing senses of such matters as politics, ethics, and values" (221). That sexual pleasure remains ineffable over time and across cultural contexts in the novels treated here is attributable to the tenacity and strength of its "antinarratability," another of Warhol's four forms.

The story of the mother's pleasure is "antinarratable," or "what shouldn't be told because of social convention" (224). Sex in nineteenth-century fiction is one of Warhol's key examples: "probably even more taboo than the body itself in Victorian literary and social discourse, the bodily details of sexuality and (especially extramarital) sexual experience fall within the realm of the unnarratable, too, for both male and female writers" ("Narrating" 85). As Warhol's model predicts, as cultural values have changed over time since the Victorian period, sex has certainly become narratable. However, on the evidence of the novels considered here, women's pleasure, and especially that of women who are mothers, remains unnarratable even in more permissive times and places, even when sex is demonstrably narratable. I would argue that this taboo has its roots in the patriarchal structure of inheritance: wealth, property, and name are traditionally passed from father to son based on the assumption (rather than, in many situations, the certain knowledge) of the son's legitimacy. A mother's sexual pleasure can only be a threat to this assumption. If the mother finds pleasure in sex, even within marriage, then she proves that she is capable of seeking sex for reasons other than procreation. Once this has been established, then the possibility exists that she may seek it outside of marriage, calling into question, if only theoretically, her son's legitimacy and thus his right to his inheritance. Therefore, any story of the mother's pleasure is unacceptable to both father and son, and the only official story the mother is allowed is of her faithfulness and of the conception of her child within her legal marriage; in this context, her pleasure is not only irrelevant but threatening.

Considering the potential drama underlying the antinarratability of the story of the mother's pleasure, that the story is also "subnarratable," or "what needn't be told because it's 'normal,'" may seem counterintuitive (Warhol 222). However, motherhood is not a rarity, and a child is (in most cases) evidence of a woman's participation in the sexual act; therefore, to an extent, such stories are "unremarkable—they need not be told" (223). If women's sexuality, which has a biological and social function, can fall below the threshold of narratability, women's pleasure in sex is even more likely to do so. As Susan Winnett writes in her influential essay on plot and pleasure, "women's orgasm and, by extension, women's pleasure can be extraneous to that culmination of heterosexual desire which is copulation" (505). Women's pleasure, then, has no biological function, and it also has no social function. David Lloyd, speaking of mothers in particular with reference to Frederick Engels's *The Origin of the Family, Private Property and the State*, explains that in any public context within patriarchy, "the mother's pleasure represents a complete excess here: an excess beyond her identity as mother, beyond the end of conception" (81). Lacking biological and social function, the story remains unnarratable. Nevertheless, both Winnett and Lloyd are interested in how this unnarratable story functions in literary texts, and that is the question I take up here.

This story certainly does function in novels of motherless daughters, though literary tradition is yet another force that renders it unnarratable. The mother's story is "paranarratable," or "what wouldn't be told because of formal convention" (226). This category helps to explain why the mother's pleasure remains unnarratable even in very contemporary novels that knowingly critique cultural norms in a variety of other ways. Even after the social taboo is weakened by progressive social mores, the generic taboo remains in force. As Jane Austen knew when she started

Northanger Abbey with a thriving mother to surprise her readers, to narrate a woman's suffering is an acceptable, even expected, literary convention, but to narrate a mother's sexual pleasure would be to lift the weight of centuries of literary tradition. Thus, as we begin reading a novel of a motherless daughter, we should expect to need unusual strategies to locate the unnarratable story of the mother's pleasure.

As we progress through these novels with the assumption that the safeguarding of legitimacy is at the root of the antinarratability of the mother's story, we can imagine that the official, public story, that the mother finds in sex only a means to procreate, might lose its hold on the imaginations of daughters sooner and more easily than on those of sons. For a son, the expectations based on his legitimacy make the mother's pleasure troubling, destabilizing, potentially delegitimating. Even for legitimate sons—Oedipus, Orestes, Hamlet—knowledge of the mother's pleasure leads to destruction as surely as that of an illegitimate son, such as *King Lear*'s Edmund. At least since Freud, the son's investment in the official version and his fear of the unnarratable story have been understood as more or less universal. However, as we progress through a novel with a daughter protagonist, we may find evidence that for her, less likely in any case to secure an inheritance of wealth, property, and name, the mother's pleasure need not be frightening but can, instead, be validating, even her true inheritance.[5] We may, accordingly, read the daughter's relationship to her mother's story as independent of the officially accepted version, even in cases in which the daughter appears to accept it, and consider that the daughter's actions and decisions may have additional motivations to those that are obvious. The fact that Jane Eyre rarely mentions her mother is not evidence that her mother's story is not her object; conversely, the fact that Esther Summerson admits to being especially interested in her mother does not mean that we should be surprised that she fails to take advantage of every possible means of finding out about her.

In fact, this additional motive remains submerged and private because everything in the daughter's experience, and in the author's, has taught her (or him) that, publicly, the only stories available for the mother are the official version of her chastity or the failure of the official version, the story of transgression. These are already all too familiar to the seeking daughter; to go beyond these public versions of the mother's story, the daughter undertakes a search that is evidence that, despite their ubiquity, she remains unconvinced by them. That the plot of the daughter's search must be submerged reflects these historical realities and is analogous to the findings of Elizabeth Abel, Marianne Hirsch, and Elizabeth Langland in their introduction to the collection *The Voyage In: Fictions of Female Development*. In the same terms I use here to reconsider the structure of plot altogether, Abel, Hirsch, and Langland write:

> Novels that depict female apprenticeship and awakening not only alter the developmental process, but also frequently change its position in the text. The tensions that shape female development may lead to a disjunction between a surface plot, which affirms social conventions, and a submerged plot, which encodes rebellion. (12)

The submerged plot of the daughter's search for the story of her mother's pleasure is a plot of rebellion against the cultural silencing of that story and against the official limits on the possibilities for her own story. Ultimately, reading for the ways the daughter's motivations differ from what we expect and understanding that her investment in the mother's official story is less committed than a son's would be, we find that the mother's pleasure is closely tied to the daughter's, and the daughter needs her mother's story to validate her own pleasure.

In most of the nineteenth- and twentieth-century novels considered here, we encounter the daughter protagonist as she approaches or reaches a marriageable age, or, in some cases, as she reaches what appears to be the limit of marriageable age. Although the more contemporary novels depart considerably from its conventions, the female protagonist's progress toward romantic love is relevant if not central to all of these works. The idea of the "marriage plot" brings with it certain associations that I, like other feminist narratologists, suggest need to be reconsidered. Robyn Warhol writes of critical responses to the marriage plot,

> Following the metaphoric reasoning of desire-centered narrative theory, feminist critics have typically read the telos of marriage as the telos of heterosexual climax: if the heroine and hero get married, they will have sex; the readers' desire to see the marriage come about is understood as the readers' desire to see the protagonists come together sexually which—for the reader—will be, metaphorically speaking, to come. (*Having a Good Cry* 63)

Warhol sees feminist critics as having adopted Peter Brooks's argument: "Desire as narrative thematic, desire as narrative motor, and desire as the very intention of narrative language and the act of telling all seem to stand in close interrelation" (Brooks 54; Warhol 61). For Warhol, not only is the relevance of Brooks's observation limited to heterosexual men, but desire itself is too limiting a concept for accessing the affect of a novel. As Warhol questions received critical assumptions about the marriage plot, so does Kay Young. Like Warhol, Young takes the focus off desire and sex; she explains, "It is the ordinary pleasures of marriage that concern me, what can come of the experience of mutuality, how play between a couple makes present an intimacy and happiness of the everyday" (4). Arguing that conversational "play" truly constitutes the reader's experience of intimacy between two protagonists and, at the same time, resists the telos of plot itself, Young, like Warhol, demonstrates that the workings of a text are more various than Brooks's formulation allows.

Like Warhol and Young, my own analysis takes the focus off desire as motive and textual motor, but I maintain a focus on sex. My analysis approaches sex as a fact of a woman's experience even as it sets the psychological power of sex to one side. In nineteenth-century marriage plots in which Victorian mores are dominant, as the female protagonist approaches marriage, she is aware, as are the novelist and the reader, that she also approaches her first, and perhaps her only, experience of sex. In such novels, a woman with no sexual experience is required to choose a man to be the only sexual partner of her life. Although the narratives, then as now, valorize the experience of being identified as "the one," hesitance about such a relatively blind commitment is also a part of the narrative. The protagonist either chooses well and ensures that her only experience of sex will be pleasurable, or she chooses (or is forced to choose) badly and ensures that she will never experience pleasurable sex. The possibility of sexual pleasure—or the foreclosure of that possibility—is central to the marriage plot. Although as twenty-first-century readers we tend to think of the unnarratability of sex in nineteenth-century fiction as the repression of what is desirable and pleasurable, we are nevertheless fully aware that the possibility of a lifetime of unpleasurable sex was a very real one for a nineteenth-century woman. Our awareness of this possibility is dramatized in Charlotte Lucas's choice to marry Mr. Collins in Austen's *Pride and Prejudice,* a choice readers could not tolerate as the end of a main character's story. This possibility is far from absent in lives lived in supposedly more permissive times and places. In Dorothy Allison's South Carolina of the 1960s and Arundhati Roy's Kerala of the late 1960s and even the early 1990s, such a possibility remains nearly as potent as in nineteenth-century England. Further, the compulsory heterosexuality of the dominant culture in all of the novels considered here makes the threat of unpleasurable sex very real for lesbian characters, as in *The Color Purple*.

Therefore, the drive to desire sex that is foremost in psychoanalytic studies is tempered in individual cases by actual social realities that are very present in the texts considered here, realities of which the novelist, the protagonist, and the reader are quite conscious. The powerful marriage plot is built on an equally powerful "negative plot," in Susan Lanser's formulation, in which the protagonist commits herself to the wrong man. Lanser defines "negative plotting" as "a situation in which opposing plots effectively operate in tandem, one shadowing the other, to produce a narrative experience. Often relying on but not requiring what Gerald Prince calls 'disnarration' [. . .], negative plotting is a cognitive process whereby readers construct one plot, as it were, on the back of and antithetically to another" ("Are We There Yet?" 38–39). For Lanser, then, negative plotting is not unrelated to the unnarratable, which Warhol characterizes as the larger category to which the disnarrated belongs. The negative plot is clearly signaled in the novel of the motherless daughter. Promising sexual partners are central to these novels, but unpromising sexual partners are prominent as well. Unpleasurable sex in the form of rape is a specter in some early novels considered here, and it is central to some of the later ones. The novelists whose work I analyze—including some who were unmarried themselves, some in unsatisfying marriages, some lesbians—are fully aware of the magnitude of their protagonists' choices in this regard, as are the protagonists themselves and readers, then and now. What Warhol refers to as "desire-centered narrative theory" cannot fully prepare us to analyze our encounter with this fact of women's lives in fiction, but reconfiguring the progression of a novel to reveal the workings of the submerged plot uncovers the ways that the possibility of sexual pleasure motivates the protagonist, conditions the reader's responses to the protagonist's decisions, and is subtly but consistently acknowledged by the author.

Of course, just as the psychological drive of desire is mitigated by the question of whether sex is likely to be pleasurable, so is the motivation to seek pleasure mitigated by other cultural influences that define virtue in women. First, in the nineteenth-century novels of motherless daughters but also in their twentieth-century successors, sexual misconduct brings dire punishment. Second, the very inaccessibility of her mother's story tells the protagonist that sexual motivation, even within marriage, is inappropriate for women. Third, even in contexts in which sexual mores are considerably more relaxed than in the Victorian novels, cultural signals suggest to the seeking daughter that focusing on her own sexual pleasure is selfish and superficial. The protagonist seeking marriage, then, is faced with the certainty of sex, which, if she knows nothing else, she knows can either be pleasurable or not. With cultural messages suggesting that her inclination toward pleasure may not be virtuous, she needs reassurance both that pleasurable sex is possible and that it is acceptable. Her search for this reassurance must be submerged, as nothing in her culture affirms it. Tracing this submerged plot has the further effect of moving the focus off the heterosexual couple who dominate the surface plot—a pairing that becomes increasingly fraught over the nearly two hundred years covered by these novels—and onto the whole web of relationships that move the plot's instabilities toward their resolution and the progression toward completion. At the center of this web of relationships we find the absent mother, whose unnarratable pleasure helps to determine the novel's plot in two ways: it has created the daughter's circumstances and it has become the object of the daughter's search for knowledge as she makes her own decisions about marriage, decisions that will determine her access (or lack of access) to sexual pleasure.

Seeking an unnarratable story, the daughter accesses it in the only way available to her: she repeats it. The tradition of literary works in which a character who has lost one or both parents accesses the experience of a dead parent by reliving that experience is a long one. Many such works have male protagonists: an early and influential example is that of Sophocles' Oedipus, who, when his father is dead, becomes the king of Thebes and the husband of Jocasta, as his father was before him. That Oedipus repeats his father's experience so exactly without being aware of it has made his story fertile ground for psychoanalysis. Repetition, from a psychoanalytic point of view, is resistance to knowing. Freud's repetition compulsion is a reproduction in action of what an analysand cannot remember. Indeed, for Freud, "the greater the resistance, the more extensively will acting out (repetition) replace remembering" (151).[6] A more instructive example for my purposes is *Hamlet,* in which, although it is not remarked upon in the play, the protagonist is knowledgeable about his father's life and conscious of his own experiences, which repeat those of his father. When Hamlet's escape from Elsinore is blocked by Claudius as well as by the ghost of his father, Hamlet begins repeating his father's experience in some important particulars. He lives in his father's house again after an absence of some time. He feels in his own right his father's resentment of Claudius, and to some extent feels his father's will to power, over Claudius and perhaps over Denmark. He shares his father's anger at Gertrude's remarriage and evident pleasure in her marriage bed, and he indulges in a passion for Ophelia that mimics his father's for Gertrude. Finally, Hamlet dies his father's death, poisoned by Claudius. Hamlet repeats his father's experiences in order to learn his father's story, and he does learn it. Nevertheless, for Hamlet as for Oedipus, repeating the parent's experiences leads to devastation.

A much later example, W. B. Yeats's 1938 play *Purgatory,* suggests why this might be so. In a scene reminiscent of Dante's *Inferno,* Yeats's Old Man watches his mother, a soul in Purgatory, repeat her transgression before his eyes. Her transgression is the lust that prompted her to make a low marriage and disgrace a proud family. Unlike Oedipus and Hamlet, the Old Man is represented as repeating, in a way, his mother's rather than his father's experience, but this difference in fact throws into relief the significant similarities. David Lloyd's reading of *Purgatory* enables us to understand these fully. For Lloyd, the two forces in the play that are frightening, to Yeats and to the Old Man, as forces of the possible, rather than the probable, are "the erotic pleasure of women" and the remorse that is inherent in the mother's purgative act and in the Old Man's response to witnessing that act (80). All three plays feature the fear of the mother's potentially delegitimating pleasure, and all share remorse, or, as Lloyd glosses it, "that emotion which [. . .] chooses to assert that things might have been otherwise. It is an appeal to the history of the possible, of what might have been" (80). For these protagonist sons, preoccupation with what might have been seems to carry with it the responsibility of attempting, unsuccessfully, to right the wrongs of the past.

For seeking daughters, repetition of the mother's experience appears to be free of both fears. The mother's erotic pleasure is not experienced as delegitimating to a daughter not expecting an inheritance, and, as they are both women, her pleasure can be validating of the daughter's own. Remorse tends not to become overwhelming for most of the seeking daughters; not brought up with a sense of active responsibility for the family's honor, the daughter tends to be better able to accept the past and not feel called upon to attempt fruitless intervention in what cannot be changed. Instead, the seeking daughter repeats her mother's experience as her male counterpart does, but, in most cases, fearlessly and with the expectation of validation. In some of the novels treated here, the similarities between the daughter's experience and what she and the reader know of her mother's experience goes unremarked, as in *Hamlet*. In others, the ways the daughter's experience repeats her mother's is as much part of the surface plot as of the submerged, as in *Purgatory*. In all cases, the repetitions serve the protagonist by making the resolution possible, and they serve the reader by calling attention to the submerged plot. In his *Fiction and Repetition*, J. Hillis Miller reminds us that "a novel is interpreted in part through the noticing of such recurrences" (2). He explains that his own project is "an exploration of some of the ways they work to generate meaning or to inhibit the too easy determination of a meaning based on the linear sequence of the story" (2). As in those Miller analyzes, in the novels considered here, recurrences both generate meaning in themselves and also call attention to elements of the text that complicate the horizontal axis. Miller argues further that "the reader's identification of recurrences may be deliberate or spontaneous, self-conscious or unreflective" (2). The repetitions on which I focus in these novels have not been considered deliberately or reflectively in the past, but that is no indication that they have not had their impact on readers' experience of these texts. Now, however, as we track the daughter's progress provided with new assumptions and reading strategies, we are prepared to witness the revelation of the unnarratable story.

We can trace the progression of the submerged plot from what James Phelan identifies as the "launch" through to the conclusion, and in doing so we find that, even when the reader is not fully aware of its intricacies, it is a constitutive factor in the novel's completeness. "Completeness," as Phelan defines it, is "the degree of resolution accompanying the closure" (*Reading People, Reading Plots* 18). Degree of resolution, in turn, refers to the degree to which the main instabilities (between and among characters) and tensions (between narrator and authorial audience) are worked out. The completeness, or lack thereof, that appears to be solely the product of the surface plot, proves also dependent on the submerged plot. Tracing and reconfiguring the progression reveals the coordinates of the vertical axis with both horizontal axes. The extent to which the submerged plot breaks the surface in the novels varies with the narration, the structure of the surface plot, and the characters. For example, in some novels of motherless daughters, including *Bleak House*, *Bastard Out of Carolina*, and *The God of Small Things*, the mother is a character about whom a great deal is known. In others, including *Persuasion*, *Jane Eyre*, and *The House of Mirth*, the mother is deceased from the novel's beginning, and we are given only the barest information about her. In novels of both kinds, the mother's pleasure remains unnarratable, but it is, nevertheless, communicated. The mother's experience remains a story, rather than a plot, because it does not generate its own track of instability-complication-resolution, in Phelan's terms, with the accompanying readerly dynamics. Instead, the mother's story becomes available to the reader as part of the instability-complication-resolution sequence for the daughter protagonist.

The submerged plot surfaces and becomes visible in a number of ways that are largely consistent throughout the novels considered here. As readers of these novels, we are often alerted to the presence of the submerged plot by what Friedman, in her work on transnationalizing narrative theory, calls a "traveling trope" ("Towards a Transnational Turn" 7).[7] As Friedman explains, "A trope is not a story; but it may contain an 'implied story' within its unnarrated figuration. An image can suggest a back story, indeed many possible back stories" (7). Friedman's example is that of "the woman writer as gifted as a man" (7), which she finds circulating through the works of Virginia Woolf, James Joyce, Rabindranath Tagore, and Swarnakumari Devi. Friedman's work on a daughter protagonist's undervalued creativity informs my work on a daughter protagonist's undervalued pleasure. Similarly, my work is influenced by a line of literary criticism that has taken an approach like Friedman's and begins with Alice Walker's "In Search of Our Mothers' Gardens." Walker's meditation on African American women, historically barred from creative expression in so many ways, seeks to recover evidence of that suppressed creativity. She finds it in their quilting and their gardening—expression manifesting itself in every available medium—and she finds it in their daughters' art: "no song or poem will bear my mother's name. Yet so many of the stories that I write, that we all write, are my mother's stories" (240).[8] Walker's theory that women inherit not only their mothers' oppression but also their ineradicable creativity forms the basis of Rachel Blau DuPlessis's work on *Künstlerromane* by women writers in *Writing Beyond the Ending* (1985). Referring specifically to Walker's essay, DuPlessis finds of the works she studies, "Such a narrative is engaged with a maternal figure and, on a biographical level, is often compensatory for her losses [. . .]. The daughter becomes an artist to extend, reveal, and elaborate her mother's often thwarted talents" (93). Like DuPlessis, Heather Ingman's analysis in *Women's Fiction between the Wars: Mothers, Daughters and Writing* (1998) takes the writers' biographies into account and arrives at a similar conclusion about the texts she considers: "Far from being a regressive influence which has to be left behind in order for the daughter to enter the symbolic order of language and culture, the mother and the recovery of the mother's voice in many cases frees the daughter's writing" (164). For these scholars, the authority of the daughter artist is based on her connection with her mother's creativity. As these writers look for what can be recovered of women's suppressed creativity, I look for what can be recovered of women's taboo sexual pleasure.

Shifting the focus from creativity to pleasure, I seek a trope that travels among the various texts considered here that carries, as Friedman explains, an "implied story" of the mother's pleasure. The "traveling trope" I identify in these novels is that of "the woman who marries despite. . . ." The trope appears in two different but related forms; indeed, we may usefully think of it as two subtropes. The first is that of a woman who marries a man despite considerable obstacles, such as her family's disapproval or even her own recognition of serious flaws in his character. The second is the trope of a woman who marries a man despite her passionate attachment to another. In quite different ways, the "implied story" in both of these scenarios is one of pleasure—whether in the man married "despite" obstacles, or the man "despite" whom she marries another. As Friedman notes, a single "traveling trope" can imply any number of stories. In these novels, I am in some cases rereading a trope that has generally been understood as implying a woman's unfortunate choice and looking past it to the pleasure against which that choice is weighed. This rereading is supported by the submerged plot of the daughter's discovery of her mother's pleasure. For Friedman, the trope stands in for that which is not narrated; in these novels, it gestures toward what is actually not narratable, and this implied story is one indicator of the presence of the submerged plot.

The trope of "the woman who marries despite . . ." usually appears early in the novel, and it resides in a direct narration of what is often a very bare outline of the absent mother's history. This history tends to be limited to her family of origin, her marriage, and her motherhood, and it is often strongly focused on the circumstances of her death. The submerged plot surfaces in this way early on, calling attention to the mother's absence and raising questions for the reader, and often for the protagonist, about whether the story is primarily characterized by suffering or whether it includes hints of pleasure. The answer often hinges on what is known of the father: in many cases the most obvious choices allowed to the mother in her lifetime were the choices of whom to love and whom to marry.

The brief history of the mother toward the narrative's beginning also prepares us to recognize the ways the daughter's experience repeats the mother's. As the daughter reaches a point in her own development at which she prepares to make her own choices about love and marriage, she begins to attend to the ways her own life repeats her mother's and to explore her mother's experience in her own. As she repeats her mother's story, the submerged plot surfaces in at least four more clearly identifiable ways. First, the daughter frequently lives in the house her mother lived in, surrounded by those who knew her mother; these relatives and friends make comparisons between the daughter and her mother. Second, and more specific, is the daughter's relationship with a mentor. The mentor is often a woman who filled the same role for the mother or was her confidante, sometimes the protagonist's aunt; alternatively, the mentor is a sister, whose relation to the mother is the same as the protagonist's. Scholars have sometimes considered these characters as substitute mother figures, but I suggest that when interactions between the protagonist and the mentor are narrated their shared connection to the mother is foregrounded and brings the submerged plot to the surface. Third, the submerged plot also surfaces in the daughter's relationships with men. As the daughter entertains one, or more often two, suitors, each is implicitly compared to the mother's choice of suitor. The novels exhibit considerable variation as to whether the false suitor or the true suitor is like the father, which emphasizes that repeating the mother's story is not an end in itself but a means of knowing her experience. Whether the daughter finds her pleasure with a man like the one her mother chose is less significant to the submerged plot than the fact that, before she makes her own choice, the daughter explores what it would mean to choose, or to be chosen by, a man like the one her mother chose. Finally, in a number of cases, the daughter's own repetition of the mother's experience is supplemented by her observation of another woman's repetition of the mother's experience, and the submerged plot surfaces in this way as well. As these recurring elements attest, the daughter's repetition of her mother's experience is largely involuntary: she usually does not choose where she lives, nor can she control whether the potential suitors she encounters resemble her father; these repetitions are in the novelist's hands. At the same time, the protagonist does choose her mentors, and her imagination sometimes determines how closely another woman's experience repeats her mother's. To an extent, then, the repetitions depend on her own interpretations of her and her mother's experience. Further, the novels include indications that the protagonist is waiting for these repetitions—those created for her and those she creates herself—to inform her own choices.[9]

That these elements of plot and their effects are quite consistent throughout the texts considered here is surprising, considering their diversity, and tracing their recurrence by means of reconfiguring the progression of each novel enables us to access the shared underlying structure. Reconsidering the textual and readerly dynamics based on the existence of two horizontal axes makes what is submerged in these texts more available for interpretation, and provides access to what is unnarratable and insight into how texts render the unnarratable. That what has been inaccessible and unavailable in the past is now accessible and available is attributable to at least two things: contemporary narrative theory and contemporary fiction. Without Robyn Warhol's fully realized theory of the unnarratable, without Susan Stanford Friedman's spatial model of the text and her concept of the transnational circulation of tropes, and without James Phelan's method of tracing the textual and readerly dynamics in tandem, the daughter's search would remain submerged. New critical approaches combine with new fiction to make the submerged evident. By changing the form of the submerged plots in ways that nevertheless resonate clearly with earlier texts, contemporary novels direct our attention to what they have in common with their predecessors. Finally, by considering together English, American, Irish, and Indian texts from two centuries, and by including authors diverse in gender, sexuality, and race, previously unnoticed commonalities alert us to that which we have felt the effects of all along.

My study begins with Jane Austen's final novel, *Persuasion*. Years after distancing herself from the convention of the absent mother in *Northanger Abbey*, Austen creates an older, more experienced protagonist through whom she shows us how a conscious, mature heroine seeks knowledge of her mother—not just as mother but as woman—and in that knowledge seeks validation for her own choices. Not only is Austen's heroine different in *Persuasion*, but the structure of the novel is different as well. Anne Elliot's search for the story of her mother's pleasure forms a submerged plot that acts on the surface "marriage plot" throughout the novel. In fact, *Persuasion* exemplifies narratives in which the surface and submerged plots are fully synchronized. Events on both horizontal axes progress steadily, with events in the surface plot working in favor of the submerged, and events in the submerged plot enabling the progression and completeness of the surface. This synchronization is what *Persuasion* has in common with Charlotte Brontë's *Jane Eyre*, and these two novels, considered together in chapter 1, illustrate that the completeness that appears to be the product purely of the successful marriage plot on the text's surface is in fact also reliant on the successful search for the mother's pleasure in the submerged plot. These two novels also introduce with particular clarity the ways that my model, even as it reconsiders the way plot works in these novels, also influences our understanding of the interrelation of plot and character. Because the model focuses on an alternative set of motives for each protagonist, our vision of the protagonist's character is altered. Also, because the model emphasizes that the daughter's pleasure is determined by more than the central romantic relationship, it enables us to reconfigure not only the progression but also the character-system. Character is a strong emphasis in chapter 1, and I continue to analyze the effects of the submerged plot on our vision of character throughout.

The surface and submerged plots of the novels analyzed in chapter 2, Charles Dickens's *Bleak House* and Wilkie Collins's *The Woman in White*, are also synchronous. In both, the search for the story of her mother's pleasure in the submerged plot facilitates and makes possible the daughter protagonist's progress toward marriage in the surface plot. However, the vibrant and complex horizontal axes of Dickens's and Collins's novels include, along with their marriage plots, mystery plots, in which the very source of the mystery is the mother's sexual history. The surface plot, then, has a double relation with the submerged plot: even as the marriage plot works steadily with the search that forms the second horizontal axis, the mystery plot works against it. The daughter's search for the unnarratable story of her mother's pleasure is impinged upon and impeded by the other characters' search for the highly narratable story of the mother's transgression. The double relation between the two plots makes demands on the narration itself in these novels. Dickens uses his dual narrators to dramatize the private search for the mother's pleasure in its struggle with the public pursuit of the mother's transgression. The relationship of Collins's serial narration to the double relation between surface and submerged plots is even more complex and involves a duality in the character narrators themselves, whose actions work against the daughter's search even as their narration works in favor of it. My focus on the complex narration of each novel in this chapter reveals the ways the submerged plot is disclosed by and also influences the narration. The submerged plots effectively resist the mystery plots to achieve resolution; as a result, *Bleak House* reaches the kind of completeness we find in *Persuasion* and *Jane Eyre*. *The Woman in White* does as well, though its ending is more likely than the other three to leave the reader with reservations about its completeness, which suggests that Collins considers the daughter's search to be central but by no means inevitably successful.

Collins's doubts about the possibility of accessing the mother's story are magnified in the early-twentieth-century novels considered in chapter 3, in which the conflicting expectations placed on the heroine in the surface plot make it impossible for her to finish her search in the submerged plot. In Edith Wharton's *The House of Mirth* and Elizabeth Bowen's *The Last September*, surface and submerged plots are synchronized, but, instead of the fulfillment of both marriage plot and search plot, the novels depict the failure of the search, which makes the success of the marriage plot impossible. The daughter protagonists of these two novels are, like Collins's Marian Halcombe, forced into the role of son in the surface plot, and this sufficiently influences their relationship to their mothers' stories as to make those stories inaccessible to them. This obstacle to their search is compounded in Bowen's novel by the repositioning of the personal in the context of Irish decolonization. Indeed, the particularity of the settings of these two novels, and the parallels between them, make them especially instructive about the ways my use of Friedman's spatialized model of the text and my vision of the daughter protagonist's experience as a search are reflected in the novels' use of space. I use *The House of Mirth* and *The Last September* to explore in detail a spatial pattern that exists in some form in all of the novels treated here, the way the daughter relies on both movement in geographical space and also a particular house in which her mother lived as sources of her mother's experience.

Chapters 4 and 5 focus on contemporary novels in which the synchronicity between the surface and submerged plots is compromised, and the relationship between them is altered in other ways as well. In Alice Walker's *The Color Purple*, Jane Smiley's *A Thousand Acres*, and Dorothy Allison's *Bastard Out of Carolina*, the search for the mother's pleasure is wrested from the submerged plot and from the daughter protagonist's control and becomes a terrifying experience when the daughter protagonist is raped by her mother's husband. The surface plot becomes a horrific and distorted version of the submerged plot when the daughter experiences what her mother has experienced before her, but, far from accessing the mother's pleasure, can feel only repulsion and pain. As in chapter 2, I focus on the character narrators of these novels and their handling of this shift. For these difficult narratives, Walker, Smiley, and Allison have been drawn to different kinds of character narrators, and I trace the disclosure of the submerged plot by each. For all their differences, these character narrators respond similarly to the forced repetition of their mothers' experiences in the surface plot, which poses a direct threat to the search for the mother's pleasure. Their narratives reveal their common agenda of protecting their mothers as far as possible from the reader's judgment while they engage in a submerged search for an alternative story from the mother's past, a story of pleasure not bound up in the daughter's pain and victimization. Each protagonist's narration of this alternative story illustrates further the demands the submerged plot makes on narration and the ways the narrative discloses the submerged plot.

In the novels considered in chapter 5, the surface plot also takes over a part of what is usually found in the submerged plot, and the latter is threatened in another way. In Helen Dunmore's *Talking to the Dead* and Arundhati Roy's *The God of Small Things*, the surface plot is revealed in two distinct narratives: the story of a devastating event in the past is revealed in a narrative that alternates with the narrative of the present, in which participants in that past event remember and confront it. In both novels, the narrative of the past, which is detailed, thorough, and fully resolved, includes the story of the end of the mother's pleasure. The daughter protagonist feels implicated in the end of her mother's pleasure, and her guilt over this and fear of knowing more of her own participation in the events that ended her mother's story delay her search. In both novels, it is in the elliptical, seemingly unresolved narrative of the present that we locate the surfacings of the submerged plot of the daughter's attempt to look beyond the end of her mother's pleasure to the pleasure itself. Because these two novels highlight the narrative functions of time by disrupting chronology, the ways the submerged plot influences and is influenced by narrative time is most productively analyzed in this chapter. Time is emphasized and then masked in *Talking to the Dead*, and it is emphasized and then reversed in *The God of Small Things*: both alert the reader to the submerged plot and also reveal the demands the submerged plot makes on the representation of time. Attention to the workings of the submerged plots of these novels reveals the ways they enable resolution in the narratives of the present and make completion in the novels possible.

The relationship between the submerged and surface plots, between the horizontal axis of a narrative and the second horizontal axis that shadows it, can vary from the straightforward to the complex, but its crucial role in enabling completeness remains the same throughout all of these novels. Analyzing its function contributes to our concept of plot even as it contributes to our grasp of the ways narratives convey the unnarratable. Revealing the unnarratable in these novels changes the way we see the daughter protagonists and their relationship to their absent mothers and to other women generally, suggesting that their vision is not so wholly constrained by the dominant culture's myths about the mother as we might have supposed and that their daughterhood affords them access to pleasure in ways we might have overlooked.

CHAPTER 1

The Submerged Plot and the Interrelation of Progression and Character

Persuasion and *Jane Eyre*

Especially given their differences—of style, sensibility, narration—Jane Austen's *Persuasion* (1818) and Charlotte Brontë's *Jane Eyre* (1847) enable us to begin to recognize the circulation of the submerged plot of the search for the mother's pleasure. These two novels offer their readers a similar experience of completeness: their degree of resolution is similarly very high, both in terms of instabilities among characters and tensions between narrator and audience. This high degree of resolution is generally attributed to Austen's and Brontë's masterful and distinctly different deployments of the conventions of the marriage plot. However, the novels' completeness rests on even greater complexities in the text: in both, the surface plot of the heroine's successful progress toward marriage is fully supported by the submerged plot of her equally successful progress toward learning about her mother's experience of and feelings about marriage. The two plots are highly synchronized, and readers can feel the effects of this synchronization even when they are not consciously aware of the second horizontal axis.

Throughout each novel, the daughter protagonist's active search for the story of her mother's pleasure forms a submerged plot that charts her engagement with the unnarratable. While they appear to be reacting purely to events in the surface plot—Anne's several relocations and her involvements with Frederick Wentworth and William Elliot, Jane's several relocations and her involvements with Edward Rochester and St. John Rivers—they are simultaneously reacting to events in the submerged plot as they repeat the mother's experiences and attempt to determine whether and where she found pleasure. Both are stories of passionate, mutual love that brings great happiness, that is then interrupted and must be denied for a time, and that finally can be expressed and enjoyed in marriage. One way of understanding why the pleasure that each protagonist ultimately experiences must be delayed is that, before that pleasure can be hers, she must find validation for it in the mother's unnarratable story.

As we reconfigure the progression of these novels with reference to not one but two horizontal axes, we are concerned especially with the protagonist's experience and also with the motives with which she approaches her choices and shapes that experience. Therefore, analysis of the submerged plot in these novels influences our understanding of plot and also of character, and it offers fresh evidence in support of the traditional view of the inextricability of the two.[1] Henry James refers in "The Art of Fiction" to "an old-fashioned distinction between the novel of character and the novel of incident" that James finds "little to the point." Rather, he considers the two to be mutually constitutive: "What is character but the determination of incident? What is incident but the illustration of character?" (174). Seymour Chatman upholds James's assertion when he argues that "stories only exist where both events and existents occur" (113). Chatman and James encourage us to understand character and plot as inextricable, and James Phelan goes a step further in his work on character and progression, claiming that "any conclusions about the nature of character in a given narrative cannot be separated from the analysis of that narrative's developing structure, or what I will call hereafter its narrative progression" ("Character, Progression" 285). My own use of Phelan's concept of progression bears this out: my analyses of the plots of novels of motherless daughters have considerable implications for our understanding of character in those novels.

Sensitivity to the submerged plot alters our understanding especially of the daughter protagonists' mimetic dimensions and thematic functions, in Phelan's terms, largely by demonstrating that their actions are the result not only of motives generated by the circumstances of the surface plot but also by a second set of motives.[2] My findings also alter our vision of what Alex Woloch calls the "character-system" of each novel, demonstrating that minor characters have additional functions in the submerged plot to those evident in the surface plot, and these additional functions can change our overall understanding of them. Attention to the submerged functions of minor characters can shift our perception of the daughter protagonist's relation to other women and our perception of how the "character-space" of the protagonist, as Woloch terms it, intersects with those of female minor characters. A primary example of this is the protagonists' mothers, who, even in novels in which they have generally been considered marginal, in light of the submerged plot, appear central.

What we do know of Elizabeth Stevenson Elliot and Jane Reed Eyre appears to leave little room for speculation, and neither, for the most part, deviates far from the norms associated with the time, place, and circumstances in which she lived. Both Anne Elliot and Jane Eyre are legitimate daughters of legal marriages, and both use their own intellects and instincts to make good marriages themselves. The protagonists and their mothers all conform in many ways to social expectations about their sexuality, remaining chaste until marriage, remaining faithful after marriage, and, assuming Anne goes on to do so, bearing children within marriage. We might imagine that, in such cases, the story of a woman's sexual pleasure would be acceptable. On the contrary, these and many other novels considered here are evidence that women's pleasure in marital sex is as antinarratable as it would be in pre- or extramarital sex and for the same reasons: pleasure in sanctioned sex implies a motive for seeking unsanctioned sex. Approaching these very different novels with a deliberate sensitivity to the steady obscuring of and the potential for representation of women's pleasure, we are in a position to reconsider our interpretation of the story implied by the "traveling trope" I am calling "the woman who marries despite. . . ."

"The youthful infatuation which made her Lady Elliot": Elizabeth Stevenson Elliot

Even before Anne Elliot is introduced to us as a woman disappointed in love, a woman who, "forced into prudence in her youth, [. . .] learned romance as she grew older" (29), she is introduced to us as a motherless daughter, one in whom Lady Russell, Anne's mentor and Lady Elliot's closest friend, "could fancy the mother to revive again" (7). In fact, the marriage plot of *Persuasion* is constantly influenced by a submerged plot in which Anne repeats her absent mother's experience in order to learn her story. The little we are told about Lady Elliot gives a glimpse into this crucial submerged plot, crucial because it significantly affects our understanding of the family situation Anne must negotiate and of her own reactions to and decisions regarding Mr. Elliot and Captain Wentworth. Tracing the progression of the second horizontal axis reveals that the novel's progression depends on Anne's discovery of that which cannot be narrated: her mother's experience of pleasure. For D. A. Miller, "the sex lives of the characters" are both "unincluded and also forbidden" in Jane Austen's novels (4). He asserts, "Subjects like these have no place—not even the shadow of a place—in the novels, and the novels never invoke them to terminate their discourse" (5). However, the submerged plot of *Persuasion* constitutes at least "the shadow of a place" in which women's pleasure in sex is evoked, and the submerged plot contributes significantly to the novel's completeness. Indeed, one way of understanding why the pleasure Anne ultimately experiences must be delayed is to recognize that, before it can be hers, she must find validation for it in her mother's unnarratable story.

The submerged plot of Anne Elliot's search for her mother's pleasure is integral to the textual and readerly dynamics of *Persuasion*; it alters our view of the progression, and it has implications for characterization as well. Each of Lady Elliot's daughters, while appearing entirely occupied with the struggle toward an acceptable marriage within the circumstances established in the surface plot, simultaneously pursues the mother's story, as best she can, with varying degrees of success. Recognizing this second set of motives enriches our understanding of each daughter and of the mother as a character, and the ways the double motivation of each daughter influences both plots emphasize the inextricability of plot and character. Indeed, in the case of each daughter, the degree of completeness achieved in the submerged plot helps to determine the degree of completeness achieved in the surface plot. Our understanding of the novel's progression, as well as our resolution of some interpretive puzzles in the narrative, depend on our reference to the submerged plot. Why are Elizabeth and Anne not married? Why should both Elizabeth and Mary behave so differently from Anne? Why must Anne's marriage to Captain Wentworth be delayed for over eight years, and what has occurred in the interim to make it possible? Why should the breach in Henrietta Musgrove's understanding with Charles Hayter be so comparatively easily healed, and what can explain the marriage between Louisa Musgrove and Captain Benwick? Why does Austen make use of Mrs. Smith to reveal crucial information about Mr. Elliot, when to do so is to rely on a number of coincidences? These questions and others can be addressed by reconsidering the progression of *Persuasion* in light of those moments in the text at which the submerged plot breaks the surface and in light of that which remains always unnarrated.

In his account of the novel's progression in *Experiencing Fiction*, James Phelan demonstrates the usefulness of focusing on what he refers to as the beginning and early middle of the narrative, identifying in them telling differences from Austen's other work. He notes that the launch of the first set of global instabilities is delayed: it follows a surprisingly lengthy mini-narrative about Sir Walter's financial situation, and it happens only at the end of the third chapter, which is also the first moment when "the narrative unequivocally establishes Anne as the protagonist" (36), when the narrator describes Anne walking alone and thinking of an unidentified "*he*" (Austen 25). Phelan's analysis identifies the launch of the surface plot, "Austen's version of the marriage plot" (37), and reveals a great deal about the significance of the delay, but the mini-narrative itself bears more scrutiny, as in it we find the launch of the submerged plot.

The mini-narrative introducing Sir Walter and his indebtedness also offers an outline of Lady Elliot's history and calls attention to the instability created by her absence. From one point of view, the novel is very much about filling the vacant social position "Lady Elliot." Lady Russell, on whom, we are told, Lady Elliot depended to act as a surrogate mother to her daughters, was the first possible candidate, but she "and Sir Walter, did *not* marry, whatever might have been anticipated on that head by their acquaintance" (7). We are further told of "one or two private disappointments" met by Sir Walter in "very unreasonable applications" (7). Mrs. Clay auditions for the parts of Lady Elliot present and future. Still, all of these possibilities, and the addition of Mr. Elliot's dead wife, are not enough to distract us from the most important contenders: Elizabeth, Lady Elliot's eldest daughter, and Anne, the daughter who most resembles her mother. The instability created by the vacancy Lady Elliot has left may help to explain why, when we meet them, Elizabeth and Anne are unmarried at twenty-nine and twenty-seven.

The narrator presents us with relatively few facts of Lady Elliot's life, and even those we may overlook as purely obligatory background information. As *Persuasion* opens we are given an excerpt from the Baronetage, in which Sir Walter finds "his own history" (5). However, the narrator communicates to the reader very quickly that what goes unnoticed by Sir Walter may well be of most interest to us, as when we are told that he undervalues his second daughter, whose qualities "must have placed her high with any people of real understanding" (7), in which category the reader will hope to be placed. Also, by contrasting Sir Walter's feelings about the "book of books" (8) with Elizabeth's, the narrator alerts us to the fact that the entry contains the stories of several people. In it we may find not only the story of Sir Walter but also a brief outline of the life of Elizabeth Stevenson, daughter of a landed gentleman in Gloucestershire, who married Walter Elliot in the summer of 1784. One year later she gave birth to a daughter named Elizabeth, and subsequently to three more children, one every other year, the third of her children a stillborn son. Ten years later she died, after seventeen years of marriage, when her daughters were sixteen, fourteen, and ten. The girls themselves are referred to as "an awful legacy for a mother to bequeath" (6), and the idea of the mother's legacy underlies the text.[3] She has left three young girls "to the authority and guidance of a conceited, silly father" (6), which is to say that she has bequeathed to her daughters Sir Walter Elliot for a father, a bequest that requires, to say the least, some explanation. The reader wonders, as her daughters must, what motivated Lady Elliot's choice of this man. The narrator, having introduced Sir Walter, anticipates our curiosity about what kind of woman would marry such a man by including the following, more direct, account of her:

> His good looks and his rank had one fair claim on his attachment; since to them he must have owed a wife of very superior character to any thing deserved by his own. Lady Elliot had been an excellent woman, sensible and amiable; whose judgment and conduct, if they might be pardoned the youthful infatuation which made her Lady Elliot, had never required indulgence afterwards.—She had humoured, or softened, or concealed

his failings, and promoted his real respectability for seventeen years; and though not the very happiest being in the world herself, had found enough in her duties, her friends, and her children, to attach her to life, and make it no matter of indifference to her when she was called on to quit them. (6)

This passage begins with the narrator's speculation as to why Lady Elliot chose this man to marry, suggesting his good looks and his rank as the primary reasons. The narrator assumes that Sir Walter's rank "must" have been a factor in Lady Elliot's decision, but also explains that she spent most of her married life trying to make Sir Walter worthy of his rank—that she does so honorably and sensibly suggests that she cannot value rank for itself but only for what it should ideally be. The use of the word "infatuation" in the next sentence seems to put more emphasis on Sir Walter's "good looks." We are told that her marriage was her only lapse in "judgment and conduct," and we may well conclude that in a woman whose values were in all other ways above reproach, only infatuation, which implies the promise of pleasure, could have blinded her to her husband's faults, however briefly, or persuaded her to marry him despite those faults.

Readers of *Persuasion* have tended to underread the mimetic component of Lady Elliot's character, assuming that her story is one of suffering only and even exaggerating the unhappiness of her marriage. Sandra Gilbert and Susan Gubar claim that Anne "realizes that her mother lived invisibly, unloved, within Sir Walter's house" (176), and Cheryl Ann Weissman asserts that Anne's legacy from her mother "includes her mother's terrible folly of marrying an unworthy man" (206). The narrator is unrelenting on the subject of Sir Walter's deficiencies but is equally insistent that Lady Elliot was well able to manage her unfortunate situation. Careful attention even to the little we are told enriches the mimetic component and alters our view of the thematic function of her character. What we know of Lady Elliot suggests that she was not invisible in her own home until after she died, and her error in judgment, which nevertheless made her the very capable and respectable mistress of a great house, does not deserve the designation "terrible folly." Indeed, that Lady Elliot is a woman who married despite shortcomings in her husband's character may well suggest that her story includes moments of pleasure—she married Sir Walter, as Lady Russell fears Anne will marry Captain Wentworth, because, despite other considerations, his appearance, his manner, and his behavior toward her promised pleasure. We are told that she was not "the very happiest being in the world," but she found comfort in many things, and the reader learns from Anne's own long experience that living with disappointment is not the thing most to be feared.

With close attention to several details that appear merely expository or else primarily to serve the development of another character, we come to understand that it is not Lady Elliot's admirable life that obscures the story of her pleasure, but her death. The insult to the excellent Lady Elliot is to have been, after her death, forgotten. Significantly, the coldness between the Kellynch family and the Dalrymples is solidified when the Dalrymples refuse condolences on the death of Lady Elliot. Thirteen years later, this refusal is entirely overlooked in Sir Walter's haste to rectify his own justifiable but "unlucky omission" on the occasion of a death in the Dalrymple family (139). Sir Walter also appears to have forgotten his wife in that, as the narrator tells us, those he has asked to marry him since her death were ill chosen (7); furthermore, he receives the attentions of the inferior Mrs. Clay with equanimity. Even more important than these proofs that she is forgotten is that, despite her years of care and planning, the family is now in such serious debt as to be forced to leave their home: "While Lady Elliot lived, there had been method, moderation, and economy [. . .] but with her had died all such right-mindedness" (10). Neither her memory, her standards, nor her example survive her in the mind of her husband.

Comparisons between Lady Elliot's experience and that of her two eldest daughters are established in the novel's first few pages; indeed, despite the fact that Elizabeth Elliot will prove to be a minor character, more than half of the first chapter is devoted to her. We learn a great deal about Elizabeth in these few pages—nearly as much, in fact, as we will ever know—and the effect of the placement of this information is not only the revelation of her character but also the establishment of a context for Anne's search. What we learn about Elizabeth is an encapsulation of her own pursuit of the mother's pleasure, which, though unsuccessful, nevertheless serves to reinforce the necessity of the attempt. This alteration of our understanding of Elizabeth's role in the progression also deepens the mimetic component of her character and changes our understanding of her function in relation to our protagonist. Her search gives her something in common with Anne, which engenders some sympathy in us, the more so because Elizabeth's attempts end in failure, as further analysis of the novel's first chapter makes clear.

Having inherited her name and, to the extent possible, her position, Elizabeth would seem well placed to know Lady Elliot's story best. We are told that "Elizabeth had succeeded, at sixteen, to all that was possible, of her mother's rights and consequence" (7). The narrator goes on to say that

> thirteen years had seen her mistress of Kellynch Hall, presiding and directing with a self-possession and decision which could never have given the idea of her being younger than she was. For thirteen years had she been doing the honours, and laying down the domestic law at home, and leading the way to the chaise and four, and walking immediately after Lady Russell out of all the drawing-rooms and dining-rooms in the country. (8)

Elizabeth appears to feel that her life will follow her mother's in other respects just as easily. We are told that "soon after Lady Elliot's death" Sir Walter insisted upon being introduced to William Walter Elliot, Esq., his "heir presumptive" (9, 6). Her father's kinsman, a man who shares his name and will inherit his house and his title, is the man Elizabeth chooses even before they have met: "she had, while a very young girl, as soon as she had known him to be, in the event of her having no brother, the future baronet, meant to marry him" (9). Elizabeth's firm belief in the appropriateness of this connection is evident when she forgets that he has disappointed her and insulted her family and welcomes his renewed attentions as soon as he deigns to pay them in Bath. Elizabeth repeats a less pleasant aspect of her mother's experience when she is confronted by her father's debts and attempts to make plans for retrenchment. Her rights as eldest daughter should give Elizabeth the advantage over her sisters in understanding her mother's story, but she focuses disproportionately on the superficial elements of rank and connection and thus misinterprets it even as she zealously seeks it. Elizabeth's experience is very like her mother's, but instead of finding in it a fuller understanding of Lady Elliot and, subsequently, moving forward in a new direction of her own, Elizabeth moves backward, confusing learning her mother's story with living her mother's life.

As she steps into Lady Elliot's place, Elizabeth appears to be in a kind of denial of her mother's death, even a denial of the passage of time. The reader wonders at Elizabeth's assumption that her father will not marry again, and at her insistence that he is in no danger from Mrs. Clay; indeed, according to Anne's friend Mrs. Smith, there is "among Sir Walter's acquaintance [. . .] general [. . .] surprise that Miss Elliot should be apparently blind to the danger" (193). Elizabeth seems to think of her father as still married; to some degree, she thinks of him as married to herself. Her response to Anne's warning is to insist haughtily, "As I have a great deal more at stake on this point than any body else can have, I think it rather unnecessary in you to be advising me" (34). Elizabeth thinks of herself as more or less settled as well; we are told that "she had the consciousness of being nine-and-twenty, to give her some regrets and some apprehensions" (8), yet she does not hurry to marry, although "the men are all wild after Miss Elliot" (167). Elizabeth is puzzling because, although she is not free from anxiety about the passing of time, she nevertheless behaves as if she has all the time in the world. She is encouraged in this feeling by her own appearance; the narrator explains,

> It sometimes happens, that a woman is handsomer at twenty-nine than she was ten years before; and, generally speaking, if there has been neither ill health nor anxiety, it is a time of life at which scarcely any charm is lost. It was so with Elizabeth; still the same handsome Miss Elliot that she had begun to be thirteen years ago; and Sir Walter might be excused, therefore, in forgetting her age, or, at least, be deemed only half a fool, for thinking himself and Elizabeth as blooming as ever. (8)

Despite her awareness of "her approach to the years of danger" (8), Elizabeth seems to feel that time has stood still, and this feeling is only enhanced by the fact that she finds herself back in the company of, and with exactly the same intentions toward and hopes regarding, her cousin Mr. Elliot, whom she last saw when she was sixteen or seventeen and "in her first bloom" (9). Her feeling that time has been suspended and her inability to distinguish Lady Elliot from the position she has vacated help to account for Elizabeth's indecision as to which Lady Elliot she intends to be, the present or the future. In this way she is comparable to her friend, Mrs. Clay, who cultivates relationships with both Sir Walter and Mr. Elliot; that she is blind to Mrs. Clay's intentions makes Elizabeth's confusion the more evident. Elizabeth tries to create her own situation in the style of her mother's—to experience for herself what her mother experienced before her. Elizabeth is dedicated to the pursuit of her mother's story, but she is a poor interpreter of it, and her failure to find pleasure, inside or outside of marriage, implies that she has been unable to find it in her mother's story, which she does not know how to value. Elizabeth's regard for rank and social forms leads her into the misapprehension that her mother's place can be filled, encourages her attempt to deny that time is passing, and stymies her in her progress toward pleasure of her own.

We are guided to judge Elizabeth's character harshly, and the explicit contrast between Elizabeth and Anne in the course of the first three chapters encourages us to hope that Anne may yet be more successful than her elder sister in this regard. Still, Elizabeth's example, which dominates the novel's opening chapter, reveals the difficulty of the search and the dangers of failure. Before we become fully aware of Anne's own search, its difficulty is emphasized again in the example of Anne's younger sister, Mary, who is introduced at length when Anne arrives in Uppercross in the fifth chapter. The characterization of Mary Elliot Musgrove as, in Jan Fergus's terms, "a relentless whiner" (69) contributes to the humor of Austen's novel, but also raises the question of why she whines. Fergus finds causes of Mary's imagined suffering in the particularities of her own life: each of her sisters was favored by a parent, but Mary was neglected; Mary was the youngest when her mother died; Mary is less attractive than Elizabeth and Anne, and even finds herself to be Charles Musgrove's second choice after Anne. These are indeed plausible causes, but rereading the progression with awareness of the submerged plot enriches the mimetic component of Mary's character and alters our perception of her place in the character-system by indicating that the primary cause may well lie in what the sisters share: a truncated version of their mother's life story in which Lady Elliot appears an underappreciated and misused wife who died young and was then forgotten by those closest to her. Mary, the only one of the sisters who has followed her mother's example and become a wife, may fear that she, like her mother, will be undervalued and forgotten, especially by her husband. This helps to explain why, although she is not, apparently, ill, Mary feels her complaints deeply and seeks the sympathy of others. In direct contrast to Elizabeth, who makes the mistake of imagining that time stands still, Mary is always moving forward in imagination to her own end, and her main concern is that others will respond to her illness and death as her father responded to her mother's.

When Anne arrives at Uppercross, summoned there because Mary was "foreseeing that she should not have a day's health all the autumn" (32), Mary complains, "So, you are come at last! I began to think I should never see you. I am so ill I can hardly speak" (36). She is especially angry at Charles, who has gone out shooting: "He would go, though I told him how ill I was" (36). Mary desires constant proof that her life has meaning for those around her, that she is thought of, that her needs and concerns are strong enough to influence the actions of others. Anne is the confidante of both husband and wife, and even as Charles tells her, "I wish you could persuade Mary not to be always fancying herself ill," Mary tells her, "I do believe if Charles were to see me dying, he would not think there was any thing the matter with me" (42). This last is the crux of the matter: Mary is compelled continually to reassure herself that Charles would miss her, would remember her, if she died. Her correct but incomplete understanding of her mother's story leaves her with the debilitating mental habit of wondering, as it were, who would come to her funeral. In Mary, the impulse toward the mother's story is a fixation on her death without a full understanding of her life. She mistakenly assumes that if she can escape the ignominy of being forgotten, as her mother was, that in itself will afford access to pleasure. Therefore, she demands constant attention, and she fears nothing more than being left behind or left out. Mary's whining strikes us as comic in the context of the surface plot, but in the context of the submerged plot her complaints are evidence that she, too, is a daughter seeking her mother's story.

These early accounts of Mary's and Elizabeth's failed searches emphasize the importance of Anne's, which also includes elements puzzling to readers. Given that Anne found the promise of pleasure at the age of nineteen with the man she loves, and that both pleasure and love prove lasting and real, what does it mean that Anne was once persuaded to reject that pleasure? Why is it necessary that she and Wentworth be separated at all, and, if only for the explicit reasons, why could they not have been reunited just two years after their broken engagement, when Wentworth had made his fortune? What is the effect on Anne of Wentworth's failure to return to her after the obstacle to their marriage has been removed? What is it that has changed after eight and a half years, and what is gained in the interval? These matters, which are difficult to account for with reference to the surface plot alone, are more fully explained by tracing both the textual and the readerly dynamics of the submerged plot of Anne's engagement with her mother's story.

James Phelan answers these questions by concluding that "the layered rhetorical communications of the progression show Austen, while ultimately committed to her narrative comedy, exploring a deeper sense of pain, loss, undeserved misfortune, and the irrevocable quality of some mistakes than she ever has before" (*Experiencing* 50). In support of this conclusion, he notes of the separation between Anne and Wentworth that "those eight years are far from being a necessary route to the happy outcome" (50).[4] Phelan's reading does not account for what is gained during the eight years—they are only to be regretted, the result of an error. Further, his reading emphasizes that, given the narrative situation as Austen defines it, to some extent Anne "can only be herself and wait" (39): she is constrained by circumstances from acting to bring about the change she desires even while her mind and heart are fully aware of what she has lost and has yet to lose.[5] He argues that one distinctive characteristic of the novel is that "Austen is working with a progression in which her protagonist has no internal instability that she needs to overcome"; that is, Anne need undergo no change of feeling or of character (38–39). Phelan observes that this challenges Austen to find ways to "make Anne a significant agent of her own happiness," which is crucial for an "aesthetically satisfying" progression (39).

Attention to the submerged plot suggests that Anne is less passive than she at first appears, that she is actively engaged in a pursuit on which the events in the surface plot depend. Indeed, Anne need not change in character, nor in her feelings for Wentworth, but her feelings about pleasure require, if not alteration, then at least validation. As a young woman, Anne embraced the promise of pleasure. However, that she was persuaded to renounce it for material and social reasons alerts us to the limitations of her confidence in that promise. Although the reader is unlikely to blame Anne for her decision or think less of her character for being persuaded by her friends, Wentworth's anger, which keeps him from her until they are thrown together by circumstance, reminds us that her choice was not self-evident. Anne's decision clearly works against her own progress toward pleasure, but it does not destroy that progress altogether. We learn that Anne hoped Wentworth would renew his proposal after he had won his fortune, just two years later: "had he wished ever to see her again, he need not have waited till this time; he would have done what she could not but believe that in his place she should have done long ago, when events had been early giving him the independence which alone had been wanting" (55). When he asks her, after their final reconciliation, whether, had he written to her then, "would you [. . .] have renewed the engagement then?" she responds, "Would I!" (231). This attention to what did not happen six years before the novel opens enables us to see the way Anne's confidence in her own pleasure has been shaken, first by her own decision, and then, perhaps even more, by his decision not to propose again when the obstacle between them has been removed. The narrator has already told us that Anne's "bloom had vanished early" (7), but Anne's changed relation to pleasure helps to explain Wentworth's surprised admission, repeated three times in the narration when Anne hears of it, that she is "so altered that he should not have known her again!" (57). Before she can be reunited with Wentworth, she must find validation for the pleasure so strongly disaffirmed by both of them. She finds that validation by recovering the story of her mother that has been denied her; her successful search for that story is as necessary for the novel's completion as the change in Wentworth's feelings.[6]

Anne learns her mother's unnarratable story by repeating elements of it. Other scholars have noted that Anne repeats her mother's experience in some respects, but ultimately rejects the opportunity, afforded by the prospect of marriage to her cousin, of living in her place. Susan Peck MacDonald observes that Anne "can and does arrive at a sort of private recreation in which she becomes a wife and (potentially) a mother—like her own mother but not a copy of her mother" (66). Diana Postlethwaite also identifies Anne's motherlessness as the central problem, and asserts that "Anne Elliot can affirm that she 'is her mother's self' without 'becoming what her mother had been'" (45). For both, repeating her mother's experience is a temptation that Anne must resist in order to find her own life; I argue, in contrast, that repeating her mother's experience is a process Anne must go through in order to embrace her own life when she finds it.

As Anne comes into focus as the novel's main character, we can identify elements of her circumstances that are shared with many other motherless protagonists, and these elements work in favor of the search. She lives in her mother's house, surrounded by the people who surrounded Lady Elliot. Anne's closest friend and mentor is Lady Russell, who was also her mother's closest friend. As her mother has been forgotten since her death, she herself is consistently overlooked and forgotten by her father and Elizabeth. Neither of them appears at first to remember her attachment to Frederick Wentworth, neither would think to consult her regarding plans for retrenchment, neither considers her feelings as they demonstrate their preference for the company of Mrs. Clay. These conditions have long been familiar to Anne; new opportunities to know her mother's experience are opened when Anne, like her mother, feels the shame of Sir Walter's debts and makes plans for the discharging of them. As readers, we recognize that these similarities function as characterization, establishing Anne as, like her mother, admirable and long-suffering among people who are unworthy of her. When we consider the second horizontal axis as well, we also recognize that these details point to events that Anne lives every day: they are matters not just of character but also of progression, and, indeed, they illustrate the intertwining of character and event.

The resolution of the initial mini-narrative is that Anne expects to leave Kellynch for Bath, a trip she has made twice before—once immediately after her mother's death, and once following the end of her engagement to Captain Wentworth (15, 28)—and which she dreads. Happily, Anne is reprieved at the last moment when "something occurred [. . .] to give her a different duty" (32): Mary requests that Anne come to stay with her. Further, her trip to Uppercross is "diversified in a way which she had not at all imagined" when she accompanies the others to Lyme (88). That Anne's visits to Uppercross and Lyme are presented as interruptions of Anne's true course, interludes in which she may well feel herself more observer than actor, may help to explain why, as Phelan describes the Uppercross section of the novel, "consistent with the narrative situation in which it is Wentworth rather than Anne who must change, Austen's approach to the voyage is to show Anne's essentially static situation as she watches Wentworth become increasingly involved with Louisa Musgrove" (*Experiencing* 40). Indeed, Anne's progress in the surface plot is minimal in this section, but her progress in the submerged plot is more substantial.

That Anne is diverted from traveling to Bath, which she associates with both the end of her mother's life and the end of her progress toward pleasure with Wentworth, is felt by her, and the reader, as a hopeful sign, and, indeed, it is in Uppercross and Lyme that Anne finds herself back in the company of the man she has never stopped loving. In her role as an observer, Anne is forced to witness as Wentworth takes a considerable and very public interest in another woman, but this is not all. She also witnesses the courtships and engagements of two sisters, which progress rapidly and, to all appearances, successfully. The reader is struck, as Anne must be, by the relative ease, compared to Anne and her sister Elizabeth, with which Henrietta and Louisa Musgrove manage their attachments. We may be tempted to think of the Musgroves as less complex, but in fact the two sets of sisters have a good deal in common. Elizabeth and Henrietta both feel an attachment of very long standing to a cousin, and Anne and Louisa both admire and are admired by the same men—Captain Wentworth and Captain Benwick. In Henrietta's relationship with Charles Hayter, as in Anne's relationship with Wentworth, an understanding is breached but healed later to the satisfaction of all. What they have in common heightens the contrast between the Musgroves' early marriages and the Elliots' deferred ones and invites us to reconsider the characters of Louisa and Henrietta and also to reconsider their relation to the protagonist in the character-system.

The Musgrove sisters are younger than the Elliots, and certainly less committed to intellectual pursuits than Anne, but the most important difference seems to be that Henrietta and Louisa manifest an openness to and a confidence in pleasure that remains out of Elizabeth's reach and that, after eight years of separation from Wentworth, six of them by his choice, Anne can only recover by completing her search. Dispiriting though the contrast must be to Anne, and painful as it is to see Louisa the object of Wentworth's attention, the similarities between the two sets of sisters suggest that Louisa, who functions primarily as a rival on the first horizontal axis, may function on the second as a model in whom Anne can observe behavior that may repeat her mother's. An implicit comparison of their families on the narrative's first page suggests that Louisa may be positioned quite similarly to the young Elizabeth Stevenson. Louisa's father is described as "Charles Musgrove, Esq. of Uppercross, in the county of Somerset," and Elizabeth's as "James Stevenson, Esq. of South Park, in the county of Gloucester" (5). If Louisa's upbringing and home life repeat Elizabeth's in some respects, then Louisa's obvious pleasure in Captain Wentworth may reveal something to Anne about the pleasure that encouraged Elizabeth Stevenson to become Lady Elliot. As Judy Van Sickle Johnson reminds us with reference to Louisa, "This is a novel in which a young woman leaps off a sea wall because the sensation of being in a man's arms is delightful to her" (60). Anne is not, as Phelan has observed, typical of Austen's protagonists, and neither is Louisa Musgrove typical of her rival characters. Louisa is, for example, no calculating and manipulative Lucy Steele, despite the fact that, like Lucy, she achieves a hold on the man the protagonist loves and then, with little explanation, marries his brother officer, as Lucy marries Edward Ferrars's brother.[7] She is not, like Lucy, merely an obstacle to the protagonist's progress, easily dismissed. Louisa's situation is central to the action of *Persuasion,* and, although we desire and expect her separation from Wentworth, we are likely to regret the loss of her youthful enthusiasm and uncomplicated motives as her character changes and as she disappears from the text following her accident. Anne herself, alone at Uppercross, contemplates the "more than former happiness" that will characterize the house if Louisa recovers, and knows that Louisa's marriage to Wentworth would bring to the house "all that was glowing and bright in prosperous love, all that was most unlike Anne Elliot!" (114–15). Anne knows that marriage to Louisa Musgrove would not be disastrous for Wentworth, which makes the particulars of Louisa's situation even more painful for Anne. At the same time, she knows that "all that was glowing and bright" should not be unlike herself, and Louisa's ability to embrace pleasure, and Wentworth's response to that element of her character, may nevertheless be instructive for Anne.

In addition to what she might learn by observing Louisa, Anne is afforded more direct knowledge of her mother's experience by the ways her own character is similar to her mother's. We are alerted to these similarities by Lady Russell as the novel opens, and they become increasingly evident as the narrative progresses. As Anne's good judgment, practicality, and compassion become more efficacious and more appreciated—by those who are capable of doing so—throughout the episodes in Uppercross and Lyme, shared character traits become shared experience between mother and daughter. At Kellynch, Anne's suggestions for retrenchment are disregarded entirely, and the situation seems little better at Uppercross, where her attention to Mary is as much taken for granted as her piano accompaniment to the dancing of the Miss Musgroves. Her nursing of her nephew after his fall is no more appreciated than her other contributions, but she herself admits its importance, and "her usefulness to little Charles would always give some sweetness to the memory of her [. . .] visit" (87). She is perhaps first appreciated by Captain Benwick, and by Captain Harville on his behalf, who tells Anne "you have done a good deed in making that poor fellow talk so much" (100). Anne's clear-headed behavior following Louisa's accident earns her Wentworth's earnest plea that she stay in Lyme and the Musgroves' "dread" of her leaving Uppercross (114). In her usefulness to others Anne is the opposite of her sisters—of Elizabeth, whose idea of retrenchment is to curtail charitable giving, and of Mary, who regards her child's accident as an imposition on her dinner plans and Captain Benwick's melancholy silence as a personal insult. Like her mother, Anne makes use of her own gifts even in service of those who cannot value them and to find friendship with those who can.

Arriving in Bath offers Anne an opportunity to repeat a final, crucial part of her mother's experience: her acquaintance with Mr. Elliot provides her with the experience of being courted and honestly admired by a man who is charming and agreeable, who is fortunate in having "something of the Elliot countenance" (99), who shares her father's name and who will inherit Kellynch Hall—a man, in fact, like the one her mother chose. Having noticed his admiration of her at Lyme, Anne is further prepared for what is to come by a brief trip back to Kellynch, where she pays a visit to the Crofts in her own childhood home, which she associates so strongly with her mother. The narrator describes Anne's feelings about going to Kellynch Hall with the Crofts in residence, and reports that she finds they deserve the great house more than the Elliots, "except when she thought of her mother, and remembered where she had been used to sit and preside" (117). That Mrs. Croft now presides where Lady Elliot did before her is an indication in the surface plot that Anne's future will ultimately be more like hers, the wife of a naval officer, than like her mother's. Anne's remembrance functions in the submerged plot as well, however, and makes her sensible of the great advantage of a marriage with Mr. Elliot voiced clearly by Lady Russell:

> I own that to be able to regard you as the future mistress of Kellynch, the future Lady Elliot—to look forward and see you occupying your dear mother's place, succeeding to all her rights, and all her popularity, as well as to all her virtues, would be the highest possible gratification to me.— You are your mother's self in countenance and disposition; and if I might be allowed to fancy you such as she was, in situation, and name, and home, presiding and blessing in the same spot, and only superior to her in being more highly valued! (150)

Lady Russell, long Anne's mentor and closely connected to Anne's mother, is still very persuasive, and her effect on Anne is strong: "For a few moments her imagination and her heart were bewitched. The idea of becoming what her mother had been; of having the precious name of 'Lady Elliot' first revived in herself; of being restored to Kellynch, calling it her home again, her home for ever, was a charm which she could not immediately resist" (150). Here the submerged plot breaks the surface: Anne considers marriage with her cousin not only because she believes Wentworth to be out of reach forever, or because her cousin is an eligible match, but also because to feel drawn to Mr. Elliot is to feel what her mother had felt before her. In Anne's case, the false suitor strongly resembles the father and provides an opportunity to understand the mother's choice.[8] The faults of both Sir Walter and Mr. Elliot include selfishness, insensitivity to the needs and even the rights of others, and irresponsibility in their handling of money. When Anne learns her cousin's true character from Mrs. Smith, her shock may be akin to what her mother experienced when, a married woman, she was forced to face the seriousness of her husband's shortcomings.

That the truth about Mr. Elliot should come to Anne through Mrs. Smith depends on more than one coincidence in the surface plot. One is that, as Anne's schoolmate and mentor, she should have met and married Charles Smith, Anne's cousin's closest companion. A second is that Anne should meet Mrs. Smith again, after twelve years, just when she becomes acquainted with her cousin. A third is that, through Nurse Rooke's attendance on both herself and Mrs. Wallis, Mrs. Smith should, once again, have access to more information about Mr. Elliot than Anne has. These coincidences in the surface plot have the effect of directing the reader's attention to the submerged plot of Anne's search for her mother's story. Mrs. Smith is associated in Anne's mind with the death of her mother: "Anne had gone unhappy to school, grieving for the loss of a mother whom she had dearly loved, feeling her separation from home, and suffering." Mrs. Smith (Miss Hamilton then), a few years older, "had been useful and good to her in a way which had considerably lessened her misery" (143). These circumstances connect Mrs. Smith with Lady Elliot directly, and Mrs. Smith's own situation connects her with Lady Elliot indirectly. What we know about Mrs. Smith is that "her husband had been extravagant" and "had left his affairs dreadfully involved" (143). Mrs. Smith, then, has known what it is to be tied to a man who is irresponsible with money; unlike Lady Elliot, Mrs. Smith was unsuccessful in curbing her husband's excesses, and she has suffered for it. Yet Mrs. Smith speaks of "my dear husband" (187), and says of his relationship with Mr. Elliot, "My poor Charles, who had the finest, most generous spirit in the world, would have divided his last farthing with him" (188). The same interview, then, that communicates to Anne the certain evils to herself of marrying this man like the one her mother chose, also communicates, through the example of Mrs. Smith's experience, that marriage to a man possessing a serious fault with dire consequences, even the same fault that her father has, does not necessarily preclude pleasure altogether. That this scene advances the submerged plot in several ways seems to justify Austen's risking a series of coincidences in the surface plot to include it.

In fact, Anne has not needed Mrs. Smith's revelation to distrust her cousin: what she does know of her mother's story has prepared her to recognize what is wrong in him. This is a man whose wife has been dead for only seven months, yet who is steadily courting another woman. Anne observes that Mr. Elliot, like her father, will not sufficiently value his wife, and he has demonstrated already that he will not remember her in her absence. Indeed, Anne finds herself the object of the attention of two men who have, it appears, forgotten their past attachments even while still in mourning. Other characters take such matters more lightly than Anne. When Anne reminds Mrs. Smith that "Mr. Elliot's wife has not been dead much above half a year. He ought not to be supposed to be paying his addresses to anyone" (184), Mrs. Smith dismisses her objection. Even Lady Russell is willing to suspend her judgment of Captain Benwick for his similar behavior; she tells Mary that she must see Captain Benwick for herself before judging whether "such a heart" is worth having (123).[9] But Anne stands by her own judgment, and she learns from their attentions to her that, whether one is the "low woman" (189) Mr. Elliot has married and lost or the saintly Fanny Harville, apparently forgotten by Benwick, one cannot depend upon being remembered for even a year after one's death.

Thus, Anne experiences the charm of her mother's attachment to her father, the disillusionment of such an attachment, and the pain of knowing oneself to be forgettable. This is the story Anne needs to know before recovering her confidence in pleasure and giving herself completely to Wentworth. Given her own experience of being separated from Wentworth, and given what she learns of her mother's story, we are not surprised that for Anne the mark of a great love is "loving longest, when existence or when hope is gone" (221). When Anne claims that women love in this way rather than men, she refers explicitly to Benwick, covertly to Wentworth, and, in the context of the submerged plot, to Sir Walter. She regrets that her mother was not the object of this kind of love, and values her love for Wentworth in part for its very longevity: love, in their case, has nearly outlived hope. Anne feels secure in Wentworth's ability to value her, and to remember her. He says, and means, "A man does not recover from such a devotion of the heart to such a woman!—He ought not—he does not" (173). Eight years have not made him forget Anne, even though "he had meant to forget her, and believed it to be done" (226). We are to understand that in her relationship with Wentworth Anne will not have to pay for her pleasure by being forgotten.

To accept Anne's judgment and Wentworth's declaration may raise questions about the aftermath of Louisa Musgrove's accident at Lyme. Wentworth's flirtation with Louisa cannot be comparable in seriousness to Mr. Elliot's marriage or Captain Benwick's engagement, but the fact remains that when Louisa is in a state resembling death, Captain Wentworth cannot get away fast enough. Austen ensures that the reader is always aware that Wentworth will not marry Louisa by allowing us to understand the significance of Wentworth's attentions to Anne even before she does (rescuing her from an overly exuberant nephew, securing her a ride when she is weary of walking). Also, we understand clearly his motives for leaving Lyme: he realizes he has "entangled himself" (227) at the same time that he realizes that he cannot love Louisa. Nevertheless, Anne is shocked by the news that Louisa is to marry Captain Benwick and not Captain Wentworth. Our comfort with Wentworth's reliability may arise in part from our understanding that when Louisa is recuperating—significantly, in the Harvilles' home—both he and Benwick are likely thinking of Fanny Harville, whom Captain Benwick's mourning has in fact kept in everyone's mind. With Louisa lying ill in the Harvilles' house, as Fanny must have lain not so long before, Wentworth realizes what it means to him that his loss of Anne may not be irrevocable. This implicit comparison between Louisa and Fanny also helps to explain Captain Benwick's proposal, which seems incomprehensible to those who know him, and to many readers, including Loraine Fletcher, who asserts that Benwick's "mourning is mainly if unintentionally fake" (84). That readers are not likely to lose all respect for Benwick or fear that Louisa is marrying someone truly unworthy may be attributable to the implication that, in Louisa, Benwick sees something of his beloved Fanny.

Although Wentworth has escaped the pain of losing Anne forever, in keeping with the tradition of sons who fear the forces of the possible, he still dwells fruitlessly on fantasies of intervening in the past, as when he asks her whether, two years after their broken engagement, when he had fulfilled his promise in his profession, she would have agreed to marry him (231). He tends toward remorse, remembering an action he might have taken had he not been ruled by resentment born, then too, of remorse. However, Wentworth benefits from Anne's example. She never entertains the idea that she can change the past, and never considers the future to be unduly shadowed by it. She tells him, "I have been thinking over the past, and trying impartially to judge of the right and wrong, I mean with regard to myself; and I must believe that I was right" (230). Certainly, Anne might as well believe that she was right, for the power to change her decision is long past, but her willingness to believe is a sign that she is not afraid of the very idea of what might have happened. She teaches him in general, as she teaches him with regard to the incident at Lyme, that "when the pain is over, the remembrance of it often becomes a pleasure. One does not love a place the less for having suffered in it, unless it has been all suffering, nothing but suffering" (173). Anne is willing to search for traces of pleasure amid suffering, and she recognizes them when she finds them. The submerged plot of Anne Elliot's successful search for the unnarratable story of her mother's pleasure is one factor that makes possible a true reconciliation with Wentworth and the completion of the surface plot.

"Against the advice of all her friends": Jane Reed Eyre

Attention to the submerged plot of *Persuasion* reveals that Anne Elliot's manifest independence of mind is matched by more independent action on her own behalf than is immediately evident. Similarly, recognition of the submerged plot of Charlotte Brontë's *Jane Eyre* influences our perception of Brontë's protagonist and of the implications of her decisions and actions. Jane Eyre has long been seen by readers and scholars as a character epitomizing independent action. Indeed, part of the appeal of *Jane Eyre* is that its protagonist, an orphan largely unprotected from the evils of the world, makes her own way and relies on herself alone. She rarely mentions her missing parents; she does not dwell on their absence or express a need for them. Barbara Thaden argues that Jane desires to be seen as a "self-creation ex-nihilo" (38). Jane appears almost entirely self-sufficient, but, even as her narrative unfolds the riveting, suspenseful surface plot of her assertion of herself in a series of oppressive circumstances, the submerged plot, visible only when we reconsider particular details that are usually underread, traces her engagement with the unnarratable story of her mother's pleasure and reveals her acknowledgment of connections and mutual dependencies between herself and other women.

The surface plot of *Jane Eyre* is very much the story of Jane's solitary pilgrim's progress, as Gilbert and Gubar express it, toward "the independent maturity which is the goal of her pilgrimage" (350). The idea of pilgrimage is reflected in the linearity of the progression, in which Jane overcomes one obstacle after another and indicates an orientation toward the future, toward that famous final result, "Reader, I married him" (473). Jane is a character narrator confident in the significance of her own story, and she rarely addresses explicitly any history beyond her own. Compared to Anne Elliot, Jane Eyre appears to leave the past behind with relative ease; implicitly, however, the past is very much with Jane.

Although her journeys nearly always take her to new places, she travels backward when she returns to Gateshead Hall to attend at her Aunt Reed's deathbed. The evening she returns to Thornfield from this journey back, she encounters Rochester in a twilit field and informs him, "I have been with my aunt, sir, who is dead." Rochester responds, "A true Janian reply! Good angels be my guard! She comes from the other world—from the abode of people who are dead" (257). Rochester's exclamation resonates through Jane's story, an apt description of her circumstances on more than one occasion. When, in her infancy, she is taken by relatives from the house in which her parents have died of typhus, Rochester's description is literally true. The early scenes at Gateshead emphasize that it is the site of her Uncle Reed's death, just as years later it is the scene of her aunt's death and inspires Rochester's remark. When Rochester learns that Jane was educated at Lowood Institution, he exclaims that she must be "tenacious of life" to have survived eight years there (127); indeed, Lowood has been the home of very many girls who are long since dead, including Helen Burns, who dies in Jane's arms. Even Moor House is the scene of her Uncle Rivers's recent death, and when Jane returns to Rochester for the last time at Ferndean, she has come from the ruins of Thornfield, where Bertha Mason Rochester leaped to her death. Rochester's remarkably accurate observation alerts us to the fact that this most independent and future-oriented of young women is figured frequently in the novel as a recent inmate of the past, as coming from "the abode of people who are dead." Jane's engagement with the past is most evident in the submerged plot of Brontë's novel, and analysis of the submerged plot reveals that its completion is a necessary component of the completion of the surface plot.

Even as the surface plot appears to provide ample motivation for Jane's decisions and actions, the submerged plot reveals another set of motives that are just as important. As Jane appears to move steadily and confidently toward her goals in the surface plot, she simultaneously seeks validation for those goals in the submerged plot by learning her mother's story. Recognizing Jane's double motivation reveals and alters our perception of elements of her character. The mimetic component is enriched by our understanding of the ways Jane does, in fact, acknowledge her connections to the past and to other women, beginning with her mother. That she does so alters her thematic function: rather than a protagonist who must sacrifice her relationships with others in order to gain her independence, Jane can be seen as a protagonist who understands the ways her independence is a product of her relationships with others. As we trace the evidence of this thematic function, we come to understand some of the novel's minor characters differently and to reconsider their places in the character-system.

Jane Eyre includes very little that is explicit about its protagonist's mother, and scholars have generally concluded that Jane's mother is presented by Brontë as at least irrelevant and at most a force to be rejected or eliminated in the interest of Jane's progress. Adrienne Rich's 1973 essay is an exception: in her "Jane Eyre: The Temptations of a Motherless Woman," Rich analyzes the effects of surrogate mothers in the novel and asserts that "individual women have helped Jane Eyre to the point of her severest trial; at that point she is in relation to the Great Mother herself" (102). Scholars since then, however, have disagreed. Just a few years later, Elaine Showalter maintained of the novel, "There is sporadic sisterhood and kindness between the women in this world [. . .] but on the whole these women are helpless to aid each other, even if they want to" (*A Literature of Their Own* 117). More recent arguments have maintained Showalter's view as the prevalent one. Penny Boumelha contends, with reference to Rich's analysis:

> It has been suggested that there is a matriarchal story within *Jane Eyre*, of Jane's turning to and learning from mother figures. There is the shadow of such a narrative in the novel, but it is, I think, a defeatist one in which Jane tests the limits of a mother-centred world and is turned back to the patriarchal determinations of kinship and inheritance. (134)

She further asserts that "this fantasied matriarchal world has no power within the world of social organisation that is necessary for survival" (137). Margaret Homans and Marianne Hirsch both suggest that Jane must actively reject the mother in order to write her story. For Homans, this means rejecting the mother's valuable gift of the literal in order to enter the father's world, in which the figurative is arbitrarily privileged. Homans concludes, with reference to *Jane Eyre,* that "the daughter's continued close connection to her mother long past her entry into androcentric culture" is "a connection that [. . .] a daughter who is a figure for the novelist, whose main allegiance is to the father's symbol making, finds very difficult to sustain and finally rejects" (94). In her article "Jane's Family Romances," Hirsch maintains that

> for most nineteenth-century heroines maternal absence actually engenders feminine fictions. Plot demands the separation of heroines from the messages of powerlessness and disinheritance which mothers tend to transmit. Maternal stories are stories not to be repeated: from the perspective of fictional plot, mothers can only be examples not to be emulated. (168)

Hirsch argues that the story of Jane Eyre's mother is an example of this: "she is the victim of the social constraints that delimit women's lives; but, from a different perspective, she has to die so that her daughter might have a story" (169). For all of these critics, the mother's story in Brontë's novel has little to offer the seeking daughter, and, to the extent that it does, must, nevertheless, be rejected.

Reconsidering the progression of the novel, however, reveals that Brontë is more interested than we may initially realize in the mother as a character in her own right. Adjusting our sense of the character-space occupied by Jane Reed Eyre enables us to further recognize that Brontë is focused on the extent to which her mother's experience has already determined Jane's situation, the effect on her of hearing her mother's story, the significance of her observation of other mother and daughter relationships, and, most importantly, the ways in which she explores her mother's life in her own. Indeed, although the reader is given only the outline of Jane Reed Eyre's life story, we come to recognize that her daughter actually repeats her experiences in many important particulars. Far from rejecting the mother's story, Jane actively seeks the story of her mother's pleasure that is unnarratable but that is necessary to the validation of Jane's own pleasure. Jane's goal, which in the surface plot seems patently to be discovery of the self, appears, in light of the submerged plot, to be fundamentally discovery of the mother. To recognize this is to gain a new understanding of Jane's character and of her relationships, with Edward Rochester and St. John Rivers, but also with other women. Attention to the unobtrusive surfacings of the submerged plot also helps to solve some interpretive puzzles created by Jane's narrative. In the context of the surface plot alone, even readers who welcome the romance elements of Jane's relationship with Rochester are likely to find the Moor House section of the novel puzzling, even extraneous. Even granted that for a variety of reasons Jane must move on from Thornfield for a time before committing herself finally to Rochester, why must the circumstances of that moving on be dependent on the unrealistic coincidence that Jane wanders in the countryside for days only to faint from inanition on the doorstep of her paternal relatives, of whose existence she has heretofore been entirely ignorant? Why is St. John Rivers given such a critical role in the novel? Why does he speak the novel's final words? The answers to these questions, not fully accessible with reference to the surface plot alone, become more evident in light of the submerged plot.

The launches of the two plots of *Jane Eyre* are simultaneous and immediate as the novel opens. As Jane retaliates against the abuse of her cousin John Reed and then fights those who would restrain her, she explains, "I resisted all the way: a new thing for me" (12). Jane selects for the starting point of her narrative the first moment when she begins to rebel against those who oppress her and to assert her own will. This marked change in Jane's responses to her world will characterize her responses to the events to come as well, and it signals the launch of the plot of Jane's progress toward independence. At the same time, from this early point the surface plot is closely bound to the submerged plot, and Jane's pursuit of her mother's story is launched in these first scenes, in which, like her mother before her, Jane asserts herself even at the risk of being expelled from her home.

We first encounter Jane in her much-interpreted window seat, and, although the scene in the drawing room, where Mrs. Reed "lay reclined on a sofa by the fire-side, and with her darlings about her" (7), may appear to be the center of maternal warmth at Gateshead, Jane's own position is an idealized maternal space. Her description implies what she never explicitly says, that this house is associated with her mother. She tells us, "I was shrined in double retirement": in the breakfast room, a place associated with nourishment, and in the window seat itself, where "folds of scarlet drapery shut in my view to the right hand; to the left were the clear panes of glass, protecting, but not separating me from the drear November day" (8). In this womb-like enclosure, Jane is protected but not separated from the world; indeed, the world intrudes all too soon in the person of her cousin.

The focus on the maternal is maintained by John Reed, as he searches his mind for an excuse for abusing Jane and arrives at this one: "You have no business to take our books: you are a dependant, mama says; you have no money; your father left you none; you ought to beg, and not to live here with gentlemen's children like us [. . .]. Now, I'll teach you to rummage my book-shelves: for they *are* mine; all the house belongs to me, or will do in a few years" (11). Jane knows as she narrates that Gateshead Hall will never belong to John Reed, that, years later, when John seeks to take possession of the property, his mother will refuse, and he will succumb to addiction and suicide before he can become Gateshead's master. Jane the child cannot know this; nevertheless, John's speech, in which he emphasizes her lack of father-conferred rights even as he invokes his "mama" as an authority, implies that mothers have power in John's world. John is fatherless, as Jane is, and his reference to "gentlemen's children" reminds us that the gentleman in question has been dead nearly as long as Jane's own father. A mother dominates this section of the novel, which may recall Jane's mother and a sense of her mother-conferred rights, those John would like to obscure. Marianne

Hirsch, who maintains that her mother's death is necessary for Jane's progress, nevertheless asserts that Jane's "individuality is firmly upheld by the class allegiance she can claim through maternal certainty" ("Jane's Family Romances" 174). Apart from her class inheritance from her mother, what Jane has of her is the Hall itself, her mother's childhood home. We know that Gateshead does not change much over time; when Jane returns to it after eight years, she notes, "There was every article of furniture looking just as it did on the morning I was first introduced to Mr. Brocklehurst [. . .]. The inanimate objects were not changed" (239). This house has not changed at all in the eighteen years of Jane's life, and we can assume that it was the same less than two years before that, when Jane Reed herself left Gateshead. John endeavors to see in the house his future, but the entire house is already a memorial to the past, and that past includes the life of Jane Reed Eyre.

Jane's narrative of the Reeds' harsh treatment of her reflects her memory of being sadly, uniquely bereft of maternal protection and, in response, germinating the rebellious attitude that will precipitate her expulsion from Gateshead. Her narrative elicits our sympathy and enlists our loyalty. At the same time, Brontë communicates to the reader that Jane's situation is not unique; in fact, in these particulars she is reliving her mother's experience. Jane Reed, whose mother is never mentioned and, in any case, failed to protect her from the wrath of her father, was alienated from her childhood home when her passion for Jane's father motivated her to act against the wishes of her family. Both Jane and her mother are cast out because of the same prejudices on the part of those at Gateshead against the less august Eyre family, and because of their strong wills and passionate natures. As in the case of Anne Elliot, these initial similarities may appear to function primarily to characterize Jane and her mother as superior to those around them. However, attention to the progression reveals that these shared characteristics motivate similar actions in both women. The traits Jane shares with her mother become experiences they share, and, even as Jane appears to react understandably to her treatment by the Reeds, she is also learning what it feels like to act as her mother did before her.

For both women, Uncle Reed's kindness and favor are a comfort. We know that Jane Reed's brother "opposed the family's disowning her when she made her low marriage" (243), and Jane reflects that he had saved her from an orphanage and that "if Mr. Reed had been alive he would have treated me kindly" (17). However, Reed is unable to save either of them, demonstrating that mothers are not alone in being unable to protect the ones they love from the harshness of the world. Jane Eyre's banishment from Gateshead is set in motion by the incident in the red-room, her Uncle Reed's bedroom, which has been interpreted by psychoanalytic critics as evidence of Jane's early negotiation of oedipal issues. In this view, Jane defies the mother figure (her aunt) and is punished by being locked in her dead uncle's bedroom, which precipitates either a fantasied consummation of a sexual relationship with the father figure (her uncle), as David Smith interprets the scene (137), or a desire to do so followed by a "strong inner repression," as John Maynard interprets it (103). These readings are supported by detailed analysis of the scene and its imagery, and also by the fact that, much later, at what is often read as the height of Jane's oedipal crisis, when she decides to flee Rochester rather than remain with him on unequal terms, she writes that she "was transported in thought to the scenes of childhood: I dreamt I lay in the red-room at Gateshead; that the night was dark, and my mind impressed with strange fears" (336). The two scenes are connected in Jane's mind, and psychoanalytic arguments encourage us to interpret the first episode as full of oedipal implications and then carry its associations over to the second.

However, the text establishes that the second vision is a fuller realization of the first, and the second vision is clearly identified as Jane's mother. During her last night at Thornfield, she dreams of a figure that "gazed and gazed on me. It spoke, to my spirit: immeasurably distant was the tone, yet so near, it whispered in my heart—'My daughter, flee temptation!' 'Mother, I will'" (337). Jane identifies what she sees in her dream as her mother and claims that it is the same as what she saw that long-ago night; therefore, we must consider the possibility that, although what Jane explicitly fears in the red-room is an encounter with the spirit of her Uncle Reed, she may unconsciously sense the presence of her mother. Indeed, Reed's similar relation to his sister and his niece means that, for Jane, thoughts of him are likely to invoke thoughts of her mother. Although much of the imagery of the red-room has been convincingly analyzed as masculine, Elaine Showalter contends that "the red-room [. . .] is a paradigm of female inner space [. . .]. With its deadly and bloody connotations, its Freudian wealth of secret compartments, wardrobes, drawers, and jewel chest, the red-room has strong associations with the adult female body" (*A Literature of Their Own* 114–15). Showalter reads this scene as the moment of Jane's "emotional menarche" (113) and suggests that "it is thus as if the mysterious crime for which the Reeds were punishing Jane were the crime of growing up" (114). Showalter urges us to read the imagery of the room as an expression of the adult female body, and suggests that the body is Jane's. However, particularly given the precedent of the womb-like window seat, we may reasonably associate the red-room with Jane Reed, the maternal body. This association need not utterly conflict with the more straightforward Freudian reading: here, we might assume, Jane Reed's own oedipal drama played out. The disinheritance of a daughter can be read as the father's attempt to discourage suitors, thwart her plans to marry, and keep her for himself. We should consider this among the motives for Grandfather Reed's disinheritance of his "disobedient" daughter, and, if Jane indeed arrives at an oedipal crisis in the red-room, she is repeating her mother's experience in this as in other details.

These initial scenes, then, invoke for the reader Jane Reed Eyre, and they prepare us to recognize the progression of the second horizontal axis. The submerged plot surfaces immediately following the scene in the red-room when, as in *Persuasion*, the reader is given an encapsulated version of the mother's life story that will guide our recognition of the ways the daughter repeats it. As Jane lies in bed, still recovering from the shock of the previous day's events, she first learns the outline of her mother's story by overhearing Miss Abbot give a brief history of her life to Bessie. Jane reports hearing

> that my father had been a poor clergyman; that my mother had married him against the wishes of her friends, who considered the match beneath her; that my grandfather Reed was so irritated at her disobedience, he cut her off without a shilling; that after my mother and father had been married a year, the latter caught the typhus fever while visiting among the poor of a large manufacturing town where his curacy was situated, and where that disease was then prevalent; that my mother took the infection from him, and both died within a month of each other. (26–27)

Jane registers no reaction to this story, either as a ten-year-old character or as a retrospective narrator. The reader, however, recognizes the trope of the woman who marries despite . . . ; in this case, Jane Reed married the man she loved despite the opposition of her family, implying a story that includes pleasure. The effect of this interpretation is to deepen the mimetic component of the mother's character and alter our understanding of her thematic function. Traditionally, the thematic function of the mother in *Jane Eyre* has depended on a reading of her mimetic component as composed of a single trait, suffering. Enriching the mimetic component by recognizing the pleasure in the mother's story changes our view of her thematic function: the character of the mother becomes important as an individual whose particular story is of value to her daughter. In addition to introducing this trope, the brief account of Jane Reed Eyre's history brings the continuities between Jane's experience in her mother's childhood home and her mother's before her into sharper focus, and we are prepared to notice others as they arise almost immediately. Despite the fact that Jane has told Mr. Lloyd, "I should not like to belong to poor people" (25), she is expelled from her uncle's house, as her mother was, and transported to Lowood Institution, which, as Helen Burns tells Jane, "is partly a charity-school: you and I, and all the rest of us are charity-children" (52). Jane is, her wishes notwithstanding, among the poor, and in the care of Mr. Brocklehurst, a clergyman. Within a year typhus rages through the school; Jane escapes the disease as her mother did not, but she is declared dead of typhus by Sarah Reed in a letter to Jane's uncle, John Eyre: "I said I was sorry for his disappointment, but Jane Eyre was dead: she had died of typhus fever at Lowood" (251). As far as her uncle knows, Jane Eyre has died the same death as Jane Reed Eyre before her. We recognize these repetitions, and we realize the extent to which Jane is able to experience her mother's experiences and thus to know them and her.

To this point, Jane is a child, and she may not speculate about the unnarratable elements of her mother's story. However, by the time she decides to leave Lowood, Jane is a woman, one beginning to understand the reasons that, as Jane explains, "at eighteen most people wish to please." She is now capable of regretting that she is, as Bessie says on her visit to Lowood, "no beauty" (96). Bessie, who learned Jane Reed Eyre's story at the same moment as Jane, who comes to visit her from her mother's home, even adds a little information to what Jane knows of her mother's story. She tells of a visit by Jane's father's brother, from which Bessie gleaned that the Eyres "may be poor; but I believe they are as much gentry as the Reeds are" (96). For Jane to learn unexpectedly as she sets out on her adult life that her father's family was not only respectable but also concerned for her well-being adds weight to what the reader has assumed from the start and what Jane must have begun to intuit: that Jane Reed's is the story of a young woman who left her home for the pleasure she found in a good man, that she may well have been right to disregard the "wishes of her friends," who were biased and mistaken from the first. Again, Jane does not comment on what she learns from Bessie, but her experience at Thornfield demonstrates that she is open to continuing the search for fuller knowledge of her mother's story.

At Thornfield, Jane relives happier parts of her mother's experience. Her mothering of Adèle reflects Jane Reed Eyre's experience of motherhood: it is brief, it is concomitant with the flowering of her passionate love, and it ends in the child, a female child, being sent away to a school with poor conditions and unforgiving policies, just as Jane was. Jane's experience of love also reflects her mother's. Jane finds with Edward Rochester the kind of deep romantic love that her mother had found with her father. Just as her mother's love transcended the prejudices of the social world against interclass marriages, so does the love between Jane and Rochester transcend the fact of her inferior social status. Jane loves Rochester, not to the exclusion of the mother, but as the mother had loved—with a passion that defies convention.

That Jane does not stay with Rochester despite all when she learns of the existence of Bertha Rochester has been interpreted as Jane's need to flee in accordance with the incest taboo. Indeed, it is widely agreed that the family romance lurking in *Jane Eyre* manifests itself in her relationship with Edward Rochester. He is, as he himself points out, "old enough to be [her] father" (140). Jane tells us, "I felt at times, as if he were my relation" (153) and "I feel akin to him" (184). Rochester is thus explicitly compared to a "relative," adding to the sense that Jane sees in him a means of consummating the forbidden sexual desire for the father. This and other evidence notwithstanding, we should consider ourselves warned when Mrs. Fairfax observes, "He might almost be your father" and Jane exclaims, "No, indeed [. . .] he is nothing like my father!" (277). This seems to be literally true; in *Jane Eyre* as in *Persuasion*, not the true suitor but the false one most closely resembles the father. Ultimately, Jane explores the forbidden oedipal drive, and experiences what her mother experienced before her, with a man who is like her father, but not in her relationship with Rochester.

In Rochester Jane finds a man who is figured not as a father but as a seeking son. Like Jane, Rochester is without parents. We are encouraged to think of Jane as the archetypal individual on her solitary pilgrimage, but Jane, though parentless, is provided with both maternal and paternal relatives. Rochester, on the other hand, is utterly alone. We hear of no relatives of his whatsoever, except for a long line of the dead stretching back even beyond "Damer de Rochester, slain at Marston Moor in the time of the civil wars" (302). Rochester, like Jane, "comes [. . .] from the abode of people who are dead." The longevity of the family and their power are commemorated in the great house, Thornfield; nevertheless, Rochester stays there infrequently and dislikes it. His discomfort there is attributable to the fact that Rochester's relationship to the past is characterized primarily by remorse. Although his power at Thornfield is his rightful inheritance, the traditional object of the seeking son, his legacy is a mixed blessing. He blames the dead—especially his father and brother—for their part in his disastrous marriage. He blames himself as well, and Thornfield contains what is to Rochester living proof, in the persons of Adèle and Bertha Mason Rochester, that sexual pleasure is only an avenue to greater remorse. With nothing in his experience to validate his own pleasure, even Rochester's love and desire for Jane cannot overcome his remorse and anger, which dominate his actions until Bertha burns Thornfield, throwing herself off its battlements in the midst of the conflagration. Rochester is blinded and maimed as he runs through the burning house in his failed attempt to save her, and scholars have tended to read Rochester's incapacitation as a disempowerment that is, in effect, a punishment for his actions toward Bertha and toward Jane. In this view, Rochester's wounds symbolize the blow to patriarchy effected by both Bertha and Jane.[10] Yet we can go further and include in our assessment the immediate cause of his injuries: what wounds Rochester is the weight of history, embodied in the house itself. We are told, "As he came down the great stair-case at last, [. . .] there was a great crash—all fell" (452). Rochester's remorse for his own past actions and his anger at the position into which others have forced him are represented by the house; its fall, as well as Bertha's death, free him from these and prepare him to benefit from the example of Jane's relationship to the past. Jane's creativity and her femaleness allow her to repeat the experiences of the dead without being possessed by them, without being forced to repudiate them, and without reproducing the social constraints that bound the dead in life.

Jane, then, contributes to but also reaps the benefits of Rochester's development, whereas the novel's surface plot demands the sacrifice of Bertha Mason Rochester's life for his and Jane's happiness. Given this contrast, readers have often concluded that Jane has insufficient sympathy for the mad woman in the attic. That Jane Eyre gains her independence of spirit, her place in the social structure, and even her power as a storyteller at the expense of other women is an argument that has come to influence our reading of the novel. For example, Susan Lanser concludes that "Jane's extraordinary narrative authority becomes insidious. [. . .] Jane's voice can be empowered only through the silencing of other women's voices" (*Fictions* 192–93). Elisabeth Bronfen moves away from strictly narratological considerations in her argument that the actual deaths of other female characters, particularly of Helen Burns and Bertha Mason Rochester, are presented in the novel as crucial to Jane's education: "What is implied is that Jane's psychic and social education requires not only an encounter with death, in the form of identificatory doubles, but also a destruction of death enacted successfully by virtue of their sacrifice" (222). The idea that Jane's empowerment is contingent on the sacrifices of other women has gained wide acceptance, largely as part of the important and necessary work of analyzing the colonialist discourses of *Jane Eyre*. Gayatri Spivak, reading *Jane Eyre* and Jean Rhys's *Wide Sargasso Sea*, argues that Antoinette/Bertha "must play out her role, act out the transformation of her 'self' into that fictive Other, set fire to the house and kill herself, so that Jane Eyre can become the feminist individualist heroine of British fiction" (681). For Susan Meyer, though the text betrays uneasiness about its "figurative tactics" (267), "Brontë's plot participates in the same activity as Jane—cleaning, purifying, trying to create a world free of oppression. [. . .] and it does so by cleaning away Bertha, the staining dark woman who has represented oppression" (266). These readings are persuasive and revealing, but, in contrast to Spivak and Meyer, I identify the source of Bertha's oppression in gender, making her more similar to than different from Jane.[11] The submerged plot of Jane's interaction with her mother's story reveals hitherto unexplored facets of Jane's relationships with other women more generally and suggest that she is less assiduously an "individualist" than Spivak (like many other scholars) asserts. Although certain minor characters clearly function as rivals to Jane for Rochester's affection in the surface plot, they have a secondary function in the submerged plot. These characters model for Jane other mother and daughter relationships that help her in her search, and, especially in the case of Bertha Mason Rochester, they emphasize the importance of the search.

That Jane identifies with Rochester's wife more fully, and more consciously, than is at first apparent is suggested by a discovery she makes during her first days at Thornfield. On a tour of the great house, outside, as she later learns, the third-floor room in which Bertha is imprisoned, Jane notices "half-effaced embroideries, wrought by fingers that for two generations had been coffin-dust" (111). In contrast to most of the house, which commemorates the rapaciousness of Rochester's father and brother and their ancestors, this room includes a memorial to feminine lives lived within the hall. Jane writes, "All these relics gave to the third story of Thornfield Hall the aspect of a home of the past: a shrine of memory" (111). Mrs. Fairfax, in sympathy with Jane's impressions, remarks that "if there were a ghost at Thornfield Hall, this would be its haunt" (111). Thus is Bertha Rochester named a ghost, but Bertha is a living memorial to centuries of Rochester women. Jane enters this room again to nurse Richard Mason after Bertha attacks him, and once more when Bertha's identity has been revealed, both times noticing embroideries wrought, perhaps, by Rochester women. The connection this implies between Bertha and "fingers that for two generations had been coffin-dust" inspires her, when Rochester asks, "If you were mad, do you think I should hate you?" to answer him, "I do indeed, sir" (317). Jane assumes that what has happened to Bertha Mason Rochester can happen to any woman. Although Rochester faults his father and brother for the disaster of his marriage, his wife's "giant propensities" do not escape his blame (323). Critics have argued that Jane projects her own instincts and desires onto Bertha and that they are contained by Bertha's demise. As Carol Pearson and Katherine Pope explain:

> Bertha is the literal equivalent of Jane's negative inner vision of sexuality; when she understands her own passion as separate from Bertha's, she is free to value her own sexuality and to love Rochester. Rochester's wound and the death of Bertha, therefore, symbolize the resolution of Jane's ambivalence about sexual passion. (167)

This argument is convincing, but the fact that Jane must flee Thornfield in the night or risk giving in to her own sexual desire suggests that Jane's passion is as fiery as Bertha's, and she has seen the catastrophe it might precipitate enacted in Bertha Mason Rochester's ruined life.

Therefore, when Jane leaves Thornfield because of the shocking events of the surface plot, she is also leaving in response to an imperative in the submerged plot. Jane has "propensities" of her own, and she needs to know how far they are likely to take her. Bertha Mason, not entirely unlike Jane Reed, left her family to marry a man from a different world, and the end, for both, was far from encouraging. To learn the power of her own passion, Jane needs to know more about her mother's experience; indeed, Jane learns at Thornfield that the mother's life predicts the daughter's. Rochester thinks of Bertha as "the true daughter of an infamous mother" (323). He explains, "Her mother, the Creole, was both a mad woman and a drunkard! [. . .] Bertha, like a dutiful child, copied her parent in both points" (306). Bertha is not the only woman who is depicted as a reproduction of her mother. Jane observes that Adèle sometimes manifests "a superficiality of character, inherited probably from her mother" (152). Blanche Ingram resembles her mother physically ("her face was like her mother's" [181]) as well as in her attitudes and ideas. Even later, at Moor House, the servant, Hannah, tells Diana and Mary: "Your mother wor mich i' your way, and a'most as book-learned. She wor the pictur' o' ye, Mary" (352). Faced with this seemingly inescapable continuity between mothers and daughters, and, by extension, among all women, Jane must learn the rest of the truth about her own mother, also a woman of great passion, before she can put herself, as she longs to do, in Rochester's power.

That Jane must learn of her mother's passion and pleasure explains more fully the necessity of the Moor House section of the novel, which can seem to be an aberration in the novel's progression. This element of Jane's journey is certainly important to the surface plot. Coming into her inheritance and finding respectable, even admirable, relatives not unlike herself establish Jane socially; her *bildung* is completed here. She gains the independence she needs to approach Rochester as an equal, and, at the same time, ceases to idolize him and returns to her sense of God as her only authority. However, even given the important functions served by this element of the progression of the surface plot, it still raises questions for the reader about coincidence and probability. Chief among these questions is why Jane should have happened upon her father's family when, had she stayed at Thornfield or returned to Lowood, they would have discovered her sooner. One answer is that, in addition to serving the surface plot, the time Jane spends living at Moor House is also crucial to the submerged plot. At Moor House, in her relationship with St. John Rivers, a clergyman and her father's nephew, Jane learns the rest of her mother's story. Her mother, appearing in a vision, gives Jane the strength to leave her great love. Her mother, in the persona of "the universal mother, Nature," keeps her alive during her four days in the wilderness without food or shelter (340). Jane writes, "As I was her child: my mother would lodge me without money and without price" (341).[12] Thus, under her mother's protection, Jane is thrown into proximity with the man who, unlike Rochester, indeed resembles Jane's father. This resemblance is emphasized for the reader when St. John, having discovered the truth about Jane's identity and her relationship to him, reveals his knowledge to Jane by telling her a story they both know but without specific details: "A poor curate [. . .] fell in love with a rich man's daughter: she fell in love with him, and married him, against the advice of all her friends; who consequently disowned her immediately after the wedding. Before two years passed, the rash pair were both dead, and laid quietly side by side under one slab" (399). The reader immediately recognizes the "rash pair" as Jane's parents, of course, but, as St. John tells the story without the particulars, the reader is also likely to find in his narration a projection of his own future. Like his uncle, Jane's father, St. John is a "poor curate." The most immediate candidate for the "rich man's daughter" is Rosamond Oliver, whom St. John loves and who, he believes, would surely die young if she agreed to share the life he has planned as a missionary in India. However, St. John does not ask Rosamond Oliver to marry him; he asks Jane, and she is the focus of St. John's projection. Jane, though not a rich man's daughter, has just found out that she, too, is an heiress, and she believes that she, too, "should not live long in that climate" (436). St. John and Jane potentially fit the template of her parents' story, and the double implications of St. John's narrative must be evident to Jane as they are to the reader.

Even though David Cowart has established that "there is maturity [. . .] in Jane's rejection of Rivers in his sternly paternal aspect in favor of the virile and husbandly Rochester" (37), St. John has rarely been considered in detail with reference to Jane's oedipal issues. This may be largely because, in contrast to Rochester, St. John refuses passion and rejects infatuation and lust in favor of more spiritual considerations. Still, to assume from this contrast that St. John is without sexual motivation is to go too far. Moments after St. John has made his proposal, Jane is already realizing that, as his wife, she would be forced to "endure all the forms of love (which I doubt not he would scrupulously observe)" (426). Jane may well envision their physical relationship, and St. John certainly does. He wonders, "How can I, a man not yet thirty, take out with me to India a girl of nineteen, unless she be married to me? How can we be for ever together—sometimes in solitudes, sometimes amidst savage tribes—and unwed?" (430). He even accuses her of suggesting they live together in sin when he admonishes her, "I before proved to you the absurdity of a single woman of your age proposing to accompany abroad a single man of mine. I proved it to you in such terms as, I should have thought, would have prevented your ever again alluding to the plan. That you have done so, I regret—for your sake" (435). Jane easily dispenses with any scruples on grounds of propriety, so his continued insistence must be on other grounds. With his repetition of their ages, it becomes clear that, while he eschews romantic love, St. John sees sex in the light of a biological imperative. Jane's instinct is correct: her cousin would "scrupulously observe" "all the forms of love." Jane dislikes this idea, but she admits to Diana: "I can imagine the possibility of conceiving an inevitable, strange, torturing kind of love for him" (438). Jane attributes the "inevitability" of such feelings to St. John's "heroic grandeur," but we can see that the attachment is inevitable in a deeper, psychological sense, for here is the man, at last, who is "like my father" (277). St. John is Jane's final opportunity to learn her mother's story by repeating her mother's experience. Jane shares the first and last of her mother's names, Jane Reed Eyre, and St. John calls forth the other in her: "I grew pliant as a *reed* under his kindness" (441, emphasis added). St. John presents the chance for Jane to marry, as her mother did, a clergyman, for her to live out her life with her father's near kinsman, and no doubt follow her mother to an early death.

For some readers, the idea that what St. John offers appeals to Jane is evident as she concludes her narrative, giving the words of St. John's letter pride of place: "Amen; even so come, Lord Jesus!" (477). Robert Keefe interprets Jane's choice to end her narrative this way as a kind of victory for death, "a peculiar coda which lies athwart the seeming optimism which Brontë's art has temporarily attained" (129). On the contrary, this choice is a gesture meant to honor the source of Jane's final happiness, to memorialize what the dead have to offer the living. She knows that St. John's most recent letter is also his last—he is, essentially, already dead, and his words come from "the abode of people who are dead" (257). Jane commemorates the dead, but she is, as ever, "tenacious of life" (127). She is not compelled to repeat her mother's story to the end, or even to choose a man like the one her mother chose; rather, she is able to find in Jane Reed Eyre's story affirmation of life and of pleasure. Unlike seeking sons, Jane attempts neither to alleviate the remorse of her dead parents nor to deny their pleasure. She has sought her mother's story by repeating her experience, and she has found it legitimating, both of her social position, marked by her inheritance, and of her pleasure, marked by her reunion with Rochester. Jane has become a reader of "half-effaced embroideries" and has discerned in them the unofficial story of women's pleasure, and thus her own.

Reconfiguring the progression of *Persuasion* and *Jane Eyre* reveals the effects of a second horizontal axis, of a submerged plot under the surface that reveals the mother's unnarratable pleasure and contributes to the satisfying completeness of these two novels. In both, the submerged surfaces similarly: in the trope of the woman who married despite . . . that we can locate in the mother's brief history, in the daughter's experience in her mother's home, in what she can learn of her mother by observing other women, and in her relationship with a man like the one her mother chose. That Anne is more strongly influenced by mentors than Jane has likely contributed to the generally accepted vision of Anne as inhabiting a more passive role than Jane does, but attention to the submerged plot influences our understanding of both characters. Reference to the second horizontal axis enables us to recognize more fully Anne's agency and independence as well as Jane's connectedness to other women. Further, our vision of female minor characters and their functions in the novels shifts as we track the submerged plot, certainly of Elizabeth Stevenson Elliot and Jane Reed Eyre, but also of sisters, mentors, and rivals.

The novels reveal how necessary the mother's story is to both of these seeking daughters, and how far they are willing to go to know it in full. In both narratives, the protagonists' searches remain submerged, for the daughter's focus on pleasure is not broadly sanctioned, and the only story available for a mother cannot include her pleasure. For Jane Eyre and Anne Elliot, the fact that their mothers find pleasure within legal marriage does not make their stories any more acceptable, any easier to access than, for example, stories of mothers who find their pleasure outside of marriage. The allowable, official story of a woman's sexuality as limited to procreation within legal marriage is as difficult to circumvent as, the protagonists considered in chapter 2 discover, is the very narratable story of a woman's transgression.

CHAPTER 2

Dual and Serial Narration and the Disclosure of the Submerged Plot

Bleak House and *The Woman in White*

Charles Dickens's *Bleak House* (1853) and Wilkie Collins's *The Woman in White* (1860) are highly plotted novels—the horizontal axes of both are thick with contingencies and coincidences, suspense and subplots. Yet completion in both novels depends not only on these carefully constructed and vivid plots but also on submerged plots similar to those in *Persuasion* and *Jane Eyre*. That we should find the same strategy circulating through two more nineteenth-century English novels, and those by two writers who worked closely together, is perhaps not surprising, yet the fact that novels by men use the same strategies as those by women to the same ends is significant and worth exploring. Dickens's deployment of the submerged plot of the search for the mother's pleasure is very like that of Austen and Brontë, and, as in their novels, it contributes significantly to the satisfyingly high degree of completion in *Bleak House*. Collins also includes highly synchronized surface and submerged plots in *The Woman in White*, but elements of the novel's completeness may trouble some readers. Like his predecessors, Collins figures the search for the mother's pleasure as central, but he evinces less optimism regarding its success. His doubt is manifested in new complexities on the second horizontal axis.

What makes *Bleak House* and *The Woman in White* different from the earlier novels is that even as the submerged plots progress steadily with the marriage plots on the surface of each novel, they are impinged upon and impeded by the mystery plots that are also part of the surface of each. This double relation between surface and submerged complicates the protagonists' searches and the workings of the second horizontal axis generally. In *Persuasion* and *Jane Eyre,* only the daughter protagonist is motivated to look past the mother's official, public story; in *Bleak House* and *The Woman in White,* in contrast, the surface plot itself is overtly concerned with the mother's sexuality. Because both novels hinge on illicit sex that results in illegitimate children, and because the absent mothers, in some cases, are not dead, the daughter protagonists are not the only characters seeking the truth about the mother's experience. The daughter's search remains distinct—she seeks knowledge of her mother's pleasure—but her search is made more difficult by and must be protected from the struggles of other characters to conceal or reveal a different story, the highly narratable story of the mother's transgression. The seeking daughter in these novels conducts her pursuit of the story of pleasure even as she resists the interference of others and even works to thwart others' manipulation of the story of transgression.

This double relation between the two plots makes demands on the narration itself, and Dickens and Collins respond to these demands somewhat similarly with their dual and multiple narrators. In both novels, the narration itself is characterized by duality. In the two alternating narratives of *Bleak House,* the omniscient narrator and the character narrator Esther Summerson share the characteristic of being both intimate with and distanced from Lady Dedlock; however, whereas the omniscient narrator uses distance to incriminate this absent mother, Esther uses distance to protect her. Whereas Dickens makes his seeking daughter a character narrator in the tradition of Jane Eyre, Collins, for all he multiplies the number of character narrators in *The Woman in White,* does not grant independent narratives to his seeking daughters but rather embeds their stories in the narratives of others. Although the novel includes numerous character narrators, the only two truly independent narrators are Walter Hartright and Marian Halcombe. Both Walter's and Marian's narration express duality, as well, in that both characters act against the search for the mother's pleasure, but both narratives reveal the search and its importance.

We might expect the stories of mothers whose sexuality exceeds the bounds of marriage—including Lady Dedlock, Mrs. Catherick, and Cecilia Jane Elster, long addressed as Lady Glyde—to be silenced to an additional degree, their antinarratability compounded by strictures against extramarital sex. In fact, their transgressive nature makes them more narratable than the pleasures of someone like Elizabeth Stevenson Elliot or Jane Reed Eyre, whose sexuality, contained within marriage, nearly escapes detection. Daughters of mothers who take their pleasure outside of marriage can find themselves confronted with versions of the story that actually obscure the truth about the mother's pleasure as effectively as what appears to be no story at all. These protagonists, then, are confronted with extra obstacles, but my analysis suggests, in contrast to traditional readings of the novels, that their illegitimacy is not an obstacle in itself. Analysis of the submerged plots of Esther Summerson's and Anne Catherick's searches suggests that illegitimacy need not in all cases have the same impact on a daughter as on a son (such as Sir Percival Glyde), and that daughters may be free to find in the mother's story not just the source of their social disenfranchisement but rather an alternative, maternal legacy. In light of this submerged plot, not only the mothers' but the daughters' experiences take on new significance altogether.

"A young and beautiful lady, then unmarried": Honoria "Barbary" Dedlock

The progression of *Bleak House* is oriented primarily toward the revelation of a sexual transgression that happened in the past, long before the beginning of the action. The narrative progression, then, is largely measurable by a series of discoveries. Individual characters—Tulkinghorn, Guppy, Krook, Hortense, Jo, Grandfather Smallweed, Bucket, and Lady Dedlock herself—knowingly or otherwise make discrete discoveries that eventually bring them (or others) nearer to the truth they seek. Notwithstanding the novel's multiplicity, nearly all of its main characters have some connection to the mystery of Esther Summerson's parentage, as Mr. Bucket insists to the suspicious Mrs. Snagsby:

> And Toughey—him as you call Jo—was mixed up in the same business, and no other; and the law-writer that you know of, was mixed up in the

same business, and no other; and your husband, with no more knowledge of it than your great grandfather, was mixed up (by Mr. Tulkinghorn, deceased, his best customer) in the same business, and no other; and the whole bileing of people was mixed up in the same business, and no other. (908)

Even as Lady Dedlock hopes to conceal the story of her long-ago affair with Captain Hawdon, others are working just as assiduously to reveal it. To the reader, the identities of Esther's parents are manifest before any of the characters has learned enough to be confident in his or her findings. Our advanced understanding is largely attributable to the alternating of the novel's two narratives; for example, the omniscient narrator gives us our first glimpse of Lady Dedlock, "who is childless," being "put quite out of temper" by the sight of a happy family (21), and this image is juxtaposed nearly immediately with Esther's account of herself as a motherless child (29). In this case as in numerous instances to come, the alternating narratives draw a connection between the two for the reader before either character is aware of it. Indeed, the reader is likely to solve the mystery of Esther's parentage fairly early on, but our interest is sustained largely by the complicating factor in this otherwise straightforward design, which is the one character who refuses to make discoveries: Esther Summerson. Esther's apparent refusal to seek information about her parents in the surface plot seems to characterize her as passive. In the context of the submerged plot, however, Esther's apparent passivity is designed to resist the selfish motives of those who seek the story of her mother's transgression and to protect her more private pursuit of the story of her mother's pleasure. Her apparent passivity on the first horizontal axis is belied by her resolute and purposeful activity on the second. Just as Esther's actions work in the interest of protecting her mother from other characters, Esther's narration works in the interest of protecting her mother from the impression the reader receives of her from the omniscient narrator's account.

In her analysis of Esther as narrator, Lisa Sternlieb begins with the assertion that "Esther appears reluctant to know anything" (75), and she refers to the history of the scholarship on this point, including work by Audrey Jaffe, who notes that Esther particularly "block[s] curiosity about her mother" (qtd. in Sternlieb 75). For Sternlieb, however, "Esther's self-effacement constitutes a narrative strategy, one that allows her to accept and reject her parentage simultaneously" (76). Sternlieb goes on to explain that, in fact, under cover of her apparent passivity, "Esther has been actively engaged all along in solving the mysteries of her parents and her parentage" (75). Sternlieb's compelling analysis enables us to locate Esther's agency, both as a narrator and as a daughter, and to recognize that, even when she appears "repressed, naive, [and] incurious," she has her own goals, toward which she progresses steadily (76). Sternlieb locates Esther's agency through analysis of Esther's narrative strategies, and concludes that Esther is engaged in a quest to learn about her parents. My own analysis of the events of the novel corroborates Sternlieb's findings by revealing a second, submerged plot that is generated by this second set of motives for Esther. Accessing Esther's search for her mother's story and its impact on her actions and decisions adds layers to our understanding of both the mimetic and the thematic components of Esther's character.

Even as analysis of the submerged plot reinforces Sternlieb's claims for Esther's agency, it reveals an alternative view of Esther's relationship to her mother's and her own sexuality. The lens through which Sternlieb reads *Bleak House* enables us to understand Esther as a sexual agent, but Sternlieb concludes that Esther's sexuality entails a rejection of her mother. She writes, "Critics may continue to read Esther as having no sexual desire, but we must not expect to find her desire expressed in positive terms, such as Jane Eyre uses, but always as a rejection of the parent in all his guises" (99–100). She explains of the scene in which Esther finds Lady Dedlock dead:

> To reach this place in the narrative Esther has literally had to follow in her mother's footsteps. She proves here that she is not insipid and naive; she is not oblivious to the sexual choices made by her mother; she actively rejects her mother's path, a path that leads to the wrong choice of sexual partner, Esther's father. (97)

We might assume, as Sternlieb and others do,[1] that Esther's relation to Lady Dedlock's story would be different from that of Anne Elliot and Jane Eyre, whose mothers were models of sexual virtue. However, attention to the progression of the submerged plot reveals that Esther resists judging her mother's sexual transgression, as everyone around her is inclined to do, and actively seeks the story of her pleasure. In order to know this story so fully as to feel what her mother has felt, Esther repeats many elements of her mother's experience.

The other important difference between Esther's mother and her literary predecessors is that Lady Dedlock has not died; therefore, a number of critics have concluded that she has abandoned her child. Hilary Schor and Nomi Stoltzenberg suggest of *Bleak House* that "what is most shocking [. . .] is not the abuse of the child by a father-figure [. . .], nor the absence of the 'real' father [. . .], but rather, the abandonment of the child by the *mother*" (111). Similarly, Marcia Renee Goodman argues that "Esther's sympathy for Lady Dedlock camouflages her fear of the anger at this abandoning mother" (154). Carolyn Dever refers to Goodman when she analyzes Esther's "desire to reject and abandon the mother who rejects and abandons her" (83). The view that Lady Dedlock must be rejected because she abandoned Esther certainly carries a great deal of weight from a psychoanalytic point of view, yet Esther tells us of Lady Dedlock's letter, "I clearly derived from it—and that was much then—that I had not been abandoned by my mother" (583). Rather than viewing Lady Dedlock as a marked contrast to the dead mothers in *Persuasion* and *Jane Eyre*, we should consider the strong association of her with images of death as evidence of the continuities between her and those other absent mothers.

After losing her lover and child, both of whom, she is told, are dead, Honoria "Barbary" becomes the mistress of Chesney Wold, a place populated by the aging and childless relatives of Sir Leicester, the seat of a family that is, as the family name implies, dying out. The description of Chesney Wold is dominated by the Ghost's Walk, which is most closely associated with Lady Dedlock. When we meet her first, we are told that "she has been 'bored to death'" (21). In "the little church in the park" (21, 289), the very place where Esther sees her mother for the first time, "there is a general smell and taste as of the ancient Dedlocks in their graves" (21); Esther notices this, too, and tells us that it "smelt as earthy as a grave" (290). These Dedlock dead, brought to our attention in the second chapter of this long novel, exert their pull, and in our final vision of Lady Dedlock she lies among them (981). As the novel opens, she clearly imagines that the rest of her life will be unbroken by any significant change, but she is soon proven mistaken in this assumption. Great change is set in motion by her accidental discovery that her lover was not drowned, but lives on; however, even this discovery, which might have revived life in her, is accompanied by "the faintness of death" (27). Furthermore, just as she finds him, she loses him to death again—this time, certainly. Similarly, Lady Dedlock learns suddenly and unexpectedly that her child did not die, but lives on. This might seem rejuvenating news, but Mr. Guppy sees her as "for the moment, dead," and, even when "her dead condition" passes, it is compared to "the features of those long-preserved dead bodies sometimes opened up in tombs, which, struck by the air like lightning, vanish in a breath" (466). Her reaction to this news is similar to her reaction to the news that her lover lives, and the same conclusion looms ominously: as soon as Lady Dedlock has learned of her child's existence, she learns that Esther is very ill, perhaps near death. Scholarship on the novel contends that Esther's second abandonment by her mother, when Lady Dedlock has revealed to Esther their relationship and also her determination to deny it henceforth, is the greatest betrayal. Yet, in completion of the pattern begun with her daughter and lover, this time Lady Dedlock believes herself to be dead before she dies. She tells Esther that she "must evermore consider her as dead" (580), explaining that "to bless and receive me [. . .] it is far too late" (579). If Esther feels abandoned by Lady Dedlock now, she nevertheless understands her request and later refers to "my living mother who had told me evermore to consider her dead" (669). Esther understands even more fully at a critical moment in her own search for pleasure, when she thinks of herself as already dead and repeats her mother's words, "too late," to describe Allan Woodcourt's declaration of love for her (937). These images of death throughout suggest that Lady Dedlock's influence on Esther is more similar to than different from the influence of a mother lost to death.

Esther asserts that from the beginning she is curious about her mother. She confides in the reader that, as a child, "I had never heard my mama spoken of. I had never heard of my papa either, but I felt more interested about my mama" (29). She asks her godmother, "O, do pray tell me something of her." What she learns on this occasion is that the story her godmother could tell her if she would is a story of Esther's mother's "disgrace" (30). Esther learns very early in life the essentials of such sexual transgression, but she always knows that the story of transgression is not what she needs. For example, in the course of Guppy's proposal of marriage, he says intriguingly, "Blest with your hand, what means might I not find of advancing your interests, and pushing your fortunes!

What might I not get to know, nearly concerning you?" (152). Although Esther assures us that she remains calm and collected when surprised with Guppy's unwelcome proposal of marriage, reporting that she "was well behind my table, and not much frightened" (150–52), she nevertheless does not pause to inquire into his meaning at all or comment on his odd statement in any way. Similarly, when Hortense leaves Lady Dedlock and applies to Esther for a position, she promises, "Receive me as your domestic, and I will serve you well. I will do more for you, than you figure to yourself now. [. . .] I will serve you well. You don't know how well!" (368). Admittedly, Esther is more flustered by the alarming Hortense than the comical Mr. Guppy, but the questions raised by these declarations that most interest the reader are the very ones Esther never asks. These two characters clearly intend to use the story of Esther's parents against them, and Esther quietly resists their attempts to enlist her help. However, even from someone with entirely different motivations and considerably more sympathy for her parents, Esther seeks no information. On her first night at Bleak House, Esther considers asking Mr. Jarndyce what he knows about her parents, but does not. Soon afterward, Mr. Jarndyce calls her to him and extends an invitation, "Esther, my dear, do you wish to ask me anything?" (122); Esther's response is, "Guardian [. . .] nothing!" (122). However various their motivations, these characters can access only the story of Lady Dedlock's transgression. Esther's refusal to pursue this information guides the reader away from an undivided focus on this story—which, in fact, we already know in outline—and emphasizes the story Esther needs and actively seeks: that of her pleasure. Even as the third-person narrator chronicles the relentless process of exposing Lady Dedlock's sexual transgression, Esther's narrative chronicles her private pursuit of the story of Lady Dedlock's pleasure. Recognizing this submerged motive enriches our understanding of the mimetic component of Esther's character, and it alters our perception of the thematic function of Lady Dedlock.

Indeed, the complexities of Lady Dedlock's character are indicated by both Esther and the omniscient narrator similarly in more than one respect. Both narrators seem simultaneously near to Lady Dedlock and far from her. The omniscient narrator sometimes appears limited to what the "fashionable intelligence" can offer (20), emphasizing a distance from her. At other times, the omniscient narrator knows what Lady Dedlock does in her home when she is alone, and, despite this narrator's confidence and authority, often appears to have a servant's view of her: witnessing her private moments without being noticed, apt to judge her but not in a position to hold her accountable for her actions. In such passages, the omniscient narrator is both close to this character and at a great remove from her. To Esther, through approximately half of the novel, Lady Dedlock is, of course, a complete stranger. After their relationship is revealed to both characters, when Esther knows she is more closely connected to Lady Dedlock than to anyone else, she also feels strongly that their connection is a danger to Lady Dedlock. Both narrators express this simultaneous proximity and distance in at least one similar way: in numerous instances in which they approach the subject of Lady Dedlock, both defer identifying her specifically, creating a moment in which the reader can imagine that she is someone else, either literally or figuratively.

That the deferring of identification by a narrator can be used to opposing ends is illustrated by two embedded narratives in which the speakers withhold Lady Dedlock's name. Mr. Tulkinghorn tells the story of Lady Dedlock's transgression to the assembled company at Chesney Wold, withholding her identity in an effort to threaten and terrify her:

> Now this lady preserved a secret under all her greatness, which she had preserved for many years. In fact, she had in early life been engaged to marry a young rake—he was a captain in the army—nothing connected with whom came to any good. She never did marry him, but she gave birth to a child of which he was the father. (650)

Tulkinghorn tells his story in this way as a display of his power to condemn, but George Rouncewell tells a part of this same story, also withholding the names, to protect those he describes. He writes to Esther that he was asked to deliver a letter "to a young and beautiful lady, then unmarried in England," by "a certain unfortunate gentleman," who, had George known him to be alive, "I never could and never would have rested until I had discovered his retreat, and shared my last farthing with him, as my duty and my inclination would have equally been" (958). The possibilities of Lady Dedlock's character (and of Captain Hawdon's) are emphasized by the lack of definite identification in these narratives. They suggest that there is more to Lady Dedlock than we know, and they demonstrate that her story can be told as one of transgression or one that implies pleasure.

As in Tulkinghorn's narrative, when the omniscient narrator employs this device of withholding Lady Dedlock's identity, it tends to incriminate her. When Lady Dedlock pays Jo to show her the places associated with Hawdon, she is described as "the woman [. . .] between whose plain dress, and her refined manner, there is something exceedingly inconsistent" (260). The narrator leaves the possibility open that this woman could be a servant or a lady, Lady Dedlock or another. The very hesitation to name her suggests that her activities on this evening are something to be ashamed of. Similarly, on the night of Tulkinghorn's murder, Lady Dedlock's movements are described without her name: "this woman, loosely muffled, goes out into the moonlight" (748). This time, we know the reference is to Lady Dedlock, but the elision of her name in the description recalls for us that earlier woman, who might have been a servant or a lady, and who might have been engaged in something shameful, or even, on this night, criminal.

Like the omniscient narrator, Esther uses this technique in describing Lady Dedlock, but with a different intention. The first time Esther sees Lady Dedlock, in the church at Chesney Wold, she describes her impressions for two paragraphs before identifying her by name. We learn after these important paragraphs that "It was easy to know [. . .] that the lady was Lady Dedlock" (292), so what Esther achieves by describing her first without naming her is worth exploring. Esther reports that "those handsome proud eyes seemed to spring out of their languor, and to hold mine!" and that, even in just a moment, "I knew the beautiful face quite well" (290). In the context of the surface plot, Esther's description is of a degree of recognition by both characters, which will lead eventually to a shared understanding of their relationship to each other. In the context of the submerged plot, the description emphasizes not only hereditary resemblance but also common experiences between the two women. Esther finds, "There was something quickened within me, associated with the lonely days at my godmother's" (290). Like Esther, Lady Dedlock has been lonely and isolated in the care of Miss Barbary. That Esther thinks of her doll at this moment may even create a comparison between Esther's imaginative play and Lady Dedlock's imaginings of the life she might have had with her own child. Like the omniscient narrator's description, Esther's description leaves open the possibility that Lady Dedlock is not who she seems to be, but, whereas the former implies that she is really a criminal, the latter implies that she is really someone similar to Esther. This is borne out when, having identified Lady Dedlock, Esther continues, "*I–I*, little Esther Summerson [. . .] seemed to arise before my own eyes, evoked out of the past by some power in this fashionable lady" (292). The difference between Esther's narration and that of the omniscient narrator is marked by this strong identification between the two women and also by Esther's report that Psalm 143:2 is being read at the moment of Lady Dedlock's entrance: "Enter not into judgment with thy servant, O Lord, for in thy sight [shall no man living be justified]" (Dickens 290; *King James Version*). Esther's invocation of the Psalm's moral imperative combines with her withholding of Lady Dedlock's identity to protect her mother from the reader's judgment. She continues to use the latter technique throughout her narrative in order to keep the possibilities of Lady Dedlock's character, which are always evident to Esther, open for the reader.

What Esther knows about her mother from childhood, which she tells her reader within three pages of the start of her narrative, is that her mother was unmarried when she gave birth to Esther. Such a story of transgression can imply a bad end, and many such characters in Victorian fiction are figured as destitute, ill, and outcast. Miss Barbary certainly communicates to her niece that her mother deserved such a fate. However, the launch of the submerged plot, as Esther confesses her fascination with her absent mother, is preceded by the launch of the surface plot, when the reader encounters Lady Dedlock, who is hiding a secret in her past but who has attained an enviable position, suggesting that not all stories of transgression must end in poverty and ostracism. Although Esther does not meet Lady Dedlock until nearly a third of the way through the novel, and although she cannot identify her as her mother until nearly two thirds of the way through, the reader makes the connection much more quickly, largely due to the juxtapositions of their stories in the alternating narratives, and partly through specific details, including Mr. Guppy's recognition of the physical resemblance between them. This juxtaposition establishes Lady Dedlock from the first as a woman who married despite the existence of another man in whom she finds pleasure, and this traveling trope provides the reader with a context for Esther's search. The trope signals to us what Esther always suspects: even if the story she seeks includes misery and suffering, it may include pleasure as well. Our introduction to Lady Dedlock reveals that she has married a courtly, wealthy, much older man who loves her, and that she has done so for security rather than for passion. She is presented as appearing bored with the life she has chosen, but this calm is belied when Lady Dedlock falls into a "swoon," for the first time in Sir Leicester's experience of her, at the sight of some familiar handwriting (27). Her response could suggest that the writer is someone she has hoped to avoid as easily as it could someone she has despaired of finding, but the juxtaposition of this scene with Esther's brief description of her mother's history works to amplify our understanding by implying continuities between Lady Dedlock and Esther's unknown mother, and the reader infers that Lady Dedlock has recognized the handwriting of a lost lover well before she confirms this by visiting the places he frequented in life as well as the place where he is buried. Therefore, quite early on a picture emerges for the reader of a woman who lost her first, great love and then entered a passionless marriage that is nonetheless characterized by respect, admiration, and advantage on both sides. This richness of the mimetic component of Lady Dedlock's character works against the traditional view of her thematic function as a fallen woman and abandoning mother who must be rejected. Remaining alert to the many facets of her character enables us to understand what she can offer her seeking daughter.

Lady Dedlock's history, which both of Dickens's narrators and all of his characters manage to avoid actually telling in its entirety, nevertheless forms the background against which we read Esther's actions and decisions, and she is in a position to be sensitive to the moments of pleasure implied by that history. Her own narrative is full of love and marriage almost from the start, reminding us that Esther is twenty years old and may be inclined to think about these subjects, however little inclined she is to mention their importance in her own life. She watches Ada and Richard fall in love, she learns of Mr. Boythorn's early disappointment, and she receives a proposal of marriage herself from Mr. Guppy. When Esther's narrative resumes again, Caddy has become engaged to Prince Turveydrop, and Esther meets Mrs. Bayham Badger, who has made not one but three prosperous marriages. At dinner at the Badgers' home, Esther meets Allan Woodcourt, a circumstance she puts off mentioning for as long as she feels she ethically can. She avoids discussing Woodcourt and the feelings he arouses in her for any number of reasons, both explicit and implicit; not the least of these is that Esther has only just begun her search for the story of her mother's pleasure, and she is still in the process of finding validation for her own pleasure.

Esther repeats her mother's experience in a number of ways, and this repetition is striking in that Lady Dedlock's experience is, at least in comparison to other works of Victorian fiction, fairly unusual. Lady Dedlock is a "fallen" woman who, nevertheless, has managed to marry a baronet and become admired and envied in her set. Esther's experience is more in keeping with other fiction of the period but is historically unusual: an illegitimate child left alone in the world by her cruel aunt who nevertheless grows up loved and cared for. Their unusual histories set them apart from other women, and the continuities between them are therefore the more notable. One way that Esther explores her mother's experience is by falling in love with Allan Woodcourt; in contrast to *Persuasion* and *Jane Eyre*, in *Bleak House* the true suitor is the one who resembles the father. When Esther first mentions Woodcourt to us as "a gentleman of dark complexion—a young surgeon" (214), she unknowingly echoes the omniscient narrator's introduction of him as "the dark young surgeon" at Captain Hawdon's deathbed (167). The alternating narration, then, encourages the reader to connect Lady Dedlock's lover with Esther's from the start. Esther also unknowingly echoes her mother's experience of falling in love with and being loved by a man who cannot offer marriage until certain obstacles have been overcome, and about whom, consequently, she feels she must remain silent. Esther's representation of Woodcourt and the omniscient narrator's representation of Hawdon are marked by parallels and oppositions; these maintain the connection between the two men in the reader's mind. We are introduced to these two men at the same time, when the "dark young surgeon" (167) attends at the death of the law writer, a man with "dark looks" (176). As a young woman, Honoria "Barbary" was in love with the reckless Captain Hawdon, and his equal feeling for her is evidenced by the fact that he kept her letters with him for twenty years when he owned almost nothing else. Captain Hawdon's indebtedness and poor prospects, it appears, prevented them from marrying, but Honoria's passion was great enough to convince her to risk her own future for the pleasure she took in him. When Hawdon goes "over the side of a transport-ship at night in an Irish harbour, within a few hours of her arrival from the West Indies" (958), he is reported drowned. He subsequently maintains this fiction, at first because, had he been found in England, he would "have been clapped into prison by the whole bill and judgment trade of London" (347), and later because, believing him to be dead, his Honoria has married Sir Leicester Dedlock.

Like Hawdon, Woodcourt finds himself at sea; as Esther tells us, "He was going to China, and to India, as a surgeon on board ship" (277). Although he never goes into debt as Hawdon did, Woodcourt accepts this employment out of financial necessity: "he had no fortune or private means, and so he was going away" (277). Like Hawdon, Woodcourt is the subject of official reports, one of which Esther reads in a newspaper clipping: she learns that he has been involved in "a terrible shipwreck over in those East-Indian seas" (568). Esther is spared the pain of believing Woodcourt to be dead—rather, "he is safe" and, furthermore, "a hero"—but she still has no hope of marrying him (568). Hawdon and Woodcourt have something else in common, as well, in their kindness to Jo. Jo reports of Hawdon, "He was wery good to me" (178, 181, 733), and Woodcourt finds a place for Jo to rest and prays with him as he dies.

The juxtaposition of these two characters and its impact on our understanding of Esther's search are also evident in the novel's progression. The section of Esther's narrative in which she first meets Woodcourt and that in which Woodcourt leaves on his voyage are separated by the omniscient narrator's report of Lady Dedlock's pilgrimage to Krook's and Snagsby's shops and the paupers' graveyard near the Inns of Court where Hawdon is buried. Despite the narrator's suspicion of her, the abiding love that Lady Dedlock habitually hides is evident in this description. Her love for Hawdon guides the reader's responses in the following section, when Esther is clearly saddened by Woodcourt's departure and also reveals to us that John Jarndyce appears troubled when she refers to him as like a "Father" to her (277). The reader understands before Esther does that she will have a decision to make that is similar to the one her mother made before her. The introduction at this point of Mrs. Woodcourt, with her firm ideas about the importance of birth, emphasizes that the story of Esther's mother's transgression will be relevant to her decision, and Jarndyce chooses this moment to tell her the little he knows about her birth. However, knowledge of the pleasure her mother took in her lover proves an equally important influence on her decision, as Esther must learn to consider her own pleasure both valid and valuable in order to make choices that favor it.

The demands of the submerged plot help to explain why, at this important juncture in the progression, Dickens represents Esther's first meeting with her mother in the keeper's lodge at Chesney Wold, the same keeper's lodge where the sight of a family—a man, woman, and child—once irritated Lady Dedlock (21). Just a week after, on first seeing her, Esther describes Lady Dedlock's face before identifying her, in this scene she describes Lady Dedlock's voice while withholding her identity. A storm rages, which Esther describes as making "creation new again" (296). Echoing the idea of the Psalm read in the Chesney Wold church that focuses on the inadequacy of all humans in the face of God's judgment, Esther sees in the storm evidence of "the tremendous powers by which our little lives are encompassed" (296). Again, the reader is discouraged from singling out Lady Dedlock for censure before she actually appears. When a voice from the dark lodge asks, "Is it not dangerous to sit in so exposed a place?" and Ada mistakenly believes that Esther has spoken, Esther tells us, "The beating at my heart came back again. I had never heard the voice, as I had never seen the face, but it affected me in the same strange way. Again, in a moment, there arose before my mind innumerable pictures of myself" (296). As before, Esther's narration advances the surface plot by emphasizing the resemblance between her and Lady Dedlock, and it advances the submerged plot by emphasizing other similarities between them. Lady Dedlock's seemingly uncharacteristically maternal concern for the two younger women's safety is so much in keeping with Esther's character that Ada believes Esther has spoken. Several more specific similarities emerge in the conversation that ensues.

In this first meeting with Lady Dedlock, Esther can observe at least two things about her. The first is her loyalty to and protectiveness of Sir Leicester, whom she mentions as involved in disputes with Mr. Boythorn that are "not of his seeking" and as "sorry not to have it in his power" to help Richard in his career (297). The second, equally strong impulse she observes is Lady Dedlock's eagerness to refer back to her youth, when she first knew Mr. Jarndyce. He does not take the liberty of raising the topic, expressing surprise that she remembers him at all (297), but she mentions the circumstances of their past acquaintance twice in the short time they are together. When she replies with irony to Jarndyce's compliment, "You have achieved so much, Lady Dedlock," she seems clearly to rate the past over the present (298). The separation that is evident between Lady Dedlock and her youth—in her long dissociation from Mr. Jarndyce, for example, and in her dissociation from her own sister, which she mentions—is a separation she obviously regrets. Even this brief meeting reveals the workings of remorse in Lady Dedlock's life, and the causes and effects of her remorse are more relevant to Esther's search than the censure of others.

Although Lady Dedlock does not say a great deal as she speaks with Mr. Jarndyce, what she says enables us to see the ways Esther's experience is repeating her mother's. Esther may remind Lady Dedlock of her young self, and Esther has come to know John Jarndyce when she is at about the age her mother had been when she knew him. This repetition of experience metamorphoses into another in that Jarndyce's relationship to Esther is, from the first, not entirely unlike Sir Leicester's relationship to Lady Dedlock. Esther's false suitor resembles, to an extent, the man her mother married despite her passion for another. Just as Lady Dedlock came to Sir Leicester twenty years before with a shameful secret, grateful for his offer of security, protection, and position, so Esther comes to John Jarndyce having been taught that the secret of her birth is a shameful one and that she has no right to the protection and position that he offers her. The reader is alerted to the commonalities between these two relationships by the representation of Jarndyce and Sir Leicester, which, like that of Hawdon and Woodcourt, is marked by parallels and oppositions. Both Sir Leicester and John Jarndyce are surrounded by cousins, but Sir Leicester's are aging hangers-on while Jarndyce's are young, hopeful lovers. Both men are cognizant of their considerable social responsibilities: Sir Leicester chooses to discharge his responsibilities by his efforts in the context of Parliament, committing himself to the system and eschewing involvement in cases of individual need, such as Richard Carstone's; Jarndyce, in contrast, distrusts the system, especially as it manifests itself in Chancery, and commits himself primarily to cases of individual need. These obvious comparisons prepare the reader for others even more central to their relationships with Lady Dedlock and Esther. Although Sir Leicester and John Jarndyce are both proven trustworthy and honorable, each keeps near him an untrustworthy companion whose defects are not obvious to him. It is Lady Dedlock who understands Tulkinghorn's will to power and the way his solicitude for Sir Leicester is used toward that end. Similarly, it is Esther who suspects that Harold Skimpole's refusal of adult responsibility is not a refreshing change but rather a con to take advantage of the generosity of others. Both women also find in their homes someone to love and foster in their young maids. As Lady Dedlock takes Rosa, the village beauty, under her wing, so Esther takes Charley. Just as Rosa is, in the end, happily settled so as to be educated and then advantageously married to Watt Rouncewell, the last we hear of Charley, after Esther has done her best to educate her, is that she is married to a miller, who is "well to do, and was in great request" (986). Esther's experience at Bleak House, then, echoes in many details her mother's experience at Chesney Wold.

Even as Esther acts consistently throughout the novel in accordance with the circumstances of the surface plot, her actions take on new meaning when we realize that they are, simultaneously, responses to the imperatives of the submerged plot of her engagement with her mother's story. Indeed, as we learn the details of Lady Dedlock's early experience, we find that Esther repeats her mother's experience in other respects as well. Miss Barbary, who was evidently her sister's confidante when Honoria was pregnant with Esther, raises Esther in her early childhood. Miss Barbary's oppressive religious principles threaten to warp Esther's vision of herself and to stunt her future. Esther does her best to think of her aunt kindly, but she is always aware of having nothing in common with her: "I felt so different from her" (28). Just as Miss Barbary is the only family Esther knows, she is apparently her sister's only relative as well, suggesting that Honoria, like Esther, may have lost her parents early in life. Honoria and her sister have been long estranged; she tells Mr. Jarndyce, "We went our several ways [. . .] and had little in common even before we agreed to differ" (298). Like Esther, Honoria feels little sympathy from this "cruel sister" (469). Esther tells us that she is made to feel "how unworthy of her I was" (28), and we learn that her response to her sister's illegitimate child is, as Lady Dedlock says, to "renounc[e] me and my name!" (469). Miss Barbary's unbending religious conviction prompts her to make her sister's life one of guilt and expiation by reporting falsely the child's death, just as she hopes to make the same of Esther's life by taking her away to be "sternly nurtured" (469). This early influence on both mother and daughter, then, is the same.

Both mother and daughter also respond similarly to this early influence, and, like her mother, Esther is saved from being overwhelmed by Miss Barbary's cruel certainties by, among other things, her own character. Although Lady Dedlock's strength of character is expressed in haughtiness and Esther's in humility, both women are certain of their own judgments and decisions, and both resist the pressures on them to make sacrifices in expiation for sins of the past. In their different ways, they are highly admired by everyone around them. The omniscient narrator informs us that, despite the initial disadvantage that "she had not even family," "for years, now, my Lady Dedlock has been at the centre of the fashionable intelligence, and at the top of the fashionable tree" (22). We learn this in our earliest introduction to Lady Dedlock, and we are offered a parallel vision of Esther when she first escapes the oppression of her aunt's guardianship. Although she arrives at the Miss Donnys' boarding school on a different footing from the others because of her illegitimacy, by the time she leaves we understand that every girl in the house is sorry to see her go, as are the Miss Donnys, the people of the neighborhood, the maids, and the gardener. In her different way, Esther is as commanding of attention as her mother, and all eyes are on her as she makes her journey to London and then to Bleak House, just as the "fashionable intelligence" tracks Lady Dedlock from Chesney Wold to London, to Paris, and back again (20). The people Esther meets in her new life—Mr. Guppy, Ada, Richard, Caddy Jellyby, Miss Flite, and John Jarndyce—all fall in love with her and remain so, and she quickly becomes, for all intents and purposes, mistress of Bleak House, and is as much admired there as Lady Dedlock is admired at Chesney Wold. These parallels, which arise from similarities of character, become similarities of experience and, thus, matters of progression that point to the intersection of the submerged plot and the surface plot.

I have emphasized, as I believe Dickens does, the similarities between Lady Dedlock as absent mother and fictional mothers who are dead, but *Bleak House* is unique among the novels considered here in that the absent mother tells her story to her daughter. For this reason, unlike other protagonists, Esther need not rely on the bare outline of her mother's life that Miss Barbary offers her, nor does she seek knowledge by observing another woman whose experience resembles her mother's. Esther's hearing some part of the story she has sought from her mother herself coincides with a crisis in Esther's life. Esther perceives that the barriers to a marriage between herself and Woodcourt—his uncertain prospects and Esther's illegitimacy—have been compounded by her changed appearance following her illness. Having just heard of Woodcourt's heroism at sea, Esther tells her reader that she is now glad that Woodcourt was never in a position to declare his feelings for her: "What should I have suffered, if I had to write to him, and tell him that the poor face he had known as mine was quite gone from me, and that I freely released him from his bondage to one whom he had never seen!" (570). At this moment when Esther feels she has lost Woodcourt altogether, Lady Dedlock appears in the clearing in the wood and explains their relationship. Their conversation with one another is centered, like all that Esther has heard implied throughout her life, on Lady Dedlock's transgression, and she expresses to Esther primarily her guilt and remorse. We may be tempted to imagine Lady Dedlock's letter, a tantalizing absence in the text, as her own narrative of her pleasure. However, Esther asserts that its content "has its own times and places in my story" (583), that all is revealed in the end. The letter, which symbolizes what Dickens could not tell, may also stand for what even Lady Dedlock herself cannot tell. The letter itself foregrounds the importance of the mother's story, and the fact that it is not reproduced in the text emphasizes its antinarratability. We can infer that even Lady Dedlock is constrained by the unnarratability of the story of her own pleasure because reading it does not change Esther's need to experience for herself what her mother has experienced.

Indeed, continuity between Lady Dedlock's experience and Esther's is expressed in this scene, signaled by Esther's narration of her vision of her mother's approach. As she has done twice before, Esther narrates Lady Dedlock's approach without identifying her first, again emphasizing the possibilities of her identity beyond those of the great lady and the fallen woman. Even as she is imagining "the female shape that was said to haunt" the Ghost's Walk, Esther sees "a figure approaching through the wood." She explains:

> The perspective was so long, and so darkened by leaves, and the shadows of the branches on the ground made it so much more intricate to the eye, that at first I could not discern what figure it was. By little and little, it revealed itself to be a woman's—a lady's—Lady Dedlock's. (576)

At first just "a figure," Lady Dedlock comes into focus by degrees, recalling the omniscient narrator's veiled description of her that vacillates in its identification as to whether she is a lady or a servant. Indeed, with reference to the surface plot, the implicit comparison Esther makes between Lady Dedlock and the ghost she imagines seeing recalls the wife of Sir Morbury Dedlock, who promised to haunt the Ghost's Walk "until the pride of this house is humbled" (113); Lady Dedlock's coming disgrace is foreshadowed in the connection. With reference to the submerged plot, however, the comparison is a connection between Lady Dedlock, whom, as Esther tells us, "I must ever more consider [. . .] as dead" (580), and Esther herself, who learns at this moment that, when she was born, she "had been laid aside as dead" (583). Although Esther's suppressing of Lady Dedlock's name in this instance allows for the fact that she is capable of disgracing Chesney Wold, it also opens the possibility that Lady Dedlock is like Esther and that they have common experiences.

Esther pursues her mother's story quite consciously after this meeting. When she agrees to marry John Jarndyce, she agrees to a marriage like her mother's: having erroneously determined that her lover is entirely lost to her, she accepts a proposal of marriage from a wealthy, older man, eschewing passion for the security and mutual respect of a different kind of marriage. That she does so seems to work against her search for pleasure, which she herself recognizes, but it attests to the impact on her of hearing her mother's story. Encouragingly, Esther may be influenced by what seems to be Lady Dedlock's true consideration for Sir Leicester, which she mentions more than once during their interview. Lady Dedlock's respect for her husband is reinforced in Esther's mind by his respect for his wife. Esther meets Sir Leicester for the first time when he visits Bleak House in order to make his sincere apologies for any lack of hospitality at Chesney Wold for Jarndyce, "a gentleman formerly known to Lady Dedlock, and indeed claiming some distant connection with her, and for whom (as I learn from my Lady herself) she entertains a high respect" (683). Sir Leicester's visit is what inspires Esther to reveal to Jarndyce her true parentage, and her telling precipitates his proposal. The courtesy between Sir Leicester and Lady Dedlock, as well as, perhaps, Lady Dedlock's declared admiration for Jarndyce, suggest to Esther that repeating her mother's experience in this way may be for the best.

Less encouragingly, even as Esther's mother insists that she be considered dead even though she lives, death begins to dominate Esther's thoughts. Our first indication of this may be that the sign by which Esther begins to realize her relationship to Lady Dedlock is "my handkerchief, with which I had covered the dead baby" (578). The invocation of Jenny's dead child resonates with what Esther learns from Lady Dedlock's letter: that the newborn Esther was thought to be dead. Esther writes, "So strangely did I hold my place in this world, that, until within a short time back, I had never, to my own mother's knowledge, breathed—had been buried—had never been endowed with life—had never borne a name" (583). The distance between knowing herself to have been believed dead and wishing that she had, in fact, died at birth is a short one for Esther, and she confesses, "I felt as if I knew it would have been better and happier for many people, if indeed I had never breathed" (583). Esther is motivated partly by a desire to protect her mother, but also partly by a strong identification with her mother. She has begun to know what it means to feel dead before death. In repeating her mother's experience, Esther feels she has outlived the possibility of pleasure. We witness the effects of this when she and Allan Woodcourt are reunited at Deal after his return from his voyage. Esther is glad that Woodcourt still cares for her enough to be, as she says a number of times, "very sorry for me" (708). She explains, "I felt for my old self as the dead may feel if they ever revisit these scenes. I was glad to be tenderly remembered, to be gently pitied, not to be quite forgotten" (708). Again, like her mother, Esther thinks of herself as dead, as having outlived pleasure.

Lady Dedlock's certainty that she has outlived pleasure, that she is as good as dead, inspires her flight and another way in which Esther repeats her experience. When Lady Dedlock leaves the safety of Sir Leicester's protection for good, she travels to St. Albans in hopes of seeing Esther one last time, and then she travels back to London to the place where her lover is buried. As Lady Dedlock makes this final journey, Esther's repetition of her experience becomes literal as she follows her. Esther and Bucket travel the road to St. Albans and stop at the brickmaker's cottage, exactly as Lady Dedlock has done a few hours earlier. They then proceed north, mistakenly believing they are following her. Even when they turn south again, heading toward London, and Esther believes they have stopped following her mother, she is actually, once again, repeating her mother's experience literally. When Esther finds her dead at the entrance to the burial ground where her father is buried, she understands that, although her mother had accustomed herself to the life she had made after her lover and child were taken from her, her early experience determines her final actions. Esther knows why her mother has chosen this place to end her life, knows that it means that her mother found pleasure once and valued it always, and this has the potential to validate Esther's own pleasure. That Woodcourt is with her at this moment certainly indicates that he is the true suitor, as John Jarndyce means to communicate to Esther when he tells her: "Allan Woodcourt stood beside your father when he lay dead—stood beside your mother" (965). The evidence that her mother valued her own pleasure is strong, but her mother's choice of death still dominates Esther's progress. When she sees the woman lying at the gate of the burial ground, she identifies her as "Jenny, the mother of the dead child" (913). Esther solidifies the identification between Jenny's dead child and her own infant self when, even after Bucket has tried to explain who the woman is, Esther insists, "I saw before me, lying on the step, the mother of the dead child" (915). She never exchanges Jenny's name for her mother's when she concludes, "And it was my mother, cold and dead" (915). At this painful point in her narrative, Esther feels as her mother had when she insisted on being considered dead before death.

Esther continues to repeat her mother's experience in this regard when Woodcourt proposes. When she tells him of his love, "I am not free to think of yours," she means because she is engaged to be married to Jarndyce (938). But the reason she is engaged to Jarndyce is evident as she echoes her mother's lament, "To bless and receive me [. . .] it is far too late" (579), in her thoughts about Woodcourt: "I learned in a moment that what I had thought was pity and compassion, was devoted, generous, faithful love. O, too late to know it now, too late, too late. That was the first ungrateful thought I had. Too late" (937). Like her mother before her, discovering too late that her lover had not died in the Irish Sea, that her child had not died at birth, Esther feels she has discovered Woodcourt's love too late. To feel this way is to have experienced all of her mother's story. Having done so, and with the patience and faithfulness of Allan Woodcourt and the insight and encouragement of John Jarndyce, Esther is eventually able to trust and believe in her own pleasure and to affirm it by marrying Woodcourt.

The submerged plot of Esther's search for the unnarratable story of her mother's pleasure is resolved successfully despite the difficulties posed by the struggles over the mother's story in the surface plot. The striking completion of the novel depends on this successful resolution just as it does on the carefully crafted resolution of the surface plot. In Dickens's novel, the fact that the mother found her pleasure outside of marriage does not alter the object of the daughter's search or its power to validate her pleasure. Instead it requires that the seeking daughter not only push past the official story of the mother's chastity but also resist those who would make the story of the mother's transgression the daughter's only legacy. In *Bleak House,* this dynamic is enacted in the dual narration: as the omniscient narration exposes relentlessly the story of Lady Dedlock's transgression, Esther's narration emphasizes the similarities between her mother and herself and insists on the story of her mother's pleasure.

"Always lived as man and wife": Cecilia Jane Elster, Jane Anne Catherick, and Mrs. Philip Fairlie

Like that of *Bleak House,* the surface plot of Wilkie Collins's *The Woman in White* is powered by competing drives to obscure and to expose the story of the mother's sexual transgression. Sir Percival Glyde is fully invested in hiding the truth about his mother's illicit sexuality, even as Walter Hartright is intent on revealing it. In keeping with the tradition, for both men, the mother's pleasure can only be a threat to legitimacy. In contrast, the novel's illegitimate daughter is an advocate for the value of the mother's story throughout. Whereas Sir Percival and Walter can recognize only the mother's transgression, Anne Catherick actively seeks the story of her mother's pleasure by repeating her mother's experience in the novel's submerged plot and resisting the machinations of others to manipulate and make use of the mother's story. Although Anne's actions appear comparatively confused and ineffectual with reference to the surface plot, attention to the submerged plot reveals that Anne has her own goals that are in complete opposition to Sir Percival's, though not in the way he thinks, and she takes decisive steps to achieve them. Anne dies before completing her search, but she is the catalyst for Laura Fairlie's. Rereading the progression of Collins's complex novel in light of the submerged plot of Anne's and Laura's searches reveals that Laura, apparently the only young woman in the novel who experiences sex, transforms from the first volume of the novel, in which she stands by her paternal inheritance and rejects her own pleasure outright, through the second volume, in which events have rendered her more receptive to her mother's story, to the third volume, in which Laura repeats her mother's experience and learns that, for the seeking daughter, the story of her mother's pleasure need not be threatening but offers validation for her own pleasure. Like Anne, Laura Fairlie is generally considered a passive victim upon whom the novel's plot hinges but whose agency has little or no impact on that plot, but reconfiguring the progression alters our view of the mimetic components and thematic functions of both characters. Reconsidering their characters encourages us to follow Laura's developing responses to the opposing influences of Anne and Sir Percival throughout the novel, enabling us to reach a new understanding of the progression of the surface plot and how it acts on and is acted upon by the submerged plot of Laura's own pursuit of the story of her mother's pleasure.

The complications of the submerged plot, focusing on two seeking daughters rather than one and with less decided success than in the earlier novels, makes demands on the narration that Collins addresses through the use of serial character narration. From one perspective, the multiple narration of *The Woman in White* appears potentially more complex than the dual narration of *Bleak House,* offering official narratives from eleven different sources. From another perspective, however, the narration is quite similar to that of *Bleak House.* Collins's novel is dominated by the narratives of Walter Hartright and Marian Halcombe, and not only because of their length. Walter's four narratives combine to over 300 pages and Marian's narrative is nearly 175 pages, in contrast to the other nine sources, none of which is afforded even fifty pages, and most of which are considerably shorter than that. More significant than their brevity is that most of the other narratives, except for the two public records, were commissioned, in one way or another, by Walter. Walter himself is the implied reader for most of them, and their authors expressly wish to please and aid him, as do Mr. Gilmore and Mrs. Michelson, or to escape him, as do Frederick Fairlie and Count Fosco. Only Marian's narrative is fully independent of this connection with Walter's goals and desires because her diary was written before Walter's design was formed. Although in this way the narration of *The Woman in White* can be seen as having common ground with the dual narration of *Bleak House,* one significant difference is that, unlike Esther Summerson, the seeking daughters in this novel, Anne Catherick and Laura Fairlie Glyde, are not granted official narratives of their own. Their stories are embedded in the narratives of others, especially those of Walter and Marian. Whereas Esther and the omniscient narrator work against each other in the submerged plot, Walter Hartright and Marian Halcombe bear a similar relation to it. The actions of both tend to work against the search for the mother's pleasure: both actively seek to expose the stories of Cecilia Jane Elster's and Mrs. Catherick's transgressions. Nevertheless, their narratives, in which they are consciously recording the key elements of the surface plot, also disclose the submerged plot, especially by including narratives written and told by Anne and Laura.

Events in the surface plot are largely determined by the actions and decisions of Sir Percival Glyde, and Sir Percival's motivation to acquire the money he needs to pay his debts and maintain his estate is matched only by his motivation to hide the story of his mother's illicit sexuality. Indeed, Sir Percival's story offers a clear illustration and reminder of why the mother's story is unnarratable. Although the reader learns Cecilia Jane Elster's story only late in the novel (from another transgressive mother, Mrs. Catherick), Sir Percival first learns it as a young man, and he understands that it renders him illegitimate, negating his right to his paternal legacy. The story of Sir Percival's mother seems to be one of sexual pleasure, and that pleasure is a constant threat to her son, who goes to great lengths to conceal it. Cecilia's genteel upbringing culminates in marriage, but she is "ill-used" by her husband, who subsequently leaves her; therefore, she cannot marry Sir Felix Glyde, but, from the time they met, they "had always lived as man and wife" (550). That Cecilia is constrained by her unsuccessful marriage from making a new start on socially acceptable terms may suggest that she turns to the reclusive, resentful, "deformed" Sir Felix as a last resort; however, the text implies otherwise, and it seems that Cecilia is a woman who "marries" despite. . . . As Sir Felix is attracted to this "accomplished musician" because "his sole happiness was in the enjoyment of music" (476), so Cecilia's painful and confining experience could well have made her a kindred spirit to a man with a reputation as "little better than a revolutionist in politics and an infidel in religion" (477). The longevity of their relationship, with no legal tie to bind them, is further evidence of their pleasure in it: from the time of their meeting until her death, they live together in defiance of convention, mostly abroad and in near-total retirement, content in one another's company. Their union produces a son who never, until his father reveals the truth after Cecilia's death, has reason to doubt the solidity of his parents' relationship. Cecilia's story illustrates the potential of the mother's pleasure to corrupt lines of inheritance and its threat to the son's legitimacy. When we meet him, Sir Percival has gone to considerable lengths for over twenty years to hide her story in order to mask his illegitimacy and protect his inheritance, including forging an entry in the church marriage registry, paying for Mrs. Catherick's silence, and incarcerating Anne.

For Carolyn Dever, all of the characters in *The Woman in White* share with Sir Percival a compelling interest in constructing the absent mother as virtuous, chaste, and faithful in support of their own legitimacy. The anxieties of the characters stem from the fact that, repeatedly, "the desire to contain female sexuality retrospectively collides with empirical evidence of maternal transgression" (109). For male and female characters alike, sexual transgression in the mother is a threat that must be contained:

> In *The Woman in White*, the virtuous mother who secures legacy by securing paternity is at all times a back-formation, a retrospective, belated construct. Yet she also represents the ideology on which the novel's detective plot predicates itself; thus the maternal ideal is at every turn, in *The Woman in White* as in mid-Victorian culture more generally, personated in the figure of a *dead* mother, against the living example of a figure such as Mrs. Catherick. For the detective plot, in its tenuous construction of "truth" and "justice" over the figure of the dead mother, exposes maternal virtue as much more than a cultural ideal; it demonstrates that it is a cultural necessity, overdetermined in its significance, and embattled in its ideology. (138)

In this view, the mother must be idealized, and idealizing the mother depends on her absence. Dever analyzes the representation of Mrs. Fairlie, and Mrs. Fairlie's burial plot, to demonstrate that "anxieties about legitimacy, inheritance, and class in *The Woman in White* focus on the relative containability of female sexuality. But the centrality of the dead mother within this novel undermines the characters' desires to read their mothers as stable and safely contained" (138). For Dever, the progression of the novel depends on the characters' attempts to construct the virtuous mother against evidence of maternal transgression.

Dever's revealing analysis, which usefully underscores the potential threat to legitimacy inherent in any mother's sexuality, nevertheless insists on the text's consistent distinction between good and bad mothers. However, though Sir Percival certainly makes this judgment, Anne Catherick appears completely innocent of such distinctions. The submerged plot suggests that mothers in the novel are not so definitively categorized, and that their daughters, though not their sons, can potentially benefit from their stories, whether of transgressive sexuality or not. Dever does not distinguish between the responses of sons and those of daughters to the mother's story, but Tamar Heller identifies in the novel male and female plots (*Dead Secrets* 112). For Heller, Sir Percival's response to his mother's story is consonant with the male plot: "the story here is of the son's fraudulent erasure of his mother's history, a plot that discredits the notion of a maternal lineage by revealing it to be a shameful deviation from the patrinomial line" (133). Heller contrasts Sir Percival's story to the novel's female plot, which is in the tradition of "the Radcliffean female Gothic narrative, where the daughter often searches for her lost mother, discovering in the process the secret of the mother's oppression" (133). She explains, "Within this carceral world, Collins represents the family romance as a Radcliffean narrative in which the daughters share the mother's invisibility; the novel's most central symbolic site is the grave of Laura and Marian's mother, which functions as an image for women's lack of identity" (113). For Heller, then, sons must reject the maternal legacy, and daughters seek their maternal inheritance but find a legacy of oppression, invisibility, and lack of identity. The submerged plot, however, suggests that the daughters seek a more rewarding maternal inheritance: the story of the mother's pleasure.

The pleasure of Cecilia Jane Elster remains obscured through most of the text; readers suspect only that Sir Percival and Anne Catherick's mother have been complicit in something they desire to keep secret, and that Anne is innocently involved. Mrs. Catherick, then, as a mother with a secret past, holds the place of Sir Percival's mother throughout, keeping the idea of the transgressive mother in the reader's mind. Anne Catherick, however, even as she is a figure for the reader in that she knows a secret exists but not what it is, knows less than the reader about her own mother and her own past. Unlike Sir Percival, and unlike Esther Summerson, who grows up aware of the story implied by the circumstances of her birth, Anne Catherick has no suspicion of her own illegitimacy, and, further, no apparent notion of illegitimacy in the abstract. Anne has had ample opportunity to observe that her mother is without a husband and she without a father, that her father is never mentioned, that her mother is isolated within their community, and that Sir Percival has considerable control over her own and her mother's lives—but she has no knowledge of why any of these things is true, nor does it occur to her that the circumstances are connected. When Walter asks her whether her own "misfortune" is that of "believing too innocently in her own virtue, and in the faith and honour of the man she loves," he reports that "she looked up at me with the artless bewilderment of a child" (124). Not only is Anne innocent of any transgressive act, but she also appears to be innocent of any knowledge of such acts. That Sir Percival believes Anne knows his secret is, therefore, the more ironic, as Anne appears to be entirely without the assumptions that would enable her to make sense of it. We may consider Anne's very naivety indicative of a simplicity of character, but her naivety can also be considered a form of resistance to the life-and-death struggles over the mother's story in the surface plot. In this as in other ways, attention to the submerged plot reveals greater complexity in Anne's character.

Walter insists from the beginning on Anne's centrality to the narrative, and his vision of Anne focuses on her sexuality. Anne's apparent inability to distinguish between illicit and sanctioned sexuality is in no way represented as indicating promiscuity, but neither is it an indication of asexuality. When Walter introduces the reader to Anne in the narrative's opening sequence, she is twenty-two years old and has just, perhaps for the first time, asserted her independent adulthood by effecting her own escape from the asylum in which she has been wrongfully imprisoned for an unspecified but apparently considerable time. The reader is given very little idea of what future Anne imagines; indeed, by the time Walter meets Anne again three months later, she stands at Mrs. Fairlie's grave and wishes for death, and only nine months after that, she is dead and buried beside Mrs. Fairlie. However, on the night of her escape, when she meets Walter on the road to London, she tells him of Mrs. Fairlie's daughter, who is nearly her own age, that she "may be married and gone away by this time" (53). We are thus alerted to the possibility that, like Anne Elliot, Jane Eyre, and Esther Summerson, Anne Catherick desires the changes that marriage can bring. Walter, whose own response to a sexually attractive and unchaperoned woman influences his presentation of her in this encounter, clarifies immediately that Anne could never have been mistaken as sexually inviting. Still, she is comfortable with this strange man, and he reports that she touches him twice—the second time, he removes her hand, admitting to a sexual response: "Remember that I was young; remember that the hand which touched me was a woman's" (50). Alert to her physical presence, Walter includes that Anne later takes his arm, and she kisses his hand when they part. Walter's narrative reveals that, for all the pain and isolation of her upbringing, Anne may be able to imagine for herself a life that includes love and marriage, and we can understand that her interest in validating a pleasure she can imagine should be quickened now.

Like other seeking daughters, Anne needs the story of her mother, who, although not altogether absent, has been very much absent from Anne's life. Anne's early childhood is mostly spent with a kind neighbor, Mrs. Clements, and she is separated from her mother again when she is committed to the asylum; they have been long estranged at the time of the novel's action. Although in the surface plot Anne and her mother are "a trouble and a fear to each other" (123)—in fact, they are ultimately divided by Sir Percival's fear of his own mother's story—in the submerged plot Anne repeats her mother's experience as other motherless daughters do. In *The Woman in White* as in *Bleak House*, the seeking daughter actively pursues the story of her mother's pleasure even as she contends with those who would use the story of the mother's transgression to their own ends.

The story of Anne's mother, Jane Anne Catherick, is not known to the reader until late in the novel—nearly simultaneously with that of Sir Percival's mother—and it is never fully known to Anne, whose progress toward her goal is prematurely cut off. Nevertheless, as Walter and Marian piece Jane Anne's story together to establish her transgression, the reader can infer that it does include moments of pleasure, however dearly she has paid for them. As a young lady's maid in a great country house, she had an affair with the handsome, charming Philip Fairlie, a frequent visitor to the house. Subsequent events suggest that Jane Anne had no expectation of marriage and acted purely in the interest of her own pleasure. She bears Philip's child apparently without ever telling him. When she and Anne visit Limmeridge on other business eleven years later, she no doubt hopes to meet him there, but, when she does not, she pursues him no further. Despite the painful consequences of the affair for Jane Anne, she speaks of Philip with fondness years later, remembering him as "one of the handsomest men in England" (555). Although Anne's experience is very limited, she learns what she can of her mother's story by repeating her experience in a number of ways.

Anne's insistence on wearing white at all times is a testament to her relationship with Mrs. Fairlie, but it also signals a connection between Anne's experience and her mother's: for both, the desire for respectability is paramount. Mrs. Catherick tells Walter, "I came here robbed of my character and determined to claim it back. I've been years and years about it—and I *have* claimed it back" (507). Walter describes her as sitting alone in her house, dressed all in sober black, with her eye on the window, never letting pass an opportunity to be bowed to by the clergyman as he walks by, never letting pass an opportunity to mention this satisfying state of affairs. Walter's attention to both women's attire enables us to compare them and realize that, much as her mother uses her black clothing as a sign of her respectability, Anne, instructed by Mrs. Fairlie, uses her white clothing for the same purpose. Mrs. Catherick herself recognizes this in Anne when she writes to Walter, "She had always had crazy notions of her own about her dignity" (557). In the surface plot, Anne's white clothing represents her attachment to Mrs. Fairlie, but it also serves the submerged plot and her need to experience what her mother has before her.

Another way Anne's experience echoes her mother's is in her relationship with Sir Percival. When Sir Percival begins to support Mrs. Catherick financially after the breakup of her marriage, he does so on two conditions—that she keep his secret, and that, as she tells Walter, "I was not to stir away from Welmingham without first letting him know, and waiting till I had obtained his permission" (553). Mrs. Catherick is entirely confined to this small town, her only periods of liberty those granted by Sir Percival. Indeed, the crisis between Sir Percival and Anne, in which she, mimicking her mother, persuades him she knows his secret, is precipitated by an instance in which Sir Percival has refused her mother permission to go away for a change of scene. Years later, Anne is literally incarcerated by Sir Percival in a suburban London asylum, and when Anne escapes he goes to great lengths to locate her and regain his control over her.

These two similarities between Jane Anne's and Anne's experience have long been central to their lives; other instances of Anne repeating her mother's experience begin as Walter's narrative begins. When Anne meets with Walter alone on the road in the middle of the night, she asks, "You don't suspect me of doing anything wrong, do you?" (48). Like her mother, Anne is always speaking from a suspect position, always having to establish her credibility before she can get to her business. Further, although Anne is chaste and her mother has "fallen," both are wrongly suspected of being Sir Percival's mistress. Mrs. Clements's account of the Cathericks' separation makes it clear that the entire community assumes that Mrs. Catherick is Sir Percival's mistress and is carrying his child. Mrs. Catherick pleads with Sir Percival to deny the truth of this assumption, but "he flatly refused in so many words. He told me plainly that it was his interest to let my husband and all my neighbours believe the falsehood—because, as long as they did so they were quite certain never to suspect the truth" (553). Twenty-two years later, Anne is a young woman who attests that she has been "cruelly used and cruelly wronged" by a man "of the rank of Baronet" (52, 51). When the baronet is identified as Sir Percival, Walter wonders if Anne's words imply a similar closeness of relationship. At this point, he suspects Sir Percival might be Anne's lover. Much later, he tells us, "At one time I had thought he might be Anne Catherick's father—at another time I had thought he might have been Anne Catherick's husband" (529–30). Mother and daughter, then, are connected to Sir Percival similarly, and mistakenly, in the minds of others.

As the surface plot progresses, Anne repeats her mother's experience in another, even more specific way when Mrs. Clements takes Anne for "the quiet and the fresh air" at Limmeridge (125). Eleven years before, when Jane Anne took her young daughter to Limmeridge, she went there to nurse her dying half-sister, hoping to inherit money from her, though in the end there was nothing to inherit (555). Now, Anne coincidentally appears at a moment of crisis in her half-sister's life. She, too, offers to help Laura, whose impending marriage to Sir Percival means, both in Anne's mind and in actuality, real danger to Laura. Although Anne has no more idea of an inheritance than she has of her real relationship to Laura, Laura's money disappears as completely as that of

Jane Anne's half-sister. Anne's actions and decisions, clearly motivated by circumstances in the surface plot, also fulfill the demands of the submerged plot.

Even as Anne's search for her mother's story progresses, she assumes responsibility for Laura Fairlie's search as well as her own when she learns that Laura is engaged to Sir Percival Glyde. Throughout the novel, while Sir Percival acts to obscure and devalue the story of the mother's pleasure, Anne acts to reorient Laura's search away from her paternal inheritance and toward her mother's story. Anne's success in this regard encourages us to reconsider her place in the character-system. Anne takes on the role of mentoring Laura, and, not unlike Lady Russell and even Miss Barbary, her own relationship with Laura's mother constantly invokes her memory, for Laura and for the reader. The progression of Collins's complex plot can best be measured by the attempts of Sir Percival and Anne Catherick to influence Laura's relation to the mother's story. In response to these influences, Laura at first values her paternal inheritance above all, even at the expense of her own pleasure, but later becomes suspicious of her inheritance and more receptive to her mother's story, and finally repeats her mother's experience, finding validation for her own pleasure in the story of her mother's.

The progression of the submerged plot of Laura's search can be tracked through the novel's three parts. The "First Epoch" begins on the day Walter Hartright learns of an available position for a drawing master at Limmeridge House. It traces the growing passion between Walter and his pupil, Laura Fairlie, and ends five months later, the day of Laura's marriage to Sir Percival Glyde. A number of interpretive questions are raised in this section of the novel. The first, likely to be the reader's immediate preoccupation throughout this section, is why Laura marries Sir Percival, when no one who takes the least interest in her believes she should. A larger and related question is why Laura Fairlie and Walter Hartright, both decent people whose love for one another proves enduring, must be separated at all. Finally, and this question is raised for the reader again and again by the events of the novel, what renders the attempts of Anne Catherick, Marian Halcombe, and even Laura herself to take control of their circumstances so utterly ineffectual? Reconsidered in light of the conflict between the surface plot's emphasis on the story of transgression and the submerged plot's emphasis on the story of pleasure, these issues become more fully explicable.

Unlike many seeking daughters, Laura Fairlie is an heiress; the responsibility and privilege of inheriting Limmeridge aligns Laura with literary sons who fear their mother's pleasure, and Laura's paternal inheritance is of central importance throughout the novel. Marian tells Walter in no uncertain terms during their first meeting, "My father was a poor man, and Miss Fairlie's father was a rich man. I have got nothing, and she has a fortune" (60). Mr. Gilmore's narrative outlines the exact extent of Laura's fortune, emphasizing the degree to which the narrative turns on it. We know that Laura is not entirely comfortable with her paternal legacy: she wears "the sort of dress which the wife or daughter of a poor man might have worn" because, with respect to her half-sister and her governess, nothing could "induce her to let the advantage in dress desert the two ladies who were poor, to lean to the side of the one lady who was rich" (80). Laura's "aversion to the slightest personal display of her own wealth" (80) and the considerable disadvantage it entails of separating her from the poor drawing master whom she loves, even should she break her previous engagement, attest to her own sense of its centrality and importance. Even before we know of Sir Percival's own unending struggle to assert his right to his inheritance, we associate Sir Percival with Laura's paternal legacy. When Marian breaks the news of Laura's prior engagement, she explains to Walter, "Her father sanctioned it on his deathbed" (97). Laura has inherited, along with her fortune, her engagement to Sir Percival.

Long before Laura or her family and friends begin to perceive her paternal inheritance as problematic, Anne Catherick recognizes its dangers. Anne takes it upon herself to fight against Sir Percival Glyde's control over her life and over Laura's, sacrificing herself in the attempt. Regrettably, her struggle is only partially successful. For herself, she gains exactly a year of freedom, but she ends her life as a prop in Sir Percival and Fosco's plan to steal Laura's fortune. Her insistence that Sir Percival hides a damaging secret provides Walter with the means to seek Laura's freedom from him, which she eventually gains, but Anne fails to stop Laura's marriage or the ensuing crimes against her. Thus, Anne's efforts in the surface plot, though valiant and indispensable, are also largely ineffectual. However, her efforts in the submerged plot succeed eventually in shifting Laura's focus from her paternal to her maternal legacy, without which reorientation Laura cannot be prepared to embrace the pleasure that she at first rejects.

Walter's narrative of his encounter with Anne Catherick on the moonlit road to London foregrounds her sexuality and also her attachment to Laura Fairlie's mother. She claims that she loves anyone of the name of Fairlie at Limmeridge House "for Mrs. Fairlie's sake" (53). Her remark plants the seed that, only two days later, has Marian Halcombe poring over her mother's correspondence for references that might explain Walter's strange meeting. The letters bring Mrs. Fairlie's voice into the text, emphasizing her significance to the reader, and are the occasion for the narration of the brief outline of her history. Just as Anne invokes the mother, the letter that Marian reads aloud to Walter from Mrs. Fairlie's correspondence also, of course, emphasizes Anne's importance. Laura is told nothing about Anne's reappearance, but "at the first safe opportunity Miss Halcombe cautiously led her half-sister to speak of their mother" (87). Anne is the catalyst that brings Laura's absent mother to her attention, and to the reader's.

Soon thereafter, Anne again brings Mrs. Fairlie to Laura's mind directly and deliberately in her warning letter. Walter chooses to reproduce Anne's letter, thus bringing her voice, like Mrs. Fairlie's, into the text. When he immediately suspects that Anne is the writer of this anonymous letter, he "began to doubt whether my own faculties were not in danger of losing their balance. It seemed almost like a monomania to be tracing back everything [. . .] always to the same hidden source" (105). Walter's suspicion is correct, yet his surprise at his own tendency to make Anne central to his narrative is also revealing: although his subsequent actions will work against the submerged plot, his narrative works for it from the start. Anne begins her letter by asking, "Do you believe in dreams?" (102), a question Laura will echo much later when she has finally understood Anne's message. Although Anne is not fully conscious of the ways her actions tend to promote the importance of the mother's story, her letter is certainly motivated by her own sense of connectedness to other women. The dream Anne narrates emphasizes this sense of connection when she reads in letters of fire this indictment of Sir Percival: "He has strewn with misery the paths of others, and he will live to strew with misery the path of this woman by his side" (103). To Anne, what she, her mother, and Laura have in common is evident, even though she remains unaware to the end of the real relationships among them. Anne fails to accuse Sir Percival of any confirmable offense, but she does end her letter by invoking Mrs. Fairlie: "Your mother's daughter has a tender place in my heart—for your mother was my first, my best, my only friend" (104). At this crucial moment, as Laura decides whether to keep her engagement to Sir Percival even though she loves Walter Hartright, Anne Catherick encourages her to think of her mother.

Indeed, Anne succeeds in bringing her beloved Mrs. Fairlie into the minds of the villagers as well, when she goes to the churchyard at twilight to tend Mrs. Fairlie's grave. She is seen there by a child who insists that he has seen "t'ghaist of Mistress Fairlie" (111). To Marian, the child's error suggests that people in the village may "have forgotten the respect and gratitude due from every soul in it to my mother's memory" (111). To Walter, his misapprehension suggests the identity of the letter writer as well as a way to get more information from her. To the reader, the absent mother remains a significant presence, as she is to Anne, and as Anne intends for her to be to others. Walter's detailed narrative of his meeting with Anne at Mrs. Fairlie's grave maintains his view of her as both potentially sexual and also naive. He reports being "roused by feeling Anne Catherick's hand laid on my shoulder" (120–21), and also finds that she is unaware of "the too common and too customary motive that has led many a woman to interpose anonymous hindrances to the marriage of the man who has ruined her" (124). He presents her as poised on the edge of sexuality, and she maintains the focus on Laura's mother: "Oh, Mrs. Fairlie! Mrs. Fairlie! tell me how to save her. Be my darling and my mother once more, and tell me what to do for the best" (127). Anne's goal is to help Laura, and, though she believes that her knowledge of Sir Percival is her surest means of doing so, her love of and attention to the memory of Mrs. Fairlie proves the most efficacious.

At this stage, Anne's attempts are outmatched by Sir Percival's own actions, past and present, designed to obscure both his mother's and Anne's mother's stories and maintain the focus on paternal inheritance. His imprisonment of Anne in an asylum damages her credibility and enables Laura and her friends to dismiss the doubts raised by her letter. However, the reader's judgment diverges from Laura's at this point, so Anne has succeeded with the reader where she has, for the moment, failed with Laura. An illustration of this difference is that the letter from Mrs. Catherick absolving Sir Percival from guilt in Anne's case helps to persuade Laura to trust him; in contrast, when Mr. Gilmore describes the letter as "short, sharp, and to the point; in form rather a business-like letter for a woman to write" (160), we are meant to suspect immediately what we learn later, that this letter was actually dictated by Sir Percival himself. Sir Percival literally replaces the absent mother's voice with his own, and his energies are concentrated on silencing Anne, whose goal is directly opposed to his.

Sir Percival, then, seeks to obscure the mother's story, and he also uses Laura's naive belief in her paternal inheritance to his advantage. When she appears to be considering ending their engagement, he pretends to be willing to release her from her commitment, asking only that she remember "what the circumstances were under which the engagement between them was made" (161). Sir Percival knows he can count on Laura's loyalty to her deceased father. At this point, Marian Halcombe takes over the narration; although her actions in the surface plot work against the submerged plot, as Walter's do, her narrative traces the submerged plot of her sister's search for validation of her pleasure. When Marian expects Laura to break the engagement, she realizes why Laura finds doing so impossible when she notices, "On the opposite wall hung the miniature portrait of her father. I bent over her, and saw that she was looking at it while her head lay on my breast" (185–86). Laura's next words clarify Marian's impression: "I can never claim my release from my engagement. [. . .] All I can do, Marian, is not to add the remembrance that I have broken my promise and forgotten my father's dying words, to make that wretchedness worse" (186). In the pages that follow, Marian reports that Laura mentions her father numerous times, including "my father's influence" (190), "my father's trust," and "my father's memory" (191). Her alignment with her father's legacy in all its forms is clear in her words to Sir Percival:

> I was guided by my father, because I had always found him the truest of advisers, the best and fondest of all protectors and friends. I have lost him now—I have only his memory to love, but my faith in that dear dead friend has never been shaken. (190)

That Laura is wrong about her father, who unthinkingly left not only Laura but Jane Anne and Anne the unprotected victims of Sir Percival's schemes, is, as yet, unknown to the reader, as it is to her and to Marian. Therefore, despite Anne's warnings and her attempt to ignite in Laura a desire for her equally important maternal legacy, Laura marries Sir Percival, consciously rejecting her own potential pleasure with Walter and accepting a future that holds no hope of pleasure whatsoever. Marian, though she questions her own actions and later regrets them sincerely, also works against Laura's search by arranging for Walter to go abroad. Nevertheless, her narrative reveals that Laura, like other seeking daughters, needs the story of her mother's pleasure before she can access her own.

The next stage in the progression develops in the Second Epoch. As Marian's diary continues, she reveals to the reader how quickly Laura discovers that sexual pleasure is by no means the only sacrifice her marriage demands of her and that her paternal legacy has proven a liability beyond her imagining. Laura, speaking of her honeymoon in Italy, confides in Marian "how soon my disappointments and my trials began" (280). By way of illustration, she tells a narrative of her own, which Marian records: the story of her and Sir Percival's visit to the tomb of Cecilia Metella. As Laura contemplates the monument, she finds in it "the remembrance that a husband's love had raised it in the old time to a wife's memory" (281), and she tries to imagine her own story in Cecilia's. However, when she asks Sir Percival whether he loves her enough to memorialize her in this way, he tells her in no uncertain terms that he loves only Laura's money, and he reinterprets Cecilia's story by imagining that Cecilia's own fortune paid for her tomb. Sir Percival is vigilant as ever against any story of the mother's pleasure: not only does Cecilia Metella share the name of Sir Percival's own mother, but the inscription on her tomb identifies her primarily as a mother.[2] Laura, however, is newly aware of the potential promise of such a story. She admits to Marian, "From that time [. . .] I never checked myself again in thinking of Walter Hartright" (281); Laura has ceased to deny her own potential pleasure.

The Second Epoch spans less than a month, from the time Laura returns from her honeymoon to live at Blackwater Park until her death is announced and she is actually incarcerated in the same asylum where Anne Catherick was held. Nevertheless, in this period Laura exhibits a greater willingness to assert herself and her own interests. Marian reports that Laura, strengthened perhaps by what her honeymoon has taught her about her marriage, resists Sir Percival's demand for her signature on papers she has not read. Marian, present in the room, intervenes on Laura's behalf, and, in her gratitude, Laura mentions her mother for the first time: "If my mother had been alive, she could have done no more for me!" (268). Like Anne, Marian mentors Laura in a way that invokes Mrs. Fairlie. Laura has awakened to a sense of what her absent mother could have done for her, and what her story can do, and she is strengthened by it. Therefore, when Anne Catherick makes another attempt at her mission, Laura is eager to learn all she can from her. Marian, having listened avidly to Laura's narrative of meeting with Anne Catherick, records it faithfully in her diary.

Marian's intention is to keep a record of all details that might lead to the exposure of Sir Percival's secret, his mother's transgression, but her narrative also serves to document the progress of Laura's search for her mother's pleasure. When Anne comes upon Laura in the boathouse, she begins by addressing her as "Miss Fairlie," as Laura describes it, "the dear, familiar name that I thought I had parted from for ever" (299). Anne's words assert as a possibility that which Laura has wished for—that she might again be as she was before her marriage. Anne is consumed with thoughts of Mrs. Fairlie, and Laura is receptive: "You knew my mother? [. . .] Was it very long ago?" (299). Anne is distressed when she feels that Laura is unlike her mother; having found Laura's lost brooch, Anne reproaches her, "Your mother would have let me pin on the brooch" (299), and she is disappointed that, as she says, "You have not got your mother's face [. . .] or your mother's heart" (300). As she has from the beginning, Anne reminds Laura that she is failing to seek her maternal legacy. Anne never has the opportunity to tell Laura "the Secret that your cruel husband is afraid of" (303), even if she were able, and thus can offer Laura no more help in the surface plot. However, what she does communicate to Laura advances the submerged plot as it emphasizes to Laura the potential power of her mother's story. When we last see Laura before her abduction, Mrs. Michelson reports seeing her off at the train station near Blackwater Park, and Laura asks her, "Do you believe in dreams?" (410). That she echoes Anne's letter is just one of the signs that she has begun to understand Anne's message.

Laura is ready to embrace her maternal inheritance, but first she learns the devastating effects of two further elements of her paternal legacy. The first is her resemblance to Anne Catherick: that the two women have inherited their physical appearance from their father enables Sir Percival and Count Fosco to use their shared inheritance of looks against them to defraud Laura of her fortune. The second is Philip Fairlie's effective disinheritance of his sister in protest against her marriage to Count

Fosco, which makes Laura the Count's target as well as Sir Percival's. As the villains force Laura and Anne into each other's identities, both, and Marian, too, recede from our direct view in the narrative, which is taken over by people less and less known to them and to us, including Sir Percival's housekeeper and Count Fosco's cook. Anne dies of heart disease in the interval, Laura is reported dead, and when Laura reappears she has suffered in an asylum for over two months and then escaped, only to be unrecognized by her father's brother and turned away from the home that is her paternal legacy. When the narrative is resumed by Walter, he explains that what has happened to Marian and to Laura has made it impossible for them to tell their "inevitably confused" stories of the past few months (435).

Having lost the independent narrative of Marian's diary, Walter narrates the story of his reunion with her and Laura twice, once from his own point of view and once based on Marian's story of her and Laura's experience. He ends the Second Epoch with an account of his own trip to Limmeridge to see Laura's grave, where he is shocked so that "the springs of my life fell low" by the appearance, much changed, of Laura herself (431). This sensational event in the surface plot has further significance in the submerged plot, and the reader is prepared to find it when Walter narrates the scene a second time. In this version, for which Marian has provided the details, we understand the changes that have been wrought in Laura: she is physically weakened and "shaken" in her "intellects" (443). An especially significant change evident in this account is Laura's new focus on her mother. When she and Marian have been rejected and even threatened at Limmeridge House, they know that they must leave the neighborhood immediately. Nevertheless, after they have walked past the churchyard, Laura

> insisted on turning back to look her last at her mother's grave. Miss Halcombe tried to shake her resolution but, in this one instance, tried in vain. She was immovable. Her dim eyes lit with a sudden fire, and flashed through the veil that hung over them—her wasted fingers strengthened moment by moment round the friendly arm by which they had held so listlessly till this time. (451)

Finally, Laura's focus is on her mother. By insisting on returning to her mother's grave, Laura is reunited with Walter, who is at the grave in the belief that Laura is buried there. This apparent coincidence in the surface plot is a risk Collins takes in support of the submerged plot: pausing at her mother's grave demonstrates that Laura has fully recognized the significance of her mother's story and its role in her own potential pleasure. This scene begins the novel's Third Epoch with Laura's focus on her mother—her father is likely buried in this churchyard as well, but there is no mention of homage at his grave—and the hope this gesture offers is clear when she finds Walter in the same moment.

With Laura experienced in the dangers of her paternal inheritance and prepared to embrace her maternal legacy, we expect the Third Epoch to proceed toward a satisfactory conclusion, and so it does. Still, many readers are troubled by the way that Laura's already tenuous voice, far from being strengthened in this final section, nearly disappears. She has no part in exposing the conspiracy against her or in her own reinstatement as Laura Fairlie Glyde Hartright of Limmeridge. Her passivity is largely attributable to the fact that she is in recovery from more than one traumatic experience, and readers are likely to be uneasy about the degree of recovery she achieves. Even though we know she loves Walter and he loves her, readers cannot feel certain that Laura is equipped to participate in a partnership of any equality.[3]

At the same time, marginal though Laura seems to the Third Epoch, she is nominally, and in some ways actually, central to it. Walter's voice dominates this section, and his one goal is "to fight her battle, and to win the way back for her to her place in the world of living beings" (434). The means by which Walter proposes to do this is to establish her identity and thus restore her paternal inheritance. Laura is not involved in this process; indeed, most of the action of this section is deliberately concealed from her in the interest of her eventual recovery. Therefore, in the surface plot Laura appears to have even less agency at this point than she has in the past, unless her passivity is regarded as deliberate resistance to the remaining vestiges of the paternal inheritance that has ruined her life. In the submerged plot, however, Laura progresses toward a fuller understanding of her mother's experiences of marriage and toward her own pleasure.

As assiduously as Anne has promoted Laura's progress, Sir Percival has impeded it. From the first, he has persuaded Laura as well as her family that to marry him will be to do as her mother had done before her: to marry a gentleman of rank, property, and wealth; to be the mistress of a great house; to bear children; and to do good among her husband's tenants. Sir Percival proves to be poor, prevents her from exerting power of any kind in his decaying house and estate, and refrains from sex to ensure that she will have no children. In this case, the false suitor pretends to resemble the father, and Sir Percival's deception has derailed Laura's search. However, his death in the burning vestry, where he is still trying to hide the story of his mother's pleasure, frees Laura to really repeat her mother's experience.

Like her mother, Laura experiences widowhood and remarriage. As Laura's first marriage seemed, superficially, to resemble her mother's marriage to Philip Fairlie, her second marriage, to the poor drawing master Walter Hartright, might seem to resemble her mother's first marriage to Mr. Halcombe, a poor man who is loved and chosen for himself alone. Further analysis suggests, however, that Laura's second marriage resembles her mother's second marriage in a number of ways, that the true suitor actually resembles the father. Philip Fairlie is described by Walter, based on information from Marian, as

> one of the notoriously handsome men of his time. [. . .] he was the spoilt darling of society, especially of the women—an easy, light-hearted, impulsive, affectionate man—generous to a fault—constitutionally lax in his principles, and notoriously thoughtless of moral obligations where women were concerned. (574)

Given that Fairlie is a sort of good-natured rake, Mrs. Halcombe may well marry him despite her better judgment—for pleasure. Although Walter's circumstances are very different from Philip Fairlie's, Walter appears to be like Laura's father in that he is attractive to women. Laura falls in love with him almost immediately, and there is evidence that Marian, too, has feelings for him.[4] Mrs. Catherick's odd letter to Walter on the occasion of Sir Percival's death includes this:

> If I was a young woman still I might say, "Come, put your arm round my waist, and kiss me, if you like." I should have been fond enough of you even to go to that length, and you would have accepted my invitation—you would, sir, twenty years ago! (548)

Even Mrs. Catherick finds him attractive. Anne Catherick touches him before she ever speaks to him, having watched him first to try to ascertain whether she can trust him. Walter, like Philip, is a man whom women find attractive. Unlike Philip, he is scrupulous about not pressing his advantage inappropriately, but this appears to be always a conscious struggle. The night he enables Anne Catherick to escape her pursuers, he questions his actions during and after the event, but he is steadfast in allowing her freedom primarily to avoid any appearance of taking sexual advantage of her himself. He admits to feeling attracted to the young ladies who are his pupils but also to schooling himself strictly to deny those impulses (89). Thus, Laura Fairlie, who, according to Mr. Gilmore, is "as amiable and attentive to every one about her as her excellent mother used to be" (151), finds pleasure in a man who is, in some ways, like the one her mother chose.

Mrs. Fairlie had the experience of being apart from her husband for long periods of time, during which they corresponded; Marian reports, "He was fond of London, and was constantly away from his country home" (63–64). Indeed, Mrs. Catherick and Anne are in Limmeridge for "a few months" and never see him (87). Walter is separated from Laura, though for very different reasons, several times throughout their relationship, including following their marriage. Both Mrs. Fairlie and Laura are kept in ignorance of facts that, unbeknownst to them, touch their lives closely. Mrs. Fairlie, in ignorance of Anne's paternity, is put in a position of vulnerability with regard to Mrs. Catherick, a woman who knows more about her than she realizes and has unacknowledged motives in coming to Limmeridge. Similarly, Walter keeps from Laura everything he and Marian have figured out about the conspiracy and their own attempts to get the better of Sir Percival and Fosco. Both women remain unharmed by these absences and silences, however, and Laura, like her mother, maintains her "perfect innocence of heart" (575). Eventually, Laura's husband takes her father's place as master of Limmeridge, and Laura shares her mother's experiences of being the mistress of Limmeridge House and of bearing a child who will inherit it.

Even as Laura finally learns the story of her mother's pleasure, she finds her own. The fact that Laura's is delayed until after she has been traumatized and weakened and has lost her memory of certain past events tempers our evaluation of Laura's marriage to Walter, as does his ultimate realization of a social position that might have been his primary object all along. At the same time, if their marriage is imperfect, that does not rule out the possibility of moments of pleasure. The intimacy of their marriage is described with reference to the marriage bed itself on the night Walter goes to confront Fosco, leaving Laura asleep, "her face turned faithfully to *my* pillow in her sleep [. . .] her hand resting open on the coverlid, as if it was waiting unconsciously for mine [. . .] She stirred in her sleep and murmured my name" (602). Her mother's story and the pleasure she finds while living secretly in London with her husband function to balance Laura's paternal inheritance when she is reinstated in her former place. The danger of that inheritance seems to have been mitigated by the fact that what is left is only a life interest in the estate; Laura's fortune of thirty thousand pounds is entirely gone.

If we are tempted to assume that Laura's search succeeds because her mother's story is of sex sanctioned by marriage, whereas Anne's fails because her mother's is a story of illicit sex, we know on the contrary that the story of the mother's pleasure is antinarratable whether that pleasure is taken within or outside of marriage, and, in *The Woman in White,* the distinction, though crucial to the plot, carries relatively little moral import. The story of Cecilia Jane Elster elicits our sympathy, and Mrs. Catherick is blamed far less for engaging in premarital sex with a single man than for her subsequent deception of the unsuspecting Catherick to falsely legitimate her pregnancy (575). Mrs. Fairlie is represented by Marian and Walter as entirely innocent and pure of heart, but Mrs. Catherick accuses her of having "entrapped one of the handsomest men in England into marrying her" (555). Mrs. Catherick has her own reasons for vindictiveness, but, whereas we easily understand why Mrs. Fairlie marries the dashing, wealthy Philip Fairlie despite his weaknesses and failings, we are not encouraged to speculate on why he marries her. She brings no money to the marriage, though she does bring a dependent daughter. Mrs. Fairlie is called "plain-looking" by Mrs. Catherick (555) (though Marian denies this [574]); she is said to resemble Marian (151), whom Walter describes as "ugly" (but who may well not be) (58). These circumstances, and the relatively brief time that elapses between the births of Anne and Laura, could support Mrs. Catherick's apparently gratuitous assertion and suggest that Mrs. Fairlie found herself in the same situation as Jane Anne, except that Philip married her. As our interrogation of the few details we have and the several narrators who provide them complicates the mimetic component of the characters of all three absent mothers, the distinctions among them become less clear, and we know that Collins himself did not value such distinctions. As our understanding of the mimetic component of each is deepened, the established interpretation of their thematic functions is destabilized. Rather than functioning primarily to emphasize cultural imperatives concerning constructions of the mother, these characters function individually as women with stories that are valuable in and of themselves.

Anne fails not because she fails to seek nor because of her mother's transgression, but because her own mother's story is bound up with that of Sir Percival's mother, and she does not live long enough to overcome the obstacle of his resistance as she helps Laura to do. Although the first time we meet Anne she is intent on her freedom, by the second time we meet her she is focused mainly on her own death. Walter finds Anne at Mrs. Fairlie's grave exclaiming, "Oh, if I could die, and be hidden and at rest with *you*!" (127). Anne has dreamed of "an angel weeping" at Laura's wedding (104), and, when she finally speaks with Laura in person, the angel of her dream is connected explicitly to Mrs. Fairlie when she tells Laura, "your mother's heart, Miss Fairlie, was the heart of an angel" (300). Anne's focus is now entirely on the afterlife, and her search is suspended as she conducts the only business she has left: she explains to Laura, "I am here to make atonement to you, before I meet your mother in the world beyond the grave" (300). Anne cannot complete her own search, but she fulfills her goal of aiding in Laura's, and ultimately, she is granted her wish to lie under the white cross in Limmeridge churchyard, repeating the experience of one who "was better than a mother to me" (121). Anne's and Laura's progress toward the mother's pleasure works against the efforts of the rest of the characters to conceal or expose the mother's transgressions. Despite their actions against the search, however, Marian's and Walter's narratives document the submerged plot and make it visible to the reader.

Of course, *The Woman in White* is the story of not two but three young, marriageable women who might reasonably be expected to seek their mothers' pleasure in order to validate their own: what of Marian Halcombe? We know from Mr. Gilmore's narrative that, unlike Laura, Marian resembles her mother physically: "Mrs. Fairlie had dark eyes and hair, and her elder daughter, Miss Halcombe, strongly reminds me of her" (151). She knows more of Mrs. Fairlie and even Mrs. Catherick than either Laura or Anne. Like them, she has also relived her mother's experience in some particulars, including living at Limmeridge

House with Philip Fairlie and mothering Laura. Her reactions to Walter Hartright and Count Fosco, as well as her comments on how marriage usually affects young women (223–24), suggest that Marian is fully conscious of sexual desire and capable of sexual pleasure. Nevertheless, she appears to have withdrawn entirely from her own search, becoming instead, as Anne Catherick envisions Marian's mother, "the good angel of our lives" (646). She does not find sexual pleasure in the course of the narrative, and her plans to eschew marriage and commit herself to Walter and Laura appear closed to it as well: "After all that we three have suffered together [. . .] there can be no parting between us till the last parting of all" (641). The failure of Marian's search may be attributable to an element of her character that tends to be underread: not unlike Laura, whose inheritance places her in the position of a son, Marian acts as a son and brother as well as daughter and sister. Walter describes Marian as physically masculine (58), and Marian disparages her own sex (59–60), but her actions speak even more loudly. Susan Balée asserts of Marian: "What she feels for Laura seems to be a chivalrous, brotherly love that deepens as Laura comes to rely on her more and more" (203). Michael Taylor expands on the idea of chivalry to find that the novel "owes a clear debt to romance, a genre dedicated to the enshrinement of women, in which servility is the chief feature of the male practitioners of knight-errantry locked into their arduous, custodial roles" (289). Taylor argues that Marian, like Walter, fills the role of knight to Laura's fair maiden. Although we should avoid overreading Laura's characterization as a maiden in distress, we should also avoid underreading the masculine element of Marian's characterization. Forced into a brother's role, a son's role, Marian's access to her maternal legacy is impeded.

We do not learn the novel's central secret—the illegitimacy of Sir Percival—until very near its conclusion. Not all readers have found the revelation satisfying; John Sutherland, for example, writes, "This, rather disappointingly, is the great 'secret,' about which eager readers of the serial were casting bets among themselves" (77–78). For Sutherland, adultery is a common transgression, but Collins has prepared us to find in the story of Sir Percival's parents not only transgression but something much less narratable, pleasure. Sir Percival rejects the possibilities of such a story, Walter remains focused on exposing transgression, and Marian, in her role as brother and son, seems unable to access it.

Nevertheless, Anne Catherick never doubts its importance, and she is responsible for Laura Fairlie's successful pursuit of pleasure.

The submerged plots of *The Woman in White* and *Bleak House* form second horizontal axes as vital to the novels as their vibrant surface plots, and the narration of each novel is put to very particular use in the disclosure of both plots. The struggle between those who would expose the mother's transgression and those who would seek her pleasure is enacted in the dual narration of Dickens's novel and in the duality inherent in the two main narratives in Collins's novel. The submerged plots demonstrate the centrality of the unnarratable story of the mother's pleasure and the difficulty of retrieving it, not only when faced with the officially accepted story of the mother's purity but also when faced with proliferating narratives of her transgression. Nevertheless, like other seeking daughters, the protagonists of these novels find that their mothers are women who married despite . . . , and they explore their mothers' experience in their relationships with suitors who are like the men their mothers chose. Laura Fairlie's progress is made possible by the mentoring of Anne Catherick. Esther's need for mentors or for other women who might model the mother's experience is obviated by her encounter with her own mother. For Esther Summerson and Anne Catherick, the fact that their mothers find pleasure outside of marriage does not make their search less necessary, less desirable, or even less effective in validating the daughter's own pleasure than those of Laura Fairlie, Anne Elliot, and Jane Eyre. That the submerged plot of *Bleak House* progresses so similarly to that of *Persuasion* and *Jane Eyre* seems to mark Dickens's confidence in the pursuit of the mother's story. Wilkie Collins employs the same method as Austen, Brontë, and Dickens in *The Woman in White*, which suggests that he was as convinced of the significance of women's pleasure as his predecessors. The very partial success of the seeking daughters in Collins's novel, however, implies that he was less optimistic about the possibilities for and effects of communicating that pleasure. Collins's doubt is reflected in the work of his early-twentieth-century successors, which I address in the next chapter.

CHAPTER 3

The House, the Journey, and the Spaces of the Submerged Plot

The House of Mirth and *The Last September*

Reconfiguring the progression of the much-studied nineteenth-century texts considered in chapters 1 and 2 enables us to understand what they have in common with twentieth-century texts from other cultures. Edith Wharton's *The House of Mirth* (1905) and Elizabeth Bowen's *The Last September* (1929) are very different in significant ways, with Wharton's style in this early work hearkening back to the nineteenth century and Bowen's decidedly twentieth-century realism shading into modernism. One important similarity, however, is that in both novels the surface plot tends toward the conventions of the marriage plot but does not end in marriage. In *The House of Mirth*, the failed marriage plot is experienced by the reader as full of drama and strong emotion; in *The Last September*, the failed marriage plot is characterized primarily by ambivalence and ambiguity, not unlike Virginia Woolf's *The Voyage Out*, which certainly influenced Bowen's novel. Even given these differences, we find the submerged plot of the search for the mother's pleasure circulating through both novels. The submerged plots of the two novels are similarly in sync with the surface plots and help to determine their endings. Both surface and submerged plots "fail" synchronously because elements of the two plots are antithetical and cannot be reconciled. Circumstances in the surface plot prevent Lily Bart from finding the story of her mother's pleasure despite her earnest search. Her inability to find the mother's pleasure is the inability to access pleasure altogether, and the synchronization of the two plots helps to explain why *The House of Mirth* achieves completion—Lily's failure is as decided as, for example, Anne Elliot's success. The two plots are also in sync in Bowen's novel, but are similarly at odds with one another. Circumstances in the surface plot impede the search in the submerged plot, and *The Last September* concludes before either plot reaches a satisfying completion. Bowen ends her novel when her protagonist is still very young, and the inconclusiveness of Lois Farquar's search leaves much in the novel unresolved, but evidence suggests that what she has managed to learn about her mother may yet enable her to find the pleasure that has eluded her thus far.

The daughter protagonists' searches in the submerged plots are strongly influenced by the novels' settings, which share some significant characteristics. In *The House of Mirth*, as in many of her other works, Wharton offers us a vision of Gilded-Age New York, and her protagonist circulates in a very exclusive social milieu of wealthy old families that is, as the novel suggests, becoming more permeable and less relevant as the newly rich become more powerful and influential. Elizabeth Bowen's *The Last September* also opens to the reader the world of an elite class in decline. Set at Danielstown, a "Big House" in County Cork, in the autumn of 1920, Bowen's novel concerns the lives of an Anglo-Irish family and their guests, who are only vaguely aware that their place in Irish society, already tenuous, will disappear completely with the signing of the Anglo-Irish Treaty in 1921. In both novels, the motherless protagonists are part of an elite by birth, but each finds herself in uneasy relationship to her social milieu because of changes in it and in herself. This similarity of setting, and the way the settings determine events on both horizontal axes, make these two novels particularly useful examples of what tracing the submerged plot can reveal about the connections between plot and space.

I have presented motherless daughters throughout this study as engaged in a search for knowledge of their mothers' experience. This figurative search is mirrored in the novels by literal movement through geographical space. Anne Elliot moves from Kellynch to Uppercross to Lyme, then back to Kellynch and finally to Bath. Jane Eyre moves from Gateshead Hall to Lowood to Thornfield, back to Gateshead, and finally to Moor House and then Ferndean. These journeys, though they cover relatively short distances, correspond with considerable change in the protagonists' lives, and, in both cases, the journeys are precipitated by ejection from the great house where the mother lived. The interplay between the great house and the journey as means of accessing the mother's experience is central to these and to most of the novels considered here. Esther Summerson's movements are even less linear than in the earlier novels, but she travels back and forth from London to St. Albans, makes two significant trips to Lincolnshire, and ends at the new Bleak House in the north of England. She never enters the great house that might offer some knowledge of her mother's experience, but Chesney Wold looms large in the novel and, after she knows who her mother is, in Esther's consciousness. Laura Fairlie's search begins, like Anne's and Jane's, in the great house associated with her mother, and Laura's journey to Italy, Blackwood Park, and London finally brings her full circle to become, as Anne Elliot at one point contemplates being, the mistress of the house where her mother was mistress before her. In all cases, the protagonist's journey works in favor of the search, but the great house provides nearly as rich a source for knowledge of the mother's experience.

The complications of this spatial pattern in *The House of Mirth* and *The Last September* reflect complications of the submerged plots in both novels. Lily Bart, like her predecessors, travels: she moves in and out of New York City, not only upstate to Bellomont but also to Europe. Because there is no great house associated with her mother, Lily's search is enacted entirely in her travels, which mirror her mother's wandering and exile; however, this homelessness is implicated in her failure to progress. Lois's mother is also associated with exile, but Bowen's narrative focuses on Lois's first experience of the great house that was her mother's childhood home. The house dominates her progress entirely during her residence there, facilitating but also frustrating her search for knowledge of her mother. Her expulsion from the house at the novel's end may promise that she continues her search more productively, benefitting both from having lived there and also from escaping.

In both novels, the third-person narrators afford us information about the protagonists' mothers. The protagonists themselves wonder about their mothers' experience even as they keep their searches private, protecting their mothers' stories and their own pursuit of them. Both mothers are described as having chosen an acceptable marriage that produced one legitimate daughter; unlike the mothers in *Bleak House* and *The Woman in White*, these mothers do not appear to have secrets. At the same time, they are not entirely similar to the mothers in *Persuasion* and *Jane Eyre*, either: we are provided with an equally bare minimum of information about them, but whereas the information we have about Elizabeth Stevenson Elliot and Jane Reed Eyre is solid and definite, what we are told about Mrs. Hudson Bart and Laura Naylor Farquar is unclear and inconclusive. The social spaces in which these two women lived only increase the obscurity of their experience. In strong contrast to the nineteenth-century novels, in these novels, a woman who has sex outside of marriage is not necessarily officially defined by the story of her transgression. Married women are afforded a great deal of freedom in Wharton's world, and Bowen's characters are not especially shocked or inhibited by broken engagements and extramarital affairs. Especially given the greater range of possibilities, the daughters' searches are very much complicated by the tantalizing vagueness of the mothers' stories, and the unnarratable story of the mother's pleasure in these novels is never fully accessed by the seeking daughters nor revealed to the reader.

"She never made clear": Mrs. Hudson Bart

The progression of Edith Wharton's *The House of Mirth* is complex by any measure, characterized by instabilities that multiply and tensions that remain at least partly unresolved. The causes of Lily Bart's plight are multiple, the opportunities she has to gain control over her situation are charged with moral ambiguity, and the reader's response to Lily's situation is likely to fluctuate as she undergoes some trials visited on her by the more ruthless members of her elite social class and other trials of her own manufacture. As we work to find meaning in the novel's progression, we come up against interpretive puzzles that are not easily solved. Is Lily consistently and reliably different from those around her? If she is, what has made her different? If not, then why does Lily, perhaps not so much more admirable than the other characters, command our sympathy? These uncertainties regarding the protagonist's character are closely related to the question about the novel's plot that we, and, as the narrator reports, Lily herself, strive to answer concerning her goal of making an advantageous marriage: "why had she failed?" (28). We are offered a number of possible answers to this question that nonetheless leave the other questions open, but recognizing the submerged plot of *The House of Mirth* enables us to reconfigure the progression in a way that addresses these interpretive difficulties more fully. The submerged plot of Lily Bart's search for the story of her mother's pleasure unlocks elements of the surface plot that are generally underread, provides a supplementary set of motives that helps stabilize our vision of her character, and helps to resolve the tension surrounding what it means to sympathize with Lily Bart.

The surface plot of *The House of Mirth* is Lily's social decline, her movement step by step from society's highest reaches to near obscurity in the course of just under two years. As the novel opens, we encounter a marriage plot that, we are told, has been too long delayed, but that promises to come to fruition quickly. Lily tells Lawrence Selden in the novel's first chapter, "I've been about too long—people are getting tired of me; they are beginning to say I ought to marry" (9). Therefore, Lily has determined that by the end of this week she will be engaged to Percy Gryce, the grindingly dull but immensely wealthy man who is exactly positioned to fulfill her one goal of a secure and powerful position among her social peers. She hesitates, however, as she has done before, at committing herself when the confinements and limitations of her chosen course loom large in their proximity. To an extent, then, her decline is attributable to her rejection of her own goal, and, by implication, of the position in which her society has placed her. The reader is likely to approve of Lily's choice, and also to be relieved. Having already experienced Lily's lively conversation with Lawrence Selden in the forbidden intimacy of his home, the reader can see as well as Lily does that Percy Gryce, in contrast, clearly represents the foreclosure of sexual pleasure.

Thus far, the logic of the progression is clear, but when Selden, as hesitant to commit as Lily, appears to offer, tentatively, an alternative to her single goal—a "republic of the spirit" based on "personal freedom" (68), and, somewhat more prosaically, a marriage based on attraction and even love—instabilities multiply. When Lily rejects Selden as she has rejected Gryce, the causes of her decline appear more complicated. As the horizontal axis of the plot intersects with the vertical axis of our interpretation, we conclude that not only is she unable to stay the course she has chosen toward material excess, but she is also unable to embrace an alternative of spiritual bounty, however seductive. We may attribute her actions to psychological or cultural conditions, but, in either case, we must accept Lily's own personal limitations. At the same time, Lily's refusal of Selden alerts us to the presence of the submerged plot. When Lily decides against a marriage that means a lifetime of unpleasurable sex, the reader approves, but when she decides against a marriage that seems to promise pleasure, she thwarts the reader's own expectations, and we seek to interpret not just her relationship to these two suitors nor to her own goals but to pleasure itself.

The instabilities in Lily's behavior and the tensions in the reader's reactions to the narrative indicate that there is more to the story than the horizontal axis provides. These interpretive problems can be more fully resolved with reference to a second horizontal axis, the submerged plot of Lily's search for the story of her mother's pleasure. As *The House of Mirth* opens, we find Lily Bart going on much as she has since her mother's death eight years earlier, but we also understand that Lily has reached a critical moment in her career as Miss Bart, and that she feels she must marry. On the evening of the day we meet Lily, as she meditates on her fears and failures—her unmarried status, her financial debt, and the signs of her own aging in the mirror—Lily thinks of her mother. At this early point, the reader is given an outline of Mrs. Bart's life. Lily recalls what she knows of her mother, with considerable emphasis on the relationship between her parents, and in what follows we can identify Lily's effort to locate her mother's pleasure in her story. Recognizing Lily's investment in this search contributes to our understanding of the mimetic component of her character, and, in doing so, helps to stabilize her thematic function. Tracing the novel's progression with attention to the submerged plot reveals a second set of motives for Lily that influences our understanding of her relationships with other women, beginning with her mother. In addition to nuancing our understanding of character and the character-system in the novel, attention to the submerged plot also alters our view of the function of space in the novel. Unlike the nineteenth-century daughter protagonists, Lily has no connections to a great house associated with her mother. Mrs. Bart is depicted as a wanderer, even an exile, and Lily both shares that experience with her and replicates it after her death. Lily's constant, restless movement enables her to access some elements of her mother's story, but her mother's apparent indifference to the idea of home obscures other elements and renders Lily unable to imagine a home of her own.

Like the other motherless daughters considered so far, Lily must learn her mother's story before she can find her own pleasure, but her repetition of her mother's experience fails to yield the validation Lily needs. Lily rejects marriage and motherhood, and she also rejects intimate relationships outside of marriage—sexual pleasure remains forever out of her reach. That Lily's search might have been successful is suggested by echoes of Austen's *Persuasion* throughout *The House of Mirth*. John Pikoulis notes a number of ways in which Lily is comparable to Anne Elliot, including that each is in her late twenties, is "reared by inadequate parents," is generally "more intelligent than the people she mixes with," and "suffers from a history of rejected suitors and discovers that her freedom of action and financial well-being are circumscribed as a result" (27). The similarities extend even further: Lily's own nascent experience of love bears some similarities to Anne's. Lily has known Selden for eight years when *The House of Mirth* begins, just as nearly eight years have elapsed since Anne's broken engagement to Frederick Wentworth when they meet again. In both novels, a kind of unacknowledged attachment exists between the male and female protagonists over the course of eight years, during which time neither of them marries someone else, although they are generally expected to do so. Further, the triangle formed between Lily, Selden, and Bertha is not unlike that between Anne Elliot, Frederick Wentworth, and Louisa Musgrove. In each case, a fairly public tie is created between the male protagonist and the rival, followed by the male protagonist's return to the female protagonist. This comparison seems complete when Lily's rival, Bertha, is finally truly consoled by Ned Silverton, with whom she falls in love, as Louisa Musgrove does with Captain Benwick, over poetry. Finally, like Anne Elliot, Lily can see that her mother's marriage did not end well, but we have reason to think that, like that of Sir Walter and Lady Elliot, Hudson and Mrs. Bart's marriage could have begun in pleasure. Why should Lily fail where Anne succeeded?

Although Lily does not lose her mother until she is twenty-one years old, she appears to know nothing at all about her mother's life before her marriage. The novel is well populated by Lily's paternal relatives— Mrs. Peniston, Ned Van Alstyne, Grace and Jack Stepney, and many others—but, among the seemingly innumerable names and characters referred to throughout, we learn of no one related to Lily's mother. After Hudson Bart's death, no maternal relatives materialize to ease the financial situation of the two women who survive him; only Mr. Bart's family help. The reader never learns her maiden name, nor even her first name: to us, she is "Mrs. Bart," just as Reynolds's subject in the painting Lily brings to life is "Mrs. Lloyd." The reader, like Lily, knows only one thing about Mrs. Bart's life before her marriage:

> She was not above the inconsistency of charging fate, rather than herself, with her own misfortunes; but she inveighed so acrimoniously against love-matches that Lily would have fancied her own marriage had been of that nature, had not Mrs. Bart frequently assured her that she had been "talked into it"—by whom, she never made clear. (34)

Lily is left with no idea whether her mother once took pleasure in her marriage only to be disappointed later, or whether it was, from its inception, the business arrangement it is in the end. Mrs. Bart has not only encountered the unnarratability of her own story, but she has gone so far as to effectively obscure any view at all of her young, unmarried self and to render ambiguous the story of how she came to be married.

What does it mean that Mrs. Bart appears to have purposefully covered any traces of her story? We might be tempted to consider this as just a part of Mrs. Bart's habitual withholding from her daughter. Because Lily's mother is presented as unrelentingly harsh, selfish, and bitter, readers tend to find Lily bereft of the maternal nurturing she needs and to identify this lack as the cause of her ultimate failure to thrive.[1] This view appears at first to be supported by the narrator's explicit admission that to be married well a girl needs her mother, and that Lily is at a disadvantage because "when a girl has no mother to palpitate for her she must needs be on the alert for herself" (22). Linda Wagner-Martin draws our attention to Lily's own rumination about the Van Osburgh daughters: "Ah, lucky girls who grow up in the shelter of a mother's love" (Wharton 91), and she observes, "The reader has no reason to doubt the honesty of Lily's statement" (Wagner-Martin 46). As a model mother, however, Mrs. Van Osburgh presents problems. She has married her oldest daughter to Herbert Melson, whom, we have reason to believe, was actually in love with Lily and married Miss Van Osburgh purely for her inheritance (65). She marries her daughter Gwen to Lily's cousin, Jack Stepney, who proposes for the same reason as Herbert Melson (47). She marries her youngest daughter to Percy Gryce, a man who is infatuated by Lily and who is in any case so unpleasant that Judy Trenor asserts bluntly to Lily, "We could none of us imagine your putting up with him for a moment unless you meant to marry him" (75). Mrs. Van Osburgh's triumph over Lily when she announces Evie's engagement to Percy Gryce—"They both wished you to be the first to know of their happiness" (98)—intimates that this desirable mother is as rock hard underneath as Mrs. Bart could have been. In fact, Lily's protestations that she is unprotected and needs a mother should, perhaps, not be taken at face value. Indeed, to take them as such we must underread evidence of Lily's own will and influence. She easily shepherds Percy Gryce toward a proposal without a mother's help; what more would she want or expect of her mother if she were still alive? What is left for a mother to do but to steady her daughter's resolve, to force her, if need be, to marry someone she cannot abide? In fact, Mrs. Bart did not succeed in doing so even when she was alive; Lily tells Selden, "I threw away one or two good chances when I first came out" (10). Lily's pattern was established during her mother's lifetime. Mrs. Bart, then, may not be much different in these ways than the mothers of the girls around her, and what Lily needs is not what Mrs. Van Osburgh could offer. What she needs is knowledge of her mother's experience of marriage and pleasure, and Mrs. Bart's undesirable qualities do not make her story less necessary to Lily than that of a kinder, more loving mother would be. The submerged plot of Lily's pursuit of the story of her mother's pleasure does not alter our understanding of Mrs. Bart's mimetic component, but it does alter our understanding of her thematic function.

Mrs. Bart's unpleasant character and faulty mothering do not explain Lily's failure to find pleasure; rather, her story remains obscured from Lily because, for all her femininity, Lily is expected by her mother to fulfill the role of son as well as of daughter, and the confusion of these roles disrupts her access to her mother's experience and her own pleasure. Lily Bart is the epitome of a particular ideal of femininity: ineffably beautiful, unerringly intuitive, skilled in the art of pleasing and apparently desiring nothing more. Cynthia Griffin Wolff explains that Lily is forced to satisfy a "requirement for an appearance of effortless, 'natural' femininity" (213), and demonstrates that Lily's entire existence is based on the performance of femininity. Therefore, we are likely to underread the significance of the rather surprising fact that Lily is charged by her mother with a responsibility traditionally associated with a son. Lily's recollections of her mother in the novel's third chapter are introduced this way: "She remembered how her mother, after they had lost their money, used to say to her with a kind of fierce vindictiveness: 'But you'll get it all back—you'll get it all back, with your face'" (28). The use of physical beauty as a means to an end is feminized, but the charge to redeem the family honor, in this case to win back the fortune presented as lost by the father's weakness and error, is traditionally associated with sons. The mother's "vindictiveness" puts her charge in the context of a quest for revenge, and the narrator tells us of Mrs. Bart that "only one thought consoled her, and that was the contemplation of Lily's beauty. She studied it with a kind of passion, as though it were some weapon she had slowly fashioned for her vengeance" (34). The reader is immediately aware that Mrs. Bart herself, with her "fierce energies" (37), is presented in masculinized terms; our understanding of the relationship between her and her daughter is deepened when we recognize that she creates for Lily a masculinized role. That she does so helps to account for Mrs. Bart's apparently deliberate obscuring of her own story: Lily is regarded by her partly as a son, to whom knowledge of the mother's pleasure would be assumed to be unwelcome.[2]

That Lily finds herself answering the demands of two different roles helps readers recognize that, throughout *The House of Mirth*, the conventions of the novel of manners,[3] supported by implicit references to *Persuasion*, compete with the conventions of another kind of plot altogether, a revenge plot, signaled by explicit references to Aeschylus's *Eumenides*. Allusions, in Friedman's model, generally function primarily on the vertical axis of the text (as those to *Persuasion* do here), but Orestes and the Furies trouble Lily's mind, placing this allusion firmly on the horizontal axis and connecting it to the plot itself. Stuart Hutchinson, arguing that *The House of Mirth* is undeserving of the designation "tragedy," asks, "In invoking them [the Furies], is not Wharton making too grandiose a claim for what is happening to Lily?" (321). I suggest that the invocation of the Furies is not intended to connect the novel to tragedy but to the revenge plot. The demands of the novel of manners place Lily firmly in the role of daughter, and this role is fully compatible with Lily's search in the submerged plot. As a daughter, Lily seeks validation for her own potential pleasure in her mother's story. However, the revenge plot requires her to act as a son. In her role as a son, her progress toward pleasure is subverted to the charge for vengeance, and her mother's story is potentially threatening. Her dual responsibilities are at odds, and their incompatibility causes the failure of Lily's search for the story of her mother's pleasure; however, that search is nevertheless necessary.

The surface and submerged plots of *The House of Mirth* are launched simultaneously, as we first encounter Lily, through the eyes of Lawrence Selden, in Grand Central Station, "wearing an air of irresolution" (3). The novel's end is foreshadowed by this apt description of a seeker who will not reach her goal, and the location of her meeting with Selden emphasizes the role that physical places will play in the novel's action. Indeed, the way place functions in Lily's progress toward marriage and her search for pleasure becomes immediately clear as Selden takes her to his apartment. She finds it "cheerful," "pleasant," and "fresh," but, even as she wishes aloud for a place of her own, she cannot quite imagine herself at home there. She jokes of her Aunt Julia's house, where she also is not at home, "If I could only do over my aunt's drawing-room I know I should be a better woman" (7–8). Not being able to imagine herself at home in the Dillworths' house explains why she hasn't married her latest conquest. When Selden asks about him, she replies that his mother "wanted me to promise that I would n't do over the drawing-room," and Selden returns, "The very thing you are marrying for!" (10). Lily, then, is figured in the novel's opening pages as a traveler who has difficulty imagining herself at home; that we see her next in a hansom cab and on a train solidifies this vision.

We do see Lily settled at Bellomont, a house she certainly covets as a home. Indeed, the single week she spends there receives disproportionate narrative attention—fully one quarter of the novel. This emphasis suggests that for Lily, as for Anne Elliot, Jane Eyre, and Laura Fairlie, a house associated with her mother would supplement her traveling and advance her search. Bellomont does inspire Lily's memories of her mother: Mrs. Bart dominates her thoughts on the first night of her stay. However, Bellomont is not her mother's home, and her being there keeps the focus on her mother's charge to vengeance, the object of which is a home like the Trenors', at the expense of her search. Indeed, Lily does not associate her mother strongly with a house at all. Sean Scanlan's insightful analysis of what Lily can remember of her own childhood home reveals that "the image of her parents' home that she recalls is one of cyclical and fragmented movement" (216). Mrs. Bart is less associated with a "house in which no one ever dined at home unless there was 'company'" than she is with "gorged trunks" and a "magnitude" of luggage (Wharton 28–29). In the absence of a family home, Lily's seeking in the submerged plot must rely on her movements as a traveler in the surface plot.

Lily's memories alert the reader to other similarities between her and Mrs. Bart. The first is a physical resemblance. The "two little lines near her mouth" (28) that Lily sees in the mirror are similar to those she remembers in her mother's face on the day her father announced their ruin: "her mother, in spite of a few lines about the mouth, and under the yellow waves on her temples, was as alert, determined and high in colour as if she had risen from an untroubled sleep" (31). Facing the end of her youth, Lily remembers the end of Mrs. Bart's youth. In addition to physical resemblance, similarities of character engender similar behavior in mother and daughter, which results in similar experience. The worries that cause lines in both women's faces are financial, and Lily's experience of being financially overextended repeats her mother's. Lily remembers in the Barts' home "a hall-table showered with square envelopes which were opened in haste, and oblong envelopes which were allowed to gather dust in the depths of a bronze jar" (28). Similarly, Lily loses herself in social engagements and avoids facing her debts, and the motivation for overspending is the same for both women: Lily "hated dinginess as much as her mother had hated it" (39). Each woman feels that a man who can support her "lively taste for splendour" is no less than she deserves (30). These similarities seem to occur to Lily because, at nearly the age of thirty and still unmarried, she has reached a low point in her experience, and her subsequent decisions, even as they are identifiably responses to events in the surface plot, are equally responses to the demands of the submerged plot of her search for validation of her pleasure. Recognizing this double set of motives enables us to reevaluate the novel's progression and see that Lily conducts her search as other motherless heroines do, by repeating her mother's experience in an attempt to learn those elements of her mother's story that are unnarratable.

Lily's troubled mind reviews what she knows about her mother's story, and this brief history provides the background the reader needs to recognize the ways that Lily repeats her mother's experience in an attempt to learn the story of her pleasure. Mrs. Bart made a marriage that placed her firmly in the highest society but without the unrestrained monetary means to enjoy it fully. Her response to this situation was simply to spend more than her husband had, and the narrator tells us that, to her, "there was something heroic in living as though one were much richer than one's bankbook denoted" (30). Her acquisitiveness kept her husband constantly at work, and her indifference to private, family life reduced him, in the child Lily's view, to a "hazy outline of a neutral-tinted father" who "filled an intermediate space between the butler and the man who came to wind the clocks" (29). When the "heavy thunder-cloud of bills" following Lily's debut burst, and Mr. Bart announced his financial ruin, Mrs. Bart blamed him (30). His subsequent death, arousing in her no more sympathy than his ruin, is redundant to her because, after he ceased to provide for her extravagant lifestyle, "to his wife he no longer counted" (33). The narrator describes Mrs. Bart awaiting her husband's death "with the provisional air of a traveller who waits for a belated train to start" (33), an image likely to strike the reader especially because our introduction to Lily is a literal rendering of this figure. The two years that followed before Mrs. Bart's own death are characterized by anger and "deep disgust" (35) at her reduced circumstances, and she is forced to alternate between visits to relatives and unfashionable, inexpensive European hotels. Lily has shared her exile, and, when Mrs. Bart dies, she leaves her twenty-one-year-old daughter still unmarried and threatened by the "dinginess" she herself fears (35).

Lily's own experience repeats her mother's in many respects. Her time at Bellomont affords Lily the opportunity to secure Percy Gryce, who appears, like her father, to be a dull, responsible, unadventurous man who can establish her in society and then be relegated to the background of her life. This likeness, however, is only a partial one, and heavily influenced by her mother's vision of her husband late in her life. Unlike Percy Gryce, Mr. Bart worked daily long hours for his money. Also unlike Gryce, whose interest is in collecting for its own sake, Lily remembers that her father appreciated art and beauty. Mr. Bart, in his wife's estimation, "had wasted his evenings in what she vaguely described as 'reading poetry': and among the effects packed off to auction after his death were a score or two of dingy volumes which had struggled for existence among the boots and medicine bottles of his dressing-room shelves" (35). He cared about literature, then, as his wife could not, and Lily remembers that he participated in his wife's social life to an extent, but that he also felt separate from it. She remembers him coming to Newport or Long Island for weekends in summer, "and he would sit for hours staring at the sea-line from a quiet corner of the verandah, while the clatter of his wife's existence went on unheeded a few feet off" (29). These memories reveal in him an independence and an affinity for higher things, however muffled by the demands of his wife. The reader recognizes in these details a truer resemblance between her father and Lawrence Selden. Like her father, Selden works for his living, and his living appears to Lily patently insufficient to support her. Like her father, Selden is a reader, and in his library Lily notes the "walls of books" (7). He tells her most of them have come from "the rubbish heap, and I go and look on at the big sales" (10), presumably sales like the one at which her father's books were auctioned. When she looks for Selden at Bellomont, she looks in the library, with its "pleasantly shabby books," for "the only member of the party in the least likely to put it to its original use" (59). Perhaps most importantly, the "social detachment" that Lily admires in Selden is similar to her father's. As in *The Woman in White*, the false suitor is superficially like the father, but the true suitor proves to resemble him more fully.

The resemblance between Selden and her father, and Lily's belated recognition of it, help to provide a more complete interpretation of her contradictory behavior toward both Gryce and Selden at Bellomont. After Percy Gryce has been frightened away from Bellomont by Bertha's gossip, Judy Trenor asks Lily outright, "You've known Lawrence Selden for years—why did you behave as if you had just discovered him?" (75). We tend to underread this exchange despite the fact that Lily herself wonders about this even before Judy asks:

> Why else had she suddenly grown interested in Selden? She had known him for eight years or more: ever since her return to America he had formed a part of her background. She had always been glad to sit next to him at dinner, had found him more agreeable than most men, and had vaguely wished that he possessed the other qualities needful to fix her attention; but till now she had been too busy with her own affairs to regard him as more than one of the pleasant accessories of life. (54)

Lily's attraction to Selden is explicable with reference to the surface plot in that he is simply different from the other men she knows, and especially different from Percy Gryce, but this fact does not explain why she has not made the comparison before, or why, at this moment of crisis, she pursues the one man who certainly cannot fulfill her single goal of marriage to an independently wealthy man. The submerged plot offers a clearer motivation: now, in her extremity, Lily seeks her mother's story, and Selden, a man like the one her mother chose or was forced to marry, offers the possibility of exploring that experience for herself.

However, with her mother's story so completely hidden from her view, Lily cannot determine whether her own feelings for Selden are at all like her mother's for her father. Did Mrs. Bart, as Lily thinks she herself might, find pleasure in a reading man who stood apart from the society he was born into, but become too much frustrated in the end by what remained out of her reach? Or did Mrs. Bart, like Bertha Dorset, marry solely for money and position? Would she have considered her husband as negligible in success as she does in his failure, and did she, as Bertha does, expect from the first to use her marriage as a cover for pleasure she always meant to find elsewhere? Alternatively, could she have resembled Judy Trenor, who, we are told, finds no pleasure in intimacy at all and "could not sustain life except in a crowd" (40)? Lily's married friends, in addition to their other functions in the character-system, provide possible models of Mrs. Bart's experience. In the case of Bertha Dorset, not only is her marriage a possible model, but so is her affair with Selden: indeed, Bertha's obvious pleasure in Selden, a man like Lily's father, further suggests that Bertha functions as more than a rival, that Lily may be observing something of her mother's experience in Bertha Dorset's. Mrs. Bart assures Lily that her marriage was a practical arrangement, though Lily is tempted to suspect otherwise, and the characterization of her father as a romantic, a man wearied by business and attracted to poetry and sea views, also suggests otherwise. Lily's attraction to Selden enables her to explore her mother's story in her own.

Lily's access to her mother's story is further impeded by the competing demands of the novel's marriage plot and its revenge plot. When Bertha Dorset recognizes the mutual attraction between Selden and Lily, she avenges herself by exposing unflattering things about Lily to Percy Gryce and ruining Lily's chance of marrying him. Bertha's revenge by no means ends with this incident: her machinations eventually cause Lily to be disowned and shunned by her friends and family altogether. Lily refuses to use the means at her disposal—illicit love letters from

Bertha to Selden—to avenge herself on Bertha and thus save herself. As we interpret Lily's decisions in the context of the surface plot, then, we are likely to understand Lily's decline as partly attributable to the maintenance of her honor among the unscrupulous. That this is so is borne out by other actions of Lily's as well, including her dealings with Gus Trenor. In this view, as Joan Lidoff explains, "Bertha becomes a malevolent presence, allowing Lily to be seen as the innocent victim of her manipulations and desires" (200). Nevertheless, attention to the submerged plot reveals Lily's capacity as Bertha's adversary; she is represented as far from blameless in their interactions. Lily's knowledge of Bertha's attachment to Selden is well established from the novel's opening scene, when Lily mentions Bertha in order to gauge Selden's reaction: "'There are to be a lot of your set—Gwen Van Osburgh, the Wetheralls, Lady Cressida Raith—and the George Dorsets.' She paused a moment before the last name, and shot a query through her lashes" (12). He reveals nothing, but in her first private talk with Judy after she arrives at Bellomont, when Judy admits that she invited Selden to entertain Bertha, we are told, "Miss Bart put down her pen and sat absently gazing at the note she had begun. 'I thought that was all over,' she said" (43). Bertha's luring of Gryce into "a confidential nook beneath the gallery" on his first night there, despite her certain knowledge of Lily's intentions, may be regarded as a provocation, but when Lily enters the library a week later to entice Selden and takes "a certain pleasure in prolonging her [Bertha's] distress," she is fully aware of the implications of her actions (25, 60). Judy Trenor chides her: "If you had a grudge against Bertha it was a stupid time to show it—you could have paid her back just as well after you were married!" (75). Judy recognizes Lily's actions at Bellomont as deliberate, and the reader can recognize Mrs. Bart's charge for vengeance at work in Lily's decisions.

Lily is responding to the demands of the submerged plot by indulging her attraction to Selden, but her mother's charge to vengeance, which is supported by the complex circumstances of the surface plot, poses a seemingly insurmountable obstacle to her progress. As long as Lily acts in such a way as to fulfill her mother's command to "get it all back" by pursuing Gryce with apparent single-mindedness, Mrs. Trenor, Mrs. Dorset, and the others support her, and she remains "the centre of that feminine solicitude which envelops a young woman in the mating season" (28, 46). In contrast, when she pursues her pleasure with Selden, she earns Bertha's enmity, underlining again the ways Bertha models for Lily her mother's experience. Motivated by two opposed imperatives, Lily's behavior appears at times inconsistent. Still, she believes she is effectively balancing her two goals: marriage that would enact her mother's vengeance and marriage that would bring her pleasure.

Lily learns incontrovertibly that her goals cannot be balanced in her interaction with Gus Trenor. The empty promise of the Trenors' great country house is fully revealed, to Lily and to the reader, when she visits their town house. In contrast to the beauty and excitement of Bellomont, the town house to which Gus lures Lily is vacant, cold, and dust-sheeted. Gus himself remarks, "Does n't this room look as if it was waiting for the body to be brought down?" (141). Another room, where Judy Trenor spends her time, is warmer, with "a general aspect of lamp-lit familiarity" (141). For a moment, Lily is comforted by this, but when she learns that Judy is not in residence, the room's "air of occupancy" takes on sinister connotations as she realizes that she has been summoned to assume Judy's vacated place (141). When Gus tries to force her to have sex with him in return for the money he has given her, the conclusion that the remorseful Lily draws from the scene is, "I've sunk lower than the lowest, for I've taken what they take, and not paid as they pay" (166). The truth, however, is that she has behaved as much like a wife of her own set as a prostitute, and she knows now what it would feel like to trade sex without pleasure for the lifestyle she craves. Lily has reached this, her lowest point, by trying to balance her irreconcilable goals in the surface and submerged plots. This episode exposes fully that her mother's charge to vengeance means a complete foreclosure of the possibility of pleasure.

Leaving the Trenors' town house, Lily feels "a stranger to herself, or rather there were two selves in her, the one she had always known, and a new abhorrent being to which it found itself chained" (148). Tormented, she compares her situation with that of Orestes, who, having carried out what he feels is justified vengeance, is nevertheless pursued by the Furies. We are told:

> She had once picked up, in a house where she was staying, a translation of the *Eumenides,* and her imagination had been seized by the high terror of the scene where Orestes, in the cave of the oracle, finds his implacable huntresses asleep, and snatches an hour's repose. Yes, the Furies might

sometimes sleep, but they were there, always there in the dark corners, and now they were awake and the iron clang of their wings was in her brain.... (148)

The comparison reveals that finally Lily can understand the dangers of her mother's charge, of her acting as a son rather than a daughter. That night, unable to sleep, she cries out, "Oh Gerty, the furies ... you know the noise of their wings—alone, at night, in the dark?" (164). The next day, facing her Aunt Julia, "The winged furies were now prowling gossips who dropped in on each other for tea" (169), and, after her aunt refuses to help her repay her debt, "the rush of the furies' wings was in her ears" (173). These references work on the horizontal axis to personify both Lily's awakened consciousness of her guilt and also those who will hold against her wrongs of which she is innocent. Lily's invocation of Orestes offers additional insight as it works on the second horizontal axis.

Orestes is hounded by the Furies for the murder of his mother, in which he feels he is justified by his right to avenge his father's death at her hands. This justified revenge is complicated by his knowledge of Clytemnestra's pleasure with Aegisthus; as is customary for sons, for Orestes his mother's story is potentially delegitimating. The power of the mother's story, however, is diminished by Apollo's claim, the claim that acquits Orestes, that mothers are not blood relations to their children. Orestes is able, in effect, to disown his mother, as he has already negated her right to avenge the death of Iphigenia, and, in so doing, further strengthen his tie to his father. Orestes is confident in his decisions from first to last; for Lily, in contrast, attempting to change the past through revenge contradicts her impulses and experience as a daughter. She desires not to interfere in but to know the story of her mother's pleasure. Already the object of the Furies' pursuit before she has steeled herself for the revenge with which her mother charged her, Lily can only fear the consequences of the act: unlike for Orestes, distancing herself from her mother cannot constitute freedom and release.

At this point in the progression, Lily is ready to put aside her mother's charge to vengeance and explore her mother's story by accepting Selden, but, as he is no longer inclined to make an offer, she finds herself instead repeating less desirable elements of her mother's experience. We are told at the beginning of the novel that, after Mr. Bart's death, "Lily and her mother wandered from place to place, now paying long visits to relations whose house-keeping Mrs. Bart criticized [. . .] and now vegetating in cheap continental refuges" (33–34). As Lily's debts have become overwhelming, she resolves to stay at her Aunt Julia's, where she finds fault with the housekeeping. Selden's defection has left her instead with an offer from Simon Rosedale, who will encourage her to resume her quest for vengeance, and an invitation from Bertha Dorset, whose own unstinting thirst for revenge will force Lily to revive her own. She chooses, for the moment, Bertha's invitation, and she escapes her aunt's home by traveling to Europe, much as her mother had.

The reader's association of Lily with restless movement is heightened when we encounter her in Book Two, living on a yacht and cruising the Mediterranean. Further than ever from being able to imagine herself at home and from understanding her mother's story, Lily is particularly vulnerable to Bertha's own desire for vengeance, and Bertha has new reasons for retaliation against her. Selden, having found his way to Monte Carlo, is told by an acquaintance that "Bertha is jealous of her success here and at Cannes" (190), and by another that Lily has a hold over Dorset, and "Mrs. Dorset was aware of it—oh, perfectly: nothing *she* did n't see!" and that "it hurts a woman's pride" (193). When we meet Lily again, enjoying the beautiful view off the yacht while breakfasting, Bertha has already completed her revenge by leaving Lily and George alone all night, a fact of which Lily is as yet entirely ignorant. As a result, Lily loses everything, mainly her paternal inheritance from her Aunt Julia, who leaves everything to the cousin who has been most assiduous about informing her of Lily's missteps.

Left with nothing else, Lily is offered two more chances to fulfill her mother's charge and, simultaneously, to avenge herself on Bertha. The first is to testify against Bertha and enable her husband to divorce her and marry Lily; George Dorset tells Lily, "I want to be free, and you can free me" (244). This opportunity Lily refuses as dishonorable, so Simon Rosedale becomes her last and best chance. He encourages Lily to fulfill her mother's charge and enact her revenge: to regain her place in society by using Bertha Dorset's illicit love letters against her, forcing her to receive Lily back into society, and by becoming Rosedale's wife, providing herself with the means to maintain her advantage over Bertha. He reminds her of her own capacity when he says, "The wonder to me is that you 've waited so long to get square with that woman, when you 've had the power in your hands" (257). Lily decides to take up Rosedale's offer, but she recognizes it as a threat to her search. Contemplating her decision, we are told:

> She did not indeed let her imagination range beyond the day of plighting [. . .]. She had learned, in her long vigils, that there were certain things not good to think of, certain midnight images that must at any cost be exorcised—and one of these was the image of her as Rosedale's wife. (248)

The phrase "midnight images" suggests that Lily foresees sex without pleasure, a concept made concrete for her by Gus Trenor's behavior when they are alone in his house after eleven o'clock with no one to call on except for servants. This vision is strengthened by her next glimpse of Rosedale, at Carry Fisher's house, where Lily feels "a sense of peace" and "an air of repose and stability" (249). This "congenial atmosphere" might almost make Lily feel at home, but her feeling of peace is disrupted when she sees "Mr. Rosedale kneeling domestically on the drawing-room hearth before his hostess's little girl" (249). Although Lily can recognize "a quality of homely goodness in his advances to the child," the narrator reports that "Rosedale in the paternal rôle was hardly a figure to soften Lily" (249). Lily takes no pleasure in the thought of the intermediate step between Rosedale as her husband and Rosedale as the father of her child. In the rest of the paragraph, she finds some consolation in imagining Rosedale treating her as he treats this child, rather than as a woman who might bear his child, and this evasion appears to sustain her. Despite failing to access validation for her own pleasure, she cannot choose to foreclose the possibility of pleasure entirely.

Instead, she repeats her mother's experience in yet other ways. We are told that in her misfortune Mrs. Bart "was especially careful to avoid her old friends and the scenes of her former successes" (34), and, at this point, Lily is forced to do the same, first working for Mrs. Hatch, and then leaving that employment for a millinery workroom. The narrator calls attention to the relationship between Lily's situation and her mother's: "something of her mother's fierce shrinking from observation and sympathy was beginning to develop in her" (287). Repeating the joyless end of her mother's experience may well inspire Lily to one last effort, supported once again by Simon Rosedale, to fulfill her charge. Rosedale finds her exhausted and hopeless, and he renews his offer to complete her revenge on all those who have shunned her by marrying her: "If you'd only let me, I'd set you up over them all—I'd put you where you could wipe your feet on 'em!" (300). Lily is tempted by Rosedale's proposal, the more so as she has realized that, "more and more, with every fresh mischance befalling her, did the pursuing furies seem to take the shape of Bertha Dorset; and close at hand, safely locked among her papers, lay the means of ending their pursuit" (296). When she still believed in the possibility of finding her mother's pleasure, the Furies were a warning against vengeance; her acceptance of the challenge now is a sign that the chance of pleasure has finally eluded her altogether.

Nevertheless, as she makes her way to Bertha to effect the transaction, she is diverted to Selden's home, and in the process, as during that long-ago week at Bellomont and so many times since, her quest for revenge gives way to her search for her mother's story. She insists on her role as daughter, even if giving up her identification with Orestes leaves her aligned with Iphigenia, who believes she is being led to a great marriage and is led, instead, to her death. We know that "after two years of hungry roaming Mrs. Bart had died—died of a deep disgust" (35). This occurs "during one of their brief visits to New York" (36) after being away for some time. Lily's death also follows immediately upon a sort of return, as Lily walks from her boarding house near the millinery shop, a place as distant in its way as Europe, toward Bertha Dorset's home, among the places she used to frequent. As she approaches Selden's flat, she thinks, "It was down this street that she had walked with Selden, that September day two years ago" (304). Lily can finally imagine in Selden's apartment a home for herself, but she has become so deeply divided by her disparate goals that her vision only applies to half of her. She tells him of "the Lily Bart you knew" that "I have brought her back to you—I am going to leave her here. When I go out presently she will not go with me. I shall like to think that she has stayed with you—and she'll be no trouble, she'll take up no room" (309). Lily still cannot imagine a home for her whole self, and that night, Lily, like her mother, dies after nearly two years of wandering. Lily repeats her mother's story to the end rather than finding in it the thing that would have enabled her to embrace a future: she never learns the truth about her mother's pleasure, and she never accesses her own.

Despite all her efforts, Lily's search for her mother's story remains incomplete, but the novel ends with the assurance that the search is necessary and, even in the world of this novel, can be successful. Lily's encounter with Nettie Struther has been interpreted in a variety of useful ways connected with Lily's view of motherhood and her need for mothering, but Nettie has yet another thematic function generated by the submerged plot. Something else the scene offers is a vision of a mother, with her infant daughter on her lap, telling her story. What Nettie tells is not, certainly, the story of her pleasure, which remains unnarratable. Indeed, Nettie explains her relief that her husband, a childhood friend, knew her story before he proposed to her; she asserts, "I never could have told another man" (315). Nevertheless, the story of Nettie's pleasure is embedded in her story of her transgression, as we might imagine Lady Dedlock's is in the letter she writes to Esther:

> You see I was n't only just *sick* that time you sent me off—I was dreadfully unhappy too. I'd known a gentleman where I was employed—I don't know as you remember I did type-writing in a big importing firm—and—well—I thought we were to be married: he 'd gone steady with me six months and given me his mother's wedding ring. But I presume he was too stylish for me—he travelled for the firm, and had seen a great deal of society. Work girls are n't looked after the way you are, and they don't always know how to look after themselves. I did n't . . . and it pretty near killed me when he went away and left off writing . . . It was then I came down sick—I thought it was the end of everything. (315)

Nettie's narrative contains the story of pleasure so tempting that she did not resist, even knowing it could be her "ruin." That she is able to tell it is evidence of her own access to pleasure and bodes well for her daughter's experience. Cynthia Griffin Wolff asserts that "Nettie Struther has found a mate who can help her formulate a new narrative of self" (223), and this is of great significance, but the old narrative is important as well, for Nettie and her daughter.

That Lily, warm in the "nest" that Nettie has built with her husband (320), talking with a young woman who has successfully married and created a home, identifies with Nettie's child is instructive: "as she continued to hold it [the baby] the weight increased, sinking deeper, and penetrating her with a strange sense of weakness, as though the child entered into her and became a part of herself" (316). Even at this late stage, Lily is still a daughter seeking her mother's story. As she takes stock of her own life in her room in the boarding house, she realizes that "her parents too had been rootless, blown hither and thither on every wind of fashion," and that "she herself had grown up without any one spot of earth being dearer to her than another" (319). She is aware of both the literal and the figurative implications of the "house":

> In whatever form a slowly-accumulated past lives in the blood—whether in the concrete image of the old house stored with visual memories, or in the conception of the house not built with hands, but made up of inherited passions and loyalties—it has the same power of broadening and deepening the individual existence, of attaching it by mysterious links of kinship to all the mighty sum of human striving. (319)

Lily has lacked both—the old house and also an unequivocal relation to her "inherited passions and loyalties." She has learned what she could from her search, but this lack has kept Lily's goal out of reach. The difficulty of the search itself—not only for Lily but for all seeking daughters—is alluded to in the novel's title, taken from Ecclesiastes 7:4, which also employs the image of the house. This verse, "The heart of the wise is in the house of mourning; but the heart of fools is in the house of mirth," raises questions about the very place of pleasure in human life, suggesting that the wise remain focused on the certainty of our common end rather than that which is not definite or lasting (*King James Version*).

Though little in her experience affirms it, Lily never gives up her search for the mother's pleasure, emphasizing the importance of the mother's story. She values her maternal inheritance and her position as a daughter to the end, and, when offered an alternative—to intervene in the past by avenging her family—she refuses, despite the cost. Her decisive failure to access her mother's pleasure, even after repeating her mother's experience, and especially her experience of wandering, blocks Lily's own access to pleasure and contributes significantly to the failure of the marriage plot. The completeness of Wharton's novel is attributable to the complex interactions of these two horizontal axes.

"I don't suppose she had made up her mind": Laura Naylor Farquar

In contrast to the completeness of *The House of Mirth*, *The Last September*, in which the daughter protagonist's goals are similarly contradictory, offers an example in which the inconclusiveness of her search in the submerged plot compromises the novel's completeness. The novel's inconclusiveness is mirrored in the indeterminacy of its central image, an Anglo-Irish "Big House" in County Cork called Danielstown. The ways the submerged plot is influenced by and influences our reading of the function of space within the novel are perhaps best exemplified by Danielstown, to which both the daughter protagonist and her mother have an ambivalent relation. Despite their ties to their ancestral home, Lois and her mother, like Lily Bart and hers, have been wanderers. Laura Naylor Farquar left Danielstown as a young woman and seems never to have returned. She likely lived in the north of Ireland with her husband when she first married, but, at some point, under circumstances the novel does not explain, she moved to England alone with her young daughter and lived there until her death. Her daughter's search is precipitated not by expulsion from her mother's home, as those of Anne Elliot and Jane Eyre are, but rather by a sudden introduction to her mother's childhood home. When Lois Farquar finishes school in England in December of 1919, she comes to Ireland, and, as the novel opens, she has been living at Danielstown for about nine months. Unlike Lily, then, Lois shares both her mother's wandering and her mother's experience of home. However, at this historical moment, in the midst of the Irish War for Independence and just over a year before the signing of the Anglo-Irish Treaty, the Big House itself embodies multiple ideas, for those who live in it and those outside. Its relation to the concept of "home" is, and has been throughout its history as the sign of a colonizing settler class, a shifting one. For Lois, who is soon to leave Danielstown again when we meet her, her relatively brief sojourn in the house in which her mother grew up precipitates her search for her mother's story but also impedes it, and we are likely to feel that Lois's seeking continues after she leaves the house, beyond the end of the narrative.

    The surface plot is a kind of marriage plot struggling to progress in the context of war and decolonization. Though she has lived her life in England, Lois is from a landed Protestant Irish family, a member of a ruling class that is soon to be unseated. As both of Lois's parents are long deceased, her mother's brother, Danielstown's current master, is Lois's guardian. Sir Richard Naylor and his wife also foster Lady Naylor's nephew, Laurence, a student at Oxford, and these make up Lois's family. Laurence appears to be the only man of marriageable age among the Anglo-Irish families the Naylors know; during the time she has been in Ireland, Lois has been entertained mainly by British soldiers stationed nearby. Sir Richard, assuring guests that they will not be shot at by Irish insurgents should they venture outside, explains, "We never have yet, not even with soldiers here and Lois dancing with officers up and down the avenue" (26). This indirect threat posed by socializing with the soldiers does not alarm Sir Richard, but when one of the soldiers falls in love with her, Sir Richard and Lady Naylor declare the idea of a marriage "impossible" (79) and "preposterous" (84). Throughout the novel, as Lois contemplates the possibility of marriage to the handsome, manly, but rather simple Gerald, we witness the influence on her decision of the guests at Danielstown, especially her mother's one-time suitor Hugo Montmorency, and the encroaching violence of the war. Finally, she accepts Gerald's proposal, but their engagement does not withstand the opposition of Lady Naylor or Lois's own misgivings, and they end their engagement almost immediately. Three days after the engagement is broken, Gerald is killed in an ambush by the Irish Republican Army (IRA). The next information we receive about Lois is that she is sent "touring" in France, so she is absent when Danielstown, like approximately two hundred houses of its kind during this period, is burned down by the IRA.[4]

The ruin of Danielstown and the historical end of the Protestant Ascendancy in Ireland would seem conclusive enough images with which to end the novel, yet completion remains elusive in *The Last September*. The strangely anticlimactic death of Gerald after Lois has severed her relation to him is followed by the end of the narrative's focalization through Lois. The reader does not accompany Lois on her seemingly pointless journey to France, but only hears a report of it. The move away from Lois's consciousness has the effect of deleting any distinction between her and the rest of the characters, and her wandering mirrors theirs, including, we can only assume, that of Sir Richard and Lady Naylor, who, despite the definitive loss of their home and their position in Irish society, are in fact still alive to make their way however they can. The surface plot appears to be a marriage plot in which none of the choices perceived as possible by the protagonist—Gerald, Laurence, and even the houseguest Hugo Montmorency—is ever really a possible choice.

Scholars have understood the implications of this plot primarily as a reflection of Anglo-Irish culture generally. Jed Esty characterizes the novel's plot as "antidevelopmental," and he argues that "Lois's dilated, inverted bildungsroman plot captures, in other words, the historically fixed, politically vexed, permanently adolescent status of the Ascendancy itself, the anachronistic class described by this novel" (181). Esty's reading of the plot identifies Lois's story as entirely analogous to the story of her class: "the frozen, virginal fate of Lois Farquar indexes the structural contradictions of settler colonialism and the larger inevitabilities of postcolonial nationalism" (181). This focus Esty shares with some earlier critics, including Phyllis Lassner, who describes Lois and her cousin Laurence as "born to inherit the myth of the ancestral home" (41), and analyzes the persistence of that myth in the face of the destruction of Danielstown itself. Lassner argues that "the characters become prisoners to those traditions upholding the 'family myth.' By living as though they are replicas of their ancestors and their aristocratic codes, they transform themselves into figures in an historical romance, important only to the imagined continuity of Danielstown" (45). Like Esty's, Lassner's reading treats the characters as figures for the Anglo-Irish, and, for both, Lois's story is significant primarily, if not solely, for the light it sheds on the violent process of decolonization in Ireland.

Nevertheless, although Lois's story is not separate from the violence around her, the inconclusiveness of her story is meaningful in itself. Tracing the progression of the submerged plot and its influence on the surface plot helps both to account for and to reveal the significance of the novel's incompleteness. Like other daughter protagonists, Lois seeks the story of her mother's pleasure to validate her own, and she accesses what she can of that story by repeating her mother's experience. Like Lily Bart, Lois fails to find what she needs; however, whereas Lily's failure becomes conclusive with her death, Lois is still just eighteen when the novel ends, and we are left with some hope for her future. Her fate may not be as decidedly "frozen" and "virginal" as Esty suggests. At the same time, Lois's is not simply an unfinished version of the nineteenth-century plots considered so far. Unlike Anne Elliot, Jane Eyre, and others, who have an early intimation of the pleasure to be found in a beloved man to reassure them that the process of validating that pleasure, however difficult, is worth it, Lois has had no such intimations, and is far from taking for granted that she will ever feel pleasure. Lois appears to us throughout as both overly conscious of what she is expected to feel and fearful that she feels so little. What makes Lois's situation even more difficult is that, in contrast to

Lily, whose ambition for wealth and luxury long overshadows her desire for pleasure, pleasure is the one ambition Lois can imagine.

The progression of *The Last September* is marked by the delayed launch of its surface plot, which gives way to the launch of the submerged plot. As the novel opens, we are aware of Lois's suitors among the British soldiers because she spends time corresponding with them. However, the narrator reveals that, to Lois, they "moved shadowless in a kind of social glare numbing to the imagination" (12). This characterization of Lois as "numbed" by her correspondents remains largely in place until Gerald actually appears in chapter 5, and is only tentatively challenged thereafter. The importance he has attained in her thinking is obscured entirely from the reader at this point as the launch of the surface plot is deferred. In contrast, the submerged plot is launched immediately, as Hugo and Francie Montmorency arrive at Danielstown on the novel's first page. Hugo has sold his own ancestral home, Rockriver, so he and Francie are homeless, making a life of visiting friends and family in Ireland's great houses. The Montmorencys' relationship to these houses, like Lois's and her mother's, is ambivalent. Indeed, Lois seeks knowledge of her mother's experience in theirs. We are told that Lois has been "nervous" all day awaiting their arrival, and she imagines admitting it to them: "'Nervous?' she would wish Mr. Montmorency to ask her searchingly, 'Why?' But she had her reserves, even in imagination; she would never tell him" (5).[5] The reader is allowed no immediate insight into what this fantasy means, but soon Mr. Montmorency is firmly connected to Lois's mother, as she tells her cousin Laurence about the time that "he came to stay with my mother and me when we were at Leamington":

> After dinner—I was allowed to sit up—Mother walked out of the house and left us. We were trying chickens at that time and I daresay she went out to shut them up and then simply stayed in the garden. Mr. Montmorency and I talked for some time, then he got solemn and went to sleep all in a moment. I sat and watched him in absolute fascination. You know the way men go to sleep after dinner? Well, that wasn't at all the way he did— Then my mother came back, very much refreshed at having been away from us, and said I was a rather bad hostess, and woke Mr. Montmorency up. I have thought since, anyone might have said *she* was a rather bad hostess. But everything she did seemed so natural. (8)

Lois tells the story for what it illustrates about Hugo Montmorency: "He was melancholy and exhausted and wise" (9); but the story also illustrates that Lois is expected to fulfill her mother's role in her absence (e.g., as hostess), but that her mother's behavior is difficult to interpret, and her role difficult to define (what constitutes a "bad" hostess?). Laura Naylor Farquar's unnarratable story is a preoccupation right from the novel's opening, and it is consistently difficult for Lois (and others) to interpret. Encountering Hugo again at Danielstown, where he knew and loved her mother, seems to offer Lois an opportunity to understand her mother's experience more clearly.

The reader's access to what Lois evidently already knows of her mother's story is delayed until the second chapter, and it comes to us not through Lois but through Hugo. Being back at Danielstown has brought Laura Naylor Farquar to mind for the Montmorencys, and, as they rest in their room and prepare for dinner, Francie asks Hugo, "*When* was it you were in love with Laura?" and "But why wouldn't she marry you?" (20). The brief history conveyed here helps us to understand in retrospect Lois's nervousness about Hugo's arrival: he is someone who has knowledge, perhaps, of her mother's pleasure. From the Montmorencys' conversation, we learn most of the details we will ever know about Laura. She grew up at Danielstown in the last two decades of the nineteenth century, and all agree that she was "lovely" (8, 20) and full of life but also tempestuous and unpredictable. As a young woman she considered marriage to Hugo Montmorency, who "had stayed at Danielstown as a boy for months together," a natural match insofar as "the Naylors and the Montmorencys had always known each other; it was an affair of generations" (13). Laura decided against marrying Hugo, after which, as Hugo expresses it, "she went up North and met Farquar, and I imagine that was all fixed up before she knew where she was or had time to get out of it. After that of course she really *had* got something to be unhappy about" (20–21). Of the end of Laura's apparently hasty marriage to Walter Farquar we know only what we can imagine based on Francie Montmorency's exclamation, "Wasn't it terribly sad about Walter!" and Lady Naylor's response: "To tell you the truth, it was what we always expected" (18). We are given very little indication of how long Laura and Walter's marriage lasted before his desertion or demise, but, by the time Lois is ten years old, she and Laura live in England alone.[6] Lois remembers Hugo's visit at that time, and we are told of a subsequent visit paid by Hugo and Francie together, and finally that "six months afterwards, without giving anyone notice of her intention, Laura had died" (21). We are not told in what year Laura died or how old Lois was at the time.[7] Hugo describes Laura to Francie as "always lovely" and "very vital." He also opines that "she was never happy at all," "she never knew what she wanted," and "she wanted her mind made up" (20). Finally, he observes, "Yet I don't believe things ever really mattered to Laura. Nothing got close to her: she was very remote," and Francie responds, "I wonder if Lois is remote?" (21). This question remains a preoccupation of both the surface and submerged plots, and the indeterminacy of the mimetic components of both Laura's and Lois's characters has significant implications for the novel's progression.

Hearing Laura's history from Hugo emphasizes for the reader what he means to Lois: he holds the possibility of learning her mother's story, of finding her mother's pleasure and thus enabling Lois to judge more accurately her own responses to Gerald. Hugo is a potential source of information in two ways: Lois will both ask him about what he knew of Laura and also imagine herself in a relationship with him as her mother had been. Seeing both Laura and Lois through the Montmorencys' eyes also clarifies for us some of the difficulties of Lois's search. Not only are Lois's memories of her mother difficult for her to interpret, but the degree to which she is like her mother is unclear.[8] Upon meeting Lois, Francie Montmorency exclaims, "Oh, *I* think she's the image of Laura—" (4). Later she repeats, "She looks sweet, I think. And surely the image of Laura" (17), but Lady Naylor replies that Lois is "not so much like Laura in character" (18). When Francie sees Lois again at dinner, she changes her mind and observes to Lois, "No, you are not like Laura" (23). Unlike, for example, the case of Anne Elliot,[9] for whom clear comparisons between herself and her mother make her mother's experience seem more accessible to her, in Lois's case opinion is clearly divided and shifting, providing no firm basis for her search.

Nevertheless, even as Lois appears to respond to circumstances more or less beyond her control—finishing school, the arrivals and departures of houseguests, Gerald's attraction to her—her decisions and actions also serve her pursuit of her mother's story. Attention to the novel's progression reveals this second plot and second set of motives as we consider the ways Lois's experience repeats her mother's. When we meet her she has lived for nearly nine months in her mother's childhood home, among her mother's family. Sir Richard, apparently at least ten years older than Laura, seems to have acted as his sister's guardian as well.[10] Hugo's arrival opens new opportunities for repeating her mother's experience, and, after dinner on the night of the Montmorencys' arrival, Lois, in imitation of her mother, walks away from the dinner guests out into the dark demesne by herself. This repeated image of a woman walking away from a house gains significance from the overbearing presence of Danielstown, which both confers power and also threatens to overpower the individual. After an evening among the assembled company in the house dominated by her thoughts of Hugo, Lois finds herself alone on "the avenue, where she had danced with Gerald" (40), and, dancing on the avenue even now, Lois thinks of Gerald, "Oh, I do want you!" (41). For the moment, Lois imagines, like her mother, turning away from the life of the big house toward the different life represented by this young English soldier. Lois may not have a clear idea of what her life with Gerald in England would be, but Lady Naylor thinks of him, as she thinks of herself, in terms of a house, and she feels certain that Gerald and his family "were just villa-ry" (80). Lois is still unsure which kind of house is likely to foster her search more effectively.

Caught between these alternative visions of her future, Lois thinks of her mother in a much-analyzed passage:

> A shrubbery path was solid with darkness, she pressed down it. Laurels breathed coldly and close: on her bare arms the tips of the leaves were timid and dank, like tongues of dead animals. Her fear of the shrubberies tugged at its chain, fear behind reason, fear before her birth; fear like the earliest germ of her life that had stirred in Laura. She went forward eagerly, daring a snap of the chain, singing, with a hand to the thump of her heart: dramatic with terror. She thought of herself as forcing a pass. In her life—deprived as she saw it—there was no occasion for courage, which like an unused muscle slackened and slept. (41)

Scholars have found in this passage evidence of fear of the mother,[11] yet this odd passage may in fact refer to something shared with her mother. Readers prepared by Lois's fascination with Hugo to note what Laura and Lois might have in common may compare this "fear before her birth" to "the earliest germ of her life that had stirred in Laura"—something conceived in each of them at the same moment. Lois's fear is not paralyzing but invigorating; we must remember that she is, as she progresses down this path, both dancing and singing. That this fear is something desirable and potentially fertile is evident throughout the passage. "She went forward eagerly, daring a snap of the chain" holding back her fear, and when she is comforted by the thought of Danielstown's nearby, warmly lit drawing room, her disappointment is suggested in the phrasing of her thoughts: "Fear curled back in defeat from the carpet-border" (41–42). Lois's need to feel anything at all is in evidence here.

The difficulties of emotional engagement are also illustrated in that even what Lois dreads is what she knows can never be: "she was [. . .] going to see a ghost" (42). Perhaps the obvious candidate is her deceased mother, so much on her mind this evening, whom Andrew Bennett and Nicholas Royle refer to as haunting Lois and the novel (17) and whom Neil Corcoran calls "the Anglo-Irish ghost *par excellence* in *The Last September*" (50).[12] However, no ghost or even ghostly vision appears; rather, an IRA agent materializes out of the darkness, and Lois, watching him unseen, feels like a ghost herself, thinking that "not to be known of seemed like a doom of extinction" (42). In this conviction she may be like her mother, but in this scene the strongest alignment is between whom Lois may have expected to see—Laura—and whom she does see: the rebel fighter. Laura, "too Irish altogether for her own country" (21), rebelled against the confinements of her social position, leaving Danielstown as a young woman, never to return. Lassner sees in Laura a failed rebel: she refers to Laura's "impulsive rebellion" as a "dubious legacy" for Lois (43) and asserts that "identifying with Lois's mother [. . .] Laurence also recognizes the futility of rebellion" (42). Neil Corcoran, too, focuses on Laura's failure: "In the entrapment and failure represented by her ghosthood, she is what Lois and Laurence understand about the entrapment and failure of the class they come from, and she is what they must overcome" (50). Like those in other novels of motherless daughters, this absent mother is generally regarded as an example of the inability to overcome oppression, a model to be rejected. However, to readers alert to the submerged plot, the alignment of Laura with the IRA agent suggests a more optimistic interpretation of the efficacy of Laura's rebellion and of its meaning for Lois. Lois's own pursuit of her mother's story, concomitant with her desire to feel things more deeply than she does, in itself demonstrates the significance and the centrality of the mother's experience to the daughter's progress.

At the same time, the experience in the demesne reveals that her muffled emotions are an obstacle to her search. Her response to the appearance of the rebel soldier is to remain hidden, if only because she cannot decide among the other possible courses of action: "'It's a fine night,' she would have liked to observe; or, to engage his sympathies: 'Up Dublin!' or even—since it was in her uncle's demesne she was trembling and straining under a holly—boldly—'What do you want?'" (42). That she chooses none of these is at least partly a function of her gender. Whether she were to choose sympathy or combat, the primary factor in the interaction would be sex; as Francie explains when considering the possibility of Lois encountering a rebel soldier alone, "at *her* age [. . .] her age isn't any protection" (75). Unlike her mother, "too Irish for her own country," Lois appears paralyzed by these complications, and we are told of her, "Here was something else that she could not share. She could not conceive of her country emotionally" (42). Indeed, neither side of the conflict galvanizes her emotions; when she speaks with Gerald about the deaths of the Royal Irish Constabulary men defending their barracks from IRA attack, Gerald tries to reassure her that there is nothing she could have done, but she exclaims, "I might at least have felt something!" (66). Unlike those of the nineteenth-century daughter protagonists, Lois's own feelings appear too indistinct to be a reliable guide.

However, the confusion of Lois's feelings is not without cause and appears to be connected not only to the position of the Anglo-Irish in 1920, but also to the confusion of her relationship to Danielstown itself. The story of Laura's pleasure is antinarratable, like those of other mothers, because of the potential threat her pleasure may pose to orderly lines of inheritance based on legal marriages. In many novels about daughters, the question of material inheritance is deemphasized, and that tradition is borne out in *The Last September,* which contains no direct reference to who will inherit Danielstown. Nevertheless, readers familiar with Bowen's life, particularly the unusual circumstance of her inheriting her family's estate, Bowen's Court,[13] may note that Lois appears to be Sir Richard's only living relation, and she may well be his heir. Imagining a future in which her aunt and the others are dead, Lois thinks that "fifty years hence she might well, if she wished, be sitting here on the steps," which gives her "a feeling of mysteriousness and destination" (36). This image of her future suggests that Lois, like Bowen, is positioned to inherit that which was meant to have been passed not to a daughter but to a son. Not unlike Lily Bart's, then, Lois's character is complicated by the expectation that she fulfill the role of a son to some degree. Readers unfamiliar with Bowen's biography may find evidence of Lois as potential heir in the contrast between her and Laurence, who appears to find himself a man in the position of daughter just as firmly as Lois finds herself a woman in the position of son.[14] His given name echoes Laura's name, the daughter of the house, and it is Laurence who resides in Laura's old room at Danielstown, who stares out a window pane "across which Laura Naylor had scratched her name with a diamond" (234–35). He is not a Naylor (but rather Lady Naylor's nephew), and even his surname is obscured: when Betty Vermont arrives at Danielstown and is met by Laurence, she attempts to introduce him to her companion, and manages only, "Denise, this is Mr.—(Oh dear, how awful)" (285–86). The house itself, which seems to offer Laurence insight into Laura's experience, tends to withhold insight from Lois, and we are made aware of expectations placed on Lois that appear to interfere with her access to her maternal inheritance.

Even this ambiguous situation is further complicated by the more immediate concern that the house will be, as it ultimately is, "executed" (303) by the IRA. Even as Lois attempts to negotiate her role at Danielstown and to locate the kinds of responses to her world that she assumes should be a given, the War for Independence being waged around the edges of the demesne seems clearly to subordinate the personal. Laurence asks Hugo, "Talking of being virginal, do you ever notice this country? Doesn't sex seem irrelevant?" (56). When Hugo responds by commenting on the number of unmarried women, Laurence goes on, "It is 'Ah, why would we?' And indeed why should they? There is no reason why one should not so one never does. It applies to everything. And children seem in every sense of the word to be inconceivable" (56). In the process of decolonization, individual concerns are perceived as subordinate to larger, public concerns. Compared to the national unrest, Laura's story is not only antinarratable but also subnarratable, "literally unremarkable" (Warhol, "Neonarrative" 223). Lois seems to perceive her own concerns as similarly subordinate; nevertheless, at nineteen years old, she still needs to know what she is to do, what she is to value, and "whether life was to hold for her, too, a man's passion" (68). She wonders if what she feels is love, if she should marry Gerald, or if she should marry at all. She attempts to settle these matters by learning what she can of Laura's experience of them, but her access to her mother's story is compromised by the confusion of her roles as daughter and son and by the way both of those roles are threatened by war.

With the submerged plot well under way in this long introductory narrative, the surface plot is launched when Gerald finally appears at Danielstown the next day for the tennis party. We are told that "he almost shone" (45), that he is "so good-looking" (49), and that Lois has "a quick response to his beauty" (70). Gerald diverts Lois's attention from Hugo to such an extent that she "did not notice him going by" (60). However, Lois remains hesitant about her own feelings and about Gerald's; she imagines that "if there could only be some change, some movement—in her, outside of her, somewhere between them [. . .]—she could love him" (71). The "movement" Lois longs for is charted in the submerged plot in which she seeks validation for her experience in her mother's story. Lois observes Hugo, the first man her mother may have chosen, and in Gerald we find a man who, unlike Hugo, may be like Lois's father, the man Laura Naylor finally chose. As an Ulsterman, Farquar is a kind of outsider to the community in which Laura was raised and closer to the English, a point of continuity between him and Gerald. However, we cannot be certain if any of these men is the "true" suitor for either woman, and Part One ends with further inconclusiveness of the kind that characterizes the novel as a whole. Lois remembers her governess, Miss Part, who loved Laura "embarrassingly," and says to Hugo, "My mother hated it—do you remember?" When Hugo asks, "Hated what?" Lois replies, "Being loved like that" (88). The reader recalls that Lois has also thought she might love Gerald "if he would not love her so, give her air to grow in, not stifle her imagination" (71). In this, she believes, she is like her mother, but she seeks further evidence when she asks Hugo, "I wonder if she would have liked being loved at my age—do you remember?" He responds, "I don't suppose she had made up her mind" (88). Lois never gets closer than this to her mother's story.

Having failed to imagine herself as Hugo's wife or to observe in the Montmorencys' marriage anything that illuminates her mother's story, Lois is provided with another source from which she might learn something about Laura's experience in Part Two of the novel—Marda Norton. Marda is a woman of twenty-nine who has been engaged to be married before but has broken her engagements; as a result, her current engagement is generally thought of as tenuous. Marda's age, her homelessness, her attractiveness to everyone around her, and her seeming inability to commit to a marriage that would offer the stability she seeks are likely to remind us of Lily Bart. Lois describes Marda as "a girl—at least a kind of a girl. She's awfully attractive" (127). Early in her short stay, Marda has commanded the attention, the admiration, and even deeper feelings of Hugo, Laurence, and Lois. Indeed, Lois's feelings for her have been considered in the context of same-sex love and desire.[15] Patricia Coughlan suggests another possibility when she observes,

> One of Marda's other functions in the book's design is certainly as an older *alter ego*: ten years on from Lois and her friends who are experimenting both in London and in Co. Cork with their first exposure to adult social life, she has been there and done that. (123)

A third, closely related, possibility is available to readers attentive to the submerged plot: rather than, or in addition to, being an object of desire or an older alter ego for Lois, Marda's character may function as a younger alter ego for Laura. Much is made of the fact that Marda, like Laura, knew Danielstown as a child (107). Now she has returned to find Laura's one-time suitor in residence, and, unlike Lois and despite her aspirations, Marda is the one who experiences, as Laura did, what it is to be desired by Hugo Montmorency. Like Laura, Marda is not overwhelmed by Hugo's attentions; indeed, she stands by her engagement, this time to Leslie Lawe, who lives in England but whose "people are in Meath" (122). Marda's fiancé has the kind of ambiguous relationship to County Cork's Anglo-Irish community that Walter Farquar, the Northerner, had before him. Watching Marda negotiate these circumstances seems to offer Lois a new means of accessing more of her mother's story than she has been able to find so far.

Just as in Part One, Gerald appears the day after the new guest's arrival, and the obstacle of Lois's remoteness from her own feelings is still central to their interaction and is even more closely tied to the house itself. Although she has been able to summon responses when thinking of him on the avenue or talking with him on the tennis lawns, their meeting inside Danielstown is dismal. For Gerald the house is a "cold shell" (124), and for Lois it is "the emptiest house in Ireland" (126). The house, then, seems partly responsible for their first kiss, of which she thinks, "So that was being kissed: just an impact, with inside blankness" (127).

Powerless against the house itself, Gerald remains unable to engage her feelings fully or consistently. Lois's feelings for the forceful Marda are stronger, but she learns that Marda can offer her no more stable vision of the possibility of pleasure for her mother or herself than she has. Marda seems to encourage a career for Lois; she is interested to see Lois's drawings and suggests writing, acting, and travel for her. However, Marda's own choices suggest a different decision, and her admission that she is engaged overrides Lois's hesitation and inspires her to think, "I must marry Gerald" (141). Marda's example is in favor of marriage, but it communicates nothing of pleasure.

When Lois's experience of encountering an IRA agent is repeated, this time in Marda's company, she is once again both aided and hindered in her pursuit of her mother's story. Laura is central to the scene, as she is in the earlier encounter, this time brought to our attention by Hugo's thoughts as he accompanies the two women on a long walk. Hugo is preoccupied with Laura's absence: "Recollections of Laura were now wiped for him from the startlingly green valley, leaving the scene dull" (175). He contemplates "her impotence to be even here," and "now guessed, in fact, he had never loved her" (176). Not unlike Lois, Hugo imagines Marda as a stand-in for Laura. As they come within sight of an old mill, other comparisons with the earlier scene among the laurels on the avenue are evident. Lois talks to Marda of her fear of the mill: "it was a fear she didn't want to get over, a kind of deliciousness" (178). This echo of the earlier scene in the shrubbery is sustained by comparisons between the mill and a ghost (178, 179). As before, Lois may be hoping to learn something about her mother in this place where, we know, Laura came with Hugo, and with Marda as a kind of surrogate for Laura. When Lois and Marda enter the mill, they find neither a ghost, nor even, as Lois thinks for a moment, a dead person, but, again, a rebel agent. He is awakened by their entrance and detains them at gunpoint. His threat against the two women and against Danielstown itself—"Yez had better keep within the house while y'have it" (181)—inspires in Lois again the thought, "I must marry Gerald" (182). However, the experience has more to offer. When the agent's gun goes off, Hugo comes running, and, before he realizes that the bullet has merely grazed Marda's hand, Lois can suddenly see that he has fallen in love with Marda. Lois tells Marda, "But I've had a . . . a revelation [. . .] About Mr. Montmorency . . . he's being awful about you, isn't he?" (185). She knows for sure at this moment that she is witnessing Marda reliving Laura's experience, and she arrives at the conclusion, "What is the good of this? It doesn't make anything" (186).

Given Marda's explicit views about Hugo and about Leslie Lawe, and given Hugo's implicit views about Marda and about Francie, the reader is likely to agree. Therefore, Marda's next remark, described by the narrator as "inconsequent," may, in fact, not be the *non sequitur* it first appears: "I hope I shall have some children; I should hate to be barren" (186). If sexual relationships among adults bring them little or no pleasure, they might, at least "make something"—children. This subject does not drop immediately, as Lois claims, "I'm glad he wasn't my father," and Marda replies, "He couldn't be anything's father" (186). The kind of sentiment that seems wholly uncharacteristic of Marda and of *The Last September* is implied here: that Laura Naylor saw the same thing in Hugo that Marda has seen, that "he couldn't be anything's father." Hugo is associated with sterility (43) and "barrenness" (250), and he himself has reminded Lois, "If she and I had married—[. . .] My dear child, you wouldn't be here" (88). Not only does he imagine Lois never having been born, but he imagines her dead, as well, in this scene, when he shouts at her, "*You* deserve to be shot!" (184). What Corcoran calls "an anxiety or terror attendant on the thought of one's own conception, which is intimately part of the characterization of Lois" (42), may well find its resolution here, as Lois realizes that, even if her mother, as is likely, failed to find pleasure in her marriage to Walter Farquar, Laura made the choice to turn away from a sterile way of life. To have a child, Laura needed to leave Danielstown altogether: Marda's childhood accident with the scraper suggests that Danielstown may not be safe for small children, and, as the young visitor Hercules tries to endure the tennis party there, Laurence tells him, "Nobody could possibly be sorrier for you than I am" (56). If Laura had not "made up her mind" about pleasure, if she married the wrong man, she did it knowingly, only after the failure of pleasure, and in service of a different kind of desire. To fulfill this other desire, for a child, and, more generally, a future, she had to leave Danielstown.

In this way, Marda's experience reveals to Lois Laura's experience. Still, we can feel Lois's frustration as any glimmers of understanding she has of herself or her mother keep slipping away. Distressed about Marda's departure, she hides in the box-room, and notices "on the whitewash, her mother, to whom also the box-room had been familiar, had written L. N., L. N., and left an insulting drawing of somebody, probably Hugo. She had scrawled with passion; she had never been able to draw" (192). In one way, Lois feels close to Laura in this moment—this was Laura's home, familiar to her, and Laura asserted herself here, writing on the wall. But what of the "insulting drawing"? Laura was not able to draw, whereas Lois is quite good at it—except that Marda suggests that Lois's drawings may not be very good after all: "I think you're cleverer than you can draw, you know" (141). Lois's two portfolios of "sinister" drawings (141) seem to imply that she is passionate about drawing, as she asserts her mother had been, but when Lady Naylor says, "She cares for her drawing intensely," Gerald rejoins, "She never speaks of it" (265). Lois ends Part Two doubly at a loss to pin down her mother and herself, and the reader can observe the ways the ambiguity of these two characters—mimetically and thematically—both contributes to and results from the contradictions in the progression that compromise the novel's completion.

Both surface and submerged plots makes considerable progress when Part Three opens with Lois away from Danielstown, attending a dance at the barracks near Clonmore. Apparently no longer expecting any further progress in her search for knowledge of her mother's pleasure, Lois is resolved to pursue her own experiment: "she intended to marry Gerald" (217). In fact, they become engaged at the dance, but this significant moment remains unnarrated, and the reader only learns of it later. Being outside of the house frees Lois to commit to Gerald, but her remoteness from her own feelings, far from being mitigated by the distance, appears magnified by the reader's temporary loss of Lois's perspective. We learn of their engagement only when Lois has returned to Danielstown the next morning. Engaged to be married as her mother had been (perhaps twice), Lois repeats what we assume was also Laura's experience when she wonders, "What have I done?" and finds that, back in the big house, "what she had done stretched everywhere, like a net" (237). Lois already feels trapped by the step she has taken; her uncertainty still dominates, and she still seeks confirmation for her decision in the experience of others. Lady Naylor has heard from Marda and reports, "She says Kent is dull, which I daresay it would be, but of course she is glad to be with Leslie" (239); Lois asks quickly, "Did she say so?" to which Lady Naylor's only response is, "She naturally would be" (240). Finally persuaded that Marda, like Laura before her, is marrying solely in response to a lack of options, Lois knows definitively that her experience is theirs. Lois need not marry Gerald to discover what these women know—she has learned it, and she is prepared to go on with fewer illusions and with a broader range of possibilities.

The change in Lois is evident to those around her as well as to the reader even before it is evident to her. Still imagining herself as Gerald's wife, Lois shocks him with her casual observation that Hugo has fallen in love with Marda. Gerald "produce[s] an appalled silence," then stammers about something he has heard that only intensifies his shock: "But about Lois's mother, he brought out finally, hadn't one heard he had once been . . . ?" (251). When Lois refuses to be scandalized that Hugo could have fallen in love any number of times ("But one can't arrange oneself; one doesn't so altogether live from inside" [252]), he understands that Lois is incapable of the proper reaction to such irregularities. Gerald's conclusion is that "above this extraordinary undercurrent, it seemed to him his Lois was poised too perfectly" (252), and he may speculate about whether Lois is capable of allowing herself to be swept away by this current. Lois shocks Francie as well. Having come to Lois's room in the night to encourage her to resist her aunt's censure and fight for her engagement, Francie declares, "Love is everything!" and "I *know* love is so important" (275). Lois's newfound knowledge—both of the realities of marriage in general and of the truth about Francie's marriage in particular—immunize her against Francie's fantasies and leave her would-be adviser disappointed and doubtful.

Lois has told Francie, "I wouldn't mind being properly tragic . . ." (275), but her own response to "Gerald's departure" (285) when their engagement is broken and to his death a few days later dispels this final illusion. She finds that her reaction to the news that Gerald is dead leaves her without "tragic" feelings but rather "wondering where to go, how long to stay there, how to come back" (297). She enters the house and goes straight upstairs without making the obligatory appearance before the assembled company, just as she had on the night of the Montmorencys' arrival, unwilling now as then to allow the others to influence how she feels. Our final view of her recalls the novel's opening scenes in other ways as well. After dinner with the Montmorencys on that first night, having walked down the avenue and "come to the holly, where two paths crossed," Lois had heard footsteps and "thought what she dreaded was coming," a ghost, perhaps Laura's ghost (42). Now, we are told, the family members are all anxious about encountering the newly bereaved Lois, and "it was Laurence who, walking about the grounds unguardedly, was exposed to what they all dreaded. He came on Lois, standing beside a holly tree" (299). Lois may be standing in this scene exactly where she stood on that first night. This time, rather than dreading a ghost, Lois is dreaded by her family. In this final way, Lois inhabits her mother's place, a ghostly figure who will soon be absent from Danielstown altogether. We know very little of what she is thinking as we glimpse her for the last time, just that she is learning what a woman feels when she has moved beyond her illusions, as her mother felt before her. When she leaves Ireland two weeks later, we may feel she has left for good, as Laura did. Perhaps most importantly, the burning of Danielstown signals the end of Lois's divided role as both daughter and son of the Big House, and we may imagine that, with this impediment removed, Lois will have greater access to her mother's story.

In both *The Last September* and *The House of Mirth,* puzzling elements of the horizontal axis—Why should the marriage plot fail? Where should the reader's sympathies lie?—are illuminated by reconfiguring the progression with reference to the second horizontal axis that tracks the daughter's search. *The Last September* suggests that knowing the mother's story is enough to keep open the possibility of pleasure for her daughter, even if that story is one of seeking pleasure but, perhaps, never finding it. Laura Naylor Farquar's life ended prematurely, before, it seems, she had "made up her mind" about such matters, but Lois's search, though impeded by some confusion in her own role as daughter, at least reveals something of her mother's own search. The submerged plot, like the surface plot, remains incomplete, in contrast to *The House of Mirth,* which demonstrates that whether or not the mother was able to find pleasure, the daughter who cannot learn her story at all has no chance of finding her own pleasure. Wharton and Bowen, like Collins before them, emphasize the deleterious effects of the unnarratability of the mother's story and are pessimistic about the possibility of overcoming those effects. Wharton offers a narrative of complete failure, and Bowen an incomplete narrative of qualified hope.

Although they are unable to determine whether their mothers were women who married despite . . . , for both protagonists, the search remains central. Both seek their mothers' stories in the experiences of other women, and Marda acts as a mentor, however ineffectual, for Lois. Both attempt to repeat their mothers' experiences with men like the ones their mothers chose—in Lois's case, with the very man she chose. For Lois, the mother's childhood home and her mother's ambiguous relationship to it loom large, both facilitating and impeding her search; for Lily, her mother's homelessness is repeated in her own and is deleterious to the search. Our understanding on the vertical axis of the implications and consequences of Lily's homelessness and Lois's confinement in the Big House is augmented by rereading the spaces in the novels in light of the reconfigured progression on the horizontal axes. Considering the function of space in these novels, particularly with reference to their nineteenth-century predecessors, deepens our understanding of the ways plot and setting are mutually constitutive.

As in all of the novels considered so far, those in the following chapters foreground the way the daughter's experience of movement through geographical space is balanced with her experience in a home associated with her mother. So far, the pursuit of the unnarratable story of the mother's pleasure, whether successful or not, and even when it is impeded by or antithetical to elements of the surface plot, has been represented as nothing short of prerequisite for the daughter's own pleasure and therefore unquestionably desirable and productive. Although this remains true throughout the novels studied here, some address the potential dangers of the search and the damage it can inflict when wrested from the daughter protagonist's control. These novels are the subject of chapter 4.

CHAPTER 4

Surviving the Submerged Plot and the Work of Character Narration

The Color Purple, A Thousand Acres, and Bastard Out of Carolina

The unnarratability of the mother's story and the circulation of the submerged plot as a strategy for revealing it persists in Alice Walker's *The Color Purple* (1982), Jane Smiley's *A Thousand Acres* (1991), and Dorothy Allison's *Bastard Out of Carolina* (1992). This shared structure brings these contemporary American novels into conversation with the older English, American, and Irish writers of the previous chapters even as they alter the use of the submerged plot considerably. The older novels attest that finding the unnarratable story of the mother's pleasure is crucial to a daughter's search for her own pleasure, and not finding the story can be debilitating in this regard. They also demonstrate that the submerged plot is threatened by the same forces that render the mother's pleasure unnarratable, primarily the preservation of lines of inheritance, to which a mother's pleasure is, at best, extraneous. When the submerged plot is threatened, the seeking daughter who tells her own story takes on the task of shielding her mother from the censure of other characters and of defending her from the reader's judgment, as the case of Esther Summerson suggests. The character narrators in Walker's, Smiley's, and Allison's novels do as Esther does in their widely various ways, and under circumstances even more devastating.

The submerged plot as we have encountered it so far tracks the daughter's pursuit of her mother's unnarratable story, and it depends upon connections between the daughter's choices and her mother's. The daughter's search is central in the three novels considered in this chapter as in the others; however, in contrast to other protagonists, who experience what their mothers did before them with similar feelings, these protagonists are forced into what their mothers chose, and they, accordingly, respond with opposite feelings. That which the mother chose, or is perceived to have chosen, is repugnant and terrifying to the daughter. In effect, the daughter's repetition of the mother's experience is wrested from the submerged plot, where it is, in some ways, under the daughter's control, and becomes part of the surface plot, where it is controlled by others. *The Color Purple, A Thousand Acres,* and *Bastard Out of Carolina* demonstrate how terrifying the process of learning the mother's story can be. In these three novels, the main character is raped by her mother's husband—Walker's Celie when she is fourteen, Smiley's Ginny at fifteen, and Allison's Bone when she is twelve. These novels raise the question of how the daughter's access to sexual pleasure is affected by being forced too early and too intimately into knowledge of her mother's pleasure through exact, not variant, repetition—not with a man like the one her mother chose, but with the very man she chose. This major change affects the way the submerged plot surfaces, the ways the second horizontal axis is referred to by the first. The daughter's repetition of the mother's experience remains the primary means by which we detect the submerged plot, and that repetition is intensified to a distressing degree. Whereas, in other novels of motherless daughters, relationships with suitors—true or false—who resemble the father are key elements of both horizontal axes, in these novels such resemblances are redundant, and male suitors are mostly absent. Especially important under the painful circumstances narrated in these novels are mentors—in most cases sisters and aunts who aid the protagonist and help her to maintain her connection to her mother. These relationships yield a range of meanings in the surface plot, and yet more in the submerged plot.

In fact, the forcing of the protagonist to repeat her mother's experience of sex exactly necessitates a considerable change in the very function of the submerged plot. Unlike novels in which the daughter retains control of her search and assumes that her mother's response to her experience must have been like her own, in these novels the daughter is faced with the knowledge that what is painful for her was pleasurable for her mother. Experiencing sex that is entirely dissociated from her own pleasure but closely associated with her mother's could annihilate the search altogether, but, although in some cases it is delayed until well into adulthood, the search remains central. What changes is its object: each of the seeking daughters in these three novels endeavors to dissociate her mother's pleasure from the story she has been forced to repeat, and each looks to the mother's distant past for another story, one without the pain of violation bound up in it. The submerged plot of this search counters the powerlessness the protagonists experience in the surface plot.

The protagonists' powerlessness is also countered by their narration, and among the ways they assert themselves as character narrators is to control the reader's response to the mothers who fail to protect them from sexual abuse. As retrospective narrators, Ginny Cook Smith and Bone Boatwright, not unlike Esther Summerson, direct our judgments of their mothers; Bone's narrative goes so far as to break the code of mimetic character narration in order to ensure that our judgments of Anney Boatwright remain in line with her own.[1] Celie's narration is not retrospective but rather epistolary, so in her narrative we do not get a distanced, considered adult point of view right from the beginning. This makes Celie's narrative even more revealing, then, of the ways that even the most abused daughter works to reserve judgment of her mother and preserve the possibility of understanding her motivations and actions.

Whereas for other motherless daughters the submerged plot is the repetition of the mother's experience, for these protagonists the submerged plot is the attempt to balance the unacceptable repetition of the mother's experience with an alternative story that enables her to survive the events of the surface plot.[2] Celie's search is completed when she finally discovers the true story of her mother's past that has been hidden from her. Bone's mother's past also offers an alternative story, although this one requires some idealizing on Bone's part as well as her concerted effort as narrator to assert its centrality and importance. Ginny cannot find an alternative story of her mother, and her relationship to pleasure is irretrievably compromised; that she is able to go on at all, however, is linked strongly to a story of her mother that she and her sister invent. These character narrators' tenacious pursuit of their mothers' stories and commitment to protecting them from readers' censure reveal the necessity, even in the most devastating circumstances, of the daughter's engagement with the mother's unnarratable story.

"A wife whom he adored": The Widow

Scholars have encountered difficulty in accounting for the plot structure of Alice Walker's *The Color Purple*. The terrible violence against women documented from the novel's first pages, and the oppression of African Americans that pervades the novel and erupts into violence at intervals throughout, situates the novel sufficiently in the realm of realism that many critics have categorized it as such and have criticized its departures from that mode. Molly Hite summarizes the initial response to the novel by referring to the

> many reviewers, who pointed out variously that in the last third of the book the narrator-protagonist Celie and her friends are propelled toward a fairy-tale happy ending with more velocity than credibility; that the letters from Nettie, with their disconcertingly literate depictions of life in an African village, intrude into the middle of the main action with little apparent motivation or warrant; and that the device of the letters to God is especially unrealistic inasmuch as it foregoes the concretizing details that have traditionally given the epistolary form its peculiar verisimilitude: the secret writing place, the cache, the ruses to enable posting letters, and especially the letters received in return. (103–4)

Scholars continue to grapple with these elements of the text, and many have found in them encouragement to recontextualize the novel generically. Hite argues that these and other elements of *The Color Purple* can be more adequately accounted for by considering its generic affinities with the romance, particularly the late romances of Shakespeare. Trudier Harris refers to the novel as "a new breed of fairy tale" (6), and Margaret Walsh argues that "many of enchantment's stock figures people its pages and that fairy-tale dimensions, such as fantastic exaggerations, turns and endings, give it shape" (89). These alternative perspectives are revealing and enriching, and they help to account for our experience of reading the novel, which, not unlike *Jane Eyre,* begins with a realistic account of an abusive childhood and moves toward the wish-fulfillment of romance.

At the same time, as in the case of *Jane Eyre,* we may account for some of the apparent vagaries of the novel's plot within the context of realism. Reconfiguring the progression of the surface plot of *The Color Purple* with reference to the submerged plot modifies our understanding of some elements of the novel that critics have found troubling.

Perhaps the most significant of these elements are the causes of Celie's transformation and the exceptionally happy ending made possible by it. For Raphaël Lambert, the happy ending is predicated primarily on Celie's financial independence, effected by her own entrepreneurship and her inheritance from her father. Lambert argues, "The story of Celie becomes a capitalist fantasy very much at odds with Walker's initial project" (43). Christine Froula also focuses on Celie and Nettie's inheritance, but with a contrasting interpretation that aligns economics more closely with Walker's apparent intentions and goes a step further: "Celie's utopian history allegorizes not only women's need to be economically independent of men but the daughter's need to inherit the symbolic estate of culture and language that has always belonged to the father" (641). Like Froula, Peter Kerry Powers focuses on the symbolic role of the father, with reference not to Celie's inheritance but rather to the much earlier revelation of Celie's true parentage. For Powers, not only do Nettie's letters provide a "model that illustrates the possibility of Celie's living a different life herself," but also, by telling Celie the true story of their parents, Nettie provides a "new personal history for Celie" (78). Perhaps most important for Powers, whose central contention is that "Walker's work is not only a domesticated history, but also a sacred history" (69), is the dismantling of Alphonso as patriarch:

> In revealing that "Pa is not our Pa," Nettie has revealed more than a genetic fact about Celie's body. Given the identification of divine authority, patriarchy, and racism—an identification that defines Celie's symbolic status as "Black Woman"—to say that "Pa is not our Pa" undermines and cracks the foundations of an oppressive form of life. To say "Pa is not our Pa" is to say that the stories that a racist and patriarchal imagination have told Celie are simply lies. With lies revealed, new possibilities for living may emerge. (79)

For Powers as for Froula, the revelation of the true history of Celie's family is significant primarily in terms of the symbolic weight of the father.

bell hooks's analysis of the significance of the story of Celie and Nettie's parents focuses not on the symbolism of the father but on the revelation that Alphonso is not Celie's biological father. For hooks, Celie's problems resolve themselves completely, and unrealistically, when the horror of incest is neutralized: "her sexual confession changes when it is revealed that she has not been raped by her real father. The tragedy and trauma of incest, so graphically and poignantly portrayed, [. . .] is trivialized as the novel progresses" (56–57). For all of these scholars, the truth about Celie's father and about Alphonso is crucial to understanding the progression of the surface plot.

I concur that the revelation of her parents' story is central to Celie's transformation, but I would suggest that, by the time we encounter this story, Celie's narration has prepared us to find in it not only the hitherto unknown father, but also the story of the mother's pleasure, and that Celie succeeds in finding that unnarratable story.[3] Understanding the submerged plot of Celie's search for the story of her mother's pleasure, and the way that search is jeopardized but not destroyed by the experience of being raped by her mother's husband, enables us to understand in a new way the function of Nettie's letters and their apparently sudden intrusion into the narrative, as well as the novel's surprisingly happy ending. The submerged plot, as well as the ways the submerged plot is disclosed through the novel's distinctive use of epistolary form, becomes evident through reconsideration of the novel's progression.

As *The Color Purple* opens, the reader understands immediately that its adolescent heroine will not progress toward marriage and motherhood as Anne Elliot, Jane Eyre, Esther Summerson, and other motherless protagonists considered so far do. Unlike the nineteenth- and early-twentieth-century novels treated in the first three chapters, in which heterosexual union is the explicit goal throughout and frequently is the condition for completion, in *The Color Purple,* the protagonist has already experienced heterosexual sex and pregnancy even before the narrative begins. When she is married just twelve pages into the novel to Albert, an abusive older man she refers to for much of her narrative only as Mr. _____ (all surnames in the novel are elided in this way), we realize in how many ways the surface plot is a departure from those of the earlier novels. At the same time, the submerged plot is still firmly in place: although Celie has experienced sex, she has not experienced sexual pleasure, and finding it becomes as much a preoccupation for her as for those other motherless daughters. The centrality of sexual pleasure is made explicit when Shug pronounces Celie "still a virgin" because she has never experienced it (77), and Celie's ultimate access to her own pleasure is facilitated by Nettie's letters, which contain, among other things, the story of their mother's past.

Scholars have suggested of all of the novels of motherless daughters treated thus far that the daughter's maturity, independence, creativity, and pleasure depend on her rejection of her mother, and we may be tempted to find that even more emphatically the case in *The Color Purple*. Celie's mother's incapacity and denial leave her young daughter vulnerable to the predatory man that the mother herself has chosen and brought into proximity with her. We know that Celie is troubled by anger she harbors toward her mother (as she is troubled by all anger she is tempted to feel). She writes, "Maybe cause my mama cuss me you think I kept mad at her. But I ain't. I felt sorry for mama" (5). We are made aware of the completeness of Celie's repression of her anger when she tells Sofia, "I can't even remember the last time I felt mad," but, when she tries, the first instance that comes to mind involves her mother: "I used to git mad at my mammy cause she put a lot of work on me. Then I see how sick she is. Couldn't stay mad at her" (41). Celie's anger, as far as we know, is more than justified: her mother has been a participant in the events that have ended Celie's sense of herself as a "good girl" (1), as a daughter, as a wife rather than just a good bargain, and even as a potential mother. bell hooks puts the problem this way in her essay on *The Color Purple:* "Mothers prove their allegiance to fathers by betraying daughters; it is only a vision of sisterhood that makes woman bonding possible" (64). Dianne Sadoff concurs that sisterhood in the novel is more efficacious than motherhood, and she goes even further to argue that the novel contains a "subterranean narrative of violence against [. . .] mothers," who "suffer death early or see their functions displaced onto sisters" (133). Nevertheless, even as the women around Celie help her to come to terms with Alphonso's violation of her and her anger at her mother's passive sacrifice of her young self, Celie still needs a story of her mother's pleasure that can validate her own. The submerged plot of Celie's search for this story alters our view of her mother's function in the novel's character-system. That she has failed to protect Celie may at first appear to be her definitive function, both mimetically and thematically, but, by the novel's end, we understand that this failure does not negate her function as the source of Celie's much-needed validation. The surface plot makes the connection between Celie's experience and her mother's explicit right from the first pages, but only attention to the submerged plot reveals that the connection is not exclusively Celie's inheritance of a history of oppression.

The novel begins with the only two sentences we will read that are not contained within a letter: "You better not never tell nobody but God. It'd kill your mammy" (1). That the first sentence is nearly always quoted in scholarly work on the novel but the second sentence far less frequently suggests that the strategies we have traditionally brought to novels of motherless daughters tend to obscure the submerged plot. Alphonso's prohibition against Celie's telling her story is intensified by the prohibition in the second sentence against sharing stories between mother and daughter. The repeat reader of *The Color Purple* knows that, just as he regulates what Celie is allowed to say to her mother, he has long regulated what her mother is allowed to say to her: we assume that he has insisted that the truth about Celie and Nettie's paternity and inheritance be kept from them. Long before Celie has learned this information from another source, and despite her mother's actual death, she refuses to believe Alphonso's assertion that knowledge of the abuse Celie has suffered would kill her mother. In contrast, she asserts, "Trying to believe his story kilt her" (5). Celie, then, establishes that she recognizes the power of stories but distrusts that which would come between her mother and herself.

This early example gives the reader fair warning that Celie's innocence is not always the same as naivety. As we read Celie's first letter, we may think of her as a naive character because her request to God, "Maybe you can give me a sign letting me know what is happening to me," implies that she is confused by the changes in her body that are signs of pregnancy. We may think of her as a naive narrator as well, because hers is the voice of a fourteen-year-old child, and, more importantly, in contrast to the retrospective narration of *A Thousand Acres* and *Bastard Out of Carolina*, the epistolary form of *The Color Purple* means that Celie is not able to shape her story retrospectively but can only report events as they occur.[4] However, close attention to this letter reveals that Celie the narrator is shaping her experience even as it occurs and that she makes connections between her own experience—especially her unwanted sexual experience—and her mother's. Celie does not begin with her occasion for writing this letter to God, "I feels sick every time I be the one to cook. My mama she fuss at me an look at me" (1). Instead, she begins her narrative with an account of her mother refusing sex with Alphonso: "Last spring after little Lucious come I heard them fussing. He was pulling on her arm. She say It too soon, Fonso, I ain't well. Finally he leave her alone. A week go by, he pulling on her arm again. She say Naw, I ain't gonna. Can't you see I'm already half dead, an all of these chilren" (1). Celie offers this scene as context for the ways her experience repeats her mother's. She has already made the connection between her mother's physical relationship with Alphonso and the children she bears and her own being forced to "do what your mammy wouldn't" and feeling sick. Celie is innocent, but she is not naive, and her attempt to make sense of "what is happening to me" (1) is closely connected to her attempt to make sense of what is happening to her mother.

Readers can recognize the complicated and contradictory messages this scene between Alphonso and Celie's mother conveys, and we learn the strengths of Celie's character as she negotiates its implications. We understand that what she overhears could teach Celie that her mother does not take pleasure in sex, that, in fact, it makes her ill and has contributed to her being "already half dead" (1). This conclusion could be reinforced by Alphonso's claim to Celie that the real danger to her mother's life would be knowing that Celie has had sex. However, Celie rejects the possibility that sex—her mother's or Celie's—is responsible for her mother's decline, and she does not acquiesce in Alphonso's attempts to separate her from her mother or from her own sexuality. In fact, we realize, as Celie must, that her mother's rejection of sex implies that, under other circumstances, she might agree and take pleasure in this act, and her choice to reject him now reminds us that she has agreed before and conceived several children with him. This view of the scene is attended by a different threat to Celie's relationship with her mother and to her sexuality. To think that sex with Alphonso, which has occasioned for Celie physical and psychic pain that stays with her always, could ever have been pleasurable to her mother brings its own kind of distress. Celie is forced by the circumstances of the surface plot to repeat her mother's experience in a number of ways, always responding with fear and horror to that which her mother, she can only imagine, once chose. Like her mother, Celie is forced to have sex with Alphonso and bear his children, to keep his house and cook his meals, to try to protect the others in the house from his predation, and then listen to him go in to another woman—all while in a state of numb shock. The conditions of Celie's marriage to Albert are similar, so, in effect, Celie repeats her mother's experience twice, once exactly and once with variation. As she tries to understand "what is happening to me" (1), Celie sees the connections between her mother and herself.

Celie is so young when forced into repeating her mother's experience that she has not yet even begun her own search for pleasure. Her first indication that sex is considered by others to be something she might choose is when Alphonso "beat me today cause he say I winked at a boy in church" (5). Celie explains that she is not interested in men, but this incident has added a new dimension to her perception of sex and pleasure, and, immediately after this incident, she reports being given a picture of Shug Avery and writes, "All night long I stare at it. An now when I dream, I dream of Shug Avery" (6). This is likely Celie's first experience of desire, and, on her wedding night, "while he on top of me," she puts the pieces—desire, sex, pleasure—together for herself as best she can: "And then I think bout Shug Avery. I know what he doing to me he done to Shug Avery and maybe she like it. I put my arm around him" (12). Her vision of Shug as a woman who desires sex and her physical desire for Shug enable her, for the first time, to imagine choosing sex.

As Celie finally begins to pursue her own sexual pleasure, the reader alert to the submerged plot is likely to note as it accumulates the evidence that her mother remains central to her way of thinking about it. From the first, when Celie writes about Shug, she also writes about her mother. When she first sees the picture of Shug, she compares the two women: "She more pretty then my mama" (6). When Albert brings Shug home to be nursed, Celie observes, "She sicker than my mama was when she die. But she more evil than my mama and that keep her alive" (47). After Shug begins to recover, Celie attends to her hair: "I work on her like she a doll or like she Olivia—or like she mama" (53). Finally, after Celie and Shug make love the first time, Celie ponders, "What it like? Little like sleeping with mama, only I can't hardly remember ever sleeping with her" (114). The repeated references demonstrate that when she tries to think through her own sexual desire she is conscious always of her mother. These references are integral to Celie's thoughts, and they are also integral to her narration. Celie modifies the vision she has given the reader of her mother in the first letters, "screaming and cussing" as she dies (2). She softens our judgments against her mother by implying that she considered her mother the most beautiful woman she had ever seen until she saw Shug (6), that she took pleasure in combing her mother's hair and would have liked to sleep with her mother more often than she was allowed to. Her mother was hurtful to Celie as Celie suffered her ordeal, but she was still less "evil" than Shug. Celie wants her reader to see her mother as she does, as she needs to in order to preserve her own connection to pleasure.[5]

The surface and submerged plots are connected even more strongly when Celie's first experience of sexual pleasure, when she and Shug finally make love, coincides with the discovery that Albert has been hiding Nettie's letters. The letters, many of which have been hidden away for years in Albert's trunk, contain exactly what Celie needs to validate the sexual pleasure she has finally found. That Celie is ready for this validation is signaled by her willingness, for the first time, to talk about Alphonso's rape of her to another person. As she and Shug lie in bed, Celie defies Alphonso's injunction and tells somebody besides God what he did to her. The telling of this story is clearly an important step in Celie's progress toward pleasure, which she finally experiences immediately following the telling. Celie's pleasure is also made possible by another element of the story she tells Shug: whereas early on, in her second letter, she recalls her mother's questioning of her about her pregnancies, in this letter she remembers her mother questioning Alphonso and beginning to realize that he is to blame rather than Celie. As before, Celie's representation of her mother works to preserve their relationship and to protect her mother from the reader's harshest judgments. The letters from Nettie complete this difficult work for Celie.

Nettie's letters have appeared to some readers, as Molly Hite expresses it, to "intrude into the middle of the main action with little apparent motivation or warrant" (103). However, the reader is not as completely unprepared for the appearance of the letters as Celie is. Celie has concluded that Nettie must be dead (18, 21, 118), but the reader likely never concurs for at least two reasons: what we know about the world that Celie and Nettie, as girls, do not yet know, and what we know of Celie's character. When Nettie, about to run away, assures Celie that she will write, and that "nothing but death can keep me from it" (18), we can imagine as the child Nettie cannot how many unforeseen circumstances could come between the sisters. We also know that Celie has difficulty imagining the possibility of escape from life as she knows it except in death. She assumes that Alphonso has killed her first infant (2), and the only alternative she can conceive of for herself is death, as when she tells Sofia that she bears her circumstances knowing that "this life soon be over" (42). We know more than Celie and Nettie at this point about life outside their community and can imagine possibilities for both girls that they cannot. Also, we are attuned to the expectations Walker creates in her characterization of Celie. The novel opens with the unsparing revelation of Celie's dire circumstances, yet it depicts her capacity for love as not only having survived abuse but as a powerful force. Helping Nettie to escape violation is Celie's first act of rebellion, which involves immense self-sacrifice. As bleak as Celie's reality is, we expect that her loving sacrifice will not be futile but will bring change eventually. Because Celie's character has not been entirely overpowered by events in the past, events in the future are likely to be more and more determined by Celie's character.[6] To this extent, the optimism of the novel's ending is present from the beginning: we are likely to feel that we start at the lowest point in her experience and that Celie's character will, eventually, save her as well as her sister. We expect Nettie to return in one way or another and aid Celie as Celie has aided her, and Nettie's letters do fulfill that function.

Recognizing the impact of the letters on Celie prompts us to reconsider them not as a sudden intrusion but rather in terms of how long they are delayed. Epistolary novels raise reader expectations for a fairly rigid chronology; therefore, even though *The Color Purple* defeats such expectations, that alternative story that Albert has prevented is still present for us.[7] If not for Albert's deliberate, malicious act, the novel would be balanced between Celie's and Nettie's letters nearly from the beginning. We can only speculate about how this might have changed Celie's life, but we do know that the withholding of the stories that Nettie can tell has delayed Celie's development and her liberation from some of the most immediate sources of her oppression. In terms of the surface plot, hearing Nettie's stories strengthens Celie to such an extent that she finally declares and then successfully fights for her own independence. Nettie's letters achieve this effect in a number of ways, not least simply in that they are evidence that someone in the world loves Celie more than she loves anyone else. They also offer Celie the wider perspective she has been denied by being denied her education. Early on, Celie tells us that Nettie has tried to explain "bout the ground not being flat" and that Celie has not been able to internalize this point of view: "I never tell her how flat it look to me" (10). Celie's historical perspective is equally limited, and when Nettie tries to teach her about Christopher Columbus, Celie finds that "it hard to think" (9). But Nettie's letters, by beginning with what Celie knows (namely, Nettie and their hometown) and proceeding to what is less familiar (for example, Corinne, whom Celie has met just once), and then to what is entirely unfamiliar (Africa), give Celie an entirely new perspective on the history of African America, and an entirely new perspective on her own personal history. The withholding of Nettie's narrative delays the progress of the surface plot of Celie's fight for independence, and it also delays the progress of the submerged plot of her search for her mother's story. Their mother is the link between the sisters, as, for example, the mother is the link between Laura Fairlie and the half-sisters who act as mentors for her, and being denied Nettie's mentoring has had considerable consequences for Celie.

Celie still needs a story of her mother's experience of marriage and sex that can validate her own pleasure, as the story she has been forced to learn can only have the opposite effect. She finds the validating story she needs in her mother's distant past, which she learns of, appropriately, through one of Nettie's long-delayed letters. The discovery of Albert's treachery and cruelty in hiding the letters threatens Celie's sexual awakening, and she reports, "Us sleep like sisters, me and Shug" (146). Celie is surprised and puzzled by her own reaction: "Much as I still want to be with her, much as I love to look, my titties stay soft, my little button never rise. Now I know I'm dead" (146). But Shug recognizes the effects of "being mad, grief, wanting to kill somebody" (146), and when Celie finally reads the story of her mother's life in one of Nettie's letters, she begins to recover. She learns of her father, her mother's only real choice, who was a "well-to-do farmer who owned his own property near town" (174) as well as a dry goods store and blacksmith shop. This successful entrepreneur also had strong family ties, depending on his brothers when his business got too large for him to run alone. This man "had a wife whom he adored," and her devotion to him was so great that, after she had been traumatized by his murder, her devotion to him was all she could remember: "she continued to fix her husband's plate at mealtimes just as she'd always done and was always full of talk about the plans she and her husband had made" (175). This story is life-changing for Celie in a number of ways. In her "daze," her first articulation is, "My daddy lynch" (177). Celie can suddenly see her life as the effect of causes that are outside herself and her community: the racism, greed, and violence of the dominant white culture. This context enlarges the world she has known, in which the violation of her own body has clearly been effected by an outside force, but which Celie has experienced as shameful and connected to something wrong within herself.

Celie's next articulation (not unlike Alphonso's "It'd kill your mammy" [1] that opens the novel) receives less critical attention, but it may be as important, and it helps Celie to change her view of that smaller world in which she has always lived: "My mama crazy" (177). This sudden addition to the mimetic component of the mother's character alters her thematic function considerably. Celie's mother, she learns, was a woman who could marry Alphonso only out of a desperation she could not mitigate on her own because "although the widow's body recovered, her mind was never the same" (175). Nettie's letter offers a vision of their mother as a woman whose physical self (her recovered body) was disconnected from her mind. From this, Celie can understand that her mother's marriage to Alphonso was never her choice, but rather that Alphonso took advantage of the young widow. She knows now that her mother was a woman who married despite a passionate and enduring love for a man who was taken from her. Having confirmed what she has read by visiting Alphonso, she finds pleasure with Shug again: "Shug say, Us each other's peoples now, and kiss me" (183). Finally, Celie has accessed pleasure, and she has a story of her mother that validates it. Celie's pursuit of this story has been largely unconscious; however, when she learns it, she is alive to its implications for her own life, and her life, accordingly, changes very quickly.

The story of her parents' great happiness together before the murder of her father and uncles, followed by the revelation that they have left Celie and Nettie a considerable inheritance, can strike readers, paradoxically, as idealized in the context of the surface plot. Christine Froula asserts that Celie and Nettie's inheritance "indulges in narrative magic that well exceeds the requirements of the plot" (641). However, as with Nettie's letters, we should pause to consider this story not in terms of its sudden, apparently "magical," appearance, but rather in terms of the delayed revelation of a story that should always have been known to Celie and Nettie, well before they needed to resort to letter writing. The story of the murder of their father and of their own inheritance is apparently deliberately kept from them, along with the story of their mother's pleasure. Clearly Alphonso is threatened by the story on every level, as it exposes his inferiority to the girls' father and the advantage he has taken of their mother. He has ample reason to hide it, enough so to make him prohibit their mother telling it herself, if she were able. Others in their small community must know this story as well, including the minister of the church they attend, the teacher Nettie so admires, and other neighbors, including Albert himself. These people must be aware of the numerous ways that knowledge of this devastating story would also be empowering for Nettie and Celie. Nettie's letter warns Celie of the shock to come when she writes that the story "made my hair stand on end" (174), but she also emphasizes the importance for Celie of knowing this story: "I pray with all my heart that you will get this letter, if none of the others" (176). The story is their connection to a time before abuse, shame, and isolation, to that successful man and his happy wife who provided for their beloved daughters. Rather than tell it, however, all of these people allow the girls to believe that their mother has always been the "beaten down" woman they have known (132); her pleasure remains taboo.

This story that seems to "[exceed] the requirements of the plot" is crucial to the submerged plot, as Celie looks to her mother's past for another story, one unconnected to the violation of Celie's own young body. Analogously, Nettie's experience in Africa provides both her and, eventually, Celie with a story of the distant past of a people. They are all too familiar with the suffering of African Americans, but the Olinka, whose way of life has remained stable in some ways over time, offer a vision of past experience before the Middle Passage and the enslavement of Africans in America. Molly Hite reminds us that the novel criticizes the African culture it depicts, but also explains that, especially when Nettie first arrives, it is represented as "an idyllic counter" to Celie's world, "with its organically round huts, its roof-leaf religion, its restorative myths of black hegemony, and its simple agrarian economy" (113). This story of pleasure that precedes great pain is echoed in that of the girls' mother, and the narrative provides evidence of the extent to which this story changes things for Celie, of which her sexual pleasure with Shug is only part, and for Nettie, who finds her own pleasure with Samuel.

Indeed, the way that the story of Nettie's pleasure reflects *Jane Eyre* helps to further define the function of the mother's story. As Hite reminds us, Nettie's letters have struck some readers as "disconcertingly literate," but Nettie does explain that in her life with Corrine and Samuel, "they teach me, and I teach the children and there's no beginning or end to the teaching and learning and working" (134). The situation described is not unlike Jane Eyre's at Moor House, where she studies with her cousins and learns from them even as she teaches girls at the local school St. John Rivers establishes. The similarities become more pronounced in the letter in which Nettie reveals the story of their parents to Celie and explains how she learned it. In effect, just as in Jane's case, a clergyman with whose family she lives tells her the story of her own parents as if it were the story of strangers, without any names, because he suspects, but is not certain of, her own connection to the story. The manner of the telling is very like St. John Rivers's narration to Jane of the story of her own parents when he seeks the heir to his (and Jane's) uncle's fortune. After Corrine's death, Samuel and Nettie continue to live in Africa; when they travel to England to enlist help for the Olinka, the English bishop implies that their relationship is improper, to which Samuel replies, "We behave as brother and sister to each other" (232). Nettie and Samuel have pursued without qualms a course Jane herself offers to St. John, though St. John takes the bishop's part and refuses to believe that such a platonic relationship between two people of a certain age is possible. Nettie's story is, in part, the alternate story Jane imagines for herself: she does become a missionary and marry a clergyman. This alternative was not where Jane Eyre's pleasure lay, but we feel no reservations about Nettie's choice because she knows the story of her mother's pleasure and is free to seek her own pleasure by making her own choice.

With the revelations of Nettie's letters, Celie regains control of her search, and she goes on to relive her mother's early, happy experience as she has been forced to relive her mother's unhappiness. Some things are gone forever: Alphonso has left his mark on Celie's life as he has on the land she recovers, and she has lost years of her life, years of her children's lives. Nevertheless, Celie owns a home on her parents' property, and she owns and runs the store as her father and his brothers had done before her. She is living on the land her mother lived on, loved and in love with another person as her mother had been, and loving her two children, as her mother had loved her and Nettie. For Celie's mother, these happy experiences lasted a relatively brief time and ended in devastation. That the novel's conclusion presents such experiences as characterizing Celie's future indefinitely helps to account for some readers' discomfort with it, as does the kind of completion made possible by the progression of both horizontal axes, which is unexpected in literature of the late twentieth century. The generic shift in the surface plot may be the only way for a protagonist to move from terrible suffering to nearly total happiness as Celie does. At the same time, readers can find in the repetition itself evidence of the steadier submerged plot, which enables a more measured advance. Celie knows her mother's story, has found a version of her mother's pleasure that she can live with, and has had her own pleasure validated. Her narration reveals this progress even as it controls the reader's response to the mother, whose failure to protect her does not change what the daughter needs from her.

"She had a history": Ann Rose Amundson Cook

Just as *The Color Purple* is dependent on its setting in a southern farm community, so is Jane Smiley's *A Thousand Acres* on its setting in a midwestern farm community.[8] In both novels, the focus is on the family, and the families are structured similarly: two sisters become vulnerable to an abusive father (or stepfather) in the absence of their mother (the other, younger children in both novels are spared). In both cases, the elder sisters are the narrators, even though they possess qualities that make them seem younger than their sisters. Their shared outlook is expressed in some similar ways: Celie begins her narrative at just fourteen years old, and in an early letter she writes that Nettie is teaching her about Columbus's voyage to America (9): "She try to tell me something bout the ground not being flat. I just say, Yeah, like I know it. I never tell her how flat it look to me" (10). Christine Froula argues that Celie's testimony reveals not only "the pathos of Celie's isolation" but also "her fidelity to the way things look to her" (638). Smiley's narrator, Ginny Cook Smith, is in her forties, and the events of her narrative have stripped away her long-held naivety, but she remembers a childhood learning experience similar to Celie's:

> It seemed to me when I was a child in school, learning about Columbus, that in spite of what my teacher said, ancient cultures might have been onto something. No globe or map fully convinced me that Zebulon County was not the center of the universe. Certainly, Zebulon County, where the earth *was* flat, was one spot where a sphere (a seed, a rubber ball, a ballbearing) must come to perfect rest and once at rest must send a taproot downward into the ten-foot-thick topsoil. (3)

Although oppression and abuse threaten Ginny's own perspective, as they do Celie's, ultimately Ginny, too, is faithful to her own point of view.

Like Celie's, Ginny's narrative does not tend toward heterosexual union in marriage, but rather toward that which she has not experienced: sexual pleasure. Ginny, who is thirty-six years old when the events she narrates begin, is married, and she has experienced pregnancy (though not childbirth). Like Celie's, Ginny's repetition of her mother's experience occurs in the surface plot, where it is out of her control, rather than in the submerged plot, and her repetition of her mother's experience is exact rather than variant. Ginny is forced in adolescence to have sex with her mother's husband, and thus to repeat her mother's experience but to find only terror and pain where her mother, she may imagine, found pleasure. Unlike clear-eyed Celie, Ginny has repressed what she knows of her mother's story, in effect suspending her search, but, as her story begins, unprecedented events in her life encourage her to resume it. Even as the surface plot of *A Thousand Acres* documents Ginny's awakening to the ways that she and the land on which she has lived her whole life have been controlled and abused by the men around her, the submerged plot reveals Ginny's attempt to salvage the possibility of and the validation of pleasure by finding a story of her mother's pleasure that is unconnected to the violation of Ginny by her mother's husband. Ginny's search is a failure, but the centrality of it to the novel attests to its necessity.

Ginny's retrospective narration, in contrast to Celie's, begins from a point well beyond the end of her story: she knows all that will happen from the start. Although her search was long delayed and then undertaken in confusion, she has mastered its implications fully by the time she shares it with the reader, and she is in control of both the surface and submerged plots of the story she has narrated. Indeed, Ginny tells us of what she refers to as her "afterlife" that she spent most of her free time reading narrative: "One author at a time, every book in the [library's] collection. I preferred them to have been productive, but now to be dead, like Daphne du Maurier or Charles Dickens" (334). Reading novels of suspense is not an entirely new pastime for Ginny; early on she loans her niece her own favorite Nancy Drew novel, suggesting that she has long experience of this kind of narrative (108). Therefore, we know that our narrator is fully conscious of narrative strategies for arousing and satisfying readers' curiosity.

Indeed, Ginny's self-consciousness as narrator is complemented by a slightly different kind of self-consciousness in Ginny the character, and the two work together to make her narrative persuasive. The narrator is self-conscious in the sense that she is fully aware of her own agenda and purposefully uses identifiable strategies that control her effect on her readers. In contrast, the character is self-conscious, as she frequently states explicitly, in the sense that she fears that others are watching and misjudging her; in effect, she fears that she lacks control over her effect on others (227, 246, 247, 278). This contrast is emphasized in a number of ways throughout the novel. The most consistent of these enables us to see how the contrast promotes Ginny's reliability: the narrator carefully details the character's uncertainty about her impact on others and depicts her as discovering her own feelings and expressions of those feelings only after the fact, often by observing the reactions they inspire in others. For example, only when her niece works to reassure her that their day together has been a good one does Ginny realize, "I must have sighed" (95). Soon after, Rose's defensive remarks convince Ginny that "I must have had some look on my face" (96) and "I must have looked doubtful" (97). As she becomes increasingly intrigued by their recently returned neighbor, Ginny admits, "I discovered that I was keeping an eye out for Jess Clark" (69), and when Caroline gets married without even telling her sisters, she tells us, "I realized that I felt the insult physically" (139). The narrator offers us a character whose recognition of her own feelings and experience is consistently delayed. This pattern in the narration is in keeping with the surface plot, in which Ginny eventually recovers memories she has repressed. This pattern also accounts for our faith in Ginny's version of events. The knowing narrator presents us with her past self as a consistently uncertain experiencing character, and the combination is what wins our trust. Ginny's habitual unsureness, in contrast, for example, to Rose's energetic efforts to persuade everyone around her, engages our sympathy. Ginny explains, "I had been the blurter, always stumbling into self-betrayal without a moment's thought. She [Rose] had been more calculating" (191). Indeed, nearly all the characters—Rose, Jess, and even Ty—come to seem calculating to Ginny, but the narrator presents Ginny as the last to know even her own desires. A character without an agenda and an authoritative narrator with a clear agenda work together to earn our affirmation, and the narrator makes use of our trust to direct our judgments not only of her father but also of her mother.

Recognizing the submerged plot of Ginny's preservation of her relationship with her mother in the face of unthinkable revelations about her father also suggests answers to questions raised by the surface plot. What is it about the events of the year 1979, when most of the action of the novel takes place, that enables Ginny to recover memories she has repressed for over twenty years? What exactly is the impact on Ginny of these memories? Why does Ginny withdraw into a world she describes as anonymous and lacking beauty, and why is the life depicted at the novel's end the most Ginny can hope for three years after making what appears to be an entirely necessary break from her old life? What accounts for the completion of the novel given the ambivalence of its conclusion? And, importantly, why does sexual pleasure remain out of Ginny's reach as it does not, for example, for Celie? These questions can be addressed more fully if we retrace the novel's progression with reference to the submerged plot.

Ginny's stated goal is to understand both of her parents, who are inaccessible to her in different ways, and scholarly discussions of the novel analyze the degree to which she succeeds. Sinead McDermott, in her study of memory and nostalgia in the novel, comments on this effort, saying:

> Ginny must transform a "disabling fiction" into an "enabling fiction" through the use of memory. This involves not simply remembering the abuse itself but also searching for memories of her mother, who died when Ginny was fourteen and whom Ginny has largely forgotten [. . .]. Ginny's search, then, is both for her lost memories of abuse and for her lost mother, and at times these seem to be the same search. (393)

McDermott argues persuasively with reference to Ginny's memories of both her parents that "remembering can be a form of resistance to the erasure of women's lives and of domestic histories of abuse within patriarchal discourse" (394). For McDermott, Ginny's attempt to remember her mother's life is important in that it signifies recognition that her mother's life was subject to the same oppressive forces as her own.

This thesis underlies other analyses of Ginny's relation to her absent mother as well, and other critics conclude that Ginny recognizes the oppression suffered by her grandmother, her mother, and herself, and then manages to mount a resistance to that oppression, mainly by telling her own story. For Susan Strehle, "Ginny's discourse is shaped by a culture that devalues and silences women" (218), but unlike, for example, her grandmother, "this ancestress, whose dependence and fear she shares" (221), Ginny ultimately acquires a "subversive style" (224). For Barbara Sheldon,

> Ginny [. . .] returns history to these women by writing about them and consciously sets herself in their tradition, without repeating their fate. [. . .] She differs from the other women in two ways: she tells her story and, in so doing, she offers an explanation of the events different from the version of her father and the farm community. (59)

Strehle and Sheldon consider that Ginny must distinguish herself from her foremothers, who were unable to overcome their oppression.

Mary Paniccia Carden and Glynis Carr concur, and both go a step further to assert that Ginny's mother has failed her daughter, and Ginny must become the mother she herself needed. Carden argues that "Ginny's desire is for the language that can, and for the mother who could, provide alternatives to Daddy's ownership, disavow paternal right, introduce the unsaid into the language" (194). What Carden finds, though, is that what Ginny needs "reside[s] not in the mother she knew, but in the possibilities she invests in a kind of mother-under-the-mother. Ginny seeks the mother covered over by the mother who acted as a representative of paternal power" (194–95). Unlike her own mother, who was forced into complicity with patriarchy, Ginny, in the end, "functions as a mother with a voice" (198). Carr's analysis of the Persephone myth in *A Thousand Acres* reaches a similar conclusion:

> Ginny recognizes herself as an abused Persephone and releases the anger she holds against her mother for not being a Demeter—a strong mother

who rages against the daughter's victimization and is able, finally, to bargain with at least some success for her daughter's return. In Demeter's absence, Ginny must recast herself in that role, becoming the strong mother she herself never had. (121–22)

All of these arguments emphasize the significance of Ginny's relation to her absent mother, but all also emphasize her need to distinguish herself from the mother.

The surface plot alone, with only a few seemingly inconclusive details from the history of Ann Rose Amundson Cook, lends itself to these interpretations. Recognizing the submerged plot of Ginny's pursuit of her mother's story, however, enables readers to account more fully for the juxtaposition of Ginny's search for the truth about her father with her search for the truth about her mother, and helps us to understand her relationship to Ann's story in a new way. It also changes our understanding of the function of the mother in the character-system of *A Thousand Acres:* she is not only a failed protector but also the object of Ginny's continued search. She functions thematically as a representation of women's suffering and oppression, but she also functions thematically as a representation of what daughters need from mothers, however circumscribed their circumstances, and however egregious their personal failings. Tracing the ways the submerged plot influences the surface plot of *A Thousand Acres* reveals that Ginny can only face her horrifying memories when she has developed a version of her mother's story that protects her relationship to her mother from being destroyed by them. What she finds is not a story of Ann Cook's pleasure—unlike Celie, Ginny discovers no relationship of her mother's that precedes the one she herself knows too well. Instead, Ginny has only a vision of her mother as a young woman, before sex, self-contained and individual, and on this vision Ginny herself builds what she calls her "afterlife" (334).

Ginny's pursuit of validation for her sexual pleasure is very much complicated by the emphasis in her community on functional sex and by her own desire to bear a child. As *A Thousand Acres* opens, the emphasis is on fertility, generativity, procreation. Ginny begins her narration with a description of the farm, including the land itself, "fertile, black, friable" (4). The first events in the narrative center on parents and children: Harold Clark holds a pig roast in honor of his returning son, Jess, and during the party Larry Cook unexpectedly offers his farm to his three daughters. The values of the community are foregrounded when nearly the first thing we learn about Jess Clark is that he has arrived back in Zebulon County with "no wife, no kids" (7). These values are also explicit when Rose says of her twenty-eight-year-old sister, Caroline, that, "According to Daddy, it's almost too late to breed her" (10). When the next chapter recounts the story of Sam and Arabella Davis's partnership with John Cook in the 1890s to reclaim and settle the land on which these characters live, the repercussions of this emphasis on fertility for women's lives is clear: Ginny offers a picture of these three adults waiting until Sam and Arabella's daughter, Edith Davis, is old enough to be married to John, which she is at sixteen years old. Edith's life is entirely circumscribed by the desire of the adults around her to maintain their hold on this fertile land and by the emphasis on procreation, of hands to work the farm and heirs to inherit it. Only much later does Ginny begin to ask herself questions about Edith's experience; at this early point, she simply accepts it, and her own "secret, passionate wishes" are all about a child of her own (27). This is the context for Ginny's confidences to the reader about her first miscarriage and her possessive love of her sister's two daughters; soon we learn that she has, in fact, been pregnant and miscarried five times.

The emphasis on functionality that results from the prizing of productivity as a cardinal virtue contrasts with Ginny's memories of the Ericsons, childhood neighbors who used to live in what is now her own home. Book Two of Ginny's narrative begins with a lengthy description of this family, whose "farm was more like a petting zoo" (43). According to Larry and Harold, Cal Ericson's method was based solely on "consult[ing] his own desires," and his goal was to "enjoy himself as much as possible" (44). Ginny's mother admired Mrs. Ericson's "remarkable powers" of being able to "relax in her own house" (46). In Ginny's world, these alternative values mean that the Ericsons cannot prosper. Ginny explains of her family: "We knew in our very sinews that the Ericsons' inevitable failure must result from the way they followed their whims. My mother surely knew it with regret, but she knew it all the same" (46). In fact the Ericson farm does fail and become part of the Cook holdings, but Ginny recognizes in her mother a yearning for what the Ericsons have, and when they leave closely following her mother's death, Ginny realizes, "I think that I did feel everything gentle and fun and happy draining away around me" (136). The Ericsons' way of life, in contrast to that of the Cooks and their other neighbors, allows for pleasure, and the events of Ginny's narrative remind her of these other values.[9]

Ginny is open to the reintroduction of these alternative values because, when we meet her, she is suddenly in a position to question the certainties upon which she has consistently relied. First, Ginny has recently been forced to face the possibility of life without her sister Rose, who has undergone treatment for breast cancer; Ginny has always thought of their companionship as "the central fact of my life" (8). Second, Ginny's father has suddenly decided to incorporate the farm and put it in his daughters' names. Although his intention may be to consolidate his power—by preventing the farm itself from being divided; by avoiding debilitating inheritance tax after his own death; by enticing his third, city-dwelling daughter back to the farm—in fact, his influence begins to diminish immediately, offering Ginny a measure of freedom from his hitherto absolute authority.

With her most fundamental relationships in flux, Ginny recognizes in Jess Clark what she had once found in the Ericsons. He envisions a method of farming that is not determined primarily by market forces. He inspires Ginny, Rose, and their husbands to spend their evenings playing games and telling stories—purely for fun. Finally, he offers the possibility of sexuality for its own sake. Just moments after her father's initial announcement of his plan to incorporate the farm, Ginny stumbles into Jess and, after he catches her, she notices, "His hand lingered on my arm" (21). Even in this moment, the long habit of sexual functionality is on their minds but has already shifted slightly: Jess tells Ginny, "You know, I've been thinking that there's something missing in this kitchen, and now I realize what it is. It's the cylinder of bull semen. I used to eat with my foot up on it" (21). This reference to the practice of artificial insemination of farm animals signifies both the pervasiveness of sex on the farm and the extraneousness of pleasure, but Jess notes the absence of this accustomed marker and holds out the promise of pleasurable sex. The next day, at the gathering to sign the incorporation papers, Ginny reports that Jess "got up and stood behind me, and I must have tensed up, because he squeezed the back of my neck" (38). As in so many other instances, the narrator is willing to admit that she may have "tensed up," though she maintains that the character only realizes it because of Jess's response. As readers, we are likely to feel in sure hands with Ginny the narrator even as we sympathize with the uncertainty, perhaps especially about sexuality, of Ginny the character.

Even as the possibility of pleasurable sex arises, Ginny finds herself thinking about her mother, Ann Cook, who died when Ginny was fourteen. As her father makes his inexplicable decision, Ginny thinks of her mother as someone who could have explained him:

> My father had no minister, no one to make him gel for us even momentarily. My mother died before she could present him to us as only a man, with habits and quirks and preferences, before she could diminish him in our eyes enough for us to understand him. (20)

At this point, Ginny thinks of her mother and father as united in what she calls "their duet" (5), and she thinks of her mother primarily in relation to her father. However, as Book Two opens, Ginny remembers that her father had "disapproved" of the Ericsons (43), whereas "my mother felt a little differently" about them (45). This slight variation of opinion is significant because the Ericsons represent a lifestyle that takes pleasure into account, and this difference between her parents is magnified when Ginny has a conversation with Mary Livingstone, an old friend of her mother. Like other mentors in novels of motherless daughters, Mary is a potential source of information about the absent mother and a sign on the surface of the submerged plot. Indeed, she surprises Ginny by telling her that Ann wanted different things for her three daughters than Larry Cook did, and that she was, essentially, afraid to leave them alone with him when she died. Mary says, "She knew what your father was like, even though I think she loved him" (91). With Mary's words, Ann is transformed in Ginny's mind from a "minister," who could explain their father, to a woman, who was capable of judging him. Now, in a line that recalls her earlier, "My mother died before she could present him to us as only a man" (20), Ginny thinks, "My mother died before I knew her, before I liked her, before I was old enough for her to be herself with me" (93). Ginny imagines finding out more about her mother, "new answers to old mysteries," by watching Rose, who resembles Ann, or even by taking up a "quest," "becom[ing] her biographer" (94). Instead, Ginny eventually gains access to her mother's story by acknowledging the ways in which her own experience has repeated her mother's. Other motherless protagonists, whom we generally encounter at an earlier stage in their development, find their mother's stories by repeating their experience; Ginny, at thirty-six years old, has already repeated her mother's experience, and she needs to find a way to survive those memories.

Ginny's memories of repeating her mother's experience are devastating, and, even as Jess Clark sets her search for her mother's pleasure in motion, the looming truth about her father's abuse threatens her progress. Even as Mary Livingstone offers Ginny a new vision of her mother, she also gives Ginny the first push toward remembering her father's abuse of her. Mary opines, "I always thought kids on farms should be made to face facts early on" (90), and Ginny admits, "I was just wondering what facts there were that I haven't faced" (92). Having told Ginny that Ann feared Larry would keep her from the opportunities Ann wanted for her, Mary says, "There was another thing, too—" (92). When Ginny shows no sign of recognition or understanding, Mary leaves the "other thing" unsaid, but Ginny feels "disconcerted" (92), and, a few paragraphs later tells us, "I realized that I was almost panting" (93). Again, the character is taken by surprise by her own reactions, and both reaction and surprise are recorded by the narrator. Neither the character nor the reader understands the full significance of this moment, but the narrator does understand, and she recreates for us the feeling of approaching realization. In addition to this affective response, we are given an interpretive clue that the impending trauma of remembering something unimaginable about her father will be closely connected to Ginny's relationship with her absent mother.

As Ginny prepares to face the full extent of the damage her father has done to her life, she must also prepare for the ways that knowledge will threaten her relationship to her mother. The closer she gets to knowledge of her father, the more important it becomes for her to locate a vision of her mother as someone other than the woman who chose this man and took pleasure in him. After her conversation with Mary, Ginny lies in bed and, as she explains, "tried to remember my father" (105). She remembers stories she has been told, including one her mother told her about how Ann and Larry met, which reveals not only things about Larry but also about Ann:

> When Mommy, who was visiting a school friend in Mason City, wouldn't dance with him at a church dance, Daddy got the manager of a local men's store, someone he knew only by name, to leave the dance and sell

him a new suit of clothes, including underwear, socks, shoes, and fedora. He looked so dapper in them, Mommy would say, that she didn't want to dance with anyone else the rest of the night. (105)

On one level, the story is meant to explain what it was in Larry's actions that long-ago night that charmed Ann. His determination to dance with her is one attraction, as well as his ability to afford to make this gesture. That he can persuade others, here the store manager, to do things just because he asks them to is amply demonstrated, as well as, paradoxically, his implicit claim that he would be willing to do anything to have Ann, including change himself. On another level, however, the story tells something of Ann's experience. One thing Ginny can understand from it is that her mother's initial impulse was to resist Larry. Subsequently, Ann was seduced by him, but the manner of the seduction suggests a kind of sustained reservation on Ann's part: focusing on his clothing, Larry appears to understand and accept that Ann will be more comfortable with physical proximity if both parties are, somehow, fully dressed. This story of Ann allowing Larry to touch her only when sufficient emphasis has been placed on the clothes that will remain between them is a safe one for Ginny, one that will enable her to protect her pursuit of her mother's story even as the truth about her father is revealed. Ginny's search becomes even more important by the end of Book Two, as Jess Clark kisses her and Ginny "discovered how much I had been waiting for it" (128). Her new freedom and Jess's offer of pleasure accelerate Ginny's search for validation of that pleasure, even as the narration emphasizes her uncertainty, even, or especially, of her own feelings and reactions.

These threads continue to develop in Book Three, which Ginny opens, similarly to Book One, with a meditation on the fertility of the land. She goes on to discuss the silences and absences of the Cook women, whose relatively short lives seemed to end with their own fertility. Although for several scholars Ginny's response to these silences is to be sure that her own voice, in contrast to those of her foremothers, is heard, I suggest that the unnarratable stories of these women, especially of her mother, remain an object for Ginny, despite what she has experienced as "the habitual fruitlessness of thinking about her" (94). The word "fruitlessness" is revealing in this context, as Ginny is still working to free herself from the model of reproductivity with which she has been inculcated.

She reveals what she needs to know to Rose, who, like Mary Livingstone, mentors Ginny and provides a link to her absent mother. Also like Mary, Rose tries to ascertain what Ginny's own experience has been by demanding of her, "Ginny, tell me what you really think about Daddy" (152). Ginny responds by talking about Larry, but soon she turns to her mother. She repeats her feeling that "Mommy hasn't been around to tell us what to think of Daddy," and she continues: "I wonder about whether they were happy. Whether she liked him. Or he liked her" (153). Her inability to resolve these questions impedes her search.

Still struggling with her inherited valuing of functional sex, Ginny finally has sex with Jess in an encounter that is intended to be purely for pleasure. This scene is both a fulfillment of the reader's expectations that ultimately Ginny will find pleasure in Jess and also a baffling of those expectations. To what extent Ginny takes pleasure in this experience is slightly ambiguous: she describes elements of this experience as "awkward" and even "humiliating" (162), but she also describes her orgasm and reports that how she feels afterward "seemed to mean that I could be satisfied as well as full of longing" (164). Even this encounter, however, is shot through with questions of sexual function. After sex, Jess asks Ginny, "How come you and Ty don't have any kids?" (164). He follows this with a revelation about nitrates in the well water, which have likely caused Ginny's miscarriages. This is new information for Ginny and for the reader, and we are likely to be surprised that she does not react to it at all. The disjunction in her mind between procreative and pleasurable sex leaves Ginny nonplussed, and Jess is affected by it as well. Discussing fertility leads Jess to wonder whether Ginny has used birth control during their sexual encounter. We learn that she has taken the necessary steps to prevent pregnancy, but Jess, though he has brought a condom to their meeting place, has not used it but claims, "I forgot I remembered to bring it" (165). Even as Ginny moves toward sex that is purely for pleasure, Jess has begun to move back toward that deeply ingrained desire for generativity. Therefore, this sexual encounter is dominated by the issue of procreation.

Our expectations for Ginny's long-awaited encounter with Jess are also stymied by the narrator's framing of the scene: she narrates it within her account of what she calls "the best ever" sex with her husband, Ty (164). Ginny has implied a number of times (and will explain at greater length later) that she and Ty are habitually uncomfortable with lovemaking, but the night before Ginny has sex with Jess, she and Ty find an unaccustomed ease with one another. Ginny tells us that the sex is "deeply exciting and simultaneously not enough" (162), but she is pleased that it is accompanied by "just a single quiver of embarrassment" (162). Here, as in her description of sex with Jess, Ginny's pleasure seems muted or incomplete. After narrating this encounter and then the one with Jess in just two pages, Ginny recounts that Ty, like Jess, inquires as to whether their sex could result in pregnancy. Upon finishing the novel, we know that these two encounters are the height of Ginny's sexual experience. Even as we read these pages, however, we understand from the tempered nature of the experience and the qualifications made by the narrator that Ginny's search for validation of sexual pleasure has little chance of success.

As if in response to these experiences, the prohibition against sex for pleasure is reiterated dramatically in Larry's demented and drunken denunciation of Ginny a few pages later when he screams at her:

> You barren whore! I know all about you, you slut. You've been creeping here and there all your life, making up to this one and that one. But you're not really a woman, are you? I don't know what you are, just a bitch is all, just a dried-up whore bitch. (181)

The terms of Larry's rant underline the general cultural taboo against women's sexual pleasure, and he verbalizes the values evident in the novel from its first pages as he accuses her of the unpardonable sin of engaging in nonprocreative sex, including sexual activity outside of marriage. As a figure for patriarchy, then, Larry decries women's sexual pleasure in general; as an individual, he has also done what he could to destroy Ginny's own sexual pleasure by raping her and, in the process of forcing her to repeat an experience her mother chose, cutting her off from the maternal legacy that could validate it.

At this point in the progression, when Ginny has experimented with pleasure and endured her father's devaluing it, Rose finally reveals what Ginny has repressed knowing: soon after her mother's death, when she was fifteen years old, her father repeatedly raped her. Rose, like Mary Livingstone, both gives Ginny cause to mistrust her father and recovers for her a bit of her mother's story. Rose forces Ginny to know that "he was having sex with you" (189), but she also, and just prior to this revelation, offers Ginny her own invented story of their mother as a kind of buffer against the full import of what Ginny has yet to accept at all. Rose, who has lived with this knowledge always, tells Ginny:

> I used to fantasize that Mommy had escaped and taken an assumed name, and someday she would be back for us. [. . .] She was a waitress at the restaurant of a nice hotel, and we lived with her in a Hollywood-style apartment, you know, its own door, two floors, two bedrooms and a bathroom up and living room and kitchen down. Nice shag carpeting, white walls, little sounds from the neighbors on either side, sliding door out to the back deck. (187)

Rose already knows what Ginny is on her way to learning: she needs a story of her mother's pleasure that is separate from the story that Rose, like Ginny, knows too well, in which what may have given the mother pleasure offers the daughter only pain and revulsion. In the absence of such a story, Rose has created one in which Larry is not Ann's choice, and she offers it to her sister. Ginny closes Book Three with a reference to Rose's fantasy, their stand-in maternal legacy. After Ginny and Rose are publicly humiliated and scorned as bad daughters at a church potluck dinner, Ginny writes, "Since then, I've often thought we could have taken our own advice, driven to the Twin Cities and found jobs as waitresses, measured out our days together in a garden apartment, the girls in one bedroom, Rose and I in the other, anonymous, ducking forever a destiny that we never asked for, that was our father's gift to us" (220). In the absence of any other acceptable version of their mother's story, Ginny holds on to Rose's fictional version.

Ginny needs more of her mother than this created story as she progresses toward her recovery of her repressed memories. Book Four opens with Ginny gathering her thoughts about her mother; entering her father's house, she tells us, "It seemed like Daddy's departure had opened up the possibility of finding my mother" (225). Despite Ginny's overt emphasis on the mother, the reader is likely to be most acutely aware of the building of suspense toward revelations about the father. As a result, we are likely to underread parts of the ensuing scene. Ginny is moments from recovering her memory of her father's abuse of her, and, just as she did when Mary Livingstone touched on those memories, Ginny constructs a vision of her mother that focuses on her relationship to clothing. Now Ginny tells us of Ann, "She had a history [...] and for us this history was to be found in her closet" (224). Although Ann was adamant that her young daughters "must *not* touch Mommy's things" (223), Ginny remembers of the closet full of her old clothes, "These were things of hers that our mother didn't mind us playing with" (224). The clothes are long gone now, taken away soon after Ann's death by "the ladies from Mommy's church club" (227), but in childhood they found in her closet high-heeled shoes, hats with veils, corsages, and dresses. Ginny describes the clothes and their significance to her and Rose:

> Although her present was measured out in aprons—she put a clean one on every day—her past included tight skirts and full skirts and gored skirts, peplum waists, kick pleats, arrowlike darts, welt pockets with six-inch-square handkerchiefs inside them, shoulder pads, Chinese collars, self-belts with self-buckles, covered buttons, a catalog of fashion that offered Rose and me as much fascination in its names as in its examples. The clothes in the closet, which were even then out of date—too narrow and high for the postwar "New Look"—intoxicated with a sense of possibility, not for us, but for our mother, lost possibilities to be sure, but somehow still present when we entered the closet. (224)

Even as small children, Ginny and Rose witness events in their home that inspire in them the need to idealize Ann's past, the time before her marriage, and to imagine the possibilities that might have been open to her then. At this crucial moment in her adult life, Ginny needs a vision of her mother fully dressed, inviolate, before marriage.

She looks at a number of old photographs as she wanders through her father's house, including one of her mother that is, significantly, an engagement picture, specifically marked as prior to marriage. Still hoping for clues from her mother about her father, wondering, "Wasn't there something to know about him that she had known that would come to me if I found something of her in his house?" (225), she admits that in this photo, "I found nothing" (226). Nevertheless, the image is significant for what it reveals about Ann herself: "The impenetrable face of a hopeful girl, dressed in the unrevealing uniform of the time; her demeanor was sturdily virtuous" (226). Ginny's choice of the word "impenetrable" helps to characterize the vision of her mother that, in lieu of a story of sexual pleasure unrelated to Ann's relationship with

Larry, Ginny needs when she remembers, two pages later, "Lying here, I knew that he had been in there to me, that my father had lain with me on that bed" (228). She tells us, "It was a memory associated with the memory of my mother's things going to the poor people of Mason City" (228). As a girl, Ginny had associated her mother's clothes with her mother's and her own safety, a defense for her against her father as they had been for Ann. Now, freshly armed with a vision of her mother as "impenetrable" and "uniformed," Ginny allows herself to remember what she has long known of her mother's story and the ways that she was forced to repeat her mother's experience.

The narrator has protected the reader, as the character protected herself, from the full knowledge of Larry's abuse of his daughters until the characterization of Ann is complete and we are prepared to recognize the complexity of her thematic function. The story we have gradually learned, with the remaining details revealed at this point in the narrative, is that when Ann Rose Amundson Cook dies in 1957, fourteen-year-old Ginny and twelve-year-old Rose begin to repeat Ann's experience. They keep her house exactly as she kept it. They raise her youngest daughter, Caroline, as Ann had raised them, with "no principles beyond those that were used with us" (64). From observing her mother, Ginny understands the work that will be required and the conditions under which it will be performed: "I knew exactly what was to come, how unrelenting it would be, the working round of the seasons, the isolation, the responsibility for Caroline" (136). About these experiences, Ginny and Rose can assume they feel much the same as their mother did, and their experience even now, in 1979, repeats their mother's in many ways. However, when as girls they are both forced to have sex with Ann's husband, their father, they may assume that their own feelings of pain and fear are different from their mother's, who chose this experience. The idea that her mother took pleasure in what is, for Ginny, a terrifying experience, is a problem for Ginny, and she comes to terms with it by fighting for her conviction that Larry Cook's sexual aggression is not the whole of Ann's story. The fact that Larry is Ann's only husband, and, almost certainly, her only lover, makes it even more difficult for Ginny to get to this tenuous point than it is for Celie. This is seemingly not because Ann withholds this part of the story, as, for example, Lily Bart's mother does, but perhaps because Ann Cook never accessed her own pleasure. That the "holy relics" (224) of Ann's life are clothes is instructive, and Ginny thinks that "her dresses, even her housedresses, were structured and public-seeming, with tucks and darts, decorative buttons and appliqué work" (93). The only reference to more intimate garments is advice Ginny remembers: "She did tell me never to wear 'pointy bras'; they were 'too suggestive.' She also advised against nylon underpants, because they were 'slippery' and 'made you feel funny'" (279). We may read in Ann's love of clothing—clothing that is specifically in no way sexy or sensual—her avoidance of the naked body. This understanding cannot validate Ginny's sexual pleasure, but it can prevent her father's crimes from dividing her further from her absent mother.

In fact, Ginny goes on to identify other continuities between her experience and her mother's as her narrative comes to its conclusion. She opens Book Five by reevaluating her experience of her own body in light of what she has remembered. Her narrative of her body is closely connected to her feelings about clothes; she can remember as a very young child, "Mommy and Daddy never complained of their clothes, but mine seemed a constant torment" (278). After her father takes from her what she calls "the memory of my body" (280), however, she remembers that nightgowns, long underwear, and washcloths shielded her body from even her own vision and touch; she retreated into clothes, as she envisions her mother doing. Ultimately, having imagined her mother in "uniform," Ginny chooses a job as a waitress in which she literally wears a uniform every day.

Ginny also repeats her mother's experience as her relationship with Rose deteriorates throughout Book Five. Rose's betrayal of Ginny with Jess Clark and her carelessness about her sister's feelings force Ginny to see things in Rose she has never acknowledged before, things her mother saw before her. Explaining herself, Rose says, "Don't you remember how Mommy said I was the most jealous child she ever knew?" (303). She goes on to say, "I'm grabby and jealous and selfish and Mommy said it would drive people away" (304). Finally, Ginny can see Rose more clearly, as her mother had, though, as with other of Ann's experiences she repeats, Ginny finds this "unbearable" (308). Ginny has long felt that Rose is the most similar to Ann: she shares with her mother "her manner, her looks, even, in part, the name" (93); her mothering of daughters; and even the cancer that threatens to end her life. At this point, however, Ginny imagines claiming more similarity for herself. Puzzled by a photograph of an unidentified baby who could be Ginny, Rose, or Caroline,

Ginny speculates for the first time that her experience of losing a child might be shared with her mother: "Maybe there was another one after all, one that came before me" (321). Ginny's recognition of the continuities between her own experience and her mother's give her a fuller understanding of Ann and of herself.

With this, Ann's story has offered up what it can, so, in the end, Ginny goes beyond repeating her mother's story and inhabits the fantasy Rose loved of their mother living in an apartment, working in a restaurant, and raising her daughters. Ginny moves to the city, finds just such an apartment, takes a job as a waitress at Perkins, and raises Rose's daughters. She tells us that "men are friendly to me at the restaurant, and sometimes they ask me to a movie [. . .] It is easier, and more seductive, to leave those doors closed" (369). She reads novels in her spare time and studies psychology at a local college, and she has become the narrator of her own story, possessed of the kind of self-consciousness that implies authority and control rather than their opposites. The resolution of the surface plot is symmetrical though uncomfortable, but completion is made possible by the submerged plot, which helps to explain why this life is the one Ginny ultimately chooses. She has not found validation for her own pleasure, but we see her last in a community of women: living with her two nieces, and working with other waitresses in a restaurant where the manager, too, is a woman. The connection she has discovered between herself and her mother has enabled her to find connections with other women as well, and has enabled the survival she has earned.

"The story Mama would have told": Anney Boatwright Parsons Waddell

Like *A Thousand Acres,* Dorothy Allison's *Bastard Out of Carolina* is told by an adult retrospective character narrator who, although forced to seek her mother's story in a state of confusion, understands, by the time she narrates, the full import of her search, and she takes clearly identifiable steps to be sure her reader understands her story as she does herself. Unlike Ginny and Celie, Bone Boatwright limits her narrative to her childhood, and when the novel ends the character Bone is still only twelve years old. Indeed, although the narrator has long been motherless, the child Bone is not, and her attempts to remain close to her mother are central to the novel's surface plot. These attempts are defeated by her mother's husband, whose physical and sexual abuse of Bone throughout her childhood effectively distance her from her mother. The loss of her mother and the trauma of the abuse are formative for Bone: at the novel's conclusion, she tells us, "I was who I was going to be" (309). The surface plot raises a number of interpretive questions, two of which are central to the narrative throughout: How are we meant to feel about Anney Boatwright Parsons Waddell, the mother who proves unable to protect her beloved daughter from abuse and who accepts being separated from her? And who, in fact, will Bone be? The latter question raises others, including about Bone's sexuality: like Celie and Ginny, Bone has been raped; her only experience of sex, then, has been terrifying and punitive, and her narrative includes details about the ways her sexuality develops in this context. Will her own access to sexual pleasure be compromised by the abuse she suffers? That *Bastard Out of Carolina* is semiautobiographical suggests that Bone's developing sexuality will prove to be lesbian: why does Allison allow us to glimpse this possibility, by making Bone's lesbian aunt central to the final scenes, but not go further? Attention to the submerged plot suggests new ways of answering these questions. Even as Bone seeks in the surface plot to secure her relationship with her mother, Anney's distance and silence, which effectively make her an absent mother, stimulate Bone's pursuit in the submerged plot of a story of her mother's pleasure that can validate her own. Glen Waddell's abuse of Bone from the time she is six years old until she is nearly thirteen is an insurmountable obstacle in the surface plot, but, though it also threatens the progress of the submerged plot, the latter is successful. Bone manages to find a story of her mother's pleasure that can validate her own, and she is able to maintain her connection to both her absent mother and her own sexuality.

Scholars agree that Bone's relationship to her mother is the novel's central concern. Tanya Horeck notes, "As most readers of the novel observe, the most traumatic event is not Bone's violation by Daddy Glen but her abandonment by her mother" (54). Similarly, Hilary Schor and Nomi Stolzenberg explain of both *Bleak House* and *Bastard Out of Carolina*, "What is most shocking [. . .] is not the abuse of the child by a father-figure [. . .], nor the absence of the 'real' father [. . .], but rather, the abandonment of the child by the *mother*" (111). Ann Cvetkovich agrees: "The novel's ultimate concern is not Bone's sexual and physical violation by her stepfather [. . .], but 'the complicated, painful story of how my mama had, and had not, saved me as a girl'" (346). These scholars also agree that Bone's own sexual desire and potential for sexual pleasure survive Glen's abuse of her, but they argue that Bone survives by renouncing the mother who has failed her. Horeck concludes that "it is only at the moment of her mother's symbolic death that the child is able to find the identification with her that she so desires" (55). That is, the absence of her mother is the "reality" (54) that Bone faces, and also a precondition for Bone to "script her life differently" (56). Cvetkovich's argument focuses more specifically on sexuality, and she writes of Bone's troubling sexual fantasy that it "also provides her with the sense of self that is her way out, that gives her the strength, for example, to renounce her mother" (349). Schor and Stolzenberg go further to identify in the novel an underlying narrative of the illegitimate mother who must be disowned. They find explicit in the novel the idea that "female sexual errancy—which is to say, female sexuality or, more precisely, erotic desire, the sexual agency of the mother—is the circumstance which haunts the daughter's progress and sooner or later wrenches her away from her mother" (120). In fact, they assert, "Renouncing the mother, the daughter claims her own powers of invention, beauty, and, above all, writing"; furthermore, "the daughter's move away from her mother is also her own move into sexuality" (126). However, Bone's narrative suggests that she cannot renounce her mother, and that doing so would not achieve the desired effect. In contrast to these scholars, Minrose Gwin observes that "oddly, though, Bone, unlike many victimized daughters, does not ultimately blame or turn away from her mother." For Gwin, Bone's ability to imaginatively transform space enables her to see "herself in relation to her mother and her mother's struggle" even after Anney has left (106). I would suggest that another element of the imaginative work Bone must perform is her attempt to solve the problem that her mother finds pleasure in the same man who causes Bone only pain and shame.

Bone's own sexual fantasies center on violent images of fire and of being beaten, and this prompts Deborah Horvitz to argue of her that, "unable to imagine anything but horror associated with sex or sexuality because her physical torture invades and pervades her thoughts as well as her body, Bone con-fuses—conflates as well as mistakes one for the other—sex with being a victim of violence" (244–45). I would argue, in contrast, that Bone is, in fact, able to imagine that pleasure is associated with sex and sexuality because she has seen the signs of it in her mother, and, given her situation, this is a problem in itself. Especially after Glen molests six-year-old Bone in his car while waiting for Anney to give birth to his son, Bone is aware of the sex between Anney and Glen. Whereas before the abuse what Bone reports noticing about her mother and Glen is hand-holding and her mother as blushing and brightening at his touch (35), afterward she notices of a kiss between them Anney's "open mouth pressing his lips hungrily" (51). She learns to recognize the signs that they are about to have sex, and explains, "Whenever they started kissing on the couch, they'd go in the bedroom and shut the door for an hour at least" (62). Further, she is familiar with the changes in each of them afterward, Glen "smiling and easy in his body," Anney "sleepy-eyed and soft all over" (62). Even in her confusion, Bone's sensitivity to sexuality has been awakened, and she cannot help contrasting her terror of Glen with her mother's pleasure in him. Even as she survives the horror of Glen's abuse, Bone must negotiate the fact that her beloved mother finds pleasure in the same acts with the same man that have been forced on Bone and have caused her repulsion, fear, and pain. Attention to the submerged plot of the novel recovers this lost element.

We can recognize the workings of the submerged plot especially in elements of the narration and in the surface plot's distinctive progression. The submerged plot surfaces immediately in the surprising omniscience of the novel's character narrator in the first chapter, omniscience that is almost never in evidence throughout the rest of the narrative and that is utterly withheld in the novel's crucial final scene. Allison uses this anomaly to guide the reader's vision of Anney and prevent us from judging her too harshly, instead aligning our responses with those of the adult retrospective narrator. As in *The Color Purple* and *A Thousand Acres*, the characterization of the mother exceeds her mimetic and thematic function as a failed protector and includes her thematic function as the source of the daughter's validation. The submerged plot also surfaces as readers respond to the alternation in the progression between Bone's experiences in the nuclear family that Anney has created with Glen and her experiences with her extended family (that is, the nuclear family into which Anney was born). At home, Glen forces Bone to do with him what Anney does with him, and being forced into what her mother has chosen threatens her pursuit of her mother's story: what Bone feels when she repeats her mother's experience couldn't be further from what Anney feels. In contrast, in the homes of her aunts, Bone repeats her mother's experience in other ways, and with the same feelings, and this enables her to avoid rejecting Anney altogether. This disjunction is one reason that our response to Anney throughout the narrative is likely to be ambivalent, but the contrasts help us to locate the intersections between the surface and submerged plots, which reveal that Bone survives her mother's story and finds a story of her mother's pleasure that validates her own.

The submerged plot is launched in chapter 1, in which readers are likely to be struck by the anomalous omniscience of the character narrator, which contrasts strongly with the limits she places on her narration throughout the rest of the novel. She calls our attention to the distinction herself when, near the beginning of the second chapter, Bone tells us of "the first thing I remember" when she was "about five years old" (18). The details she recounts in chapter 1 occur prior to this time, and, we later learn, have been recounted to her over and over by her grandmother and her aunts (25–26, 126, 261). Yet Bone goes beyond even the stories she has heard to report details no one could have told her. For example, she narrates what the nearby farmhands said and thought when Anney's first husband, Lyle Parsons, was killed in a car accident that was witnessed neither by her four-year-old self nor by any of her family members. She reports dialogue and, perhaps even more surprisingly, that "everybody kept expecting him to get up" (7). The narrator reports how Glen Waddell felt when he was first introduced to Anney by her brother in the White Horse Cafe: "He would have her, he told himself. He would marry Black Earle's baby sister, marry the whole Boatwright legend, shame his daddy and shock his brothers" (13). Bone as narrator takes liberties with her position in this chapter, and Dorothy Allison takes a chance with this inconsistency, in order to achieve a very particular effect. Dispensing with techniques that will dominate the rest of the narrative (which, for example, would demand that the stories told in the novel's first chapter be revealed only later, as Bone learns them), the narrator deliberately prefaces her narrative with what she knows of her mother's history before she marries Glen. The concentration of this story on Anney's sexual experience alerts the reader to the narrator's desire to establish and even to idealize a story of her mother's pleasure that is separate from her relationship with Glen Waddell.

We might expect that what Bone seeks in her mother's sexual past is information about her own biological father, but this expectation is immediately defeated. That we learn little more about Bone's own father, in this chapter and throughout, than that he was a "soft-talking black-eyed man" (4), emphasizes how narrowly the narrator's focus is on Anney. This is manifestly not a search for her own origins, but rather for "the story Mama would have told" (31). Bone may be able to imagine that Anney found pleasure in this first sexual relationship based on the risks she took for it, but she appears to prefer the story of Anney's marriage to Lyle Parsons. Lyle is the man who is able to shift Anney's focus from legitimating her first sexual experience and the child that resulted to a new relationship that Anney chooses unreservedly; Lyle inspires Anney to start "thinking more about marrying him than dragging down to the courthouse again" (5). Bone tells us that "Lyle was one of the sweetest boys the Parsonses ever produced, a soft-eyed, soft-spoken, too-pretty boy tired of being his mama's baby. Totally serious about providing well for his family and proving himself a man" (6). Unusually for Anney, she shares stories of her relationship with Lyle that focus on the sexual: "She [. . .] whispered to her sisters about the soft blond hairs on his belly, the way he slept with one leg thrown over her hip" (6). Anney takes pleasure in this man, who seems more like an angel when he dies in the bright sun with a smile on his face and "not a mark on him" (7), and his death emphasizes his connection to Anney, who was, like Lyle, thrown from a car and ended lying on the pavement with few evident wounds (2). Anney's love for Lyle is also demonstrated in that his death changes her; Ruth tells her, "You're as old as you're ever gonna get, girl" (8). Lyle's death marks an irrevocable change in Anney, and Bone feels free to imagine, much as Celie and Nettie are enabled to do, that after being widowed Anney never quite recovered, and all of her subsequent decisions were made in a state of limited capacity. The adult narrator works to overshadow the image of her mother as a woman who married Glen Waddell despite his shortcomings with an image of her mother as a woman who married Glen despite her great love for Lyle Parsons.

The power of the story of her mother's pleasure with Lyle is also evident in that Glen is clearly threatened by it. Bone's half-sister, Reese, who is Lyle's daughter, "kept his picture hidden in her underwear drawer where Daddy Glen wouldn't see it and get his feelings hurt" (59). When a $250 death benefit from Lyle's service in the army is at issue, Glen considers it a point of honor to deal aggressively with the Parsons family to get the money for Reese. He convinces himself that he is forcing from the Parsonses that which they in fact intend to give freely, and he nearly alienates these "stuck-up mountain people" altogether (56). Glen is clearly jealous of the memory of "the best-loved boy in the county" (56), who was "pretty as a girl and so white-blond he could have been a model in magazines" (59), and that he is cowed by the image of Lyle may be a reason Glen never abuses Reese. The memory of Lyle appears to protect Reese, and Bone envies her inheritance of his smile (56), a granny who actually looks like a granny (55), and "another side of herself to think about, something more than Mama and me and the Boatwrights" (59). Bone's retelling of the story includes indications that Lyle is not perfect: in a photograph Anney takes of him, he has "a grin so wide you could smell the beer" (7), but Bone, and, very likely, those who told her the story, idealize this experience of Anney's as a consolation for her life with Glen.

The function of this one chapter of omniscience is emphasized by the withholding of all that the narrator certainly knows in the final chapter of the novel. The adult narrator, who does not hesitate to make clear references to the future in chapter 1, as when she reports, "I *know* that the first time I ever saw Uncle Travis sober was when I was seventeen" (2), ends her narrative abruptly, with no further clues to her reader about the future, just before her thirteenth birthday. The final chapter leaves the reader with many pressing questions unanswered: Does Bone tell her story to the police, and is Glen arrested? Does Glen survive the Boatwright men's vengeance? Has Anney left alone or with Glen? Does she stay away, or are she and Bone reunited later? Bone gives no indications of the answers, leaving us with only what she knew on that day: "I knew nothing, understood nothing" (309). We may assume that knowing what happens next would intensify our harshest judgment of Anney, and Bone chooses to withhold the facts that would justify that judgment. Instead, she refers back to chapter 1; when she takes her last look at her mother's face, she remembers that "Aunt Ruth had told her after Lyle Parsons's funeral that she would look the same till she died," but observes that "now that face was made new" (305–6). Losing Bone has changed Anney as nothing has since the death of her beloved Lyle, and Bone recognizes the connection. The memory of Anney's pleasure in Lyle remains a significant part of Bone's vision of her mother through this final scene, and she is careful to keep it in the reader's mind as well.

Bone the adult narrator has had to earnestly seek what she knows of her mother's story, unnarratable even by a mother who is present. Indeed, Anney's absence even when present is a theme in the novel that reinforces her story's unnarratability. This central element of the surface plot is introduced in the novel's first sentences when Bone explains that Anney was, in a sense, absent even from her daughter's birth. Bone knows that she was named "for and by" her Aunt Ruth because Bone was born while Anney was unconscious following a car accident; as Bone explains, "Strictly speaking, she wasn't there" (1). In this way the motherlessness that has become familiar to the adult narrator is experienced by Bone even before Anney leaves altogether. This image of Anney as physically present but unable to speak recurs throughout Bone's narrative and maintains the focus on the unnarratability of the mother's story. The threat that the story of Anney's pleasure, uncontained by marriage, poses to patriarchy is not only theoretical but actual, and Anney knows it is taboo. Every smirk and knowing glance she encounters in the Greenville, South Carolina, courthouse, to which she returns annually in the early 1950s in an effort to procure for Bone an unmarked birth certificate, is evidence that, whereas the story of her transgression is widely known, the story of her pleasure is unnarratable.[10] The fierce sanctions on Anney's pleasure are far more than Anney could fight under the best of circumstances, and her status as "trash" (3) emphasizes her powerlessness. Anney's silence is partly attributable to her shame at being an unwed, teenaged mother, fulfilling all of the dominant society's expectations of her, and partly attributable to her pride in the face of others' scorn.

Although storytelling is a strong tradition in the Boatwright family, Anney is figured mostly in terms of what she will not say. As readers, we are likely to feel increasingly frustrated by Anney's silence, especially as it becomes increasingly painful for Bone. Anney avoids answering when Bone asks about her father, and Bone explains:

> It wasn't even that I was so insistent on knowing anything about my missing father. I wouldn't have minded a lie. I just wanted the story Mama would have told. What was the thing she wouldn't tell me, the first thing, the place where she had made herself different from all her brothers and sisters and shut her mouth on her life? (31)

Anney keeps that "first thing" to herself, and "shut her mouth on" stories of her own past; she has difficulty telling stories of herself to anyone, we learn.¹¹ Aunt Raylene is a forthcoming storyteller who tells her niece Deedee on the day of her mother's funeral, "Tonight or tomorrow, I'll talk to you about your mama" (237), and we can feel Deedee's relief that Raylene can do this for her. In contrast, after Anney leaves Bone violated and broken, Raylene takes her home and shelters her but tells her, "You want to know about your mama, I know. But I can't tell you anything. None of us can" (301). Her mother's real story remains a mystery, even in this close and garrulous family.

Anney's silence deepens after her marriage to Glen, at least partly as a result of his disapproval of the Boatwrights and their ways:

> She just got quiet, more and more quiet all the time. I begged her to tell me stories like Granny did, but she said I was too young to hear such things. Maybe when I was grown and had my own family she would tell me what few things she thought I needed to know, but until then she expected me to ask no questions she didn't want to answer. (110)

Not only is Anney unwilling to tell stories about herself, but speaking with Anney at all becomes nearly impossible for Bone when Anney leaves Glen after her family has seen the marks of his beating on Bone's body. Bone tells us, "Mama and I did not talk at all" (248) and "She clearly didn't want to talk" (249). "It was impossible to talk to her," Bone tells us (256). Anney's silence sets the example for Bone, and she will not testify to her abuse when asked to do so by the doctor (114), the sheriff (296), or even her Aunt Ruth (123). Bone keeps the truth especially from her mother:

> [Glen] would show me just how much he hurt when Mama left him in that parking lot, and then when he beat me, we would both know why. But Mama wouldn't know. More terrified of hurting her than of anything that might happen to me, I would work as hard as he did to make sure she never knew. (118)

At this point Bone tells us, "It was as if I was her mother now, holding her safe, and she was my child" (118). As Bone comes to feel she mothers Anney, Anney is increasingly absent as a mother to Bone. When Anney deserts Bone at the end of the novel, she does so in accordance with the difficult decision—to live away from Glen, even if that means living away from Anney—forced on her twelve-year-old daughter by her own silence and abdication of responsibility.

Although Bone is not technically motherless as a child, then, and the surface plot traces Bone's desperate attempt to maintain their relationship, Anney is essentially absent, and her absence sets the submerged plot in motion. Like other motherless daughters, Bone seeks validation in the story of her mother's pleasure even as she recounts the way that the child's nascent search for that story is nearly derailed altogether. In the absence of explanation, Bone seeks her mother's story by repeating her experience of growing up a Boatwright, and she is simultaneously forced to repeat it too exactly and too intimately by her mother's husband. From the beginning, repeating her mother's experience in the context of her extended family saves the search that could otherwise have been destroyed by repeating her mother's experience with Glen. The alternation between these two threads defines the progression of Bone's narrative.

In contrast to Celie and Ginny, who, as children, identify in their (step)fathers absolute authority, Bone experiences Glen's assertion of his power without recognizing him as an authority, and this helps to explain why, unlike Celie and Ginny, Bone's survival strategy is not acceptance or repression but aggression. Her aunts, uncles, and cousins are the models for Bone's aggressive behavior and also the force that undermines Glen's authority, which both Bone and Glen recognize very clearly. Like Lyle Parsons before him, Glen imagines that his ability to win and to satisfy a woman like Anney Boatwright will solidify his patriarchal rights, and Anney strives to maintain this illusion for him. However, in the context of the Boatwright clan, Glen retains the status of boy and outsider, and Bone's narrative focuses not only on the great damage he does but also on the ways that the family overpowers him.[12]

In the novel's opening chapters, which narrate the events leading up to Anney's marriage to Glen, Bone's experiences with the Boatwrights and Glen are mixed and interrelated. Especially prominent in the early chapters is Anney's favorite brother, Earle, whom Bone clearly imagines as preferable to Glen as a father and even as a husband to Anney. We are well able to understand the way Bone as a child romanticizes her mother's relationship to her brother in much the way she romanticizes

Anney's relationship to Lyle. We are likely to be more surprised by the degree to which the adult narrator maintains this view of him. Apparently deliberately, Earle introduces Anney to Glen by bringing him to lunch in the diner where she works. As Bone, omniscient in this first chapter, narrates this meeting, she stresses Glen's physical response to Anney, but she also implies that both Anney and Glen are as attracted to Earle as to each other. She tells us that "more than anything in the world, Glen Waddell wanted Earle Boatwright to like him" (12), and reports that Anney's voice is "buttery and sweet" when she asks her brother, "You coming over tonight, Earle?" (13). Earle seems to regret bringing the two together in the charged atmosphere for which he is largely responsible (he is described as "made for sex" [24]), and, later, in a rare moment of omniscience outside of chapter 1, Bone chooses to tell us that Earle tries to dissuade Anney from marrying Glen:

> "You sure, now, Anney?" Earle must have asked Mama twice before he drove her down to the courthouse in his pickup truck to meet Glen and get the license. It seemed he just couldn't take her ready smile for an answer [. . .]. He asked her one more time before he let her out of the truck. (40)

Earle recognizes his mistake in offering Glen as a substitute—for himself, for Lyle—and tries, ineffectually, to correct it.

Bone notices that Anney relies on Earle when Glen fails. When Glen loses his job, Anney reassures him, "We can get Earle's help to move, maybe stay with Alma" (64). Earle "insisted on loaning Mama a little money" (67), but "Daddy Glen got mad at Mama for taking the money" (68). Bone tells us,

> Before Mama had decided she was going to marry Daddy Glen, Uncle Earle was always around, but we saw less and less of him all the time. For a moment then, I wished we lived with him so Mama could take proper care of him and he could give us coins and make Mama laugh. (68)

Bone does not relinquish this vision of the relationship between her mother and her favorite uncle. When Uncle Earle has given Anney another gift and sits at her table eating her gravy and biscuits as on the day he introduced her to Glen, he says, "A man belongs to the woman that feeds him" (150), to which Alma objects: "It's the other way around and you know it. It's the woman belongs to the ones she feeds" (150). In Bone's view, just as Glen's relationship with Anney can only ever be a shadow of Anney's marriage to Lyle, so it is only a shadow of this primary tie between Anney and Earle. Readers are likely to be acutely aware of the blurring of family relationships in Bone's fantasy of Earle as Anney's husband, and Glen himself is responsible for this fantasy: he makes it necessary by creating an untenable situation and he models such blurring when he forces himself sexually on his stepdaughter.

Because Glen's first abuse of Bone occurs just hours before the stillbirth of Anney and Glen's son, Bone finds herself, in the aftermath of the traumatic experience of being molested, surrounded by her extended Boatwright family. Bone reports that "after Mama got home from the hospital, her sisters came around to see us every day" (48). They cook, clean, and sit talking to Anney, and the uncles come, too, and stand in the yard drinking. The aunts and uncles are unaware of what Bone has been through, but she observes what it is like for her mother to be a part of this family—how loved Anney is, and how her family congregates to take care of her in her time of need. She may realize already what her narrative bears out: that she, too, will be loved and cared for by this family. Glen resents the power of the Boatwrights to comfort his wife, so he moves Anney and the girls into a house "well away from the rest of the family" (51). From this point, rather than being interrelated, Bone's experience with her extended family alternates with her experience of the nuclear family, and, as the reader responds to this alternation, the submerged plot reveals itself.

This set of textual and readerly dynamics is exemplified immediately in a pair of scenes, the first in Glen and Anney's home and the second at Anney's sister's. Glen and Anney become angry with one another over dinner in the kitchen, and Glen displaces his anger onto Bone, bruising her arm. She reports that this kind of incident has become typical: "More and more those hands seemed to move before he could think. [. . .] I could not avoid them" (70). Anney excuses Glen for hurting Bone when she exclaims, "You don't know your own strength!" (70), but the kitchen has become the site of continual conflict because they can't afford enough food, and Anney does not excuse Glen for failing to find work while Bone and Reese eat soda crackers and ketchup for dinner. This scene is followed by another in which Bone and Reese stay with Alma and Wade while Anney takes on the task of providing food, apparently by, to some degree, prostituting herself. The girls feel at home in their aunt's house: "Reese was asleep in Aunt Alma's bed, but I was sitting up with Uncle Wade, nodding over the picture puzzle he worked at when he couldn't sleep" (76). Bone begins to notice the difference between the "unloved" tract houses Glen chooses for the family and the homes her aunts choose, places Glen "sneered" at (79), but which Bone finds "alive [. . .], warm, always humming with voices and laughter and children running around" (80). She explains, "There was something icy in Daddy Glen's houses that melted out of us when we were over at our aunts'" (80), and this contrast defines the novel's progression.

In the next pair of scenes, Bone's experience begins explicitly to repeat her mother's. Glen himself calls attention to this, watching Bone constantly, at one time opining ominously, "You don't look like your mama [. . .] except when you're asleep" (105), at another, even more ominously, "You're just like your mama" (108). Bone's narrative accelerates through the next year or two and arrives at the first time Glen beats her with a belt when she is ten years old (after which he does this regularly). Bone explains that as Glen's violence has escalated it has become consistently sexual as well: "It wasn't sex, not like a man and woman pushing their naked bodies into each other, but then, it was something like sex, something powerful and frightening that he wanted badly and I did not understand at all" (109). Because Glen compares Bone to Anney and forces himself on her sexually, Bone perceives her experience as a repetition of Anney's. However, whereas she knows very well that her mother takes pleasure in sex with Glen, including immediately after he beats Bone with his belt, Bone feels only "ashamed" and "afraid" (108).

The progression shifts from Bone's experience in her nuclear family to her experience in her extended family when, because of Glen's anger and violence, Anney sends Bone to stay for the summer with her sister Ruth, who is ill. Ruth is a mentor to Bone, as all of her mother's sisters are throughout her narrative from this point; they help Bone to develop and to stay connected to her mother. When Ruth tells Bone, "You know, when you close your eyes, you look just like your mama when she was a girl" (122), the frightening connotations of Glen's similar observation are gone, and Bone seems to take her busy, working mother's place as companion to Ruth, to do what her mother would if she could, and likely to repeat experiences her mother has had in the past. Anney tells Bone that Ruth was like a mother to her:

Truth is, she just about raised me. Daddy was gone by then, and Granny was always running after the boys or your aunt Alma, who was always getting herself in some trouble or other. Ruth was the one that was there for me, that I could talk to. (230)

Bone, too, is mothered by Ruth when her own parents are absent: Ruth is the one family member who asks the question, "Bone, has Daddy Glen ever . . . well . . . touched you?" (124), and Ruth is the one who realizes that Bone "an't never gonna be safe with him" (132). Bone does not fully confide in Ruth, but she spends a safe summer being mothered by her when her own nuclear family is in turmoil, just as Anney had before her.

This alternation in the progression occurs again immediately. Bone reports that, for a time after her summer at Ruth's, she is spared Glen's abuse. She tells us, "It had been a long time since he had caught me alone, and sometimes I could almost convince myself that he had never held me tight to his hips, never put his hands down inside my clothes" (142). Eventually, though, Glen's anger begins to build, and, as usual, he expresses it against Bone in assertions of his power laced with his sexual preoccupation with her: "He'd yell at me one day that I was getting too big to run around in a T-shirt with no bra, and the next accuse me of pretending to be grown-up" (176). This time, Anney sends Bone to her sister Raylene's house. Bone is disappointed that her mother hasn't suggested that Bone resume working with her at the diner: "I liked it down there. I liked listening to the waitresses tell jokes and watching the truckers flirt with Mama like she was still the prettiest woman in the county" (177). The progression of the surface plot hinges on Bone's desire to be with her mother; the progression of the submerged plot hinges on her goal of repeating her mother's experience, so much of which is work. Although denied the job at the diner, Bone's eagerness and ability to work are emphasized, and Aunt Raylene compliments her to her mother when she says, "Ah, Anney, Bone's the best you got, works like a dog, she does, just like you and me" (188). Raylene makes explicit the comparison between Bone and her mother, as well as between Bone and herself, and Bone tells us, "I loved her praise more than the money, loved being good at something, loved hearing Aunt Raylene tell Uncle Beau what a worker I was" (182). Her duties include picking, peeling, and canning vegetables, and we see her most often sitting in Raylene's kitchen watching the boiling pots, sometimes with both her aunt and her mother present. In this way, then, she repeats her mother's experience with a great deal of satisfaction.

Her stay at Aunt Raylene's is framed by her tumultuous friendship with Shannon Pearl, a memorable aberration from the progression that nevertheless is entirely contained in just the two chapters before and after that in which Bone narrates the events of her summer with Raylene. The episodes involving Shannon function to create a comparison between the two girls, but they also provide an image of another girl's family relationships. From the beginning, Bone is very aware of Shannon as part of a family: "I'd seen her with her family at the revival tent" (153). With the exception of Glen Waddell's family, in which all of the children are male, the Pearls are the only other family we see, and Bone can observe in Shannon another girl in her role as daughter. Bone experiments in her imagination with being a part of the Pearl family. She says of Shannon, "I felt a fierce and protective love, as if she were more my sister than Reese" (156). Further, she explains, "I was so careful with the Pearls, so quiet and restrained and politely attentive, I might have been a cousin of theirs. It was worth it to me to play at being one of them" (158). Bone observes that Shannon's mother is unable to see clearly her daughter's suffering. Mrs. Pearl insists that Shannon is a beautiful child; as a result, she cannot suspect the truth when she witnesses Bone shouting obscenities at a gospel singer who has just said to Shannon, "Child, you are the ugliest thing I have ever seen" (165). Mrs. Pearl cannot and does not imagine a man treating her child this way, assumes that Bone is to blame, and responds to him with a "half giggle," saying "I love it when you sing" (166). Bone reports that "Shannon pulled away from her and stared up at them both. The hate in her face was terrible" (166). Watching Shannon's loving mother fail her this way is like a mirror of Bone's own experience; however, though Bone clearly shares her desire for revenge against the hurtful man, she does not share Shannon's hatred of her mother. Bone is able to see Mrs. Pearl's love as Shannon no longer can, and her example reinforces her faith in her own mother's love.

Having seen Shannon in her nuclear family, we see her among her extended family in the only other chapter in which she appears. Bone, arriving late to the barbeque at the Pearls' home in honor of Shannon's "Daddy's people from Mississippi" (196), notices that "there were a lot of people there, and they all looked like Pearls" (199). She can see immediately, however, that, in contrast to the Boatwrights, this extended family is no comfort or protection for Shannon, who looks "as miserable as any human being could" and "looked like she had been crying" (199). Bone hears one of Shannon's cousins call her a "fat old thing" and a "hog" (199), and understands by contrast that her own extended family is a refuge for her. Shannon's horrific death is the catalyst for Bone's efforts to reinforce her connections to her family. Bone's observation of Mrs. Pearl at Shannon's funeral tells her what Shannon never knew, that her mother loved her completely, even though she was unable to save her. Mrs. Pearl begins to moan, "softly, tonelessly" (202), even as Bone, leaning against her own mother, hears Anney "[croon] under her breath her own song—muted, toneless, the same hum I'd been hearing all my life" (203). Suddenly, Bone reports, "All my hardheaded anger was gone" (203). Bone's anger will return, but she understands more now about what family can and cannot be, and she determines to return to her own. She has thought of Shannon, temporarily, as a replacement for Reese, and when she "tried to make up with Reese" (204), she finds that her sister has become inseparable from their cousin Patsy Ruth. While Bone has been gaining a new perspective on her family, Reese has needed none and has cemented her relations with the Boatwrights. Bone is well able to reconnect, however, and, inspired by a visit to Uncle Earle at the county farm, she and her cousin Grey become partners in crime when they break into and loot the Woolworth's. Committing this dangerous and illegal act as a protest against the conditions of her life, Bone once again feels fully integrated into her extended family.

In the final chapters, as in the first few, Bone's experiences in her nuclear and extended families become entangled. When Glen beats Bone until she is unconscious on the day before Ruth's funeral, she compares herself to her aunt: "The belt went up and came down. Fire along my thighs. Pain. Had Aunt Ruth felt pain like this? Had she screamed? I would not scream. I would not, would not, would not scream" (234). Anney wonders, "Is it because of Ruth? Is that why you started yelling at Glen?" (235), and, in a sense, Anney is correct. As before, Bone finds strength in her connection to her Boatwright family, and, as is usual for him, Glen is threatened by this connection: "You think 'cause your aunt died you can mouth off to me?" (233–34). He is right to feel threatened: when Raylene discovers the cuts Glen has made all over Bone's thighs, she charges her brothers to avenge Bone: "I'd kill him" (245).

The Boatwright men do beat Glen, and he spends a night in the hospital, during which time Anney and the girls move out.

Bone does not appear to relish this revenge, but her need for her extended family remains so strong as Glen's violence escalates that, even as she complains bitterly to Raylene about being born a "piece of trash" (258), she idealizes Earle as she always has, as she has always idealized Lyle Parsons. He arrives at Ruth's funeral with a new, young girlfriend, and Raylene criticizes his treatment of women. Bone, furious, defends him: "He loves them more than they deserve" (258). Raylene accuses Bone of being "seriously confused about love" (258), but Bone needs Earle in ways that Raylene may not recognize. Although Anney, too, has criticized Earle for being a "cradle robber" (257), Bone's narrative presents them once again as a kind of couple when the two of them respond to Alma's breakdown. Bone is a witness as her mother and Earle come together to stop Alma's destructive rampage, to nurse Alma and comfort her frightened children. Earle is important to Bone's survival, and Alma is as well. Bone watches Anney and Alma together, and notices that "they seemed more alike than ever" (269). This resemblance is significant in that, soon after, Anney tells Bone, "I never realized before how much you look like Alma. [. . .] You're gonna be as pretty as Alma was when she was a girl, prettier than you can imagine" (274). Perhaps foreseeing that she and Bone will be parted, Anney is, as she has throughout Bone's life, ensuring that her child will be tied closely to the Boatwrights, that she will share her mother's experience if not her mother's life. That Anney has always worked to ensure this connection is evident in the ways this emphasis on resemblance echoes that in chapter 2, when Bone notices how much her mother and Alma are alike, and when both women notice the similarities between themselves and Bone. Anney entrusts her daughter to her sisters, knowing they will advise Bone as she would have herself, and knowing they will be a connection between her and Bone even when they are separated.

That Bone is again sent out of her nuclear family and into her extended family to nurse Alma through her recovery in her mother's place seems a hopeful sign that Bone will continue to repeat her mother's experience of growing up among her mother's sisters, as she has with Ruth and Raylene. However, Glen does not allow this, and the peace Bone feels at Alma's lasts only a short time before Glen arrives to force Bone to repeat Anney's experience of sex with him by raping her. Explicitly, Glen is punishing Bone for coming between him and Anney; implicitly, he feels driven to assert his authority in Alma's home, while Wade is absent and Alma is weakened by the loss of her child (whose name, Annie, asserts the family's hold on Anney). Having been beaten severely by the Boatwright men, Glen retaliates viciously against Bone and tries to force her out of the refuge of her extended family and back into the nuclear family he has made with Anney: "You're gonna have to tell her you want us all to be together again" (281). When she refuses, he rapes her. Glen's attempt to undermine Bone's connection to her family as refuge fails; her first words to her mother are, "Ruth's, Mama [. . .] Take me to Ruth's" (288). She imagines using her Uncle Travis's shotgun, which she knows is in Ruth's closet, to kill Glen. Instead, Bone is taken (via the hospital) to Raylene's, where Earle is also staying. Her picture from the newspaper appears (to her chagrin) in Alma's scrapbook, along with clippings featuring her Uncle Earle and "Granny, my mama, uncles, aunts, cousins" (293). Bone maintains her connection to her mother's family.

Although Glen has succeeded in separating Bone from Anney, Bone has managed to find in her extended family and in her mother's experience before her marriage to Glen a story of her mother's pleasure that can validate her own. We can imagine that the story of Raylene's pleasure, which she finds with a woman, is important for Bone and enables her sexuality to develop in healthy ways; however, Allison ends Bone's narrative here and thereby maintains the focus on the connection between sexual pleasure and the mother's story. Bone's narrative is evidence of the ways she has fought to find this story against terrible obstacles and succeeded. Anney has left her daughter, but she has also left her the Boatwrights, and among them Bone will continue to know her mother better by repeating her experiences. Despite all, Bone tells us, "I was who I was going to be, someone like her [Raylene], like Mama, a Boatwright woman" (309). Despite the many unresolved questions at the narrative's end, the surface and submerged plots work together to create completion.

All three of these seeking daughters survive the trauma visited upon them by the men their mothers have chosen, and, although their mothers are in some ways complicit in the abuse, their daughters do not reject or disown them. Each daughter keeps searching until she finds a story from her mother's past that she can live with, as Celie does, even if she must idealize it, as Bone does, and even if it offers no revelation of pleasure at all, as in the story Ginny seeks. These stories are necessary to protect the protagonist's relationship with her mother and her pursuit of her own pleasure. Even as they seek, each narrator works in her own way to manage the reader's judgment of her mother and insist on her own vision of their relationship.

The surface plots of these three novels amplify and intensify to a horrific degree the ways that cultural norms consistently seek to render the mother's pleasure inaccessible to the daughter. Alphonso, Larry Cook, and Glen Waddell stand between the mothers and daughters in these novels in more than one way, and they are supported by their communities as they do it. In utter defiance of the surface plot that threatens to stymie the daughter's search and destroy her connection to her mother altogether, the submerged plot of the daughter's engagement with the unnarratable story of the mother's pleasure progresses steadily and contributes to the completion of each of these novels. The submerged plots enrich our understanding of the three tenacious protagonists who retain, despite all, their faith in their maternal birthright, and whose narratives insist on the importance of their mothers' stories. The submerged plots also emphasize the roles of mentors, especially sisters and aunts in these novels, in maintaining the daughter's threatened connection to her mother.

Interpretive questions raised by the horizontal axis in each novel that are difficult to answer with reference to its interaction with the vertical axis are more fully addressed with reference to the second horizontal axis. The second horizontal axis in these novels progresses differently from those in the earlier works. The daughter protagonist's repetition of her mother's experience has been co-opted by the surface plot, and the submerged plot traces the daughter's pursuit of, and in some cases creation of, a manageable, alternative story of her mother's pleasure. We are unlikely to be surprised that the searches of these daughter protagonists take a different form from the others; what is startling is that these protagonists are willing to undertake the search at all. These novels demonstrate that the mother's pleasure remains the daughter's object even when it poses a threat to the search; the novels considered in the next chapter reveal that the search can also be threatened, though, again, not destroyed, by the end of the mother's pleasure.

CHAPTER 5

The End of Pleasure and the Function of Time in the Submerged Plot

Talking to the Dead
and *The God of Small Things*

The submerged plot as a strategy for rendering the unnarratable is still in circulation, not only in the American novels addressed in chapter 4, but also in the English novel *Talking to the Dead*, by Helen Dunmore (1996), and the Indian novel *The God of Small Things*, by Arundhati Roy (1997). The unnarratability of the mother's story and its necessity remain central even in these late-twentieth-century novels, and the consequences of this for the progression are just as pronounced as in the nineteenth- and early-twentieth-century novels. Indeed, in Dunmore's and Roy's novels the very legibility of elements of the surface plot's progression and its availability for interpretation depend heavily on the submerged plot of the daughter's search for her mother's story. Sensitivity to the novels' submerged plots reveals additional elements of the progression of the surface plots and offers a fuller understanding of the grounds on which completeness in the novels is based.

These novels, like those of Walker, Smiley, and Allison, introduce another kind of threat to the search for the mother's pleasure. The previous chapters have argued that, most often, if the seeking daughter can find a manageable story of her mother's pleasure, that story, despite almost anything, can validate the daughter's own pleasure. However, in *Talking to the Dead* and *The God of Small Things*, the search is beset by another kind of difficulty altogether: in both, the daughter's certain knowledge of the end of her mother's pleasure stands between her and the pleasure itself. The end of pleasure is figured in less dramatic ways in many of the novels treated here; indeed, we might assume that novels in which the daughter is the product of an illicit union would fall into this category—that the daughter in such novels might feel that her own birth disrupted her mother's pleasure. However, the evidence of *Bleak House, The Woman in White, Bastard Out of Carolina*, and others suggests that this kind of inherited guilt is not a strong influence on the daughter's search: the illegitimate child in these novels tends to be a sign of pleasure rather than of its destruction. *Talking to the Dead* and *The God of Small Things* are centered on more sudden and undeniably devastating circumstances in which the daughters, at least in their own minds, play an active, not a passive, role. In Dunmore's novel, the traumatic event is the death of the mother's youngest child, an infant conceived in the mother's final moment of sexual pleasure; in Roy's novel, it is the brutal murder of the lover who has given the mother her life's first pleasure. In both cases, the daughter who feels responsible was a small child when the event occurred, and, in each, the action covers a short period approximately twenty-five years after the event, during which the now-adult daughter attempts to untangle and confront the facts of her own involvement in her mother's story.

Therefore, both novels are characterized by the markedly dual structure of the surface plot: the narrative of the present alternates throughout with a narrative of past events. In both, the narrative of the past circles back repeatedly to a critical moment, revealing more information each time until, by the novel's end, the reader feels that the story of the past has been completely uncovered. What is puzzling in both novels is the narratives of the present, which, by contrast, appear elliptical and unresolved. However complex the narratives of the past, readers can agree on a set of possible interpretations that arise clearly from the events reported, and the novels' completion appears to rest primarily on the resolution of these narratives. The narratives of the present, in contrast, appear to resist interpretation. In each novel, although the movement toward uncovering past events is steady and clearly identifiable, the progression forward is baffling.

Reconfiguring the progression of each of these two novels with particular attention to the representation of time both alerts us to the submerged plot and also reveals the ways that time in the surface plot supports the function of the submerged plot. Both novels defy chronology by beginning with the present but focusing intensely on the past. Having established the narrative of the present, both assiduously deemphasize it. In Dunmore's novel, this is accomplished by the character narrator's masking of both the time of her narrating and also the relation between time and event in her narration. In Roy's novel, the deemphasis is effected by reversals that privilege the past: the mother's and daughter's stories are reversed so that the daughter's, rather than the mother's, appears to have ended while the mother's goes on. The final scenes are reversed from what we would expect if the narrative of the present were allowed to truly frame the novel, thus contributing to the sense that the mother's story, rather than the daughter's, continues beyond the ending. These unusual narrative techniques serve to mark the surfacings of the submerged plots, and the submerged plots, in turn, offer another context in which to reinterpret the overshadowed narratives of the present.

The submerged plots trace the belated searches of the protagonists for their mothers' stories, despite the fact that Dunmore's Nina appears at first to have no need for validation of her pleasure and that Roy's Rahel appears to refuse adamantly to search. Even in these contemporary novels, in which we would assume very little would be considered taboo and which in fact treat infanticide and incest, among other social problems, the unnarratability of the mother's pleasure remains central. The daughters' searches for this unnarratable story are documented in the submerged plots, as they are in novels from Austen to Allison. At the same time, the roles of other characters in the daughters' searches vary the patterns identified in the previous novels. In *Talking to the Dead*, the daughter's mentor is an older sister whom the protagonist has always perceived as a second mother, and the confusion of these roles has considerable implications for the daughter's search. In *The God of Small Things*, the protagonist's brother functions as a kind of mentor but also as a suitor like the man her mother chose, and this even greater confusion complicates the search in other ways. In both, as in Austen's *Persuasion*, the siblings are also seeking the mother's story; in contrast to *Persuasion*, however, for good or for ill, these siblings' searches are inextricably interdependent. Finally, *The God of Small Things* introduces what seems to have been impossible in the earlier texts: a son seeking the story of his mother's pleasure.

"It was very important to her to be accurate about things like that": Mrs. Close

Helen Dunmore's *Talking to the Dead* is the story of eleven days during which Nina Close, a London-based photographer, makes an unplanned visit to Sussex, where her much-admired, much-loved older sister has just been through the difficult birth of her first child and an emergency hysterectomy. For both Nina and her sister, Isabel, Antony's birth recalls the birth of their brother, Colin, when they were four and seven years old; Colin died in infancy, apparently of SIDS. During her visit, Nina becomes increasingly preoccupied with this twenty-five-year-old tragedy and its effects on their family. In the course of the narrative she recovers repressed memories of the actual circumstances of Colin's death, which implicate both herself and Isabel. Nina's narrative documents her attempt to establish the truth about Colin's death, trying to reconcile her own memories, as they surface in fragments, with Isabel's version of events. We are given to understand that Colin's death is also very much on Isabel's mind, dangerously so, and her memories of it, intensified by Antony's birth and combined with postpartum depression and emotional instability of longer standing, cause her breakdown and suicide.[1]

The progression, then, tends strongly toward a recovery of the past, and the narrative seems, eventually, to answer all of the reader's questions about that past. The novel's completion may appear to rest entirely on these answered questions, especially because the progression's trajectory forward is more puzzling. Our questions about the narrative of the present are left largely unanswered: What is it exactly that finally compels Isabel to suicide? Is Nina implicated in Isabel's death? Why does Nina tell this story, and to whom? What does Dunmore offer her readers in the brief prologue, and why is it positioned as such rather than as an epilogue? Why does the prologue reveal so little of Nina's life since Isabel's death, and what has her life become? In this past-oriented narrative, the significance of certain events in the present appears murky, perhaps especially the sudden and surprising beginning of an intense affair between Nina and Isabel's husband, Richard. The significance of this affair for the novel's progression and for the characterization of Nina is difficult to assess, and it raises questions about Nina as narrator as well. Like Walker, Smiley, and Allison, Dunmore is drawn to a particular kind of character narration to effect the disclosure of her dual surface plot as well as the submerged plot. Whereas we consistently believe that Celie, Ginny, and Bone are reliable reporters of events as they experience them, even when we know more or judge differently than they do, Nina's reliability is presented as questionable on all three levels.[2] In a novel of competing versions of the truth, Nina's voice dominates, and our interpretation of the novel depends on our determination of how reliable her knowledge, judgments, and telling are.

These interpretive puzzles become easier to solve if we recognize the novel's submerged plot, that of Isabel's and Nina's searches for the unnarratable story of their mother's pleasure, and its impact on the surface plot. Tracing the progression of the surface and submerged plots of this brief, sultry, suspenseful novel, with particular attention to the ways that the representation of time influences both textual and readerly dynamics, offers solid ground on which to make difficult interpretive judgments. The eleven days between Nina's arrival and Isabel's suicide constitute the present in the novel and are narrated by Nina in the present tense. Events in the present precipitate Nina's recovery of childhood memories, and her narration of these in the past tense, a total of about 40 pages scattered throughout this 300-page novel, constitutes a narrative of the past.[3] The complex surface plot comprises these two narratives; however, even the complexities of the interaction between the narratives of the present and past cannot account fully for either Isabel's or Nina's actions: recognizing the progression of the submerged plot allows us further insight into their motivations. For both sisters, their mother's pleasure is inaccessible; it lies behind the overwhelming presence of the death of Colin, which the sisters apprehend as the end of their mother's happiness and pleasure. In all of the novels treated here, the mother's suffering is evident to the daughter—hence the need for the validation of pleasure. The difference in this novel is that both daughters feel personally implicated in their mother's suffering. Indeed, they feel they have caused the end of their mother's pleasure; thus, even more than other fictional daughters, Nina and Isabel cannot help focusing on that end to the exclusion of the pleasure itself. This exclusion threatens both of their searches, and proves insurmountable for Isabel, who consistently eschews the pleasure of sex and even of food, and who finally rejects life altogether.

The progress of Nina's search is more difficult to determine because her narration obscures the extent to which she acts as opposed to being acted upon. As readers, we are very aware that characterization is in her hands. She presents herself as the younger, more awkward, less confident sister of the beautiful, entirely self-sufficient Isabel. She presents Isabel as possessing qualities and a life that Nina could never hope to achieve. At the same time, in the course of the few days during which Isabel becomes increasingly unstable and finally commits suicide, Nina seems to repeat Isabel's experience—not with variation, but exactly. She becomes the person who cares for Isabel's beloved garden, she becomes the lover of Isabel's desirable husband, and, ultimately, she becomes the caregiver for Isabel's baby son. What this course of events means and how readers are meant to feel about it seem to vary throughout the novel among at least three irreconcilable interpretations that arise from instabilities in both the mimetic and thematic components of the characterization of both sisters and tensions created as we seek to determine how reliable Nina's narration is. At some points in the narrative, we may suspect that Nina, stronger and more manipulative than she admits, is robbing Isabel of her own experience as Isabel lies in bed ill. At other points we may think of Isabel as more fully in control, as when some details in the text imply that Isabel is consciously relinquishing her experience, which has exhausted her capabilities, to Nina. At still other points, Isabel seems to be so controlling as to be destructive: we may feel we are watching as Isabel, resigning her experience entirely and moving toward suicide, beckons Nina, who, as the younger sister, is habituated to following her, to share the final experience of death. This third possibility would suggest that Nina's actions throughout the novel can be read as her resistance to Isabel's resignation, her affirmation of life to fend off the seduction of Isabel's invitation to death.

The ambiguities of Nina's character—is she manipulating Isabel or being manipulated by her?—are mirrored in the ambiguities of her narration. Nina's present-tense, or simultaneous, narration, implies that she has disowned the power that comes with retrospective narration: the power to reflect on experience and shape an authoritative narrative based on one's own goals and purposes.[4] However, although it poses as present-tense narration, the narrative of *Talking to the Dead* appears upon closer inspection to be what Per Krogh Hansen calls "covered past tense," otherwise known as the historical present (319). In such cases, the narration's pretense of simultaneity is breached in those moments when we realize that the story "is told with the knowledge gained by temporal distance" (319). Few moments of this kind appear, but they are certainly deliberate—Nina refers to herself as "a meticulous noter of tenses" (93)—and they tell us that Nina's narration is fully in her control, and that that control is consciously masked throughout. The most obvious indicator that Nina's present-tense narration is a mask is the prologue, which tells of Isabel's funeral and describes her grave, months, at least, after the end of the story. Because of the prologue, we know that the story will end with Isabel's death, though Nina's narration throughout makes it possible for us to forget that she, too, knows the end. Having read in the prologue, which is narrated in the present tense, that Isabel is dead, we begin the first chapter, in which Isabel is still alive, encountering a present tense that we can already identify as earlier than that of the prologue. We are not asked to question the temporal order of the events, which remains definite; therefore, we are especially likely to question the temporal representation of the narration.

The next overt slipping of the mask of simultaneous narration is an observation of Nina's early on that indicates her knowledge of the future. Nina works to explain her relationship with Isabel: "Isabel and I were in the habit of exaggerating our own lives, and each other's. [. . .] All this began as a game we played, the kind of game sisters play when they need to find out how different they are. But it turned into a game that played us" (26). This reference is indefinite—when did the game start to play the sisters?—but could refer to the events Nina will soon narrate, which reveals her knowledge of what is represented as the future. The final slipping of the mask is also indefinite. Fully the final third of the novel, over 100 pages and ten chapters, narrates the day of Isabel's death, so when Nina tells us, "What began then, in the back room of the café, is still going on" (245), she could simply mean as the seemingly endless day progresses, but it seems to be a comment on the persistence of these events beyond the frame of the story. The latter possibility is supported by Nina quoting from Isabel's diary twelve pages before she narrates finding it (278, 290). These details suggest the possibility that what appears to be simultaneous narration of this disastrous day is actually being narrated in retrospect. If this is the case, then not only is Nina in greater control of her narrative than she appears to be, but also she deliberately obscures that control for her own ends, which we can only imagine.

At some points, we may be tempted to interpret Nina's narrative as deliberately misleading the reader about her own intentions and motives. Ultimately, however, we are likely to conclude that Nina's narration is designed to both confess to the role her own actions played in her sister's death and also remind the reader that she acted with no knowledge of the future and did not intend the consequences that ensued. In the aftermath of her sister's suicide, Nina must acknowledge that her own actions contributed to it, just as she has had to face her child self's role in her baby brother's death. She takes responsibility for this, and she uses the prologue to admit that she tells her story in full knowledge of its end. At the same time, in order not to be judged prematurely by her reader, Nina needs to recreate for us the experience she had of acting in response to the situations in which she found herself without knowing the outcome. If her motives are not altogether admirable, neither are they altogether blameworthy. Nevertheless, the narrative risks Nina takes in order to protect herself raise questions about her reliability.

These issues can be resolved with a greater degree of confidence if we reconsider the progression of the surface plot with reference to the submerged plot. Doing so reveals a great deal about Nina's and Isabel's relationships to each other and to their mother and explains the sympathy we are likely to feel for both of them that their own actions in the surface plot do not warrant, increasing our faith in Nina's narration. Andrea Adolph, in her work on *Talking to the Dead*, also finds that Nina is ultimately more reliable than we expect; for Adolph, this reliability is a result of her "embodiment," which is so much fuller than Isabel's: "What ultimately allows for Nina's narration to emerge as more believable than her transgressions might allow, however, is the very fact of her body, regardless of the ambivalent status of that body as it relates to her sexual expression" (372–73). Heightened attention to the novel's progression affirms Adolph's findings and suggests a way of accounting for the fact that Nina's reliability survives her "sexual expression." Indeed, reconfiguring the progression not only reveals the workings of the submerged plot but also clarifies significant elements of the surface plot that can be underread.

With relatively few explicit time markers throughout, Nina's apparently present-tense narration serves to obscure what is, upon examination, a very specific and surprising relation between time and event in the novel. The first-time reader is likely to come away from the novel with a vision of Nina somewhat gradually, over the course of a week or two, recovering repressed memories of childhood and pursuing a sexual relationship with her brother-in-law, Richard. In fact, nearly the first third of the novel (nine chapters of thirty) cover eight days, most of Nina's stay, during which neither of these things happens. What we imagine happens during these eight days is that Nina spends time with her recovering sister, her purpose in coming to Sussex. We learn toward the narrative's end that Nina has spent a great deal of this time drawing Antony—in the garden, in the bath, asleep (221). What Nina mainly narrates is her interactions with Richard; in fact, her narration skips those periods within the first eight days of her stay when Richard is traveling for work. In this instance, our determination about the nature of Nina's present-tense narration has strong implications for our interpretation of her character. If Nina's narration is truly to be considered simultaneous, then this focus suggests that Nina's real purpose in coming to Sussex is to seduce Richard—her focus is on him from the novel's first chapter. However, the centrality of Richard in Nina's account of these days can also be seen as further evidence that the present-tense narration is a mask, and that, in light of after-events, these moments with Richard have taken on great significance for Nina and dominate her memory of that time.

When, in chapter 10, Nina and Richard have sex for the first time, the reader is meant to be shocked, and, especially given that the sex immediately follows Nina and Richard's mutual acknowledgement that Isabel's depression is advancing so that she is unable even to leave the house, we are likely to blame Nina for this apparently unmotivated betrayal. At the same time, in the preceding chapters, we do find evidence that Isabel is stepping aside and beckoning Nina to inhabit her life. Isabel tells Nina of Antony, "You know, *you* could feed him, Neen [. . .]. Did you know that? Women who've never had babies can breast-feed if they keep on letting the baby suck" (53). Nina negates this, "'He's not my baby,' I say" (53). Isabel continues, though, when she asks Nina, "Does Richard talk to you?" (54). Nina answers that he does not and never has, and Isabel replies, "Maybe he will, while you're here. After all, you're my sister. If he can't talk to you, who can he talk to? It'd do him good" (54).

If this contains an implication that Isabel is giving Nina permission to become intimate with Richard, so does her suggestion to Richard, in the presence of Nina and others, that he not sleep with her in their bed but rather stay on the sofa (76). Nina's affair with Richard appears selfish, but the evidence suggests that Isabel, if she does not orchestrate it to some extent, at least condones it.

This first phase of the novel culminates in a lovely dinner Nina cooks for herself, Richard and Isabel, and two guests. The dinner enacts the same tensions with reference to Isabel's and Nina's motives as does Nina and Richard's affair and serves as an illustration of the three competing interpretive possibilities regarding the novel's progression. Whereas Nina takes pleasure in good food, is an excellent cook, and brings people together for cooking and eating in the course of the novel, Isabel eats very little and is incapable of eating at a table with other people. These traits go far to define the mimetic component of each character, but their thematic functions are less stable. These characterizations may be usefully analyzed as independent of one another,[5] but the stark contrast creates the suspicion of a causal relationship between Nina's indulgence and Isabel's abstinence, the sense that there is only so much food and only so much enjoyment to go around, and either Nina is taking it from Isabel, or Isabel is leaving it for Nina, or Nina is using it to protect herself from Isabel. When Nina arrives at Isabel's home to help during her recovery, that she helps by cooking healthy, delicious food appears natural and commendable, a desire to nurture her sister's ailing body in a way that Isabel will not do for herself. As we learn more about both sisters, however, we may regard Nina's actions in another light: she has entered Isabel's home at a time when her body has been battered by giving birth and undergoing major surgery. Knowing this, and knowing that Isabel eats almost nothing and never eats in company at the best of times, Nina creates a bounteous, rich meal for five people. Especially because Nina is forthcoming about her own less admirable qualities, we may suspect her of more insidious motives, of taunting her apparently anorectic sister with her own and others' enjoyment of food and isolating Isabel from those closest to her. As we come to know Isabel better, however, and recognize that her frail body belies her steely will, a third possibility seems equally possible—that Isabel, who is soon to commit suicide, is, at some level, already willing herself to death, and that Nina is a victim of a kind of advance survivor guilt. Beginning in childhood but especially recently, Isabel has steadily withdrawn further and further from the life-affirming activities of eating, having sex, gardening—the birth of Antony appears, in this light, to be a final, and unsuccessful, effort to hold onto creativity and vitality. We can imagine that, witnessing this withdrawal in her sister, Nina has had to fight her own urge, present in her from her earliest memories, to follow Isabel. Given this reading, we might understand Nina's feast as self-defense, as a tremendous effort not to succumb to the guilt she feels as Isabel approaches death and nothing Nina does can save her. Food is one of the novel's most pronounced motifs, but these conflicting and seemingly irreconcilable possibilities exist in nearly all of the elements of Isabel and Nina's relationship. Reference to the submerged plot of Nina's search enables us to arrive at an interpretation that helps to account for some of these complexities.

Even as the surface plot is occupied with these issues, the novel's initial chapters also launch the submerged plot as they establish the ambivalence of each sister's relationship to the experience of their mother. The first reference to Mrs. Close, who is never referred to by name, is when Isabel shouts to Nina from her bedroom, and Nina remembers, "Our mother wouldn't let us shout from room to room" (23). Nina presents Isabel as consciously distinguishing herself from their mother. Isabel has followed Mrs. Close into motherhood, in circumstances that, we later learn, are surprisingly similar to those under which her mother had Colin, but Richard tells Nina, "Before she had the baby, she said all she'd have to do was think of what your mother did with you two, and then do the opposite" (36). Nina has refused motherhood altogether, and, although she feels at home in Isabel's house because Isabel models her housekeeping on their mother's, Nina tells the reader, "I've made myself stop doing this, but Isabel goes on" (67). At the same time, Nina is explicit in reporting that she has repeated her mother's experience in her work. Her first recollection of Mrs. Close not allowing them to shout in the house is tied to her vision of her mother as artist:

> If we wanted to speak to our mother, we could go in and speak to her. We rarely did. The door of her studio was shut, and behind it she was working. If we went in she would glance up, her slippery hands controlling the live clay by touch, and most of the things we were going to say would seem not worth saying. (23–24)

For Isabel, this fact about Mrs. Close is evidence of neglectful parenting; for Nina, it means that her mother's work was important, to herself and others. She recalls, "My mother was the first person who taught me to draw" (34), and not only to draw but to really look and gain perspective. Richard, watching Nina draw, observes, "I've never seen it before, but you do look like your mother, don't you? There's a photo of her working that looks like you did just then" (36). He makes the connection, and Nina confirms it: when Richard implies that Nina might be mishandling her own photography business financially, she insists that she is not and rejoins, "Artists don't have to be stupid. My mother wasn't. She was very good with money" (49). Consciously, then, both sisters have repeated their mother's experience in some ways and in other ways rejected it.

In the course of the action, each repeats her mother's experience in other ways; true to form, Nina seeks her experience of pleasure, while Isabel appears to be limited to repeating her mother's experience of the end of pleasure. The reader's perceptions of their actions are influenced by the narrative's representation of time. The next phase of the progression does begin with an explicit time marker: Nina reminds Richard, "I've only been here eight days" (90). What the reader does not realize yet, however, is that the rest of the novel will take place over just three days, and that the narration of the ninth will be extensive. The ninth day of Nina's visit is covered by nearly the same amount of text as her entire stay to that point—eight chapters, and nearly the same number of pages. The reader must exert a good deal of attention to recognize clearly that the many events narrated in this part of the novel occur on a single day. In the course of it, Isabel's mental and physical decline accelerates noticeably, Nina begins a passionate sexual affair with her hitherto rather distant brother-in-law, and Nina begins to question, apparently for the first time in her life, whether her baby brother's death was actually attributable to natural causes. In this phase of the progression, the submerged plot acts most strongly on the surface plot as we witness Nina's own search for pleasure become closely linked to her search for the story of her mother's pleasure and the truth about its end. What is unnarratable becomes evident, and the desire to learn the unnarratable story becomes as strong for Nina as all of her motives in the surface plot.

In the course of the ninth day, Nina recovers three sets of memories about the circumstances of Colin's birth and death, and each recovery is preceded by a sexual encounter with Richard. They first have sex on the morning of this day, and, involved as we are in the ethical problems this raises, what is likely to surprise the reader as much as the encounter itself is the tone in which Nina conducts it and relates it, which is nearly affectless even as it is quite detailed. They suddenly kiss, and Nina invites more in this way: "'I'm not talking about love,' I say, and look him full in the face. 'But we can have a good fuck and none the wiser'" (94). Her description of sex with Richard begins this way: "I have short hair, so it doesn't get in my way, hanging down and trailing on the ground. The position is awkward and the bench would be rough if I hadn't spread Richard's white shirt carefully over it, and used his jeans to make a pillow under my stomach" (96). A number of interpretations of Nina's tone are possible, but a reader alert to the submerged plot may connect it to something she tells us about her mother later in the day. Nina remembers learning the story of Colin's conception from her mother, which occurred after her father already had a mistress in London:

> Colin was a fluke, not an attempt at reconciliation. I found out later that my parents hadn't slept together for two years before he was born. But my father was down from London for a few days and they sat for a long time over a meal after we went to bed, drinking rich red wine that my father had brought back from France. And so they stumbled into bed, and later there was Colin. No, not stumbled. They weren't that drunk, my mother said. They still knew what they were doing. It was very important to her to be accurate about things like that, and not to give us false ideas about what had happened between them. I suppose it was a good thing, but it could feel a bit bleak. (129)

The bleak accuracy Nina remembers from her mother's account characterizes her own; she repeats her mother's experience in this way perhaps more than she realizes. We may question whether Nina, who explains in no uncertain terms that she is sexually active and sexually satisfied, needs validation for her pleasure, but her account of the sex between herself and Richard affirms that she does. She mimics her mother's style of narration, and both narratives focus on physical facts (sexual positions, degrees of intoxication) and exclude emotions. This may be a sign that Nina does not give herself completely even to pleasurable experiences, that she maintains a certain distance from them, as she may believe her mother did.

Nina's experience of sex, then, which may at first seem to be evidence that she has no need to seek, appears, in fact, to be part of her search. This is confirmed by the more obvious element of repetition in this scene: Nina repeats Isabel's experience, not with variation, as she repeats her mother's, but by having sex with Isabel's husband. This repetition is in the surface plot rather than in the submerged, but the motivations for it originate in both plots. On the surface, Nina either covets what is her sister's, or she accepts her sister's invitation to fill the space she is vacating, or she has sex with Richard as a kind of resistance against Isabel's denial of pleasure. In the submerged plot, in order to validate her own pleasure, Nina needs to know why Isabel denies her own.

Her repetition of Isabel's experience is a way of learning Isabel's story, which, despite their lifelong intimacy, has always been inaccessible to Nina, as both plots affirm. Isabel's function as a mentor to Nina as she pursues her mother's story is complicated by Isabel's function as a second mother. This day ends with Nina telling the reader, "I always knew that Isabel loved me even more than my mother did, because she told me so" (148). She goes on to say, "What life I possess, I possess because Isabel's given it to me. Isabel is my mother" (151). Nina is mistaken about this last, but these passages suggest that Isabel's story has been, like their mother's, an object of Nina's search. As an object of the search, though, Isabel is nearly as elusive as an absent mother. Just as Nina's actions can always be attributed to seemingly mutually exclusive motives in the surface plot, Isabel's can as well. Possibly, Isabel filled in for Mrs. Close, who was, by Nina's account, not a strongly attentive mother. However, some evidence suggests that Isabel stood between Nina and their mother. Throughout the course of this eventful day, Nina tries to work through this instability. In trying to identify clearly the object of her search, Nina is brought face to face with the event to which all of the confusion and contradictions of that search are attributable: Colin's death.

Immediately after this first sexual encounter, Nina finds herself focused on childhood memories, and these memories bear on the mystery of Colin's death in the surface plot and also on the problem of Nina's search in the submerged plot. She recalls several events from her childhood, especially one in which Isabel christens her own doll in a bowl of water, and then, while christening Nina's doll, enacts drowning her. As Nina screams uncontrollably, Mrs. Close comes running and enacts reviving Nina's doll. With reference to the surface plot, this story is meant to cause the reader to wonder how far the child Isabel was willing to go to assert her will. She easily appropriates, in the context of their play, the power of the priest as well as the power of their parents. Nina remembers in this passage that Isabel once took Nina to Sunday school, and that she explained their presence there by lying and saying their parents meant to keep them from church. When she declares Sunday school "a load of shit" (99), she also, at least in Nina's world, appropriates the power of God. Nina connects the "drowning" of the doll explicitly to her brother's death by explaining that it happened shortly afterward, and this is the first shift in our understanding of the circumstances of Colin's death. With reference to the submerged plot, this scene pits Isabel against their mother in small ways; Isabel lies about their mother as well as to her, and the mother steps in to undo the damage Isabel has done. The contest between them in Nina's mind is exhibited in other memories as the day progresses.

The pattern established in this chapter—sexual encounter followed by memories of childhood connected with Colin's brief life—repeats itself twice more in this phase of the progression, once just before lunch, and again in the late evening. Nina leaves the actual sex of their second encounter unnarrated, focusing even more pointedly on the memories that follow of Colin's funeral, the dramatic effect of his death on the child Isabel and her relationship to eating, and their mother's attempts to help her. This memory seems to impel Nina to make her pursuit explicit, and she speaks with Isabel, recounting her memory of how Colin's death changed things for the Close family:

> "You know what it was like, it seemed as if he'd just disappeared. You remember how we looked in his room and the bed was gone, and everything. And Mum never being happy again, it all seemed completely pointless." It's only at that moment, as I say those words, that I admit to myself that my mother never was happy again after Colin's death. (119)

Our awareness of Isabel's distress as Nina speaks makes us question Nina's motives in raising this memory at this time. We wonder if Nina can see the danger, as we do, of making connections between the past and the present with Isabel recovering from the birth of her own new son. However, we may also begin to realize at this point that, although Isabel is obviously in crisis, Nina, too, has reached a point of crisis. Perhaps significantly, Nina reveals at this stage her age, which is twenty-nine; Wharton's Lily Bart also finds this a critical age, as she tries to understand finally why she has not yet married.[6] That Nina should have this in common with Lily is certainly surprising, but the comparison suggests that those things Nina has claimed not to want, including marriage and children, have in fact been unavailable to her with her search unfinished.

Isabel offers nothing in response to Nina's implied questions, but their discussion is followed by a sustained reflection on her parents, the most we ever hear of them, including the passage in which Nina recalls her mother's narrative of Colin's conception. This story is significant because Nina, like the reader, can detect the hint of unnarratable pleasure in the "bleak" narration. The act that conceives Colin is an isolated one, not carrying the weight of an "attempt at reconciliation," and not artificially created by drunkenness that gives way later to regret. On that night, in spite of everything, they chose each other, and Colin was created in a moment of sexual pleasure. Nina and Isabel are very aware that this was their mother's last moment of pleasure. Following Colin's death, she had a breakdown and was hospitalized for a time. That we learn these details for the first time at this point in the narrative makes the divergent directions of Nina's and Isabel's searches even more evident. Isabel, who, in a scene that frames these memories, collapses in the garden, repeats her mother's experience of grief and mental breakdown, whereas Nina doggedly pursues the gleam of pleasure in Mrs. Close's story.

The third repetition of the pattern commences with Nina's next sexual encounter with Richard that evening in the garden. This account is more detailed, and Nina certainly attempts to describe her pleasure: "I don't often get to the point where I forget who I am. [. . .] I got there with Richard" (138). Nevertheless, the main focus, even in this passage, is on Nina's unwillingness to engage emotionally with Richard; she asserts, "It's not a matter of emotions, it's a physical thing" (138). This encounter culminates in his accusation that Nina is like Isabel: "You give with one hand and you take back with the other" (140). Nina's search remains focused on pleasure, but what she knows of her mother's story and of Isabel's story colors her experience. For Nina to this point, sex is desirable but remains insulated from emotion.

As with their other two encounters, the third precipitates another memory in Nina. She walks into Isabel's room, sees her bent over

Antony in his crib, and remembers seeing Isabel at seven years old bent over Colin in his crib smothering him, not unlike the way she pretended to drown Nina's doll. This discovery, which could advance Nina's progress by explaining Isabel's self-denial as arising from feelings of guilt, is quickly negated by Isabel. When confronted, Isabel tells Nina that Nina killed Colin and repressed the memory, and that Isabel has kept it a secret for twenty-five years. Shocked and horrified, Nina tells her sister, "I don't feel like me anymore" (149), but she feels grateful for Isabel's protection, and this is what prompts her to report, "What life I possess, I possess because Isabel's given it to me. Isabel is my mother" (151). This confusion precipitates two dreams, which appear to be memories of actual events that place Mrs. Close and Isabel in opposition to one another with reference to Nina. The opposition of these two characters focuses our attention on the ambiguities of their thematic functions in much the same way that the opposition between Nina and Isabel does. In the first, Nina hears a neighbor report to her mother that Isabel, out pushing the child Nina in a pram, put her in danger. In the second, her mother tries to interest Nina in drawing, something the two of them can do together without Isabel, and Nina feels she is being disloyal to her sister. These incidents not only indicate the complexities of the relationships among the mother and daughters, but also the complexities of Nina's search, the object of which is not quite clear.

The increasing instability of these relationships, combined with Isabel's accusation that it was Nina who was responsible for the end of their mother's pleasure, creates a breach in the pattern and in Nina's progress. This is observable in the next two chapters, which take place on the next day, when she is working to assimilate Isabel's version of the past. In contrast to the previous day, Nina and Richard contemplate sex twice but do not follow through. What rights the threatened search is that, at this juncture, both Richard and Isabel tell Nina the truth about their marriage. Isabel confesses that her marriage has "been difficult for a long time" and "was never much good" (183). Nina is surprised, and tells the reader:

> The mystery of Isabel and Richard used to be one of my touchstones. That was the way you could be, if you found the right person. I thought they possessed a happiness they hid to keep it safe from outsiders. They were the adults, the ones who knew how life worked. (183)

That Nina has intervened in a marriage that she believed to be happy may make her unlikable, but, in the context of the submerged plot, it makes sense: Nina seeks knowledge of her sister's pleasure. Only now does she learn that, in marriage, Isabel has, once again, denied herself pleasure. She has desired pleasure, and she seems to have found it before she married with men, according to Isabel, of "the sort who aren't any good to her" (212). Though capable of pleasure, Isabel refuses it and gives it away. Richard's account confirms Isabel's, and adds crucial information: "She doesn't sleep with me anymore, you know" (179). Nina cites Isabel's pregnancy as evidence to the contrary, but Richard rejoins, "That didn't take long. She'd got it worked out so it only took one go" (179). This detail echoes the story of their parents' conception of Colin—one sexual encounter following a separation. This information compounds the previously established connection that both Mrs. Close and Isabel wanted a home birth but, because of potential or actual complications, gave birth in a hospital. Nina begins to recognize Isabel's repetition of their mother's experience, and to be aware of Isabel's pursuit of the story of their mother's pleasure.

Even as she gains this insight, the utter failure of Isabel's search is borne in on Nina. Isabel confides to Nina that her feelings about sex are similar to her feelings about food, and that she believes both are equally unnecessary:

> I don't [need sex], though, do you? Not really. You soon get used to not having it. I remember thinking the same about food. All those people thinking they had to have food all the time or they'd die, always thinking about it and talking about it and going out to the shops for it and then sitting chomping it down, and yet it wasn't really necessary at all. All the world turned on something you could do without. I wanted to shout out and tell everyone the truth. (185)

Isabel's search has not brought her validation for her own pleasure, but rather has had the opposite effect. After Nina recovers a fuller, more solid memory of Isabel at seven years old suffocating Colin in his crib, Nina and the reader begin to conclude that Isabel's conviction that she brought an end to her mother's pleasure invalidates her own to such a degree that she eschews food and sex, and it seems clear she is afraid to search further. After she has given birth to her son, when she cannot help but recall that terrible time when her mother's baby son died, Isabel also ceases to enjoy the garden she has created from wilderness; indeed, she no longer leaves the house at all. Her refusal to progress in her search is signified by her increasing immobility.

Even more significant to Isabel's failure to progress than her inability to move in space is her inability to move in time. Whereas Nina strives to maintain control of time—by masking her present-tense narration, by deemphasizing the surprising temporal relation between story and narrative throughout—time has escaped Isabel's control. For Isabel, the past has crept into the present in a way that Nina tries to resist. When Nina realizes Isabel is alone with Antony, she runs back to the house with the feeling that "I've got to get there first, before anyone else sees" (172). Despite Isabel's assertion that Nina smothered Colin, something in Nina feels that Isabel did it, and that she could do the same to Antony. As she enters the house, Nina hears Isabel singing; of the song, Nina writes, "I know it well. That song's lodged in my bones, like all the songs Isabel once sang me" (173). But Isabel claims she is not aware she has been singing, and when Nina tells her which song it was, "Isabel laughs. 'I haven't thought of that for years, Neen'" (174). Isabel has clearly entered a mental state in which the past and the present are becoming indistinguishable, and her extremity helps us to understand Nina's own dedication to ordering both in her own way.

The rest of the novel, comprising eleven chapters and over a hundred pages, takes place on the day of Isabel's death. The day begins with further evidence that Isabel is slipping into the past mentally. Nina describes what she observes:

> Isabel rubs a hand over her face, to and fro, pressing so hard I see the flesh whiten round her fingers. When she speaks it's as if she's wiped away herself to let out a new voice. Or perhaps an old one. It echoes like something I've heard before, and know well. It's a high, sweet voice that makes the hairs rise on my arms. A child's voice. "Is that what you want, Neen? All right. I promise." I stare at her and the voice trickles into the silence. I'm not sure she even knows I'm still here. Then she looks down, focuses on the shears, and then up at me. She's herself again. (207)

By the end of the narrative, Nina will remember that what is being "echoed" is seven-year-old Isabel's response to her own request, as a four-year-old, that her big sister make her little brother go away. What Nina can understand at this point is that Isabel's past and present are becoming indistinguishable to her, and she is no longer able to progress.

This is the longest phase of the progression, and the proportions of the narrative imply that Nina considers the details of this day well worth scrutiny, despite the fact that Isabel herself appears only in the initial two chapters. The events of the surface plot are easily recounted: Isabel sends everyone off running errands; then she leaves the house for the first time in weeks, goes to the beach, leaves Antony with a young mother enjoying a day by the sea, walks into the water, and drowns. The police search for her body while Richard and Nina piece together the last hours of Isabel's life. That evening, Nina and Richard have sex, and, as in the novel's second phase, this precipitates further memories for Nina that finally clarify the circumstances of Colin's death. Nina's memories confirm her conviction that it was Isabel who smothered their infant brother, but also reveal that Isabel's act was committed at Nina's request, making Nina feel she is to blame as well. In the surface plot, the reason for the immense detail is Nina's exploration of the extent to which she is culpable in the deaths of both of her siblings.

At the same time, this long phase of the novel also narrates the culmination of Nina's search in the submerged plot. We might expect that Nina's final realization of her own share of responsibility for the long-ago death of Colin would render the success of her pursuit impossible, as it did for Isabel. However, the prologue, which is narrated some time after the events of the novel, reveals a Nina still closely connected to her sister—she narrates lying on Isabel's grave—and unchanged in her belief that, despite all, life must be affirmed. As she is "talking to the dead," she tells Isabel, "After a funeral you have to eat, to prove you're still alive" (3). Nina withholds any information about what her life has become since Isabel's death, perhaps knowing that the reader is likely to judge her harshly for it.[7] We can imagine that Nina's search has concluded in her exact repetition of Isabel's experience: that Nina is now in a relationship with Richard and that she acts as a mother to Antony. Soon after Isabel's disappearance, Nina holds Antony, and she reports, "The baby looks as if he belongs in my arms" (243). When Isabel's death has become a near certainty, Nina looks in on Antony as he sleeps: "'It's all right, Ant, I'll look after you,' I tell him in a whisper, but he's asleep, and anyway he knows it already" (285–86). We are to understand that she will fill these roles that Isabel has vacated, but, rather than invite our further judgment, Dunmore maintains the ambivalence she has created in the reader throughout.

Nina's exact repetition of Isabel's experience also serves as a more distanced connection to her mother's experience of marriage, sex, and motherhood. She continues to repeat her mother's mode of narrating "accurately" when she and Richard have sex the night of Isabel's death: "I am under Richard, my head scrubbed into the muddy ground" (276). In this phase of the progression, the emphasis is on another way Nina repeats her mother's experience: by surviving. At the scene of Isabel's disappearance, with police beginning their investigation, Nina thinks:

> I never stare at accidents. If I'm traveling somewhere and an ambulance pulls onto the station concourse and two men with a stretcher run toward a train, I don't look. My mother taught me that. You don't watch people when they're being hauled out of one life into another. (243)

Among the ways this passage is significant in the novel is that Mrs. Close's advice is about the ethics of survival. She is a survivor herself, and she tries to teach her daughters about how survivors should act. Indeed, what remains unnarrated between the end of Nina's narrative and the prologue is the recovery of Isabel's body; this, Nina has clearly decided, should not be "watched" by the reader.

Mrs. Close is also figured as a survivor the next time she is referred to, as Nina remembers her father reciting Louis MacNeice's "Autobiography" (from which Dunmore's title is taken), in which the speaker remembers the loss of his mother when he is five years old. Nina's memory focuses first on the third stanza of MacNeice's poem: "*My mother wore a yellow dress, / Gently, gently, gentleness. / Come back early or never come*" (282). Although Nina has been preoccupied with the event when she was four years old that ended her mother's happiness, in this passage Nina approaches her memory of her mother another way. She thinks,

> My mother never wore a yellow dress. She wore smocks that smelled of clay and dust, and she worked all day long and earned more money than my father. She had to. What he earned was less than he needed for drink. She was strong. (282)

Nina distinguishes her own mother from the gentle, lost mother of the poem. Her own mother was a passionate woman who married the man she wanted despite his obvious failings. Although Mrs. Close suffered a breakdown when Nina was a child, she survived the loss of Colin and continued to raise her daughters and create art until her death from breast cancer years later. Mrs. Close's story validates Nina's very survival. This validation is necessary, but it does not inspire a great deal of hope for the future. MacNeice's poem is dominated by images of solitude, including "nobody, nobody was there" and "nobody, nobody replied," and we are reminded that Nina is now without either of her parents, without either of her siblings. The poem's refrain, which Nina quotes twice, "Come back early or never come," keeps the poem's reader, like the novel's reader, suspended between the idea of time as relative ("early") and time as absolute ("never"). When the child Isabel refers to the refrain as "stupid" and insists, "I'd just say what I meant," her father responds, "It's never as easy as that [. . .] as you'll find" (282–83). Isabel fails to negotiate both the contradictions in experiencing time and the difficulties of saying what one means, but Nina faces both with all her resources.

Among the final images of Mrs. Close is a photograph of her holding Colin, in which Nina sees "Love, and hope. Those things my mother had felt when Colin was born" (293). This photograph Isabel has kept, and, Nina assumes, tormented herself with. Nina, in contrast, having found it among Isabel's things, discovers, "It's easy to tear the photo. I tear it along the creases, then again, into pieces no one could ever recognize" (294). This moment is further evidence of Nina's capacity for survival, and of her refusal of remorse. She can see in her mother's face the joy that Nina's and Isabel's acts destroyed, and she can also see the way that joy excluded herself and Isabel and left them alone. Unlike Isabel, who was overwhelmed by the photograph, Nina, a photographer herself, can see how it is constructed and is not intimidated by it. She knows that photographs can be "deliberate [. . .] composition[s]," such as "a photograph of a begging child, alone on a barren street, carefully angled to exclude the mother three yards away" (19). That is, she knows that a photograph may be manipulated to produce a particular narrative for the viewer. What is excluded from the photograph Nina destroys is not the mother but her two needy daughters. This particular photograph, Nina insists, has a meaning that no one else would be able to understand in the way that she and Isabel do. Yet even the sisters' understanding is not identical: whereas Isabel can see in it only what was subsequently lost, Nina can also see in it what was, finally, saved, and this is evident in her memories of her mother in the time after Colin's death throughout the text. Isabel witnesses her mother's joy and can think only of her suffering, whereas Nina can accept both.

As narrator of the novel, Nina repeats Isabel's experience in one final way: whereas Nina has always been "the artistic one" (42), Isabel was always the storyteller. Nina remembers of their one trip to Sunday school, "I was coloring a donkey while Isabel won the prize for telling a Bible story in her own words" (99). Nina tells us, "I'm in the habit of believing Isabel's version" (19), and "I have Isabel's stories" (130). To Nina, Isabel's stories have always been powerful enough to create truth, as when she "decided one summer that Rosina [her doll] had long raven hair," and insisted so completely that "on her coarse, vigorous, yellow hair I thought I detected a faint sheen of black" (186). When Isabel tells her version of Colin's death, in which Nina has smothered him and Isabel later found him dead, Nina reports "beginning to see the bulk of Isabel's truth, advancing like an iceberg to blot out my world" (145). However, in *Talking to the Dead*, Nina makes her own attempt at storytelling and decides to be the narrator, as Isabel has been, and her narrative protects her. In this as in so many things, repeating Isabel's experience is also repeating their mother's. Although, like Nina, Mrs. Close is connected to other arts, at one point Nina thinks of her mother as a storyteller. When Isabel tells Nina her own version of the events surrounding Colin's death, Nina is shocked, and she thinks to herself: "There is no evidence, so it's Isabel's word against mine. Even my mother is firmly dead, and I think that only she could ever dare to put together the threads of such a story" (151). Of the three, however, Nina is the one who succeeds in weaving the story that, for all the uncertainty inherent in it, is finally convincing.

Despite the ambiguities of her own character and those of her mother and sister, the submerged plot of Nina's narrative manages to garner more sympathy for all three women than their actions in the surface plot might warrant, and, ultimately, we are likely to affirm Nina's strength as a survivor. If Nina's decisions as narrator, to obscure her own retrospection and her choices about the relationship between time and event in her narrative, seem deceptive, we can see that they also serve to protect Nina from the blending of past and present that preys on her sister. The success of Nina's search in the submerged plot validates her entitlement to pleasure, and recognizing the effects of this second plot enables us to understand the narrative of the present in *Talking to the Dead* in a new way that manifests its contribution to the novel's completion.

"She wanted her body back": Ammu Ipe "Un-known"

Like *Talking to the Dead,* Arundhati Roy's *The God of Small Things* centers on a motherless daughter attempting to manage her memories of her own involvement in long-ago events that devastated her family and ended her mother's pleasure. In *Talking to the Dead,* the narrative of the present communicates the story of Nina's recovery of memories of the past that she has repressed; unlike Nina, however, Roy's Rahel has not repressed her memories of the past but has lived in full knowledge of them for twenty-three years. The narrative of the present in *The God of Small Things,* then, is not about recovering lost memories, and, indeed, its function is not altogether obvious with reference to the novel's surface plot. The narrative of Rahel's and Estha's return to Ayemenem and reunion with one another is puzzling as an ending to the novel's story, and has been accounted for as the depiction of a static condition resultant from social ills of various kinds, and, at best, the belated and tentative beginnings of healing for the twins. To find what is conclusive in the narrative of the present, and thus locate its contribution to the novel's completeness, we must analyze its progression. Such an analysis reveals connections between the story's end and the narrative's end; completeness is not easily identifiable in either, but, taken together, these two endings are the culmination of the submerged plot of Rahel's search for the story of her mother's pleasure, a search that has been derailed by her fear that she herself is responsible for the end of Ammu's pleasure. By refusing to know any more than she does, Rahel holds her own potential pleasure at bay. She wanders through adulthood, avoiding seeking anything at all, until Estha's sudden return to Ayemenem necessitates Rahel's just as they themselves reach the age at which their mother died. Her reunion with Estha functions in two ways for Rahel: it both enables her to undertake the rest of her search and it makes possible the success of the search, however qualified.

The narrative structure of *The God of Small Things* has drawn considerable critical attention.[8] The novel alternates between the narrative of the traumatic events of two weeks in 1969 that destroy the Ipe family and the narrative of the reconciliation twenty-three years later of the traumatized twins, Rahel and Estha. The imbalance in the pattern of alternation has influenced readings of the novel's progression to focus on the past: the narrative of the present (an unspecified number of days in 1992) constitutes not half but approximately one fifth of the text (only 66 pages[9] of Roy's 321-page novel). The present is characterized by decay and degeneration, and we are encouraged to mine the past for causes—near and remote, personal and social—of the state of affairs with which we are presented. Of Rahel and Estha's childhood home, the narrator tells us "Filth had laid siege to the Ayemenem House" and describes it as "graying" under layers of "grime," "grease," and "a film of oil" (84). The once powerful Meenachal River is now "just a slow, sludging green ribbon lawn that ferried fetid garbage to the sea" (119). The rubber plantation across the river has been turned into a resort where the wealthy guests are shielded from the poverty around them and where abbreviated versions of Kerala's traditional kathakali performances are offered as local color background to the guests' sunbathing. The performers, traditionally "the most beautiful of men" (219), are forced by necessity to accept this shaming employment, and they are portrayed as despairing, stoned, abusive. To this place, from which their beloved mother, grandmother, and uncle have disappeared, Rahel and Estha return, themselves only shadows of the children they had been. The novel appears to be entirely oriented toward the past, toward identifying the factors that determined the characters' current circumstances. The reader is likely to have difficulty finding signs of hope for the future or of any way forward at all.

These elements of the surface plot suggest two mutually informative interpretations, both focused on the implications of the representation of time in the novel. For Madhu Benoit, the dual structure alerts us to a more overarching duality between chronological time, represented by the two main and several other "temporal levels," and "a-chronological or historical time," which creates "a constant awareness in the reader's mind of the inflexible cultural codes, which govern the lives of the protagonists" (100). Benoit's conclusion is that "the basic reason for the book's multiple-time structure" is that Roy "is writing an angry book, a book which is a political statement" (105). He characterizes the novel as "a head-on attack on the Keralese caste-ridden society, and the cruel destiny it reserves for both women and untouchables" (106). Benoit's reading is certainly convincing and accurately characterizes the narrative of the past, but it explains less about the narrative of the present. The death of Velutha, the banishment and demise of Ammu, and the abandonment of the twins would be sufficient to convey the important ideas identified by Benoit, and we would feel their significance even without the decaying house, the dying river, and the threatened traditional culture, which in fact point to a different political statement about the effects of a globalized economy. What the narrative of the present contributes to the "attack on the Keralese caste-ridden society" is not immediately clear.

For Elsa Sacksick, too, the dual structure points to a larger duality: the alternation of the two narratives represents both entanglement and careful, patterned interlacing. Whereas Benoit locates in the dual structure a technique in service of social protest, Sacksick finds in it an image of the mind, represented by Rahel and Estha in the present, coming to terms with a life-shattering past event, represented by the narrative of "the Terror" (Roy 181). Sacksick views the narrative as reflective of "a traumatised mind which can only go round in circles. The only possible dynamic for the main characters as well as for the narrative is to progress through detours" (59). Susan Stanford Friedman observes similarly of the novel, "The narration of trauma and its disastrous effects unfolds out of temporal sequence, in fragments of the story that keep emerging as returns of the repressed" ("Spatial Poetics" 198). In the same analytical vein, Elizabeth Outka develops a theory of "temporal hybridity" to explore "the central role of trauma in creating the temporal mix experienced by the characters" (22). This persuasive reading of the novel as reflecting the experience of the traumatized individual accounts for both the narrative of the past and of the present. Nevertheless, in this reading, the narrative of the present is apparently the beginning, not the end, of a process of psychological healing, and we are offered no assurance of its eventual success or, in fact, any vision of what psychological healing might make possible for either Estha or Rahel.

Neither of these readings accounts fully for the specifics of the narrative of the present; thus, in comparison to the end of the narrative, the end of the story has received relatively little concentrated attention in the scholarship on the novel.[10] The reader understands that the occasion for the narrative is the reunion of the twins, but their reunion raises questions for us. Why now? Why should incestuous sex be their only means to reach one another? Why are we left with this image and given no indication of its aftermath? What is the purpose of the clearly demarcated and discrete narrative of the present, which reveals only a fraction of what the reader would wish to know? These questions are difficult to answer without the submerged plot, which reveals that Estha and Rahel, after years of shock and grief over the deaths of Velutha, Sophie Mol, and their mother, and bewildered horror at the events that culminated in those deaths, have finally reached a point at which they are able to seek among the wreckage for a glimpse of their mother's pleasure.

As children, the twins are aware only of horrifying events and their own feelings of responsibility for them. We know that they have struggled even to understand the events themselves: the one thing they know for sure is that they, along with Ammu, "had loved a man to death" (307). What they fear from knowing more of their mother's story is being forced to face even more responsibility. For the reader as for the children, untangling the confusion of "the Terror" to find the moment of pleasure that precedes it is difficult. Before Sophie Mol has drowned, before Velutha has been betrayed and beaten to death, before Chacko's anger and grief break up Ammu's family, Ammu's mother has discovered that she has had sex with Velutha and has locked her in her bedroom. Ammu's sexual transgression has been exposed. The twins have sufficient understanding of all of these events except for the first, the event that precedes the rest. With no understanding of Ammu's pleasure, they understand only her fury when it is taken from her. Enraged "at being locked away like the family lunatic in a medieval household," she screams through the door at the twins, "Because of you! [. . .] If it wasn't for you I wouldn't be here! None of this would have happened! I wouldn't be here! I would have been free! I should have dumped you in an orphanage the day you were born! *You're* the millstones round my neck!" (239–40). This blame, augmented by Ammu's despairing "Why can't you just go away and leave me alone?!" (240), sets off the disastrous chain of events. Estha and Rahel, then, feel implicated in every stage of the catastrophe that befalls their family. Their guilt began with the tie they constituted between Ammu and their father, the man who beat her and would prostitute her if he could. It was compounded by the necessity they created for Ammu to come back to Ayemenem, cloistered, demeaned, finished. They understand all that has hurt their mother, but the narrator tells us at the novel's end that "it took the twins years to understand Ammu's part in what had happened" (307). They know the story of her pain, grief, and death without any understanding at all of the pleasure she so briefly found. The narrative of the past, then, is primarily focalized through the children, but includes information about the relationship between Ammu and Velutha that they did not observe, could not have understood at seven years old, and can only imagine now, at thirty-one years old.[11] As being reunited and back in Ayemenem forces them to traverse this old ground again, they finally allow themselves to seek the story of the mother's pleasure that preceded the devastation that has possessed them so thoroughly.

Reconfiguring the progression of *The God of Small Things* to reveal the workings of the submerged plot helps to clarify the function of the narrative of the present and to identify the contributions of both surface and submerged plots to the novel's completion. Central to the novel's progression is its handling of time. Despite the extensive use of analepsis and prolepsis throughout *The God of Small Things,* its dual surface plots are more discrete than those in *Talking to the Dead*. The disjunction between the narrative of the past and that of the present is enacted in what is presented as two beginnings of the novel. Chapter 1 launches the narrative of the present, interrupting itself frequently and at length with analepses to various points in the past twenty-three years and earlier. The chapter ends with a meditation on the ethics of choosing a starting point for a narrative, and chapter 2 presents us with an entirely different beginning, this one acting as the launch of the narrative of the past (although chapter 1 has already familiarized the reader with elements of it). The distinction between the two is maintained throughout and emphasized by the novel's final two scenes, in which, rather than reversing the order and ending with the narrative of the present, which might grant it less equivocal status as a frame narrative, the order is maintained and the novel ends with the narrative of the past.

Like *Talking to the Dead,* Roy's novel begins with the narrative of the present, and even includes some present-tense narration in its first three pages, as when the narrator tells us of Rahel: "Anyway, now she thinks of Estha and Rahel as *Them,* because, separately, the two of them are no longer what *They* were or ever thought *They'd* be" (5). This particular sentence alerts us to another way the discrete narratives of past and present are maintained: whereas Nina narrates both past and present in *Talking to the Dead*, and her narration of her memories preserves the continuities between her childhood self and her adult self, the narrator of *The God of Small Things* focalizes through Rahel and Estha in the narrative of the present as adults and through these same characters in the narrative of the past as children, in effect treating each as two different characters, "no longer what *They* were" (5). We might assume that the separation between the two narratives is a reference to the adult twins' lack of memories, but Roy does not naturalize her strategy in this way. The narrator in fact emphasizes Rahel's memories by listing several and commenting, "She has other memories too that she has no right to have," and going on to say, "And these are only the small things" (5). Estha, in contrast, has repressed his memories insofar as he can: "he grew accustomed to the uneasy octopus that lived inside him and squirted its inky tranquilizer on his past" (13). Nevertheless, we are also told that there is an element of his past that "Estha's octopus couldn't get at," and therefore some part of his memory has remained conscious (32). Although the adult twins' memories could be a link between the narratives of past and present, they are not used as such. That the dual narratives remain insistently separate alerts us to the separate function of the narrative of the present.

The reader is likely to feel temporally disoriented in the narrative of the present. The period of time covered by this narrative, in contrast to that of the past, is unclear. Readers can easily imagine that the events in the present take place in one day (Friedman, "Spatial Poetics" 198; Outka 25), though we learn toward the novel's end that at least "a few mornings" have passed (Roy 283). The relationship between time and event in the narrative of the present, then, is masked, as in Dunmore's novel. Already a smaller proportion of the novel, much of this narrative is consumed by analepses to the past, which maintains the emphasis on the narrative of the past and obscures the function of the narrative of the present. Indeed, analepses in both of the beginning chapters function as brief histories of each character's life up to the moment he or she appears in the narrative. In contrast to other novels of motherless daughters, which often provide a brief sketch of the absent mother's history that is subsequently filled in by the daughter's similar experience throughout the narrative, Roy provides us with a sketch of the daughter's life first, which we learn is a repetition of her mother's experience only gradually, as the narrative of the past reveals Ammu's story in great detail. This has at least two effects evident to the reader, perhaps especially the reader considering the novel in the context of the other works treated here. The first is that the encapsulation of Rahel's life, and of Estha's, in chapter 1, gives the impression that their lives, rather than their deceased mother's life, are over. The second is that we realize as we read that the parallels between Rahel's experience and her mother's have been mounting, but that Rahel has refused to acknowledge them. The surfacings of the submerged plot in the narrative of the present enable us to see the ways Rahel finally acknowledges her mother's experience in her own, repeats her mother's experience in new ways, and transcends her own sense at the novel's beginning that her life is over.

The analepsis in chapter 1 that summarizes Rahel's life from the time of her mother's death until her return to Ayemenem creates a considerable contrast between her and other seeking daughters. In the lives of Anne Elliot, Jane Eyre, Esther Summerson, and even Anne Catherick, the submerged plot of the search for the mother's pleasure manifests itself in the surface plot in a great deal of activity and purposefulness. Often the determination to be educated in the surface plot mirrors the submerged search, as in the case of Jane, and also of Walker's Celie and Allison's Bone. In contrast, Rahel's adolescence and adult life are clearly characterized by wandering. We are told in the novel's first chapter that "after Ammu died [...] Rahel drifted" (16). Rahel's "almost fierce lack of ambition" (19) leaves her to "drift" from school to school, to "happen" into the university where she never takes a degree, to "drift" into marriage and out again, to take jobs as a waitress and a night clerk. Although a number of scholars, in response to Estha's evident psychological distress, think of Rahel as stronger than he, strong enough to help him to heal, Rahel also exhibits signs of distress.[12] Rahel's experience of wandering is simply a less literal manifestation of Estha's habitual walking, the characterization of him as "a quiet bubble floating on a sea of noise" (13). Rahel's inner scars and their outward manifestations are not dissimilar from "mad" Estha's: both adamantly choose to wander rather than seek, and we understand that they are terrified that seeking their mother's story might mean finding further guilt and responsibility for themselves.

Indeed, Rahel is so overwhelmed by the story of the end of her mother's pleasure that she remains distanced from pleasure itself, her mother's and her own. We are told of Rahel's husband that "when they made love he was offended by her eyes. They behaved as though they belonged to someone else. Someone watching. Looking out of the window at the sea. At a boat in the river. Or a passerby in the mist in a hat" (20). Clearly, what Rahel has learned about sexual pleasure she has learned from the end of her mother's story; the narrator explains that

> [in] the country that Rahel came from [. . .] *personal* despair could never be desperate enough. That something happened when personal turmoil dropped by at the wayside shrine of the vast, violent, circling, driving, ridiculous, insane, unfeasible, public turmoil of a nation. That Big God howled like a hot wind, and demanded obeisance. Then Small God (cozy and contained, private and limited) came away cauterized, laughing numbly at his own temerity. Inured by the confirmation of his own inconsequence, he became resilient and truly indifferent. Nothing mattered much. Nothing much mattered. And the less it mattered, the less it mattered. It was never important enough. Because Worse Things had happened. In the country that she came from, poised forever between the terror of war and the horror of peace, Worse Things kept happening. (20)

In a world in which personal despair can never be important enough to merit attention, how much less important yet must personal pleasure be? It appears that not only does Rahel fear to look further into her mother's past to locate the pleasure that preceded disaster, but, not unlike Elizabeth Bowen's Lois, she has grown up believing that sexual pleasure is extraneous, at least in comparison to the collective concerns of the postcolonial nation.

Although she has not sought her mother's story, has in fact feared knowing more of it than she does, her own experience has, in some important respects, repeated her mother's. For example, we are told of Rahel in the novel's first chapter that she married an American and moved with him to Boston; we will later learn that her mother married a man of another religion, a Hindu, and moved from southwest India to the northeast. Rahel's marriage, we are told, ends in divorce, as we will learn her mother's did. Like her mother, she is vulnerable to insult as a result: Rahel remembers the police inspector who referred to her mother as a "*veshya*" (9), or prostitute, and Rahel herself, working as a night clerk at a gas station, finds that "pimps propositioned her with more lucrative job offers" (21). Indeed, Rahel's experience of work for which she is overqualified and to which she is not attached—night clerk, waitress—mirrors her mother's experience of a "succession of jobs," the last "a receptionist in a cheap hotel" (152), after which she had hoped to become "someone's secretary" (154). These details alert the reader to the submerged plot, and the effect of the reversal is to suggest that, although Rahel's experience has in fact repeated her mother's in a number of significant ways, Rahel has refused to seek in her own story more details of her mother's, but also that she is open to doing so now that Estha is with her.

In the course of the narrative, we learn even more ways that Rahel's experience has repeated her mother's, mostly in connection with the fact that, for both women, the Ayemenem house is home, and both spend considerable time there as children. For Rahel, as for her mother, this is the place most strongly associated with family and childhood. Both are mothered, to some extent, by Mammachi. Ammu's abusive father, who appeared "charming and urbane" to the community but was to his family a "monstrous, suspicious bully, with a streak of vicious cunning" (171–72), is not entirely unlike Rahel's father, whose alcoholism and abuse remain hidden from others, even Ammu's own family (42). Both women, dowryless, are denied (or freed from) traditional marriages, and both women find themselves with no rights to their ancestral home, no "Locusts Stand I" (56, 179, 220) because they are female and also because they are divorced. An equally important repetition is the relationship of both women to Velutha. We know only one detail about the time Ammu spends in the village as a child: that Velutha was a significant presence there. A few years younger than she, he called her by a familiar nickname, "Ammukutty" (72), and he brought her gifts he had made: "tiny windmills, rattles, minute jewel boxes out of dried palm reeds; he could carve perfect boats out of tapioca stems and figurines on cashew nuts" (71). Velutha is also an important part of Rahel's life in Ayemenem, and he makes her gifts as well: "It was Velutha who made Rahel her luckiest-ever fishing rod and taught her and Estha to fish" (75). He also makes up a nickname for Estha, "Esthapappychachen Kutappen Peter Mon" (173), which he and Rahel use and which Rahel remembers when they are reunited.

Like many other motherless daughters considered here, Rahel further repeats her mother's experience in feeling drawn toward a man like the one her mother chose. In Rahel's case, that man is Estha. However, as Rahel's twin, and as another protagonist who shares with her the role of focalizer, Estha's role as "suitor" is complicated considerably. Indeed, what he shares with Rahel suggests that the resemblances between Estha and Velutha function not only as an element of Rahel's search but as an element of his own. The submerged plot of *The God of Small Things* alters the established pattern by including a seeking son. As with Rahel and Ammu, we are given a brief sketch of Estha's life early in the narrative, and only gradually, as Velutha's story unfolds, do we see the similarities between the men's stories. We are told that "Estha had always been a quiet child, so no one could pinpoint with any degree of accuracy exactly when [. . .] he had stopped talking" (12). Velutha, too, is described as quiet; his father notices "the quiet way he offered suggestions without being asked. Or the quiet way in which he disregarded suggestions without appearing to rebel" (73). Estha's school reports that he "*Does not participate in Group Activities*" (12); we first encounter Velutha as part of a large group of Naxalites protesting, but we come to see the ways that his caste isolates him even within this group, as it does among the employees of the factory where he works. When Velutha as a youth believes his father resents him, he spends less time at home and gravitates toward the river, cooking fish on its banks and sleeping there. Estha, too, thinks of the river as an escape. Velutha disappears and is gone for four years; Estha is gone for a much longer period. Neither is home when his mother dies. Both love two women: Ammu and Rahel.

Estha's resemblance to Velutha enables him to help Rahel in her pursuit and makes him crucial to the submerged plot; his resemblance to herself may suggest that he, too, needs the story of his mother's pleasure, and the submerged plot accommodates Estha's search as well. Conventional gender roles work against Estha's search, which seems to be suspended altogether during the twenty-three years he lives, in silence, with his father in Calcutta. Preparing to send him away, Ammu whispers, "Maybe they're right [. . .]. Maybe a boy does need a Baba" (31). In the aftermath of the event that, traditionally, would be kept from a son—his mother's experience of sexual pleasure—Estha is separated from his mother and sister and sent to learn to be an adult, a man, from his father. This tactic fails utterly; indeed, one of the few things we know about Estha's adult life is that he has "embarrassed" his father and stepmother by choosing to do housework, traditionally women's work (12).[13] Estha is more lost when we meet him again at thirty-one years old than he was when last encountered at the age of seven, but, as his does for her, Rahel's presence changes things for Estha: "The world, locked out for years, suddenly flooded in, and now Estha couldn't hear himself for the noise" (16). The novel's ending suggests that being deprived of his mother's story is a problem for him as it is for Rahel, and that she can help him to find it as he helps her.

The identifications between Estha and Velutha and between Rahel and Ammu are made explicit in the next chapter of the narrative of the present, advancing the submerged plot and preparing the reader for the culmination of this narrative. As the adult twins meet for the first time, their searches, so long delayed, are already in motion as they repeat their mother's experience in new ways. Estha returns from his walk in the rain, and Rahel follows him into the room he is staying in, "Ammu's room. Once" (87). The narrator, focalizing through Estha, reports of Rahel that "at first glance she appeared to have grown into the skin of her mother" (88). Not only does Rahel look like her mother to some extent, but she also feels like her mother. As Estha takes off his wet clothes, Rahel "searched her brother's nakedness for signs of herself" (88), but she also "watched Estha with the curiosity of a mother watching her wet child" (89). To feel what her mother must have felt, and to see Estha as a beloved child, enhances the identification between her and her mother. This scene also, by extension, creates identification between Estha and Velutha. Rahel is seeing Estha as a man for the first time, and she notes of his body, among other things, "the sculpted hollows on either side of his taut, beautiful buns. Tight plums. Men's bums never grow up" (88–89). Later in the narrative, when Ammu sees Velutha playing with the child Rahel, "she wondered at how his body had changed—so quietly, from a flat-muscled boy's body into a man's body," and, like Rahel with Estha, she notices that which has not changed as well: "it was his smile that reminded Ammu of Velutha as a little boy" (167). In both cases, a much-loved boy from childhood is suddenly seen as a man in a way he was never meant to be seen by the woman watching him. These similar scenes, with that involving Rahel narrated first, maintain the reversed orientation and portray Rahel as finally finding in what she can imagine of her mother's life analogues to her own experience.

The progression offers more conventional ways to access the past in the next two chapters of the narrative of the present. In the first, Rahel goes for a walk around the village. She is followed by a "band of children," but, rather than finding in them an image of her own past self, when one of them throws a stone at her, "her childhood fled, flailing its thin arms" (121–22). When she passes Comrade Pillai's home and business, he shows her photographs, one of his son with Rahel, Estha, and Sophie Mol as children. Rahel needs no reminder of her cousin, but this photo is actually a reminder of what is perhaps her introduction to the concept of sex. Rahel remembers that, just before the photo was taken, Sophie Mol had lectured her younger cousins about sex: "See what they do is . . ." (129). She finds little insight into her young self by watching the village children or even photographs from her childhood, but Comrade Pillai's photo is an indication to Rahel of her childhood self's nascent search, soon afterward suspended. Back at the Ayemenem house, in the next chapter in the narrative of the present, Rahel finds mementos of herself and Estha as children, particularly notebooks in which they had done their schoolwork, including one headed "Esthappen Unknown. (His surname postponed for the Time Being)" (149–50). Rahel reads exercises written by Estha and corrected by their mother, apparently preserved by Ammu in what the children believed was their own secret hiding place. That Ammu was aware of their hiding place and valued their childhood work is comforting, and the exercises themselves are marked with Ammu's comments, reviving Ammu's and Estha's voices from before the terrible events of December 1969. These conventional ways of connecting with the past—returning to familiar places, encountering evidence of a childhood self—open doors, but they are not enough to break through to a time when pleasure was possible.

The progression of the submerged plot accelerates when we next return to the narrative of the present. Rahel is in the garden looking in at her brother, sitting in his room looking out but unable to see her in the darkness. Focalizing through Rahel, the narrator describes the twins as "a pair of actors trapped in a recondite play with no hint of plot or narrative" (182). Rahel connects her own and Estha's plotlessness with the absence of their mother, who, following Velutha into death, "left them behind, spinning in the dark, with no moorings, in a place with no foundation" (182). Their mother left them terrified of knowing the rest of her story, but tonight, back in Ayemenem and reunited with Estha, Rahel is attracted to narrative: "The direction of the breeze changed and brought her the sound of drums. A gift. The promise of a story"

(182). She follows the sound to the temple, where the kathakali dancers employed by the hotel "stopped at the temple to ask pardon of their gods. To apologize for corrupting their stories" (218). After a time, Estha joins her there, and the two spend the night watching the performances. The stories performed that night, "Karna's Oath" and "Death of Duryodhana," do for the characters what they do for the reader: they clearly reflect the story of the past, but they also enable Rahel and Estha to see the connections we are already aware of between their own lives and those of Ammu and Velutha. Even as these comparisons between them and well-known figures from Indian epic foreground what Phelan terms the synthetic components of all four characters, they also help to solidify their thematic functions in the surface plot by emphasizing continuity of experience, not just over decades but over centuries. The function of these comparisons in the submerged plot is to help Rahel and Estha to negotiate their troubled relationship to narrative itself.

Karna bears some resemblance to both Estha and Velutha. Like Karna, Estha is the son of an unmarried mother. Circumstances conspire to make Estha, like Karna, feel undervalued by his mother in comparison to other children: the advent of the white, English Sophie Mol, the vision of the lovable "peppermint" children from *The Sound of Music*, and, of course, being sent away while Rahel remains in Ayemenem with Ammu. More generally, the events of the novel make Ammu appear to him a mother whose desires are centered on something besides his own well-being, as Karna's mother's are. Velutha, too, is like Karna, knowing that he was born equal to anyone, but arbitrarily raised as a member of a lower class. Like Karna, Velutha is approached only when he can be of use to others, as to Mammachi and Chacko, and dispensed with when he ceases to be useful, as by Comrade Pillai. In her article on "Religious Myth and Subversion" in the novel, Chelva Kanaganayakam notes that "the destruction of Karna finds a parallel in the killing of Velutha. Like Karna, he, too, is 'condemned goods. A prince raised in poverty. Born to die unfairly, unarmed and alone . . . Majestic in his complete despair'" (146). Both directly and in their shared resemblance to this epic hero, then, Estha has repeated Velutha's experience.

To overcome the fear of plot and narrative is important for the twins, and Karna's story is helpful in this regard, but Dushasana's story acts as a warning against relying too implicitly on literary parallels rather than lived experience. The Pandavas have lost Draupadi to the Kauravas in a game of dice, and Dushasana has tried to humiliate her publicly by undressing her. The story is Bhima's avenging of Draupadi's honor by murdering and dismembering Dushasana. The narrator reports, "It was no performance. Esthappen and Rahel recognized it" (224): they have witnessed the vicious beating to death of Velutha by the police. At the same time, they know that, although Velutha's story appears to most of the community to parallel that of the "vile Dushasana" (223), it does not. In love with a woman forbidden to him, Velutha's love can only be seen by her family as dishonoring, but Ammu loves Velutha and goes to him willingly, and, far from wishing to bathe in his blood, she is destroyed by his death. Also, Draupadi, who, unusually, had five husbands, is revered and saved from being stripped by divine intervention, whereas Ammu and Rahel, each of whom leaves a husband and, eventually, goes to another man, are in fact stripped of their standing in the community and remain entirely unprotected. The kathakali dances enable the twins to revive their interest in story and to see necessary connections between themselves and their mother, but they also discourage the twins from seeking their mother's pleasure in literary parallels.

The only way to access the mother's pleasure proves to be the repetition of Ammu and Velutha's experience in their own. A few days after the kathakali performances, when the narrative of the present resumes, we find Estha "on his bed in the dark. He sat very straight. Shoulders squared. Hands in his lap. As though he was next in line for some sort of inspection. Or waiting to be arrested" (279). The feeling that he is about to be arrested is one he shares with Velutha, we learn in the novel's final scene. Touching Ammu for the first time in the river, Velutha imagines, "This was a trap. There were people in the bushes" (316). Estha thinks of Ammu and Rahel as one because he was forced to leave them both in 1969—both are associated for him with the "sound of passing trains" (283). He thinks again of Rahel as "grown into their mother's skin" (283). When the adult twins have sex, then, we are not wholly unprepared, but we are nevertheless likely to be shocked. Rahel has chosen a man like the one her mother chose, but she has made this choice despite his relationship to herself. With reference to the surface plot, we are told that their sexual union is not an attempt to find pleasure: "what they shared that night was not happiness, but hideous grief" (311). Their union is a way to grieve for what is lost and give up the terrible guilt that keeps them "Quiet" and "Empty." The scene is also crucial to the submerged plot, the final element in their repetition of Ammu and Velutha's experience, and it contains echoes of that earlier pleasure, which is narrated next. The scenes are explicitly connected by their proximity to one another and by the narrator's repetition in both scenes, with only minor variation, of this description: "It was a little cold. A little wet. But very quiet. The Air" (310, 320). Like Ammu and Velutha, Rahel and Estha are breaking the Love Laws "that lay down who should be loved. And how. And how much" (311). Having relived the other parts of Ammu's and Velutha's lives, the twins attempt to find their way to the pleasure they shared. Although their own experience is heavily sorrowful, the possibilities of it are emphasized by the ending of the narrative and its focus on the mother's pleasure.

In this scene we find the completion of both plots, though their resolution is not without ambivalence. We are authorized to be hopeful when we read that, for the first time, "no Watcher watched through Rahel's eyes" (310); this sexual experience is different from those she has had before. The placement of the scene is also grounds for understanding that the search has been completed. Whereas the scene is preceded by the fraught, climactic separation of the little family at the train station in Cochin, it is succeeded by the scene of Ammu and Velutha's pleasure. Their pleasure is narrated for the reader as it cannot be for Rahel, but the order of the scenes suggests that she has learned it in essence by completing her search. At the same time, the novel emphasizes how individual the struggle for pleasure must be, and how tenuous a hold on it Estha and Rahel, and their entire family, can maintain. The Ipes have found nothing solid enough to consider passing on, and have created no line through which to pass any legacy. Both Chacko and Ammu marry people from outside their own social group, forming marriages the family clearly would prefer to have no issue, especially in the case of Ammu's two "Half-Hindu Hybrids" (44). A child Ammu might have with Velutha would be immeasurably worse.[14] In the case of the three children who are born to this brother and sister, Chacko feels he has cause to doubt his daughter's legitimacy (though the narrator tells us otherwise) (111, 235). Sophie Mol herself explains to the twins "how there was a pretty good chance that they were bastards, and what bastard really meant" (129), and the Kottayam police inspector refers to them as "illegitimate" (9). In any case, Chacko's child is dead at nine years old. Rahel appears to people around her as not physically made to bear children: Comrade

Pillai thinks she is "*probably barren*" (124), and a drunken gynecologist once told Rahel's husband, with reference to her slim hips, "Tell her she'll need a cesarean!" (88). Rahel and Estha's intercourse only confirms that this family has not found any encouragement to procreate for the purpose of establishing a line of inheritance; their incest, as Janet Thormann observes, is "the violation of the basis of social exchange, of generational succession in time, and hence of history" (304). Any validation Estha and Rahel find for any pleasure they might, finally, access, has been too hard-won to inspire confidence that they could preserve such validation and pass it on to children of their own.

Nevertheless, *The God of Small Things* maintains the emphasis on pleasure as momentary and finds it no less valuable for being so. Roy's narrative ends with a beautiful recounting of the first moment of sexual pleasure between Ammu and Velutha. This scene is unique among the eleven novels considered here as the only narrative rendering of the mother's pleasure. The detailed description of Ammu and Velutha's love-making challenges the unnarratability of the mother's pleasure. It defies social and generic taboos, insists on its own relevance and necessity, and even represents a moving effort to confront the ineffability of sexual pleasure:

> Clouded eyes held clouded eyes in a steady gaze and a luminous woman opened herself to a luminous man. She was as wide and deep as a river in spate. He sailed on her waters. She could feel him moving deeper and deeper into her. Frantic. Frenzied. Asking to be let in further. Further. Stopped only by the shape of her. The shape of him. And when he was refused, when he had touched the deepest depths of her, with a sobbing, shuddering sigh, he drowned. (318)

This passage culminates in Velutha's pleasure, and we are also told of Ammu's, when "she cried and laughed at once" and "seven years of oblivion lifted off her and flew into the shadows on weighty, quaking wings" (319). We know that Ammu achieves at this moment a goal she expresses in a different context earlier: "she wanted her body back" (211).

Despite its challenge to unnarratability, however, the scene has been a source of serious criticism, and may suggest that the mother's story, even in very contemporary literature, remains unnarratable. A lawsuit was brought against Roy almost immediately upon the novel's publication by a resident of Kerala who found the scene offensive for its graphic depiction of sex between a "Touchable" woman and an "Untouchable" man, suggesting that, at least in some contexts, the story is still taboo. In contrast to the plaintiff in the case, Aijaz Ahmad argues that "the problem with Arundhati Roy's handling of sexuality is not that it is pornographic but that it is so thoroughly conventional as not even to surprise anyone who reads English fiction with any degree of regularity" (104). Ahmad's assertion illustrates the dynamic by which the mother's pleasure, should it cease, however tentatively, to be antinarratable, becomes immediately subnarratable. For Ahmad, the novel's final scene is so common that we need not read it again. That we are being asked to read it again is harmful, Ahmad argues, because, like all such narratives, this one embraces

> the theme of the privatisation of both pleasure and politics, which leads then to sheer aggrandisement of the erotic relation in human life, as a utopic moment of private transgression and pleasure so intense that it transcends all social conflicts of class, caste, and race. (104)

Ahmad goes on to explain that this privatization is nearly always manifested in a specifically phallocentric utopia in which transgression, such as sex outside of one's caste, is titillating but that, however overtly political the pleasure is made to appear because of such transgression, "in depicting the erotic as Truth it also dismisses the actually constituted field of politics as either irrelevant or a zone of bad faith" (104). For him, then, the narrative's end fails the novel's political agenda.

Ahmad's charge is assailable on a number of counts.[15] Although he refers to the "utopic moment," his further arguments reveal that he is not treating pleasure as momentary but as a sustained state that can draw the individual away from the ideological battles in which all are necessarily embroiled. However, the novel represents moments of pleasure as fleeting, and almost impossible to validate, especially in a postcolonial situation. Sex in Roy's novel is not generally represented as the "aggrandisement of the erotic relation in human life": we need only the examples of the Orangedrink Lemondrink Man's abuse of Estha behind the Refreshments Counter of the Abhilash Talkies and the sexual intercourse between Rahel and Estha to establish that (Ahmad 104).

Sex abounds—in Roy's novel and in life—but moments of pleasure are unfortunately rare. With reference to Ammu and Velutha's pleasure, Ahmad argues that Roy's novel "construct[s] eroticism as that transcendence which takes individuals beyond history and society, straight into the real truth of their beings" (105). If it does so, it also evinces awareness that such transcendence can only be momentary. Ahmad notes that when the sexual encounter is transgressive, it is "all the more pleasurable" to the reader, but that the "deep structure" of such narratives really erases the political significance of the transgression (104). In Roy's novel, however, the fact that the lovers cross traditionally rigid social boundaries functions to underline the very fleetingness of the pleasure they find. Neither is freed from history or society, and neither ever believes such freedom is possible. They do not escape from politics, even momentarily. Still, Velutha and Ammu insist on the relevance of pleasure, and Roy's choice to end her novel with their union validates the importance of those rare moments, in whatever circumstances they are found.

Tracing the submerged plot of Rahel's, and Estha's, search for the story of the mother's pleasure offers insight into the seemingly static and inconclusive narrative of the present. Reconfiguring the novel's progression with reference to the second horizontal axis enables us to recognize the ways the protagonists' wandering becomes searching during these few days back in their family home where they lived with their mother. That a son seeks his mother's story in this novel suggests that, when disillusionment with what the father has to offer frees him from the official story the mother is allowed, a son may learn to find the value in his mother's story. His means of searching cannot be identical to his sister's, but he can conduct his own pursuit, and, having recognized its necessity, he can become a kind of mentor to his sister on her search as other women are in most of the novels considered here. The detailed treatment of and thorough resolution of the narrative of the past in *The God of Small Things* may seem to be the source of the novel's completeness, but analysis of the interaction between the narrative of the present and the submerged plot reveals their constitutive roles.

Reconfiguring the progression of *The God of Small Things* and *Talking to the Dead* to take into account both horizontal axes enables us to understand more fully the complication of the representation of time in both novels. That both eschew chronology in order to begin with narratives of the present and yet consistently deemphasize the present in favor of the past alerts us to the surfacings of the submerged plot. In turn, our recognition of the workings of the submerged plot renders the narratives of the present more fully legible in both novels.

The destruction of the mother's pleasure looms large in the surface plots of the two novels, and this threat to the searches of these daughters—and one son—influences the ways the submerged plot surfaces. The daughters are more closely bound to their siblings by the guilt they assume, and their searches are dependent on their siblings' searches. The role of mentor becomes confused with more intimate roles. In *Talking to the Dead,* the protagonist's sister functions not only as mentor and model for the mother's experience, but as a second mother and therefore an object herself of the protagonist's search. In *The God of Small Things,* the protagonist's brother functions as a mentor in that the relationship to the mother he shares with the protagonist keeps the search central, but he also functions as the suitor like the one her mother chose who enables the protagonist to experience what her mother did before her. Although the relationships between the pairs of siblings in these two novels can be read in multiple ways, one possible reading is to see in each their willingness to go to extreme lengths to save one another from remorse and to enable one another to find pleasure. In Dunmore's novel, only one sister is saved; in Roy's, the saving is of a very tenuous and unstable kind. Roy offers the first son in the novels considered here who seeks his mother's pleasure. The officially allowable story of the mother's life, never quite compelling enough for the seeking daughters, can also cease to be adequate for a son whose illusions about his paternal inheritance have been destroyed. In these novels as in their predecessors, the significance of the mother's pleasure and its unnarratability is a force that breaks the bounds of our conceptions of plot and manifests itself in multiple elements of the progression.

CONCLUSION

The Evolution of the Search

That the mother's pleasure remains unnarratable from the early nineteenth through the late twentieth centuries, in novels from England, the United States, Ireland, and India, is a surprising testament to the tenacity of traditional social structures concerning paternity and inheritance. Paternal inheritance is problematic in the surface plots of nearly all of the novels considered here, from the entailment of Kellynch Hall away from the Elliot sisters to the suspicion of Baby Kochamma that her grandniece and grandnephew might have designs on the decaying house in Ayemenem. The possibility of a daughter's inheritance of property appears to be unmentionable in *The Last September,* a community seems to conspire to conceal it in *The Color Purple,* and the actuality proves disastrous in *A Thousand Acres.* Jane Eyre's inheritance of a fortune enables her, once she has given much of it away, to enter a more equal partnership with Edward Rochester than she could otherwise have done, as Lily Bart's lack of inheritance demonstrates by contrast. However, Bertha Mason Rochester's inheritance makes her the object of a fortune-hunter, as Laura Fairlie's does, and costs her her life, as it nearly does for Laura. Troubling as the material element of the paternal inheritance is, the material is matched by less tangible trouble in that the very structure of inheritance is predicated on the silencing of mothers' stories of pleasure. Whereas these daughters' paternal inheritance, when it is not withheld, is not actively sought, all of the protagonists considered here seek their maternal inheritance, which is possible for all of them, even Esther Summerson, Anne Catherick, and Bone Boatwright, with no paternal inheritance at all.

Despite what remains rigidly the same over this period and in these several cultures, the daughters' searches do change over time as the range of possibilities open to their mothers widens. As Anne Elliot and Jane Eyre pursue the stories of their mothers' pleasure, their searches are limited to discerning whether the mother could have found pleasure in her husband. For Anne Catherick and Esther Summerson, the possibility of the mother's pleasure must be traced in her relationships with two men—lover and husband—and Laura Fairlie, too, as the daughter of a woman who married twice, seeks a story in which pleasure may have been experienced in more than one sexual relationship. For Lily Bart and Lois Farquar, the range of possibilities for their mothers' stories is broadened by the fact that, although strict sexual mores characterize their social worlds as in the earlier novels, women are not in all cases fully defined by their sexual behavior. In Lily's New York, although single women are subject to the most minute moral scrutiny, married women have a great deal of latitude, and, once protected by their status as wives, they may experience sex with multiple partners, as Mrs. Bart could conceivably have done. Lois's Ireland is certainly ruled by attention to proprieties, and the Anglo-Irish presented in *The Last September* enjoy the sense that their moral discriminations are finer than those of the English. Nevertheless, the general indifference toward sex manifested by the characters suggests that a young woman who experienced sex before marriage would not, as in the nineteenth-century novels, be marked for life, and that this experience may have been possible for Laura Naylor or Marda Norton even though it is not defining of their stories. When the mother's story can take several possible shapes, the daughter's search is made more difficult.

In the more contemporary novels, sex outside of marriage is portrayed as more likely to be known but less likely to define a woman's future. That we know of no lover of Ann Cook or Mrs. Close except for their husbands seems to indicate that no such lover exists. Similarly, we are likely to assume that Celie's mother's sexual experience is limited to her two marriages because we know of no other lover. Women who have sex outside of marriage are known in Celie's world, including Annie Julia, Shug Avery, Sofia, and Mary Agnes, which does not necessarily preclude them from choosing future relationships and even careers. This reality is reflected in Bone Boatwright's social world as well, and Anney Boatwright's affair with Bone's father is as publicly known as her two marriages. Anney may well experience the public knowledge of her transgressive sex as defining, but it does not preclude her from marrying or from earning her living, as it might have in the nineteenth-century novels. Similarly, Ammu's affair with Velutha is as much known as her marriage, and, though the consequences of this affair are catastrophic, Ammu's plan to start a school and reunite her family suggest that they need not necessarily have been so.

As the range of possibilities for the mothers expands over time, so does the range of possibilities for the daughters, making the search important in different ways. For Anne Elliot and Jane Eyre, the search for the story of the mother's pleasure must be successfully completed before marriage, as a single marriage is likely the protagonist's only option and will mean a lifetime of either pleasurable sex or unpleasurable sex. Esther Summerson and Laura Fairlie both illustrate the importance of completing the search before marriage as well, as Esther nearly enters a marriage without validation for her pleasure and Laura actually does so but then is offered a second chance by her husband's death. That Lily Bart and Lois Farquar seem to have more options open to them means the search may serve an additional purpose in preparing them to commit to just one choice. Lily witnesses the love affairs of Bertha Dorset and the marriages and affairs of Carry Fisher, and the lack of finality of marriage in Lily's world is what keeps her goal of an advantageous marriage, even if it means sacrificing pleasure, alive for her. Similarly, Lois knows her own mother to have vacillated between two men, and she knows that Marda has tried and discarded several relationships; choosing among her options may well seem at least fraught and perhaps impossible. In the contemporary novels, the range of possibilities for the daughters is even wider. As for their mothers, extramarital affairs like Ginny's or Nina's need not be defining for these protagonists; indeed, Nina can claim nineteen past affairs. Marriages need not be final but can end in divorce, as do Ginny's and Rahel's. Daughters can find their pleasure in other women, as Celie does, and as Bone Boatwright may. With more options open to them, the possibilities of the search need not be cut off by an early marriage or even by childhood sexual abuse. The search can be begun or resumed at later points in the protagonist's experience and still yield validation for the daughter's pleasure.

The impact of social change over time on the deployment of the submerged plot as a means of revealing the story of the mother's pleasure could be traced further in other texts of motherless daughters. For example, in Elizabeth Gaskell's *Wives and Daughters* (1866), the motherless protagonist Molly Gibson, like Jane Eyre and Esther Summerson, ultimately finds her pleasure. In Virginia Woolf's *The Voyage Out* (1915), Rachel Vinrace, like Lily Bart and Lois Farquar, seemingly fails to access pleasure. Indeed, *The Voyage Out*, with its explicit references to *Persuasion*, its implicit references to *The House of Mirth*, and its clearly marked influence on *The Last September*, is itself a nexus of the common concerns found in the novels considered here. Jennifer Johnston's 1987 *Fool's Sanctuary*, an Anglo-Irish Big House novel in the tradition of *The Last September*, depicts a protagonist who refuses her own pleasure outright, while Edna O'Brien's *The Country Girls Trilogy* of the 1960s gives us a protagonist as insistent as any we have encountered that her mother's pleasure must exist and as persistent in her attempt to access it. Eudora Welty's 1972 *The Optimist's Daughter* (like *Wives and Daughters*) complicates the interactions of the surface and submerged plots with a stepmother, and Jeanette Winterson's 1985 *Oranges Are Not the Only Fruit* complicates those interactions with an adoptive mother. The network of texts is extensive, with the unnarratability of the mother's pleasure troubling the plotting of all.

Although traditionally the search for the mother's pleasure is conducted by a daughter protagonist, with less investment in her own actual or theoretical legitimacy than a son, contemporary fiction offers novels of seeking sons who, disinherited by patriarchy themselves, seek to validate their own pleasure not in their fathers' stories but in their mothers'. As for Roy's Estha, the avenues for seeking sons are different from those of their sisters, but such novels' different representations of the unnarratable story are also instructive. Graham Swift's 1983 novel *Waterland* and John Irving's 1989 *A Prayer for Owen Meaney* have a great deal in common in this regard. Both overtly stories of attempts to determine paternal origin, they are also both histories of war in the twentieth century. The violence of the dominant culture leaves the protagonist narrators suspicious of their paternal inheritance and seeking the stories of their mothers that are left out of the official record. Unable to repeat their mothers' experiences as seeking daughters do, each protagonist's access to the story of his mother's pleasure is clouded by cultural artifacts—novels, fairy tales, the classical and biblical traditions—that, rather than rendering the mother's story clearer, increase its ambivalence and keep the seeking son distant from the mother's and his own pleasure. Although these two novels depict unsuccessful searches, they emphasize the significance of the search itself. Richard Russo offers a somewhat more promising example of a son's pursuit of his mother's story in his 2001 *Empire Falls*, in which the protagonist does, in fact, repeat his mother's experience in some important respects, and in which, we may imagine, validation for his own pleasure finally comes within his reach.

That the mother's pleasure is unnarratable is a consuming problem for generations of seeking daughters in literature, and, more recently, for seeking sons. My work establishes the submerged plot as a means of revealing that unnarratable story that is used by novelists over time and in various geographical and social contexts. But the submerged plot is not only at the service of the story of the mother's pleasure; unnarratable stories of various kinds may be found with attention to the submerged plot of any novel. We will usually notice first its occasional surfacings, and, upon further investigation, begin to recognize the existence of an entire second plot submerged under the plot we recognize. We will be prepared to observe those surfacings if we approach a text with the knowledge that, far from being one-dimensional and easily accessible, plot is multiple and works in texts in ways we have not yet fully imagined.

NOTES

Introduction

1. Susan Peck MacDonald (59) and Susan Greenfield (13, 145) both identify this important moment in the history of the novel of the motherless daughter.

2. This history includes Nancy K. Miller's *The Heroine's Text* (1980), Rachel Blau DuPlessis's *Writing Beyond the Ending* (1985), and Susan Winnett's "Coming Unstrung: Women, Men, Narrative, and Principles of Pleasure" (1990), and it extends to more recent work including Ruth Page's *Literary and Linguistic Approaches to Feminist Narratology* (2006) and Susan Lanser's "Are We There Yet? The Intersectional Future of Feminist Narratology" (2010).

3. The duality in Friedman's model makes it strongly compatible with Phelan's concept of progression, a connection she makes: "For Phelan, the mimetic aspect suppresses the reader's awareness of the character as authorial construction while the synthetic foregrounds this construction as part of a communication between author and reader [. . .]. For him, it is the play between the mimetic and the synthetic that accounts for narrative progression, a theory that assumes, like spatialization of narrative axes, that the text operates on an interplay between two different chronotopes—the mimetic world of the characters, and the synthetic realm of the author and reader" ("Spatialization" 19). For Friedman, the two models strive for similar goals by not entirely dissimilar means; for me, Phelan's progression is a means of tracing the coordinates of the horizontal and vertical axes in Friedman's spatialized model.

4. Robyn Warhol's "Neonarrative; or, How to Render the Unnarratable in Realist Fiction and Contemporary Film" revives and elaborates on Gerald Prince's "The Disnarrated."

5. Ruth Perry, in her *Novel Relations,* explains that the rise in England of "a lineage system defined predominantly through the marriage of first-born sons, a change that gathered momentum in the seventeenth century, had the consequence of disinheriting daughters" (40). She explains that the change, firmly in place by the end of the eighteenth century, "had been building slowly for several centuries, with the erosion of provisions for daughters (and wives and widows) in equity, manorial, and ecclesiastical as well as common law" (46).

6. Similarly, repetition is an irresistible unconscious compulsion in Fraiberg, Adelson, and Shapiro's study of impaired infant-mother relationships, which argues, as in Freud's formulation, that repetition is part of a parent's resistance to remembering "the tragedy" of his or her own childhood (388).

7. Friedman's interest in what is not narrated, explored in her early work on "spatializing" narrative, is further elaborated here.

8. I locate Walker's essay as the source of a line of scholarship that focuses on the role that mother and daughter relationships play in women's creativity. Of course, Walker's essay is also part of a long tradition of scholarship on mothering and matrilineage in African American literature. Among the many scholars who have contributed to this tradition are Gloria Wade-Gayles, Elizabeth Brown-Guillory, Jean Wyatt, Cheryl A. Wall, Teresa N. Washington, Gloria Thomas Pillow, and others I cite in the context of my analysis of *The Color Purple* in chapter 4. Maternity may have received more attention in this tradition than motherlessness: Jill Bergman argues that "the significance of the mother—and specifically the lack or loss of the mother—as a literary pattern that has psychoanalytic and postcolonial, personal, and political relevance has not yet received its critical due" (2). Bergman's psychoanalytic approach to motherlessness in African American fiction draws on theoretical assumptions similar to those of Homans, Hirsch, and Dever to reach conclusions about both "the personal condition of motherlessness" and "the political condition of civic alienation and powerlessness" (3). The feminist narratological concept of the submerged plot offers an alternative to a psychoanalytic approach to many African American novels, as my work on *The Color Purple* suggests, but it may function differently, or not at all, in texts in which the protagonist's mother was enslaved. The submerged plot of the search for the mother's pleasure depends on both mother and daughter exercising a certain degree of choice, however circumscribed by their culture. The radical circumscription of the choices of enslaved women can separate mothers and daughters in ways not overcome by the daughter's repetition of the mother's experiences. As Hortense Spillers argues, in slavery "the

customary lexis of sexuality, including 'reproduction,' 'motherhood,' 'pleasure,' and 'desire' are thrown into unrelieved crisis" (399). This crisis itself remains central to nineteenth-century African American texts and also contemporary historical novels, including Toni Morrison's *Beloved* and *A Mercy*.

9. Because the plot of the daughter's search remains submerged, accessible only through interpretation of these recurring signs, it would seem to resemble what psychoanalysts label the "implicit" because it remains "nondeclarative," or unstated. James Fosshage explains, "The non-declarative memory systems influence experience and behavior, but typically cannot be explicitly or consciously recalled" (519). Donnel Stern discusses the "implicit" in terms of "unformulated experience": "In this sense, unformulated experience is the sum total of all the knowable, communicable implications that have never been spelled out, perceptions that have been habitually passed over, and so forth" (44). My own concept of the submerged, although it shares the characteristic of being unstated, remains distinct from this technical use of the term "implicit" in that to make the implicit explicit, the analysand must look inward, and the barriers to formulating his or her experience are psychological. In contrast, the daughter protagonist's undeclared experience is that of her relationship to a story outside herself, and social and cultural barriers stand between her and the declaration of formulated knowledge of that story.

Chapter 1

1. Not all theorists have subscribed to this view; some have given precedence to one or the other. For example, Vladimir Propp and other formalists, following Aristotle, consider plot dominant and character secondary. In contrast, E. M. Forster, disagreeing outright with Aristotle, gives the precedence to character in his *Aspects of the Novel*.

2. As Phelan argues in *Reading People, Reading Plots*, "character [. . .] is a literary element composed of three components, the mimetic, thematic, and synthetic, and [. . .] the mimetic and thematic components may be more or less developed, whereas the synthetic component, though always present, may be more or less foregrounded" (3). He distinguishes further between a "dimension" and a "function": the former "is any attribute a character may be said to possess when that character is considered in isolation from the work in which he or she appears," and the latter "is a particular application of that attribute made by the text through its developing structure" (9).

3. As Julia Prewitt Brown has observed, "The question of inheritance is central to many English novels and crucial to those of Jane Austen. Because she

centred on the destinies of women, this question has been overlooked" (132). Austen constructs the inheritance plot differently from those who came before her: in an article tracing the influence of Sir Walter Scott on *Persuasion,* Jane Millgate observes, "Inheritance, which possesses in the plots of Scott's early novels a redemptive power linking older and younger generations, remains in *Persuasion* simply an arid legal procedure" (121–22). Austen indeed rejects the kind of inheritance plot central to some of Scott's novels: not unlike *Pride and Prejudice* and *Sense and Sensibility, Persuasion* is the story of a family of daughters whose paternal inheritance has in some way failed them. However, I suggest that, with no faith in an official, public inheritance from the father, Austen turns to a kind of inheritance that is even further from "arid legal procedure," a private, maternal inheritance.

4. Phelan's reading corroborates, to an extent, D. A. Miller's reading of *Persuasion.* Considering the ambiguities in the closure of *Persuasion,* Miller also analyzes the problem of the lost years of Anne and Wentworth's relationship. He explains, "On one view, the narrative delay has added nothing ('six years might have been spared'); on another, it has produced a superfluity, what the original version called an 'overplus of Bliss'" (105). I argue that the submerged plot, and what her search makes possible for Anne, works against this apparent problem in the surface plot.

5. Robyn Warhol also analyzes the constraints on Anne's ability to act. She finds that looking is a "source of power and control" for Anne ("The Look, the Body" 30), but also that Anne's position as focal character forces her to be present and experience circumstances that are "painful" or "agitating" without being able to seek relief (24).

6. Elizabeth Dalton, in her application of Freud's "Mourning and Melancholia" to *Persuasion,* reaches conclusions that are opposite to mine and argues that the daughter must reject what her mother stands for in order to access her own pleasure. Dalton establishes the mother as an obstacle between the daughter and her pleasure: "like the self-sacrificing Lady Elliot, Lady Russell stands for the renunciation of pleasure; she and her persuasion suggest the repressive superego founded on feelings of guilt toward the dead parent" (52). Dalton concludes that Anne is reunited with Wentworth because "she has finally freed herself from the persuasion of Lady Russell, and more important, from that of the dead Lady Elliot" (59). One problem is that this reading relies on Anne's final happiness to prove that she has freed herself from the guilt and repression of the mother, but it does not explain what has changed to make this freedom possible.

7. Lucy Steele is Elinor Dashwood's rival for Edward Ferrars's affections in Austen's *Sense and Sensibility.*

8. Linda Raphael finds that the true suitor in *Persuasion* also resembles the father, especially in his "egoism," and that Anne repeats her mother's experience in her relationship with Wentworth, too (43-44).

9. In accordance with her own fears of being forgotten after death, Mary is the harshest in her judgment of a man who appears to mourn insufficiently for a woman he claims to have loved.

10. Diane Hoeveler's description of Rochester after the fire comprises the prevalent interpretations of what has happened to him: Jane's "gothic hero has been tamed and ritualistically wounded. [. . .] He is daddy wounded; he is the safe husband; he is the punished patriarch; he is man. Or rather, he is the weakened man that the gothic feminist must have if she is to live with a man at all" (204).

11. Both Spivak's and Meyer's readings assume that the oppression of Bertha Mason Rochester is based on different grounds from that of Jane Eyre. Spivak describes Bertha as a "white Jamaican Creole" (678), but she attributes her oppression to her role as "self-immolating colonial subject" (681). Meyer, in contrast, argues that the novel constructs Bertha as "an actual Jamaican black woman" (250), and attributes her oppression to racial difference (266). My own reading of Bertha depends on the continuities between her and the other women in the novel, as it depends on the continuities between Jane and other women. Like Spivak (and others), I read Bertha as white; less influenced than Spivak by Rhys's implied reading of *Jane Eyre*, I consider her as part of the colonial power structure in the Caribbean. In this view, her oppression, like Jane's, has its roots predominantly in gender. Like other women characters in nineteenth-century fiction, her fortune, far from empowering her, makes her vulnerable to a destructive marriage. The similarity is augmented when Jane inherits a fortune that originates in the same place as Bertha's, from an uncle who is employed by the Mason family, and, perhaps recognizing the danger, gives three quarters of it away. For Meyer, Bertha's distance from power is signified by physical descriptions of her that seem to identify her as black. I argue, in contrast, that the physical description of Bertha is similar to that of other powerful characters throughout the novel: Aunt Reed, John Reed, Rochester, and Blanche Ingram. The physical descriptions of characters who pose a threat of some kind to Jane reveal Brontë's racial prejudice as well as her confrontation with Britain's role in the oppression of other peoples, but I argue that they do not single out Bertha.

12. This reference to Isaiah 55:1, with its promise of blessings for the people of Judah should they repent and return to God, functions in the surface plot to emphasize Jane's decision to renounce her idol and obey God's laws. At the same time, she attributes her survival to "Nature," referred to specifically as

"my mother," suggesting that the mother, too, has blessings to offer an errant daughter.

Chapter 2

1. Other scholars, too, have suggested that Esther's connection to Lady Dedlock is one she must eschew, not just for Lady Dedlock's benefit, as Esther herself recognizes, but for her own. Carolyn Dever concludes that "the daughter's virtue is constructed in contrast to the counter-example of her mother, the eroticized, transgressive woman, the sinful abandoning mother begging at her feet for forgiveness" (101). Dever's argument, like Sternlieb's, is concerned with Esther as a speaking subject, and Dever asserts that Lady Dedlock must die for Esther to construct her own identity and control her own narrative: "Esther's ability to represent herself as a subject, as an agent, is dependent on her status as a mourner; there is a direct relationship between abandonment and articulation, and specifically, between the death of a mother and the birth of an authorial subject" (81). Hilary M. Schor and Nomi M. Stoltzenberg, in their work on *Bastard Out of Carolina* and *Bleak House,* also argue that "female sexual errancy—which is to say, female sexuality, or, more precisely, erotic desire, the sexual agency of the mother—is the circumstance which haunts the daughter's progress and sooner or later wrenches her away from her mother" (120). They assert that "both daughters, accordingly, close their mothers out of their narratives" (121). Like Dever, Schor and Stolzenberg assert that "renouncing the mother, the daughter claims her own powers of invention, beauty, and, above all, writing" (126).

2. J. M. C. Toynbee, in his *Death and Burial in the Roman World*, explains that "the tomb's inscription should be interpreted as meaning that Caecilia Metella was the mother of the Marcus Licinius Crassus who in 27 BC was accorded a triumph for his conquest of Germanic, Dacian, and Moesian tribesmen in 29 or 28" (155).

3. See, for example, Judith Sanders's work on "The Horrors of the 'Happy Ending' in *The Woman in White*."

4. Shirley Stave argues convincingly that "Marian herself grows attracted to Walter, an attraction which he reveals without comment, as though he seemingly were unaware of her feelings for him" (291).

Chapter 3

1. A number of scholars connect Lily's inability to reverse her steady decline to her mother and her motherlessness. Linda Wagner-Martin suggests

that "viewed from the perspective of her being a girl in need of mothering, Wharton's sometimes baffling protagonist is more nearly explicable" (46), and she concludes that "throughout the whole course of Lily's life, there is only a vestige of anything bearing a resemblance to a mother" (48). Joan Lidoff agrees: "The array of mother figures in *The House of Mirth* also suggests a pervasive psychic configuration of inadequate maternal nurturance and support" (199). This, Lidoff argues, is the root problem, of which "Lily's troubles with sexual love and adult responsibility are symptomatic" (199). Like Lidoff, Ellie Ragland Sullivan approaches the novel from a psychoanalytic point of view, and she suggests that Lily is an hysteric, and that "the dialectical basis of hysteria in which the daughter identifies primarily with her opposite-sex parent arises out of the mother's emotional abandonment of her child" (465). Sullivan argues that Lily fails because "she can find no exit" from this "childhood drama" (468).

2. In this, Lily Bart is similar to Collins's Marian Halcombe, who adopts the roles of son and brother in her courtly behavior toward her sister. Other protagonists whose actions and decisions are motivated by a similar duality include Collins's Magdalen Vanstone and George Eliot's Gwendolen Harleth, to whom Lily has been compared by other scholars, including Stuart Hutchinson.

3. The novel is characterized as such in Gary Lindberg's *Edith Wharton and the Novel of Manners*, and subsequently by Carol J. Singley (3) and Linda S. Watts (187).

4. Vera Kreilkamp explains, "During the struggle for independence from 1919 to 1921 and the subsequent civil war, nearly two hundred Irish country houses were destroyed as the symbols of a colonizing force" (5–6).

5. This instance of disnarration depicts Lois as certain of her feelings and bold enough to communicate them, however elliptically. Another such instance is when Lois imagines the possible attitudes with which she could have greeted the IRA agent she sees in the demesne, instead of which she remains hidden (42). Considered in light of these examples, Laurence's extended fantasy of a world in which Laura Naylor actually married Hugo Montmorency (53) may suggest that disnarration is used in the novel generally to depict a certainty and decision the characters do not possess. These imagined scenarios emphasize the characters' actual uncertainty about their own emotions and inability to express them in a way that connects them to other people.

6. That Lois's parents share the first names of Wilkie Collins's Laura Fairlie and Walter Hartright may not be simply coincidence. Bowen writes about Wilkie Collins's expert handling of the country house, from which he "wrings the last drop of effect," in *The Woman in White* ("Uncle Silas" 101).

7. Bowen lost her own mother at the age of thirteen, which may be relevant to our reading of this semiautobiographical novel.

8. John Coates, in his article about the relationship of the novel to modernism, traces several comparisons between Laura and Lois. He points out that "Laura had 'wanted her mind made up' [. . .] by a relationship with a man" (212), and that this is true of Lois as well. Also, Laura's "endless talk was a camouflage, he [Hugo] felt, for a wish to avoid personal contact or being known," and Coates provides evidence that this is also true of Lois (212). Coates concludes: "The comparison which the reader is invited to draw between Lois and her mother is a vital part of the novel's historical dimension, a reinforcement of the sense, fundamental to *The Last September*, of changes in moral feeling and emotional response" (212). Coates, then, uses the comparisons to highlight the differences between generations, and he argues persuasively for the centrality to the novel of historical change; in contrast, I maintain a focus on the similarities and continuities.

9. Anne Elliot may, in fact, be evoked for us with humor in the novel's opening pages when Lois remembers her embarrassment at inadvertently discussing a houseguest within her hearing, "a Miss Elliot—a very musical woman," who was "English and honorable" and therefore "began to rattle her chest of drawers" to stop Lois from continuing her discussion (10–11).

10. When Laurence imagines Laura as a young woman, he thinks of her raging not against her parents, who are never mentioned or even alluded to, but against Richard (154).

11. For Andrew Bennett and Nicholas Royle, the focus is on the etymology of the shared root of the words "laurel" and "Laura," and they suggest that "Lois's fear seems to be a fear of the name of the mother: the 'laurel', plant of poets, the signifier of linguistic profusion, is also the path down which Lois walks in the name of her mother Laura" (17). Neil Corcoran analyzes the same account of Lois's solitary walk and other passages referring to laurels, arguing that they raise the issue of anxiety of origin: "Clearly, this passage anchors Lois's lack of secure identity in thoughts of her dead mother and associates her fundamental anxiety with her very genetic constitution, in her now dead mother's womb" (50).

12. Why Laura Naylor, who could have married Hugo Montmorency and created a new family in the traditional Anglo-Irish style as the mistress of Hugo's Rockriver but refuses outright, should be considered "the Anglo-Irish ghost *par excellence*" is not clear. Francie Montmorency, bewildered, well-meaning, rather sickly, and, as we first encounter her after her long car ride, dusty, may be a more convincing figure of the Anglo-Irish in 1920. Indeed, Lassner refers to "Francie's ghost-like presence" (45).

13. Eluned Summers-Bremmer explains that "the inheritance of Bowen's Court was passed from son to son," and she quotes W. J. McCormack, writing about the Protestant Ascendancy in literature, as explaining, "a female cannot hope to claim property except by way of exception" (138–39).

14. He aligns himself with daughters more than once. Unlike the others, he believes Marda Norton unlikely to break off her engagement because by marrying she will gain "money, assurance and scope. He himself only wished he could do so as easily" (172). Laurence also lies awake contemplating Laura's story, wondering why she married Mr. Farquar and what her life with Hugo might have been like (153–54). For Corcoran, Laurence's reimaginings of Laura's life story are evidence of his desire to be a novelist (41), but I suggest that Laurence's relation to Laura's story is more intimate and not so different from Lois's relation to the same story.

15. Margot Gayle Backus compares the relationship revealingly to that between Sally Seton and Clarissa Dalloway. Similarly, Ellen Crowell compares them to the "Ladies of Llangollen," Eleanor Butler and Sarah Ponsonby, two young Irish women who eloped to Wales to live together in 1778. Backus and Crowell cite the considerable textual evidence that Lois is ambivalent about her relationship with Gerald, which seems not strongly sexual, and considerably more certain about her relationship with Marda, which is described in terms that can be read as sexual, and they agree that the text is inconclusive on the subject. Patricia Coughlan also agrees, and argues that "Bowen's text characterises the relation of Lois to Marda with delicate impulses of yearning and attraction, but there are no false dawns" (125).

Chapter 4

1. I take the idea of a "code of mimetic character narration" from James Phelan's work on the subject in his "Implausibilities, Crossovers, and Impossibilities: A Rhetorical Approach to Breaks in the Code of Mimetic Character Narration."

2. The construction of these narratives has also been analyzed in the context of survivor discourse; Minrose Gwin considers all three texts (and others) together, seeking, as she explains, to define "the role of the feminist reader of the daughter's survival discourse within fiction" (114). Given her focus on "non-felicitous space," Gwin traces "the convergences of material, textual, and cultural spaces in contemporary U.S. women's fiction about father-daughter incest" (58). My analysis offers the submerged plot as an additional textual space that adds to our view of what Gwin calls "the equivocal discourses of victimization and survivorship" (114).

3. Critics rarely focus on Celie's relationship with her actual mother, but they have analyzed mothering and matrilineage in *The Color Purple,* especially in the context of Walker's essay "In Search of Our Mothers' Gardens." Gail Keating's 1994 essay, "Alice Walker: In Praise of Maternal Heritage," observes

that quilt-making in the novel places the female characters into a matrilineage. She concludes, "And just like the black women Walker refers to in 'In Search of Our Mothers' Gardens,' Celie has managed 'to hold on' [. . .], carrying forth the legacy of so many generations of black women before her, and setting an example for those to follow" (37). Janet Montelaro, in her *Producing a Womanist Text: The Maternal as Signifier in Alice Walker's* The Color Purple, considers the essay "a prologue to *The Color Purple*" (21). She brings together the work of Henry Louis Gates and Molly Hite, explaining that both, like Montelaro, consider the novel itself "a matrilineal text" (22); Montelaro argues that "Walker recreates [. . .] a maternal ancestry in her novel" (15).

4. See Robyn Warhol's *Having a Good Cry* for a discussion of the limits on homodiegetic narrators in *The Color Purple* and Alison Case's *Plotting Women* for a discussion of the limits on narrators in epistolary fiction more generally.

5. Tamar Katz's thorough analysis of the function of epistolary form in *The Color Purple* is helpful in identifying the sources of authority and persuasiveness in the novel. She argues that readers of didactic epistolary fiction receive a "directed message" (the novel itself) that is supported by "documentary authority" (the letters), the power of which lies in the fact that they are not addressed to the reader (188). She further argues that, as Celie "gains control over the reporting of actions," her own messages to her reader become more direct (191). I would add only that Celie is able to persuade her reader of beliefs that are important to her, including those about her mother, from early in her narrative, and that she is likely to wish to influence her stated addressee, God, on the subject of her mother's goodness as well as her own.

6. Years later, Celie opens a fortune cookie to find the message "Because you are who you are, the future look happy and bright." The fortune is ironic, both in the context of Celie's life as a poor, African American woman in her time and place and also in the immediate situation, in which Shug tells her that she has "the hots for a boy of nineteen" (248). Despite the levels of irony, however, the fortune is also true to Walker's representation of Celie throughout the novel.

7. As Tamar Katz explains, "Walker has given us a series of letters that almost never reach their addressees, a series of letters with absent, unhearing, or impotent readers." In these ways the novel "truncates traditional epistolary form," rendering "most of the novel's epistolary exchanges [. . .] nonfunctional" (189). The novel defies our expectations about chronology in this way, and also in that, as Steven C. Weisenburger proves in his "Errant Narrative and *The Color Purple*," it is characterized by "startling errors of simple narrative chronology" (258).

8. To the evocation of a very particular time and place that provide the setting of *A Thousand Acres*, Smiley adds an implicit reference to *King Lear* by grounding her plot in the play's action. Accordingly, the novel begins with two

unusual events in the quiet lives of two Iowa farm families: the sudden decision by Larry Cook, owner of an enviable thousand acres, to incorporate his farm and divide it into equal shares for his three daughters, and the return of neighboring farmer Harold Clark's oldest son, disowned by his father thirteen years earlier when he left the United States for Canada to avoid fighting in the Vietnam War. The plot is a close adaptation of Shakespeare's, but the point of view is entirely changed: Smiley's narrator is Larry Cook's oldest daughter, Ginny Cook Smith, and her narrative reveals the effects of these events not on Larry and Harold, nor on Larry's favorite youngest daughter or on Harold's faithful younger son, but rather on Ginny and her sister Rose, whose place in the plot is analogous to that of Goneril and Regan, and on Jess Clark, Smiley's Edmund.

9. Catherine Cowen Olson's "You Are What You Eat: Food and Power in Jane Smiley's *A Thousand Acres*" analyzes an analogous element in the novel and argues that the characters in the novel seem resistant to taking pleasure in food, preparing only bland, heavy, filling dishes.

10. John Duvall explains that, in Anney's small-town postwar South, her story takes on added implications: "More than enforcing moral values regarding female chastity, 'bastard' polices racial lines. If the father is unknown or unnamed, the specter of the ultimate southern horror—miscegenation between black men and white women—arises" (131).

11. This description of Anney appears to be one of the many autobiographical elements of the novel. In her nonfiction work *Two or Three Things I Know for Sure*, Allison writes, "My mama never told me stories. [. . .] Mostly my aunts respected Mama's sense of propriety. They wouldn't tell stories she didn't want them to tell, nothing of my father or the husband she had loved and lost" (24–25). As in the novel, these two men from her mother's past are of equal interest to Allison, and, as this is the only mention of either, we can conclude that Allison's depiction of Lyle Parsons in the novel is mainly created by her and the attention to this character is deliberate.

12. Allison's *Two or Three Things I Know for Sure* tells us that Glen's abuse of Bone is based on actual events in Dorothy Allison's own life, but the powerful and avenging family is a fictional creation: "When I told, only my mama believed me, only my mama did anything at all, [. . .] thirty years later one of my aunts could still say to me that she didn't really believe it" (42).

Chapter 5

1. Isabel is connected with Virginia Woolf, not only by her suicide by drowning, but also by her and Nina's childhood in St. Ives and Isabel's comfortable home and beautiful garden not far from Lewes.

2. I am indebted for these distinctions to James Phelan's taxonomy of types of unreliability in *Living to Tell about It: A Rhetoric and Ethics of Character Narration*.

3. This dual structure has been labeled as such by Andrea Adolph: in her article establishing *Talking to the Dead* as "a model of embodied reading," she asserts that "the two narratives within the novel [. . .] play out the inseparable natures of reader and text, of mind and body" (356). For Adolph, the narrative of Nina's visit "mask[s] the hidden narrative of Colin's death and of who may have been responsible for it" (366). Adolph is certainly correct in identifying the two narratives in the text, and her reading of the significance of this dual structure is illuminating. However, her term "hidden narrative," elaborated further as "submerged narrative" (370, 373), is problematic. Defined as a particular telling, a "narrative" cannot be hidden or submerged in the way that a story or plot can be. Whereas Adolph refers to the "narrative" of Colin's death as submerged, perhaps more accurate would be to argue that the *story* of Colin's death has been submerged in his sisters' memories. The *narrative* of the past is not hidden; Nina narrates this story as she learns it, and she appears to narrate it in its entirety—indeed, we learn that seven-year-old Isabel smothered the baby Colin halfway through the novel. The story of the past has been hidden, repressed, and denied, but the narrative of the past unfolds alongside the narrative of the present. I argue that what is submerged is a plot that accounts for Nina's sudden recovery of her repressed childhood memories at this particular point in her life.

4. My analysis of this element of Nina's narration is indebted to Alison Case's concept of "feminine narration" and her analysis of the complex ways character narrators negotiate authority.

5. Andrea Adolph treats the two characters independently and argues that their opposing relationships to food function primarily as a narrative technique on Dunmore's part. She concludes that the reader is likely to trust Nina as a narrator because of her more insistent embodiment.

6. Elaine Showalter, with reference to *The House of Mirth*, writes, "The threshold of thirty established for women by nineteenth-century conventions of 'girlhood' and marriageability continued in the twentieth century as a psychological observation about the formation of feminine identity" (*Sister's Choice* 86). Dunmore is likely drawing on this traditional view.

7. In this, Nina is like Bone Boatwright, who withholds any information about the further consequences of the story she has told, in Bone's case to protect her mother from readers' judgments.

8. Surprisingly little of the scholarship on the novel has focused on mothers or mother and daughter relationships. Perhaps many readers have found what Mohini Khot has; in her article on the feminist voice in the novel, Khot argues that "the overall tone is one that underscores the weakness of women,

their subservience and their silence" (213), and that "there is indeed a conspicuous absence of female camaraderie, closeness, and support in Roy's Ayemenem" (217). Katherine Sutherland focuses on mothers in her article on "Maternity, Mourning, and Nation" in three novels, and her findings are in line with Khot's: she reads Ammu as a figure for Mother England and the twins as India and Pakistan, separated from their mother and then from one another. The relative dearth of attention to mothering in the novel may also result from the fact that the relationship between Ammu and her twins is frequently deemphasized in studies of the novel compared to her relationship with Velutha and the motivations of the other adults involved. My analysis focuses on the relationship between Ammu and Rahel, much of which is traceable only in the submerged plot, and the important part that Estha plays in this relationship in both the submerged and the surface plots.

9. Including analepses referring to the period between 1969 and 1992 but excluding those that are earlier.

10. Outka's work is an exception; she argues that "Roy offers little sense that recovery is possible" and argues of the narrative of the present that it "records the permanent damage caused by trauma and asks the reader to face—and to bear witness to—this destruction" (47).

11. Perhaps drawing on the same traditions regarding the age of thirty as Dunmore and Wharton (see note 6), Roy's choice of the age of thirty-one for her protagonists is as significant in its way as the age of twenty-nine is in the earlier novels. Referred to as "a viable die-able age" (5, 310), the age, in fact, at which the twins' mother died, to reach the age of thirty-one without a settled life of one's own appears to signal the end. That Estha and Rahel seem positioned to survive this age as their mother did not may imply new possibilities after the age of thirty, akin to the sense of possibility on a grander scale implied by the number 1,001.

12. Fox describes Rahel as "more resilient and rebellious" than Estha (54). Ahmad writes that Rahel returns to Ayemenem "wiser and surer of herself, takes him [Estha] into her arms and reaches out to heal his psychic wounds through the bereaved solace of incest" (105). Bose, too, writes of "the sexual solace that Rahel offers Estha for his unspeakable pain" (67). These interpretations overlook Rahel's needs and so obscure the effects of the twins' sexual union on her.

13. The attempt to ensure that the children would learn conventional gender roles fails equally with Rahel, whose teachers conclude, "It was [. . .] *as though she didn't know how to be a girl*" (18).

14. In a discussion of caste in the novel, Pumla Dineo Gqola observes that if Ammu had borne Velutha a child, the child would take on her caste membership because "one takes on the caste membership of one's mother," and "this might translate as the introduction of impurity into the upper caste" (112).

15. Others have refuted Ahmad's arguments about *The God of Small Things*. Brinda Bose argues that "erotics can also be a politics" (68), claiming that "the sublimely erotic experience is also the pursuit of a utopia in which ideas and ideals, greater than what a momentary sexual pleasure offers, coalesce" (59–60). Bose, then, confronts Ahmad's basic point, but she changes direction by focusing on desire rather than pleasure. L. Chris Fox also confronts the basis of Ahmad's argument on slightly different grounds, contending that Ahmad's reading "misrepresents the social and political nature of the novel" (40). Fox considers Bose's reading "compelling," but makes it her project to go even further to trace the social, politicized roots of the personal in every aspect of the novel. I agree with both Bose and Fox that the novel by no means offers the erotic as depoliticized, but I center my own refutation not on abjection and trauma, as Fox does, or on desire, as Bose does, but on pleasure itself.

WORKS CITED

Abel, Elizabeth, Marianne Hirsch, and Elizabeth Langland, eds. *The Voyage In: Fictions of Female Development*. Hanover: UP New England, 1983.

Adolph, Andrea. "The Reader's Body: Reader Response and the Consuming Body in Helen Dunmore's *Talking to the Dead*." *Literature Interpretation Theory* 17 (2006): 353–77.

Ahmad, Aijaz. "Reading Arundhati Roy Politically." *Frontline* 8 Aug. 1997: 103–8.

Allison, Dorothy. *Bastard Out of Carolina*. 1992; New York: Plume, 2005.

———. *Two or Three Things I Know for Sure*. New York: Dutton, 1995.

Austen, Jane. *Northanger Abbey*. 1818; Harmondsworth: Penguin, 1987.

———. *Persuasion*. 1818; London: Penguin, 2003.

Backus, Margot Gayle. "Woolf and Same-Sex Love." *Re:Reading, Re:Writing, Re:Teaching Virginia Woolf*. Selected Papers From the Fourth Annual Conference on Virginia Woolf, Bard College. Ed. Eileen Barrett, Patricia Cramer, and Paul Connolly. New York: Pace UP, 1995. 102–5.

Balée, Susan. "Wilkie Collins and Surplus Women: The Case of Marian Halcombe." *Victorian Literature and Culture* 20 (1992): 197–215.

Bennett, Andrew, and Nicholas Royle. *Elizabeth Bowen and the Dissolution of the Novel: Still Lives*. New York: St. Martin's, 1995.

Benoit, Madhu. "Circular Time: A Study of Narrative Techniques in Arundhati Roy's *The God of Small Things*." *World Literature Written in English* 38.1 (1998): 98–106.

Bergman, Jill. *The Motherless Child in the Novels of Pauline Hopkins*. Baton Rouge: Louisiana State UP, 2012.

Bose, Brinda. "In Desire and in Death: Eroticism as Politics in Arundhati Roy's *The God of Small Things*. *ARIEL* 29:2 (1998): 59–72.

Boumelha, Penny. "*Jane Eyre.*" *New Casebooks:* Jane Eyre. Ed. Heather Glen. New York: St. Martin's, 1997.

Bowen, Elizabeth. *The Last September.* 1929; New York: Anchor, 2000.

———. "*Uncle Silas* by Sheridan Le Fanu." *The Mulberry Tree: Writings of Elizabeth Bowen.* Ed. Hermione Lee. NY: Harcourt Brace Jovanovich, 1987. 100–113.

Bronfen, Elisabeth. *Over Her Dead Body: Death, Femininity and the Aesthetic.* Manchester: Manchester UP, 1992.

Brontë, Charlotte. *Jane Eyre.* 1847; Oxford: Oxford UP, 1998.

Brooks, Peter. *Reading for the Plot: Design and Intention in Narrative.* Cambridge: Harvard UP, 1984.

Brown, Julia Prewitt. "The Radical Pessimism of *Persuasion.*" *New Casebooks: Mansfield Park & Persuasion.* Ed. Judy Simons. London: Macmillan, 1997. 124–36.

Brown-Guillory, Elizabeth, ed. *Women of Color: Mother-Daughter Relationships in 20th-Century Literature.* Austin: U of Texas P, 1996.

Carden, Mary Paniccia. "Remembering/Engendering the Heartland: Sexed Language, Embodied Space, and America's Foundational Fictions in Jane Smiley's *A Thousand Acres. Frontiers* 18.2 (1997): 181–202.

Carr, Glynis. "Persephone's Daughters: Jane Smiley's *A Thousand Acres* and Classical Myth." *Bucknell Review* 44.1 (2000): 120–36.

Case, Alison. *Plotting Women: Gender and Narration in the Eighteenth- and Nineteenth-Century British Novel.* Charlottesville: UP Virginia, 1999.

Chatman, Seymour. *Story and Discourse: Narrative Structure in Fiction and Film.* Ithaca: Cornell UP, 1978.

Coates, John. "Elizabeth Bowen's *The Last September:* The Loss of the Past and the Modern Consciousness." *Durham University Journal* 51:2 (1990): 205–16.

Collins, Wilkie. *The Woman in White.* 1860; London: Penguin, 1985.

Corcoran, Neil. *Elizabeth Bowen: The Enforced Return.* Oxford: Oxford University Press, 2004.

Coughlan, Patricia. "Women and Desire in the Work of Elizabeth Bowen." *Sex, Nation, and Dissent in Irish Writing.* Ed. Éibhear Walshe. New York: St. Martin's, 1997. 103–34.

Cowart, David. "Oedipal Dynamics in *Jane Eyre.*" *Literature and Psychology* 31:1 (1981): 33–38.

Crowell, Ellen. "Ghosting the Llangollen Ladies: Female Intimacies, Ascendancy Exiles, and the Anglo-Irish Novel." *Éire-Ireland* 39:3/4 (2004): 203–27.

Cvetkovich, Ann. "Sexual Trauma/Queer Memory: Incest, Lesbianism, and Therapeutic Culture." *Incest and the Literary Imagination.* Ed. Elizabeth Barnes. Gainsville: UP Florida, 2002. 329–57.

Dalton, Elizabeth. "Mourning and Melancholia in *Persuasion*." *Partisan Review* 62:1 (1995) 49–59.

DeKoven, Marianne. "*Jouissance*, Cyborgs, and Companion Species: Feminist Experiment." *PMLA* 121.5 (2006): 1690–96.

Dever, Carolyn. *Death and the Mother from Dickens to Freud: Victorian Fiction and the Anxiety of Origins*. Cambridge: Cambridge UP, 1998.

Dickens, Charles. *Bleak House*. 1853; London: Penguin, 1996.

Dunmore, Helen. *Talking to the Dead*. 1996; Boston: Back Bay, 1998.

DuPlessis, Rachel Blau. *Writing Beyond the Ending: Narrative Strategies of Twentieth-Century Women Writers*. Bloomington: Indiana UP, 1985.

Duvall, John N. *Race and White Identity in Southern Fiction from Faulkner to Morrison*. Houndsmills: Palgrave, 2008.

Esty, Jed. *Unseasonable Youth: Modernism, Colonialism, and the Fiction of Development*. New York: Oxford UP, 2012.

Fergus, Jan. "'My sore-throats, you know, are always worse than anybody's': Mary Musgrove and Jane Austen's Art of Whining." *Jane Austen's Business: Her World and Her Profession*. Ed. Juliet McMaster and Bruce Stovel. London: Macmillan, 1996. 69–80.

Fletcher, Loraine. "Time and Mourning in *Persuasion*." *Women's Writing* 5:1 (1998) 81–90.

Forster, E. M. *Aspects of the Novel*. New York: Harcourt, 1927.

Fosshage, James L. "The Explicit and Implicit Domains in Psychoanalytic Change." *Psychoanalytic Inquiry* 25.4 (2005): 516–39.

Fox, L. Chris. "A Martyrology of the Abject: Witnessing and Trauma in Arundhati Roy's *The God of Small Things*." *ARIEL* 33:3–4 (2002): 35–60.

Fraiberg, Selma, Edna Adelson, and Vivian Shapiro. "Ghosts in the Nursery: A Psychoanalytic Approach to the Problems of Impaired Infant-Mother Relationships." *Journal of the American Academy of Child Psychiatry* 14.3 (1975): 387–421.

Freud, Sigmund. "Remembering, Repeating and Working-Through (Further Recommendations on the Technique of Psycho-Analysis II)." *The Standard Edition of the Complete Psychological Works of Sigmund Freud, Volume XII (1911–1913): The Case of Shreber, Papers on Technique and Other Works*. Ed. James Strachey. London: The Hogarth Press, 1962. 145–56.

Friedman, Susan Stanford. "Spatial Poetics and Arundhati Roy's *The God of Small Things*." *A Companion to Narrative Theory*. Ed. James Phelan and Peter J. Rabinowitz. 2005; Malden: Blackwell, 2008. 192–205.

———. "Spatialization: A Strategy for Reading Narrative." *Narrative* 1:1 (1993): 12–23.

———. "Towards a Transnational Turn in Narrative Theory: Literary Narratives, Traveling Tropes, and the Case of Virginia Woolf and the Tagores." *Narrative* 19.1 (2011): 1–32.

Froula, Christine. "The Daughter's Seduction: Sexual Violence and Literary History." *Signs* 11:4 (1986): 621–44.

Gallop, Jane. *Thinking through the Body*. New York: Columbia University Press, 1988.

Gilbert, Sandra M., and Susan Gubar. *The Madwoman in the Attic: The Woman Writer and the Nineteenth-Century Literary Imagination*. Second Edition. New Haven: Yale UP, 2000.

Goodman, Marcia Renee. "'I'll Follow the Other': Tracing the (M)other in *Bleak House*." *Dickens Studies Annual* 19 (1990): 147–67.

Gqola, Pumla Dineo. "'History Was Wrong-Footed, Caught Off Guard': Gendered Caste, Class, and Manipulation in Arundhati Roy's *The God of Small Things*." *Commonwealth Essays and Studies* 26:2 (2004): 107–19.

Greenfield, Susan C. *Mothering Daughters: Novels and the Politics of Family Romance, Frances Burney to Jane Austen*. Detroit: Wayne State UP, 2002.

Gwin, Minrose C. *The Woman in the Red Dress: Gender, Space, and Reading*. Urbana and Chicago: U of Illinois P, 2002.

Hansen, Per Krogh. "First Person, Present Tense: Authorial Presence and Unreliable Narration in Simultaneous Narration." *Narrative Unreliability in the Twentieth-Century First-Person Novel*. Ed. Elke D'hoker and Gunther Martens. New York: Walter de Gruyter, 2008. 317–38.

Harris, Trudier. "From Victimization to Free Enterprise: Alice Walker's *The Color Purple*." *Studies in American Fiction* 14.1 (1986): 1–17.

Heller, Tamar. *Dead Secrets: Wilkie Collins and the Female Gothic*. New Haven: Yale UP, 1992.

———. "Victorian Sensationalism and the Silence of Maternal Sexuality in Edith Wharton's *The Mother's Recompense*." *Narrative* 5.2 (1997): 135–42.

Hirsch, Marianne. "Jane's Family Romances." *Borderwork: Feminist Engagements with Comparative Literature*. Ed. Margaret R. Higonnet. Ithaca: Cornell UP, 1994. 162–85.

———. *The Mother/Daughter Plot: Narrative, Psychoanalysis, Feminism*. Bloomington: Indiana UP, 1989.

Hite, Molly. *The Other Side of the Story: Structures and Strategies of Contemporary Feminist Narrative*. Ithaca: Cornell UP, 1989.

Hoeveler, Diane Long. *Gothic Feminism: The Professionalization of Gender from Charlotte Smith to the Brontës*. University Park: The Pennsylvania State UP, 1998.

Homans, Margaret. *Bearing the Word: Language and Female Experience in Nineteenth-Century Women's Writing*. Chicago: U of Chicago P, 1986.

hooks, bell. "Writing the Subject: Reading *The Color Purple*." *Alice Walker's* The Color Purple. Ed. Harold Bloom. Philadelphia: Chelsea House, 2000. 53–66.

Horeck, Tanya. "'Let Me Tell You a Story': Writing the Fiction of Childhood in Dorothy Allison's *Bastard Out of Carolina*." *New Formations* 42 (2000): 47–56.

Horvitz, Deborah. "'Sadism Demands a Story': Oedipus, Feminism, and Sexuality in Gayl Jones's *Corregidora* and Dorothy Allison's *Bastard Out of Carolina*." *Contemporary Literature* 39:2 (1998): 238–61.

Hutchinson, Stuart. "From *Daniel Deronda* to *The House of Mirth*." *Essays in Criticism* 47.4 (1997): 315–31.

Ingman, Heather: *Women's Fiction between the Wars: Mothers, Daughters and Writing.* New York: St. Martin's, 1998.

James, Henry. "The Art of Fiction." *The Art of Criticism: Henry James on the Theory and the Practice of Fiction.* Ed. William Veeder and Susan M. Griffin. Chicago: U Chicago P, 1986. 165–83.

Johnson, Judy Van Sickle. "The Bodily Frame: Learning Romance in *Persuasion.*" *Nineteenth Century Fiction* 38:1 (1983) 43–61.

Kanaganayakam, Chelva. "Religious Myth and Subversion in *The God of Small Things.* *Literary Canons and Religious Identity.* Ed. Erik Borgman, Bart Philipsen, and Lea Verstricht. Aldershot: Ashgate, 2000. 141–49.

Katz, Tamar. "'Show Me How to Do Like You': Didacticism and Epistolary Form in *The Color Purple.*" *Alice Walker.* Ed. Harold Bloom. New York: Chelsea House, 1989. 185–93.

Keating, Gail. "Alice Walker: In Praise of Maternal Heritage." *The Literary Griot* 6:1 (1994): 26–37.

Keefe, Robert. *Charlotte Brontë's World of Death.* Austin: U of Texas P, 1979.

Khot, Mohini. "The Feminist Voice in Arundhati Roy's *The God of Small Things.*" *Indian Feminisms.* Ed. Jasbir Jain and Avadhesh Kumar Singh. New Delhi: Creative, 2001. 213–22.

Kreilkamp, Vera. *The Anglo-Irish Novel and the Big House.* Syracuse: Syracuse UP, 1998.

Lambert, Raphaël. "Alice Walker's *The Color Purple:* Womanist Folk Tale and Capitalist Fairy Tale." *Alice Walker's* The Color Purple. Ed. Kheven LaGrone. Amsterdam: Rodopi, 2009. 43–57.

Lanser, Susan Sniader. "Are We There Yet? The Intersectional Future of Feminist Narratology." *Foreign Literature Studies/Wai Guo Wen Xue Yan Jiu* 32.4 [144] (2010): 32–41.

———. *Fictions of Authority: Women Writers and Narrative Voice.* Ithaca: Cornell UP, 1992.

Lassner, Phyllis. "The Past is a Burning Pattern: Elizabeth Bowen's *The Last September.*" *Éire-Ireland* 21:1 (1986): 40–54.

Lidoff, Joan. "Another Sleeping Beauty: Narcissism in *The House of Mirth.*" *Edith Wharton's* The House of Mirth. Ed. Carol J. Singley. Oxford: Oxford UP, 2003. 181–207.

Lindberg, Gary. *Edith Wharton and the Novel of Manners.* Charlottesville: UP Virginia, 1975.

Lloyd, David. *Anomalous States: Irish Writing and the Post-Colonial Moment.* Durham: Duke UP, 1993.

MacDonald, Susan Peck. "Jane Austen and the Tradition of the Absent Mother." *The Lost Tradition: Mothers and Daughters in Literature.* Ed. Cathy N. Davidson and E. M. Broner. New York: Frederick Ungar, 1980. 58–69.

MacNeice, Louis. "Autobiography." *Collected Poems 1925–1948.* London: Faber and Faber, 1949.

Maynard, John. *Charlotte Brontë and Sexuality.* Cambridge: Cambridge University Press, 1984.

McDermott, Sinead. "Memory, Nostalgia, and Gender in *A Thousand Acres*." *Signs* 28:1 (2002): 389–407.

Meyer, Susan L. "Colonialism and the Figurative Strategy of *Jane Eyre*." *Victorian Studies* 33.2 (1990): 247–68.

Miller, D. A. *Narrative and Its Discontents: Problems of Closure in the Traditional Novel*. Princeton: Princeton UP, 1981.

Miller, J. Hillis. *Fiction and Repetition: Seven English Novels*. Cambridge: Harvard UP, 1982.

Miller, Nancy K. *The Heroine's Text: Readings in the French and English Novel, 1722–1782*. New York: Columbia UP, 1980.

Millgate, Jane. "Prudential Lovers and Lost Heirs: *Persuasion* and the Presence of Scott." *Jane Austen's Business: Her World and Her Profession*. Ed. Juliet McMaster and Bruce Stovel. London: Macmillan, 1996. 109–23.

Montelaro, Janet J. *Producing a Womanist Text: The Maternal as Signifier in Alice Walker's The Color Purple*, The ELS Monograph Ser. 70. Victoria: U Victoria, 1996.

Olson, Catherine Cowen. "You Are What You Eat: Food and Power in Jane Smiley's *A Thousand Acres*." *Midwest Quarterly* 40.1 (1998): 21–33.

Outka, Elizabeth. "Trauma and Temporal Hybridity in Arundhati Roy's *The God of Small Things*." *Contemporary Literature* 52.1 (2011): 21–53.

Page, Ruth E. *Literary and Linguistic Approaches to Feminist Narratology*. Houndsmills: Palgrave Macmillan, 2006.

Pearson, Carol, and Katherine Pope. *The Female Hero in American and British Literature*. New York: R. R. Bowker, 1981.

Perry, Ruth. *Novel Relations: The Transformation of Kinship in English Literature and Culture, 1748–1818*. Cambridge: Cambridge UP, 2004.

Phelan, James. "Character, Progression, and the Mimetic-Didactic Distinction." *Modern Philology* 84.3 (1987): 282–99.

———. *Experiencing Fiction: Judgments, Progressions, and the Rhetorical Theory of Narrative*. Columbus: Ohio State UP, 2007.

———. "Implausibilities, Crossovers, and Impossibilities: A Rhetorical Approach to Breaks in the Code of Mimetic Character Narration." *A Poetics of Unnatural Narrative*. Ed. Jan Alber, Henrik Skov Nielson, and Brian Richardson. Columbus: Ohio State UP, 2013. 167–84.

———. *Living to Tell about It: A Rhetoric and Ethics of Character Narration*. Ithaca: Cornell UP, 2005.

———. *Reading People, Reading Plots: Character, Progression, and the Interpretation of Narrative*. Chicago: U Chicago P, 1989.

Pikoulis, John. "Reading and Writing in *Persuasion*. *Modern Language Review* 100:1 (2005): 20–36.

Pillow, Gloria Thomas. *Motherlove in Shades of Black: The Maternal Psyche in the Novels of African American Women*. Jefferson: McFarland, 2010.

Postlethwaite, Diana. "Sometimes I Feel Like a Motherless Child: Austen's Anne Elliot and Freud's Anna O." *The Anna Book: Searching for Anna in Literary History.* Ed. Mickey Pearlman. Westport: Greenwood, 1992. 37–48.

Powers, Peter Kerry. "'Pa is not our Pa': Sacred History and Political Imagination in *The Color Purple.*" *South Atlantic Review* 60.2 (1995): 69–92.

Prince, Gerald. "The Disnarrated." *Style* 22.1 (1988): 1–8.

Rabinowitz, Peter J. *Before Reading: Narrative Conventions and the Politics of Interpretation.* Ithaca: Cornell UP, 1987.

Raphael, Linda S. *Narrative Skepticism: Moral Agency and Representations of Consciousness in Fiction.* Madison & Teaneck: Fairleigh Dickinson UP, 2001.

Rich, Adrienne. "Jane Eyre: The Temptations of a Motherless Woman." *On Lies, Secrets, and Silence: Selected Prose 1966–1978.* New York: Norton, 1979. 89–106.

Roy, Arundhati. *The God of Small Things.* 1997; New York: Harper Perennial, 1998.

Sacksick, Elsa. "The Aesthetics of Interlacing in *The God of Small Things.*" *Reading Arundhati Roy's* The God of Small Things. Ed. Carole Durix and Jean-Pierre Durix. Dijon: Editions Universitaires de Dijon, 2002. 59–73.

Sadoff, Dianne F. "Black Matrilineage: The Case of Alice Walker and Zora Neale Hurston." *Alice Walker.* Ed. Harold Bloom. New York: Chelsea House, 1989. 115–34.

Sanders, Judith. "A Shock to the System, a System to the Shocks: The Horrors of the 'Happy Ending' in *The Woman in White.*" *From Wollstonecraft to Stoker: Essays on Gothic and Victorian Sensation Fiction.* Ed. Marilyn Brock. Jefferson: McFarland, 2009. 62–78.

Scanlan, Sean. "Going No Place?: Foreground Nostalgia and Psychological Spaces in Wharton's *The House of Mirth.*" *Style* 44.1–2 (2010): 207–29.

Schor, Hilary M., and Nomi M. Stolzenberg. "Bastard Daughters and Illegitimate Mothers: Burning Down the Courthouse in *Bastard Out of Carolina* and *Bleak House.*" *REAL: The Yearbook of Research in English and American Literature* 18 (2002): 109–29.

Sheldon, Barbara H. *Daughters and Fathers in Feminist Novels.* Frankfurt am Main: Peter Lang, 1997.

Showalter, Elaine. *A Literature of Their Own: British Women Novelists from Brontë to Lessing.* Princeton: Princeton UP, 1977.

———. *Sister's Choice: Tradition and Change in American Women's Writing.* New York: Oxford University Press, 1991.

Singley, Carol J. *Edith Wharton's* The House of Mirth. Oxford: Oxford UP, 2003.

Smiley, Jane. *A Thousand Acres.* 1991; New York: Fawcett Columbine, 1992.

Smith, David. "Incest Patterns in Two Victorian Novels." *Literature and Psychology* 15 (1965): 135–62.

Spillers, Hortense. "Mama's Baby, Papa's Maybe: An American Grammar Book." 1987. Reprinted in *Feminisms: An Anthology of Literary Theory and Criticism.* Ed. Robyn R. Warhol and Diane Price Herndl. New Brunswick: Rutgers UP, 1997.

Spivak, Gayatri Chakravorty. "Three Women's Texts and a Critique of Imperialism." *The Novel: An Anthology of Criticism and Theory 1900–2000*. Ed. Dorothy J. Hale. Malden: Blackwell, 2006. 674–90.

Stave, Shirley A. "The Perfect Murder: Patterns of Repetition and Doubling in Wilkie Collins's *The Woman in White*. *Dickens Studies Annual* 25 (1996): 287–303.

Stern, Donnel B. *Unformulated Experience: From Dissociation to Imagination in Psychoanalysis*. New York: Psychology Press, 2003.

Sternlieb, Lisa. *The Female Narrator in the British Novel: Hidden Agendas*. Houndsmills: Palgrave, 2002.

Strehle, Susan. "The Daughter's Subversion in Jane Smiley's *A Thousand Acres*." *Critique* 41:3 (2000): 211–26.

Sullivan, Ellie Ragland. "The Daughter's Dilemma: Psychoanalytic Interpretation and Edith Wharton's *The House of Mirth*." *Edith Wharton: The House of Edith*. Ed. Shari Benstock. New York: St. Martins, 1993. 464–81.

Summers-Bremmer, Eluned. "Heart(h) and Home: Elizabeth Bowen's Irishness." *Etudes Irlandaises* 29.2 (2004): 135–50.

Sutherland, John. "Wilkie Collins and the Origins of the Sensation Novel." *Wilkie Collins to the Forefront: Some Reassessments*. Ed. Nelson Smith and R. C. Terry. New York: AMS Press, 1995. 75–90.

Sutherland, Katherine G. "Land of Their Graves: Maternity, Mourning and Nation in Janet Frame, Sara Suleri, and Arundhati Roy." *Canadian Review of Comparative Literature/Revue Canadienne de Littérature Comparée* 30:1 (2003): 201–16.

Taylor, Michael. "'In the name of her sacred weakness': Romance, Destiny, and Woman's Revenge in Wilkie Collins's *The Woman in White*." *University of Toronto Quarterly* 64:2 (1995): 289–304.

Thaden, Barbara. "Elizabeth Gaskell and The Dead Mother Plot." *New Essays on The Maternal Voice in the Nineteenth Century*. Ed. Barbara Thaden. Dallas: Contemporary Research Press, 1995. 31–50.

Thormann, Janet. "The Ethical Subject of *The God of Small Things*." *JPCS: Journal for the Psychoanalysis of Culture and Society* 8:2 (2003): 299–307.

Toynbee, J. M. C. *Death and Burial in the Roman World*. Ithaca: Cornell UP, 1971.

Wade-Gayles, Gloria. "She Who Is Black and Mother: In Sociology and Fiction, 1940–1970." *The Black Woman*. Ed. La Frances Rodgers-Rose. Beverly Hills: Sage, 1980. 89–106.

———. "The Truths of Our Mothers' Lives: Mother-Daughter Relationships in Black Women's Fiction." *SAGE* 1.2 (1984): 8–12.

Wagner-Martin, Linda. The House of Mirth: *A Novel of Admonition*. Boston: Twayne, 1990.

Walker, Alice. *The Color Purple*. 1982; Orlando: Harcourt, 2003.

———. "In Search of Our Mothers' Gardens." *In Search of Our Mothers' Gardens*. San Diego: Harcourt Brace Jovanovich, 1983. 231–43.

Wall, Cheryl A. *Worrying the Line: Black Women Writers, Lineage, and Literary Tradition.* Chapel Hill: U North Carolina P, 2005.

Walsh, Margaret. "The Enchanted World of *The Color Purple.*" *The Southern Quarterly* 25.2 (1987): 89–101.

Warhol, Robyn R. *Having a Good Cry: Effeminate Feelings and Pop-Culture Forms.* Columbus: Ohio State UP, 2003.

———. "The Look, the Body, and the Heroine of *Persuasion:* A Feminist-Narratological View of Jane Austen." *Ambiguous Discourse: Feminist Narratology and British Women Writers.* Ed. Kathy Mezei. Chapel Hill: U North Carolina P, 1996. 21–39.

———. "Narrating the Unnarratable: Gender and Metonymy in the Victorian Novel." *Style* 28:1 (1994): 74–96.

———. "Neonarrative; or, How to Render the Unnarratable in Realist Fiction and Contemporary Film." 2005; *A Companion to Narrative Theory.* Ed. James Phelan and Peter J. Rabinowitz. Malden: Blackwell, 2008. 220–31.

Washington, Teresa N. *Our Mothers, Our Powers, Our Texts: Manifestations of Àjé in Africana Literature.* Bloomington: Indiana UP, 2005.

Watts, Linda S. "The Bachelor Girl and the Body Politic: The Built Environment, Self-Possession, and the Never-Married Woman in *The House of Mirth.*" *Memorial Boxes and Guarded Interiors: Edith Wharton and Material Culture.* Ed. Gary Totten. Tuscaloosa: U of Alabama P, 2007. 187–208.

Weisenburger, Steven C. "Errant Narrative and *The Color Purple.*" *Journal of Narrative Technique* 19.3 (1989): 257–75.

Weissman, Cheryl Ann. "Doubleness and Refrain in Jane Austen's *Persuasion.*" *New Casebooks: Mansfield Park & Persuasion.* Ed. Judy Simons. London: Macmillan, 1997. 205–11.

Wharton, Edith. *The House of Mirth.* 1905; New York: Penguin, 1993.

Winnett, Susan. "Coming Unstrung: Women, Men, Narrative, and Principles of Pleasure." *PMLA* 105.3 (1990): 505–18.

Wolff, Cynthia Griffin. "Lily Bart and the Drama of Femininity." *Edith Wharton's* The House of Mirth. Ed. Carol J. Singley. Oxford: Oxford UP, 2003. 209–28.

Woloch, Alex. *The One vs. the Many: Minor Characters and the Space of the Protagonist in the Novel.* Princeton: Princeton UP, 2003.

Wyatt, Jean. "Failed Messages, Maternal Loss, and Narrative Form in Toni Morrison's *A Mercy.*" *Modern Fiction Studies* 58:1 (2012): 128–51.

———. "Giving Body to the Word: The Maternal Symbolic in Toni Morrison's *Beloved.*" *PMLA* 108.3 (1993): 474–88.

Young, Kay. *Ordinary Pleasures: Couples, Conversation, and Comedy.* Columbus: Ohio State UP, 2001.

INDEX

Abel, Elizabeth, 12
Adelson, Edna, 254n6
Adolph, Andrea, 212, 264n3, 264n5
Aeschylus. See *The Eumenides*
Ahmad, Aijaz, 244–45, 265n12, 266n15
Allison, Dorothy, 14, 209. See also *Bastard Out of Carolina*; *Two or Three Things I Know for Sure*
antinarratable, 9–11, 28, 68, 84, 108, 143, 144, 244. See also paranarratable; subnarratable; supranarratable, unnarratable
Aristotle, 255n1
Austen, Jane, 2, 4, 10, 66, 111, 255–56n3. See also *Northanger Abbey*; *Persuasion*; *Pride and Prejudice*; *Sense and Sensibility*

Backus, Margot Gayle, 261n15
Balée, Susan, 110
Bastard Out of Carolina (Allison), 18, 24, 153–54, 160, 186–204, 205–7, 234, 258n1

before reading, 4, 6, 9,
Beloved (Morrison), 2–3, 255n8
Bennett, Andrew, 142, 260n11
Benoit, Madhu, 229–30
Bergman, Jill, 254n8
Bleak House (Dickens), 11, 18, 22–23, 66–88, 89–90, 93, 94, 111, 114, 115, 133, 153, 155, 158, 171, 187, 206, 234, 248–250, 258n1
Bose, Brinda, 265n12, 266n15
Boumelha, Penny, 50
Bowen, Elizabeth, 144, 151, 259n6, 259n7, 260n13. See also *The Last September*; "*Uncle Silas* by Sheridan Le Fanu"
Bronfen, Elisabeth, 59
Brontë, Charlotte. See *Jane Eyre*
Brooks, Peter, 13
Brown, Julia Prewitt, 255–56n3
Brown-Guillory, Elizabeth, 254n8

Carden, Mary Paniccia, 173
Carr, Glynis, 173–74

Case, Alison, 262n4, 264n4

character, 20, 22, 27–28, 29, 32, 33, 36, 38, 39, 40, 41–42, 49, 51, 53, 56, 59, 64, 69, 70, 73, 74, 76, 77, 79, 80, 83, 89, 93, 97, 108–9, 110, 115–17, 123, 126, 137, 138, 140, 146, 148, 149, 159, 160, 163, 164, 171–72, 174, 176–77, 178, 184, 189, 207, 210, 214, 221, 227, 233, 240, 253n3, 255n1, 255n2, 256n5, 263n11, 264n5. *See also* character narration; character-space; character-system; mimetic component; mimetic function; thematic component; thematic function; synthetic component

character narration, 23, 24, 48, 51–53, 55, 59, 63, 67, 69–70, 73–74, 75–77, 79–80, 84–85, 88, 89–90, 96, 98–104, 108, 109, 111, 153, 155, 156, 158, 160–162, 165, 169–72, 174–81, 184–85, 186–204, 207, 208–228, 258n1, 261n2, 262n4, 264n2, 264n3, 264n4. *See also* code of mimetic character narration; dual narration; epistolary narration; serial narration; simultaneous narration

character-space, 28, 51. *See also* character; character-system

character-system, 22, 28, 36, 41, 49, 97, 117, 126, 159, 174. *See also* character; character-space

Chatman, Seymour, 27

Coates, John, 260n8

code of mimetic character narration 155, 189–93, 261n1. *See also* character narration; dual narration; epistolary narration; serial narration; simultaneous narration

Collins, Wilkie, 108, 111, 151. *See also No Name; The Woman in White*

Color Purple, The (Walker), 14, 24, 153–55, 156–69, 170, 172, 174, 184, 186, 187, 189, 191, 195, 204, 205, 209, 234, 247–49, 254n8, 261–62n3, 262n4, 262n5, 262n6, 262n7

completeness, 15, 17–18, 22, 23, 25, 26, 29, 39, 47, 49, 61, 64, 66, 72, 88, 109, 113, 130–32, 134–35, 136–37, 149, 151, 155, 158, 169, 172, 186, 203, 204, 205–6, 208, 228, 232, 242, 245, 249

Corcoran, Neil, 142, 148, 260n11, 261n14

Coughlan, Patricia, 146, 261n15

Country Girls Trilogy, The (O'Brien), 250

Cowart, David, 62

Crowell, Ellen, 260n15

Cvetkovich, Ann, 187–88

Dalton, Elizabeth, 256n5

Daniel Deronda (Eliot), 259n2

daughter's pleasure, 12–13, 15, 17, 18, 21, 22, 24, 27, 36, 37–42, 45–47, 51, 64, 72, 78, 80, 85–88, 89, 94, 97–98, 101–2, 105, 107, 110–11, 113, 116–18, 120–22, 126–28, 131–32, 134, 137–38, 151–52, 153–55, 158–59, 162–63, 165–169, 170, 172, 174, 179–81, 185–86, 187–88, 204, 206–7, 210, 214, 216–18, 220, 222, 228, 234–35, 239, 241–46, 249–51, 256n6. *See also* mother's pleasure; submerged plot

DeKoven, Marianne, 8

Dever, Carolyn, 2, 4, 5, 71, 91–92, 254n8, 258n1

Dickens, Charles. *See Bleak House*

disnarration, 14, 254n4, 259n5

dual narration, 23, 67, 69, 73–74, 75–80, 84–85, 88, 89–90, 111. *See also* character narration; code of mimetic character narration; epistolary narration; serial narration; simultaneous narration

Dunmore, Helen. *See Talking to the Dead*

DuPlessis, Rachel Blau, 19, 253n2

Duvall, John N., 263n10

Eliot, George, 259n2. *See also Daniel Deronda*

Empire Falls (Russo), 251

epistolary narration, 155, 156–68, 262n4, 262n5, 262n7. *See also* character narration; code of mimetic character narration; dual narration; serial narration; simultaneous narration
Esty, Jed, 136–37
Eumenides, The (Aeschylus), 11, 121, 128–29, 132

Fergus, Jan, 36
Fletcher, Loraine, 46–47
Fool's Sanctuary (Johnston), 250
Forster, E.M, 255n1
Fosshage, James L., 255n9
Fox, L. Chris, 265n12, 266n15
Fraiberg, Selma, 254n6
Freud, Sigmund, 11, 15–16, 54–55, 254n6, 256n6
Friedman, Susan Stanford, 6–8, 18–20, 21, 24, 121, 230, 233, 253n3
Froula, Christine, 157, 166, 169

Gallop, Jane, 8
Gaskell, Elizabeth. See *Wives and Daughters*
Gilbert, Sandra M., 32, 48
God of Small Things, The (Roy), 3, 18, 25, 205–8, 228–46, 247, 249, 250, 264–65n8, 265n9, 265n10, 265n11, 265n12, 265n13, 265n14, 266n15
Goodman, Marcia Renee, 71
Gqola, Pumla Dineo, 265n14
Greenfield, Susan C., 2, 253n1
Gubar, Susan, 32, 48
Gwin, Minrose, 188, 261n2

Hamlet (Shakespeare), 11, 16, 17
Hansen, Per Krogh, 211
Harris, Trudier, 156
Heller, Tamar, 8, 92
Hirsch, Marianne, 2–3, 8, 12, 50, 52–53, 254n8

Hite, Molly, 156, 163, 167, 168, 262
Hoeveler, Diane, 257n10
Homans, Margaret, 2, 5, 8, 50, 254
hooks, bell, 158, 159
Horeck, Tanya, 187–88
horizontal axis, 7–8, 17, 18, 21–23, 25, 26–27, 29, 40, 41, 55, 64, 66, 69, 111, 113, 116–17, 121, 129, 134, 151–52, 154, 169, 204, 245, 253n3. *See also* submerged plot; vertical axis
Horvitz, Deborah, 188
house, 20, 24, 32, 39, 43, 48, 52–53, 56, 58–60, 82–83, 85, 97, 99, 104, 106, 107, 109–10, 113, 114, 117–18, 122–23, 128, 131, 134, 135–36, 138, 141, 144, 146–47, 149–51, 152, 182–84, 197–98, 213, 215, 223–24, 229–30, 236, 239, 247, 250, 259n4, 259n6. *See also* narrative space; journey
House of Mirth, The (Wharton), 18, 23–24, 112–134, 135, 137–38, 144, 146, 151–52, 184, 220, 247–250, 258–59n1, 259n2, 259n3, 264n6, 265n11
Hutchinson, Stuart, 121, 259n2

"In Search of Our Mothers' Gardens" (Walker), 18–19, 254n8, 261–62n3
Ingman, Heather, 19
instabilities, 5, 15, 18, 26, 30, 31, 38, 115–17, 210, 218, 221. *See also* tensions
Irving, John. See *A Prayer for Owen Meany*

James, Henry, 27
Jane Eyre (Brontë), 11, 18, 22, 23, 26–28, 47–65, 66–68, 70–71, 78, 94, 111, 113–15, 122, 135, 137, 156–57, 158, 168, 234, 247–250, 257n10, 257n11, 257–58n12
Johnson, Judy Van Sickle, 41
Johnston, Jennifer. See *Fool's Sanctuary*
journey, 48, 61, 83, 86, 114, 136. *See also* house, narrative space

Kanaganayakam, Chelva, 240
Katz, Tamar, 262n5, 262n7
Keating, Gail, 261–62n3
Keefe, Robert, 63
Khot, Mohini, 264–65n8
King Lear (Shakespeare), 11, 262–63n8
Kreilkamp, Vera, 259n4

Lambert, Raphaël, 157
Langland, Elizabeth, 12
Lanser, Susan Sniader, 14, 59, 253n2
Lassner, Phyllis, 137, 142, 260n12
Last September, The (Bowen), 23–24, 112–15, 134–152, 235, 247–50, 259n5, 259n6, 259n7, 260n8, 260n9, 260n10, 260n11, 260n12, 261n14, 261n15
launch, 17, 30, 51, 52, 76, 122, 138, 145, 190, 215, 232
Lidoff, Joan, 127, 259n1
Lindberg, Gary, 259n3
Lloyd, David, 10, 16

MacDonald, Susan Peck, 39, 253n1
MacNeice, Louis, 225–26
marriage plot, 3, 5, 12–14, 22, 23, 26, 29–30, 67, 112, 116, 126, 134, 135–36, 151
Maynard, John, 54
McDermott, Sinead, 172–73
Mercy, A (Morrison), 255n8
Meyer, Susan, 59, 257n11
Miller, D. A., 29, 256n4
Miller, J. Hillis, 17
Miller, Nancy K., 253n2
Millgate, Jane, 256n3
mimetic component, 27, 32, 33, 36, 49, 56, 70, 73, 77, 89, 108–9, 117, 120, 140, 149, 166, 210, 214, 255n2. *See also* character; mimetic function; thematic component; thematic function; synthetic component

mimetic function, 159, 189, 253n3, 255n2. *See also* character; mimetic component; thematic component; thematic function; synthetic component
Montelaro, Janet, 262n3
Morrison, Toni. *See Beloved*; *A Mercy*
mother's pleasure, 4, 8–12, 16–25, 26–29, 32–33, 37, 41, 45–47, 48, 51, 56–57, 61, 64–65, 66–68, 69–70, 73, 75–79, 84, 86–88, 89–98, 102–3, 106–110, 112–123, 126, 129, 132–34, 137, 139, 140, 143, 147–49, 151–52, 153–55, 158–59, 161, 165–169, 170, 176, 178, 182–84, 187–91, 193, 195, 198, 203–4, 205–8, 209, 216, 220–22, 228, 231–32, 234, 237, 241–46, 247–51, 254n8, 254–55n8, 266n15. *See also* daughter's pleasure; submerged plot
Mother's Recompense, The (Wharton), 8

narrative space, 6–7, 21, 24, 113–15, 117, 152, 223, 261n2. *See also* house; journey
narrative time, 7–8, 25, 164, 207, 209, 213, 216, 223, 226, 229, 232, 233, 246, 253n3, 262n7
negative plot, 14
No Name (Collins), 259n2
Northanger Abbey (Austen), 1, 4, 11, 22

O'Brien, Edna. *See The Country Girls Trilogy*
Oedipus the King (Sophocles), 2, 11, 15–16
Olson, Catherine Cowen, 263n9
Optimist's Daughter, The (Welty), 250
Oranges Are Not the Only Fruit (Winterson), 250
Outka, Elizabeth, 230, 233, 265n10

Page, Ruth E., 253n2
paranarratable, 10–11. *See also* antinarratable; subnarratable; supranarratable; unnarratable
Pearson, Carol, 60

Perry, Ruth, 254n5
Persuasion (Austen), 3, 18, 22, 23, 26–47, 48, 53, 64–65, 66–68, 70–71, 78, 94, 111, 113–14, 118, 121, 122, 135, 137, 140, 158, 234, 248, 249, 207, 256n3, 256n4, 256n6, 260n9, 257n8
Phelan, James, 5, 8, 17, 18, 21, 27, 30, 38, 40, 42, 240, 253n3, 255n2, 256n4, 261n1, 264n2
Pikoulis, John, 118
Pillow, Gloria Thomas, 254n8
Pope, Katherine, 60
Postlethwaite, Diana, 39
Powers, Peter Kerry, 157
Prayer for Owen Meany, A (Irving), 250
Pride and Prejudice (Austen), 13, 256n3
Prince, Gerald, 14, 254n4
progression, 6, 8, 14, 15, 17–18, 21, 22, 27, 29–30, 33, 36, 38, 40, 48, 51, 53, 55, 61, 64, 68, 70, 80, 83, 88–89, 97, 102, 112, 115–17, 123, 129, 137, 137–38, 140, 149, 151, 152, 157–58, 169, 172, 181, 189, 195, 198–200, 205–7, 208–9, 212, 214, 216, 219, 224–25, 228–29, 232, 238–39, 245–46, 253n3. *See also* readerly dynamics; textual dynamics
Propp, Vladimir, 255n1
Purgatory (Yeats), 16–17

Rabinowitz, Peter J., 4, 5
Raphael, Linda S., 257n8
readerly dynamics, 5–6, 18, 21, 29, 37, 197, 209. *See also* progression; textual dynamics
Rich, Adrienne, 49–50
Roy, Arundhati, 14. *See also The God of Small Things*
Royle, Nicholas, 142, 260n11
Russo, Richard. *See Empire Falls*

Sacksick, Elsa, 230
Sadoff, Dianne F., 159
Sanders, Judith, 258n3

Scanlan, Sean, 122–23
Schor, Hilary M., 71, 187, 188, 258n1
Sense and Sensibility (Austen), 42, 256n3, 256n7
serial narration, 23, 67, 89–90, 98–104, 108, 109, 111. *See also* character narration; code of mimetic character narration; dual narration; epistolary narration; simultaneous narration
Shakespeare, William. *See also Hamlet*; *King Lear*
Shapiro, Vivian, 254n6
Sheldon, Barbara H., 173
Showalter, Elaine, 50, 54–55, 264n6
simultaneous narration, 209–212, 223. *See also* character narration; code of mimetic character narration; dual narration; epistolary narration; serial narration
Singley, Carol J., 259n3
Smiley, Jane, 24. *See also A Thousand Acres*
Smith, David, 54
Sophocles. *See Oedipus the King*
Spillers, Hortense, 254n8
Spivak, Gayatri Chakravorty, 59, 257n11
Stave, Shirley A., 258n4
Stern, Donnel B., 255n9
Sternlieb, Lisa, 69–70, 258n1
Stolzenberg, Nomi M., 71, 187, 188, 258n1
Strehle, Susan, 173
submerged plot, 6–8, 11–12, 14–15, 17–18, 20–25, 26–30, 36–38, 43–47, 48–49, 51–52, 55, 59, 61, 64, 66–68, 69–70, 73, 75, 76, 80, 82–83, 85, 88–90, 92–93, 95, 97–99, 101, 103–5, 109, 111, 112–14, 116–17, 120–23, 126–28, 133, 135, 137–38, 140, 142, 145–46, 149, 151, 153–55, 158–169, 170, 172, 174, 177, 186, 187, 189–90, 195, 197, 199, 203, 204, 205, 207, 209, 212, 215–19, 222, 224, 227–228, 231–32, 234, 236–240, 242, 245, 246, 250–51, 254n8, 255n9, 256n4, 261n2, 264n3, 265n8. *See also*

daughter's pleasure; horizontal axis; mother's pleasure; vertical axis
subnarratable, 10, 144, 244. *See also* antinarratable; paranarratable; supranarratable; unnarratable
Sullivan, Ellie Ragland, 259n1
Summers-Bremmer, Eluned, 260n13
supranarratable, 9. *See also* antinarratable; paranarratable; subnarratable; unnarratable
Sutherland, John, 110
Sutherland, Katherine, 265n8
Swift, Graham. See *Waterland*
synthetic component, 240, 253n3, 255n2. *See also* character; mimetic component; mimetic function; thematic component; thematic function

Talking to the Dead (Dunmore), 25, 205–28, 232–33, 245–46, 249, 263n1, 264n3, 264n4, 264n5, 264n6, 264n7, 265n11
Taylor, Michael, 110
tensions, 5, 18, 26, 115–17, 210. *See also* instabilities
textual dynamics, 5–6, 18, 21, 29, 37, 197, 209. *See also* progression; readerly dynamics
Thaden, Barbara, 48
thematic component, 70, 149, 210, 255n2. *See also* character; mimetic component; mimetic function; thematic function; synthetic component
thematic functions, 27, 89, 117, 159, 189, 255n2. *See also* character; mimetic component; mimetic function; thematic component; synthetic component
Thormann, Janet, 243
Thousand Acres, A (Smiley), 24, 153–155, 160, 169–86, 187, 189, 195, 204, 205, 209, 247–49, 262–63n8, 263n9
Toynbee, J. M. C., 258n2

traveling trope, 18–20, 21, 28, 55–56, 64, 76. *See also* woman who marries despite . . .
Two or Three Things I Know for Sure (Allison), 263n11, 263n12

"*Uncle Silas* by Sheridan Le Fanu" (Bowen), 259n6
unnarratable, 4, 6, 8–11, 15, 17, 21, 23, 25, 26–27, 29, 39, 47, 48, 51, 56, 64, 88, 90, 111, 115, 123, 133, 139, 152, 153–54, 156, 158, 179, 193, 204, 205, 207, 209, 216, 220, 243, 247, 251, 254n4. *See also* antinarratable; paranarratable; subnarratable; supranarratable

vertical axis, 7–8, 18, 116, 121, 152, 204, 253n3. *See also* horizontal axis; submerged plot
Voyage Out, The (Woolf), 112, 250

Wade-Gayles, Gloria, 254n8
Wagner-Martin, Linda, 119, 258–59n1
Walker, Alice, 24. See also *The Color Purple*; "In Search of Our Mothers' Gardens"
Wall, Cheryl A., 254n8
Walsh, Margaret, 156
Warhol, Robyn R., 6, 9–10, 12–13, 14, 21, 144, 254n4, 256n5, 262n4
Washington, Teresa N., 254n8
Waterland (Swift), 250
Watts, Linda S., 259n3
Weisenburger, Steven C., 262n7
Weissman, Cheryl Ann, 32
Welty, Eudora. See *The Optimist's Daughter*
Wharton, Edith. See *The House of Mirth*; *The Mother's Recompense*
Winnett, Susan, 10, 253n2
Winterson, Jeanette. See *Oranges Are Not the Only Fruit*
Wives and Daughters (Gaskell), 250
Wolff, Cynthia Griffin, 120, 133

Woloch, Alex, 28

Woman in White, The (Collins), 22–23, 66–68, 88–111, 114, 115, 125, 165, 206, 234, 247–49, 258n2, 258n3, 258n4, 259n2, 259n5, 259n6

woman who marries despite . . . , 19–20, 28, 32, 55–56, 64, 76, 81, 90, 106, 108, 111, 152, 166, 191, 226. *See also* traveling trope

Woolf, Virginia, 18, 263n1. See also *The Voyage Out*

Wyatt, Jean, 254n8

Yeats, W. B. See *Purgatory*

Young, Kay, 13

THEORY AND INTERPRETATION OF NARRATIVE

James Phelan, Peter J. Rabinowitz, and Robyn Warhol, Series Editors

Because the series editors believe that the most significant work in narrative studies today contributes both to our knowledge of specific narratives and to our understanding of narrative in general, studies in the series typically offer interpretations of individual narratives and address significant theoretical issues underlying those interpretations. The series does not privilege one critical perspective but is open to work from any strong theoretical position.

The Submerged Plot and the Mother's Pleasure from Jane Austen to Arundhati Roy
KELLY A. MARSH

Narrative Theory Unbound: Queer and Feminist Interventions
EDITED BY ROBYN WARHOL AND SUSAN S. LANSER

Unnatural Narrative: Theory, History, and Practice
BRIAN RICHARDSON

Ethics and the Dynamic Observer Narrator: Reckoning with Past and Present in German Literature
KATRA A. BYRAM

Narrative Paths: African Travel in Modern Fiction and Nonfiction
KAI MIKKONEN

The Reader as Peeping Tom: Nonreciprocal Gazing in Narrative Fiction and Film
JEREMY HAWTHORN

Thomas Hardy's Brains: Psychology, Neurology, and Hardy's Imagination
SUZANNE KEEN

The Return of the Omniscient Narrator: Authorship and Authority in Twenty-First Century Fiction
PAUL DAWSON

Feminist Narrative Ethics: Tacit Persuasion in Modernist Form
KATHERINE SAUNDERS NASH

Real Mysteries: Narrative and the Unknowable
H. PORTER ABBOTT

A Poetics of Unnatural Narrative
EDITED BY JAN ALBER, HENRIK SKOV NIELSEN, AND BRIAN RICHARDSON

Narrative Discourse: Authors and Narrators in Literature, Film, and Art
PATRICK COLM HOGAN

Literary Identification from Charlotte Brontë to Tsitsi Dangarembga
LAURA GREEN

An Aesthetics of Narrative Performance: Transnational Theater, Literature, and Film in Contemporary Germany
CLAUDIA BREGER

Narrative Theory: Core Concepts and Critical Debates
DAVID HERMAN, JAMES PHELAN AND PETER J. RABINOWITZ, BRIAN RICHARDSON, AND ROBYN WARHOL

After Testimony: The Ethics and Aesthetics of Holocaust Narrative for the Future
EDITED BY JAKOB LOTHE, SUSAN RUBIN SULEIMAN, AND JAMES PHELAN

The Vitality of Allegory: Figural Narrative in Modern and Contemporary Fiction
GARY JOHNSON

Narrative Middles: Navigating the Nineteenth-Century British Novel
EDITED BY CAROLINE LEVINE AND MARIO ORTIZ-ROBLES

Fact, Fiction, and Form: Selected Essays
RALPH W. RADER. EDITED BY JAMES PHELAN AND DAVID H. RICHTER

The Real, the True, and the Told: Postmodern Historical Narrative and the Ethics of Representation
ERIC L. BERLATSKY

Franz Kafka: Narration, Rhetoric, and Reading
EDITED BY JAKOB LOTHE, BEATRICE SANDBERG, AND RONALD SPEIRS

Social Minds in the Novel
ALAN PALMER

Narrative Structures and the Language of the Self
MATTHEW CLARK

Imagining Minds: The Neuro-Aesthetics of Austen, Eliot, and Hardy
KAY YOUNG

Postclassical Narratology: Approaches and Analyses
EDITED BY JAN ALBER AND MONIKA FLUDERNIK

Techniques for Living: Fiction and Theory in the Work of Christine Brooke-Rose
KAREN R. LAWRENCE

Towards the Ethics of Form in Fiction: Narratives of Cultural Remission
LEONA TOKER

Tabloid, Inc.: Crimes, Newspapers, Narratives
V. PENELOPE PELIZZON AND NANCY M. WEST

Narrative Means, Lyric Ends: Temporality in the Nineteenth-Century British Long Poem
MONIQUE R. MORGAN

Joseph Conrad: Voice, Sequence, History, Genre
EDITED BY JAKOB LOTHE, JEREMY HAWTHORN, AND JAMES PHELAN

Understanding Nationalism: On Narrative, Cognitive Science, and Identity
PATRICK COLM HOGAN

The Rhetoric of Fictionality: Narrative Theory and the Idea of Fiction
RICHARD WALSH

Experiencing Fiction: Judgments, Progressions, and the Rhetorical Theory of Narrative
JAMES PHELAN

Unnatural Voices: Extreme Narration in Modern and Contemporary Fiction
BRIAN RICHARDSON

Narrative Causalities
EMMA KAFALENOS

Why We Read Fiction: Theory of Mind and the Novel
LISA ZUNSHINE

I Know That You Know That I Know: Narrating Subjects from Moll Flanders *to* Marnie
GEORGE BUTTE

Bloodscripts: Writing the Violent Subject
ELANA GOMEL

Surprised by Shame: Dostoevsky's Liars and Narrative Exposure
DEBORAH A. MARTINSEN

Having a Good Cry: Effeminate Feelings and Pop-Culture Forms
ROBYN R. WARHOL

Politics, Persuasion, and Pragmatism: A Rhetoric of Feminist Utopian Fiction
ELLEN PEEL

Telling Tales: Gender and Narrative Form in Victorian Literature and Culture
ELIZABETH LANGLAND

Narrative Dynamics: Essays on Time, Plot, Closure, and Frames
EDITED BY BRIAN RICHARDSON

Breaking the Frame: Metalepsis and the Construction of the Subject
DEBRA MALINA

Invisible Author: Last Essays
CHRISTINE BROOKE-ROSE

Ordinary Pleasures: Couples, Conversation, and Comedy
KAY YOUNG

Narratologies: New Perspectives on Narrative Analysis
EDITED BY DAVID HERMAN

Before Reading: Narrative Conventions and the Politics of Interpretation
PETER J. RABINOWITZ

Matters of Fact: Reading Nonfiction over the Edge
DANIEL W. LEHMAN

*The Progress of Romance: Literary
Historiography and the Gothic Novel*
DAVID H. RICHTER

*A Glance Beyond Doubt: Narration,
Representation, Subjectivity*
SHLOMITH RIMMON-KENAN

*Narrative as Rhetoric: Technique, Audiences,
Ethics, Ideology*
JAMES PHELAN

Misreading Jane Eyre: *A Postformalist
Paradigm*
JEROME BEATY

*Psychological Politics of the American Dream:
The Commodification of Subjectivity in
Twentieth-Century American Literature*
LOIS TYSON

Understanding Narrative
EDITED BY JAMES PHELAN
AND PETER J. RABINOWITZ

Framing Anna Karenina: *Tolstoy, the Woman
Question, and the Victorian Novel*
AMY MANDELKER

*Gendered Interventions: Narrative
Discourse in the Victorian Novel*
ROBYN R. WARHOL

*Reading People, Reading Plots: Character,
Progression, and the Interpretation of
Narrative*
JAMES PHELAN

www.ingramcontent.com/pod-product-compliance
Lightning Source LLC
Chambersburg PA
CBHW030131240426
43672CB00005B/97